Post-Theory,
Games, and
Discursive Resistance

SUNY Series, The Margins of Literature
Mihai I. Spariosu, Editor

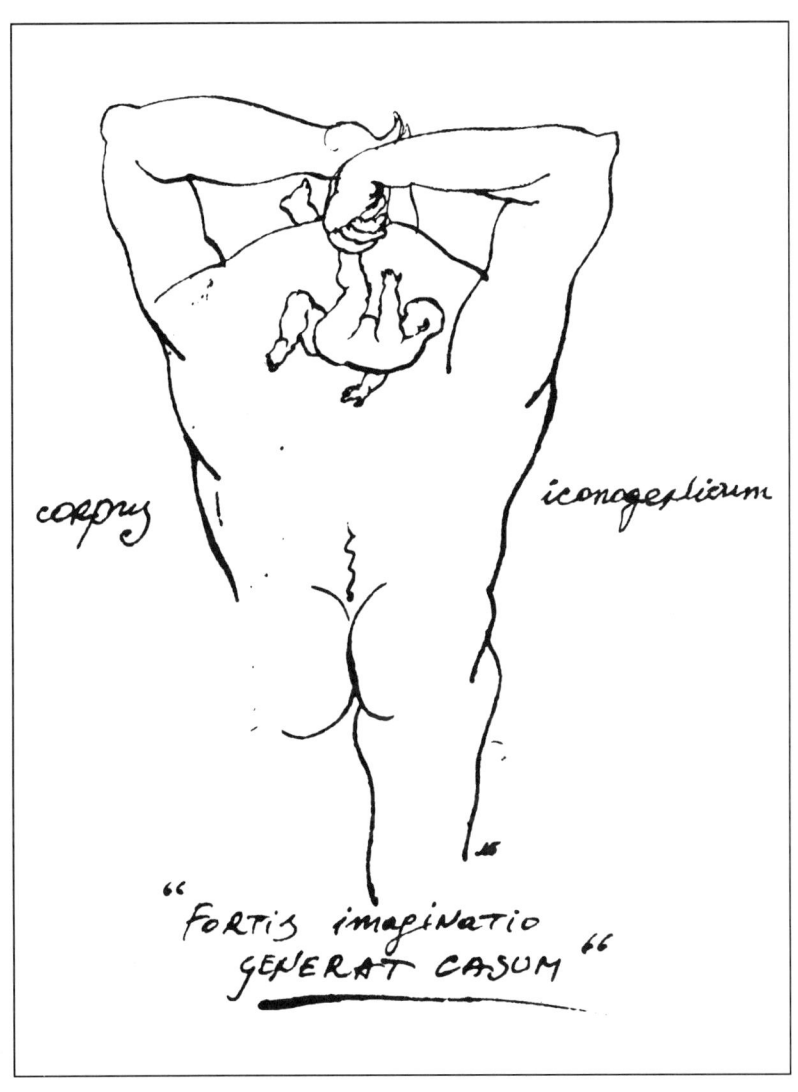

Luchezar Boyadjiev, b. 1957, Bulgaria
Cover for "ARS Simulacri," 1989, pen and ink on paper

Post-Theory, Games, and Discursive Resistance
The Bulgarian Case

Edited by
Alexander Kiossev

State University of New York Press

Production by Ruth Fisher
Marketing by Nancy Farrell

Published by
State University of New York Press, Albany

© 1995 State University of New York

All rights reserved

Printed in the United States of America

No part of this book may be used or reproduced
in any manner whatsoever without written permission
except in the case of brief quotations embodied in
critical articles and reviews.

For information, address the State University of New York Press,
State University Plaza, Albany, NY 12246

Library of Congress Cataloging-in-Publication Data

Post-theory, games, and discursive resistance : the Bulgarian case /
   edited by Alexander Kiossev.
      p.   cm. — (SUNY series, the margins of literature)
   Includes index.
      ISBN 0-7914-2357-3 (alk. paper). — ISBN 0-7914-2358-1 (pbk. :
alk. paper)
      1. Underground literature—Bulgaria—Translations into English.
2. Bulgaria—Intellectual life—1945–1990. I. K'osev, Aleksandŭr,
1953– . II. Series.
PG1145.E8P67   1995
891.8'108003—dc20   94-33220
                                                                                           CIP

10 9 8 7 6 5 4 3 2 1

Contents

Introduction: A Broken Promise   ix
Alexander Kiossev

Part I   Ars Simulacri

The Transparent Book   1
Ivaylo Ditchev

Literalisms   3
Ivaylo Ditchev

Angulus: The Figure of Sameness   11
Vladislav Todorov

The Four Luxembourgs, Civitas Peregrina   15
Vladislav Todorov

Pierre Menard, the Author of *Don Quixote*   25
Ivan Kristev

Goethe's Indigo   33
Alexander Kiossev, etc.

Part II   Political Aesthetics of Communism

Introduction to the Political Aesthetics of Communism   65
Vladislav Todorov

From Anatomy of the Political Body   95
    I.   A Political Anatomy of Communism   95
    II.   The Guillotine and Acid   97
Ivan Kristev

Part III The Post-Paranoid Condition

The Post-Paranoid Condition *Ivaylo Ditchev*	105
Epitaph for Sacrifice, Epitaph for the Left *Ivaylo Ditchev*	119
An Essay on Terror *Alexander Kiossev*	135
An Essay on Theoretical Terror *Ivan Kristev*	147
Epilogue: Health Takes the Power *Alexander Kiossev*	155
Contributors	179
Index	181

Introduction:
A Broken Promise
Alexander Kiossev

This text is an introduction. This means that its own genre makes it face problems that are insoluble. (In fact every introduction is impossible, but we will not elaborate on that now.)

The author made a promise to his American publishers to explain very clearly in this introduction the **context** of the whole collection: the chain of recurrent circumstances and events, the sharing of a common political and intellectual (besides a very private—that of close friends) milieu, and the particular plots of events that made the writing of the texts in this book possible. This would be a background which could make the texts, at least relatively, comprehensible.

As it happens, the promise, frivolously made, was impossible to keep.

And this is so not only because, as according to the general deconstructivist "truth," the context can never be described in a way that will guide and lead to a satisfactory and adequate understanding/using of the text. Every "representation" and "narrating" of a context always involves some totalizing procedures: politics of representation, control over the myths that set the semantic scale of an intellectual community, self-proclamation of the narrator (introductor) as the "legal" heir of this context, etc. The narrative about this context is impossible—and not because of the general reasons mentioned above, but because of some very specific ones.

In the first place this context does not exist anymore. The circle of friends, where "The Transparent Book," "Goethe's Indigo," or "Political Aesthetics of Communism" were born is gone. This could, of course, serve rather then disserve the narration: there is no easier way to take control of the mythology of a community than the act of retrospectively re-writing it, especially when nobody is there to contradict the narrator. But what actually happened to this community, to this intellectual circle, is something besides disintegration—it was a destruction of its potential to construct meaning, an effort to throw away and lose for good the hermeneutic key to it. In order to make possible its own disintegration it had to stop understanding itself: this was a necessary precondition for its destruction. Once the key is completely lost, the human and intellectual experience of this community begins to fade and escapes the totalizing mechanisms of the narration; today this experience seems to the author of the introduction himself somewhat unreal, and the effort to revive it—full of suspicious sentimentality and retrospective ideologies.

So the narrative has to narrate its own impossibility—to tell why this community cannot be told about.

Three of the four authors presented here were close friends for about ten years and the texts that they produced then bear the traces of this friendship: traces of discussions and arguments in pubs and streets of nighttime Sofia, of shared depressions and exaltations, of shared books—lived through together, of countless talks, dialogues and disputes, of reactions and reactions to the reactions, which nobody would manage to reconstruct now. This was as much discussing-things-together as it was living together, and everyone—under the influence of the other, under the influence of their own influences reflected in the other, etc.—was gradually losing (obliterating) his traditional, ideologically and professionally permissible profile, fixed by the totalitarian surroundings. And in the communal intellectual happenings Ivaylo Ditchev was less and less "a young writer," Alexander Kiossev—a "young literary critic," and Vladislav

Todorov—a "young theater critic" (that this was a natural process of shaping each other became clear later when Ivan Kristev joined the group and had to give up the perspective careers of a "young philosopher" and a "young poet" as well). These men not only ceased to be "young," but were also gradually turning into—for good or bad—something different, something for which the completely pieced-out-into-strict-categories totalitarian culture of Bulgaria simply had no name (nomenclature). The combination of studying the postmodern writers and leading a totalitarian/posttotalitarian existence created a common hybrid discourse and a community of obscure but passionate intellectual positions. From an orthodox-totalitarian point of view (including the totalitarian point of view of a narrative about them) they appeared like an intolerable monster. At the same time the new discourse they tried to create was not enough to explain everything. To slip away from professional nomenclatures did not suffice. This friendly debating circle was a "form of life"—vivid intertextuality, which the participants themselves experienced as an intellectual oasis. But in the cramped space of the oasis the bodies clutched at each other, the thoughts existed only in the ambivalent tension of aggression/erotics one towards the other. Thus the eroticism of the situation was paralleled by a claustrophobic feeling in a closed space: later Vladislav Todorov would call all this "promiscuous closeness." Like every oasis, this one would also at some point lose meaning and disintegrate (although at the time nobody was clearly aware of this)—and the disintegration would leave behind not only an intellectual but a corporeal void too.

Then came the political changes in Bulgaria: the "desert" of totalitarianism was taken over by a melancholic flora growing in the post-totalitarian chaos; the intuitions of space all of a sudden changed and the claustrophobic Eros of the oasis cooled down.

This introduction should try to hold the texts in a contextual unity and offer the reader the general form of their meaning. In addition, it is meant to perform this impossible hermeneutic operation at a point of time when the centrifugal energies of that very context dispersed the circle all over the world. Today Ivaylo Ditchev is in Paris, Vladislav Todorov in Philadelphia, Alexander Kiossev in Goettingen, and Ivan Kristev is on the way between Sofia, Oxford, Saarbruecken, and Boston. This suggests that the feeling of community the circle had created had been cracked and crumbling from the very beginning and probably had never been totally communal.

What is more, the "story" that each member of the group took away with them after the disintegration turns out to be quite different—not to say incompatible and hostile—from the other stories; denying the basic conceptual patterns of the rest, recalling different details and nuances of the relationship, continuing different (forgotten by the rest of the group) lines of former discussions. In this sense the hermeneutic key to the group was not lost, it was broken into pieces. And this introduction holds just one piece, one fragment of it. The rest, with which it could build up again the hermeneutic whole, the **symbol** ('symbolon'— the Hellenic piece, which the other carries to identify the community) are not only distant, but do not fit together. The elements of the hermeneutic puzzle were not simply transpositioned, they were transformed; the shape and contour of each fragment participates already in some other, completely different linguistic and human game; and joins together into other symbolons. The former fragments do not fit each other.

The impossibility of a proper introduction is increased as well by the fact that in a certain sense the texts published here owe something to a larger intellectual milieu, for which—*mutatis mutandis*—the above is also true. In the period between 1987 and 1990 the friendly circle of the authors existed amongst a crazy intellectual amalgamation of young university professors, graduate and undergraduate students—men and women of letters, philosophers, theater people, artists, sociologists, poets, and simply snobs—and this society sometimes perceived itself as involved in some act of resistance against totalitarianism still parasitizing inside its system of institutionalized languages and genres. The group "Synthesis," which gathered occasionally in the house-museum of the late Bulgarian writer Angel Karaliichev (this certainly with some effort could be interpreted symbolically—the group parasitized on the living space that had belonged to one of the numerous official Bulgarian authors, whom nobody read anymore) was not a dissident organization. It did not make the effort to "live in truth"—as "typical" dissidents like Vaclav Havel did (by the way, such people hardly existed in Bulgaria). Its strategy was to transgress the safeguarded totalitarian genres like fiction, philosophy, sociology, and theater which were ideologically limited and rigid. These genres had to be mixed and cross-fertilized to reach the point of appearing scandalous and becoming unregulated strategies of expression—"mystification," "inflammations," "disfiguring figures"—as the group itself defined the genres of its own writing and talking (indeed "Synthesis" existed mostly orally). For these "genres" the totalitarian state simply had no controlling mechanisms. The "radicalism" of that kind of intellectual-artistic behavior was certainly hyperbolized— and this hyperbolization was due to the fact that to the most part of the members of "Synthesis" totalitarianism itself, being in its late stage, was a purely linguistic phenomenon—a self-reproducing semiosphere with its own automatisms, which need to be broken.

The group "Synthesis" itself, was only a part of an even wider semi-academic, semi-artistic milieu without a common ideology. In this milieu "Synthesis" existed at times together, at times versus and against other different groups; in relations which ranged from overlapping and mixing of the groups to rivalry and open hostility. To this milieu belonged Marxist circles and secret Christian Orthodox communions, avant-guard theater groups, and students' research teams. These societies preserved their identity with an unerring instinct, drawing the line between themselves and totalitarian organizations like "Club of the Young

Writer" or "Council of the Young Scholar" that the official Communist power in Bulgaria carefully bred. In addition, they had the clear and sometimes condescending self-awareness of being a "generation" different from the preceding one of cultural clerks serving the totalitarianism.

All the groups and the loose communities referred to here were strange formations. They were naturally born as an inevitable intellectual alternative to the communist public code. They masked themselves as seminars and conferences, summer schools for young scholars—and workshops, philosophy salons, and poetic clubs. This was an attempt to outwit the system by simulative quoting of its own organizational-institutional and controlling forms (these were total, the whole life had to be "organized"—according to the totalitarian strategy).

In that kind of intellectual circle it was **possible** to mention the names of Max Weber, Vatimo, pseudo-Dionysius the Areopagite, de Sade, Fyodorov or Lyotard without the corresponding ritualistic Marxist formulas, which necessarily had to accompany them in other cases. Such an absurd list of names is not accidental. It reflects just how much this circle was productively lacking a single authority-center, that it did not have one and just one intellectual discourse—it was decisively *not* belonging to a common intellectual paradigm, a school. These authors could be mentioned, and their ideas passionately discussed without fear of sanctions. In this chaos of phenomenologists, structuralists, Orthodox believers, neo-Marxists and men of letters, postmodernists, sociologists, ethnologists, theater directors, and feminists, you could even expect that someone had read these authors. Actually the erudition was rather partial and very artistically fragmented—all these people were still semi-phenomenologists, not yet converted Christians, fresh and green postmodernists (the average age was between 25–30), the communities were organized "in pace"; this was an intellectual milieu in *status nascendi*, one that would never reach the point of being complete. In this respect the friendships, the rivalries, the discussions and the "dialogue," the latter brought to the status of an ideology (Bakhtin's ideas were in the air), were not just a form of communication but also a form of the self-generation of the intellectual communities. Dilettantism was both their sin and their vital atmosphere; it was though legitimated through the dream of "inter-disciplinarity"—another ideologeme important for the community—which hardly anyone was able to clearly formulate as an intellectual program. But on the other hand the feeling of being somehow in opposition was shared by everyone.

It is very hard to describe this intellectual milieu because of its ambiguity. Its inexplicitness was not only the characteristic feature of an intellectual puberty, it had some deeper dimensions—it could be defined as structural or even logical. None of the groups that it comprised could clearly state its ideas and did not even want to. Yearnings, biases, and feuds were not very much articulated. The amazing thing by this milieu was the very act of somehow managing to stand on the very edge of totalitarian permission and legality. It played games with the power (were they dangerous or harmless?), games of dissimulations and double dissimulations; this was a milieu where every intellectual had in one way or another masked in conspiracy his/her "true mission" so that even for the participants in this game was hard to identify the cultural or political roles of his fellows in the public space. A very refined political and cultural as well as psychological intuition was needed to be able to distinguish between a totalitarian mask and the cultural face of your neighbor; who is with you, who is against you, and what is actually your own position. The act of identifying "who is who" in this milieu built on defense strategies, conspiracy, and a problematic resistance to the all-controlling eye of the Big Brother resembled the endless process of opening a Russian doll. The identification was structurally impossible. If the distinctions could be easily made, if one could clearly and without doubt distinguish the conformist writer from the religious thinker, the potential dissident from the undercover informer, the radical community from the official institution, the postmodernist from the conservative Slavophil, this would be the end of the intellectual community. The ideological cops were always the first ones to make these distinctions. And this whole very ambiguous, but nevertheless fertile, intellectualism would be swept away in one single blow of repression by the created-for-that-very-purpose state services. Any clarity and perspicuity would actually fulfill their police ideal—total control. The ambiguity, the obscurity, the confusing and confused dissimulations, the blend of mimicry and resistance, all these were flaws of the milieu—but they were at the same time a condition for its existence, its constitutive basis. Its being in semiopposition, its nontransparent eclecticism (probably extremely repulsive for the current Western and Eastern lovers of historical *post factum* moralizing) were conditions necessary for its existence. And what is more—a prerequisite for its birth too.

In this sense the hermeneutic disintegrity of this milieu was not something that appeared later in time, it was a virus existing in in from the very beginning. As I have already said, for most of us this loosely woven network was an oasis: an intellectual island inhabited by friendly rivalry and sometimes hostile communities, which often stood at a different distance from the official ideology and official cultural institutions. This, parallel to the erotic tension, naturally created the feeling of solidarity and trust—they were not spoken about, but they were the oxygen, the condition for the existence of this milieu. But besides the solidarity—this was a paranoid space as well—a space of suspicion and distrust. Since the totalitarian system allowed for almost only impossible ways of resistance and "life in truth," nobody was completely certain, and could not be, that he/she had chosen the most correct position; everyone needed to fanaticize oneself—some procedure of self-persuasion and autohypnosis that he/she had made the "only possible choice." This inevitably caused great suspicion and distrust as far as other people's choices were different—and everyone secretly watched the conspiratorial games of the others surrounding him/her, drew their own lines between masks and faces, questioned the authenticity of the motivation of the others. Everybody wanted to know to what extent these games could be harmlessly integrated into the totalitarian mechanism, evaluated the behavior of the other not only as a covered-up resistance, but measured it against another scale too—as a probably successful strategy for an official career in the totalitarian hierarchy. In this respect, things were really getting worse due to the fact that Bulgarian science and literature of the 50s and 60s were an outstanding example of whole generations that had "started" on their way with an authentic cultural impulse and had wound up as a complacent mob of communist officials; informal circles had merged into official organizations like the "Union of Bulgarian Writers." "Dissidents" had wound up as secret agents of the ideological police or as belonging to the establishment totalitarian writers. So the structural ambiguity of the milieu had this dimension as well—from the very beginning of its existence the suspicion doubled the feeling of unity; different auto-interpretations haunted this milieu, the identities of its protagonists proliferated in number in a paranoid way, and the community itself managed to stay somehow on the edge between a solidarity of people in opposition and the secret hostile suspicion of everyone for everyone.

In the autumn of 1988, Vladislav Todorov and Alexander Kiossev—after knocking on door after door of the official institutions, after dissimulation, despair, and exaltation, after bottles of brandy for the printers and almost unbelievable luck—turned a semilegal manuscript with the title *Ars Simulacri* into 200 copies of a book. It was printed on an awful yellowish-gray paper with a flimsy binding. Later, in Ivaylo Ditchev's house, the four authors together with the illustrator Luchezar Boyadjiev, spouses and friends had to glue the illustrations, carbon sheets, etc. And, for the simulation to be complete, they put on the back cover of the book-simulation a stamp of the New York Bakers of 1913 (which somebody had accidentally come across), to parody the stamp of permission given by the official authorities.

Not by accident, in the first part of this book there is a recurrent trope. This is the trope of repetition: twins and carbon paper copies; doubling bodies, cities, and figures. The figure of Pierre Menar stands for this principle—a plagiarist of a greater genius than the author himself. This figure of the impossible identity is a symptomatic one. It bears the symptom of structural ambiguity which signifies the "recurrence of the suppressed." Thus the pattern of the Double was pervading the political unconscious of the milieu.

The authors were not aware then of how stable were the configurations of their communal political unconscious. What they wanted to do was to bring *Ars Simulacri* to the utmost because they had just made their first enthusiastic steps in reading Baudrillard.

But today it is easy to realize how little the totalitarian simulations had in common with the "precession of simulacra," that Baudrillard writes about. Because what he has in mind are virtual models whose only purpose is to produce reality—a tempting and luxurious one; the productivity (virtuality) of these models is not just a token of the disintegrating opposition between images and things, but also a sign for **potentiality** ("to produce means to materialize something by means of force," says Baudrillard) and for **potency.** To produce in Western society is not a problem. The problem is the overproduction. **Reality** is set aside just by a command on a computer because "the force" has acquired sheer informational dimensions. The real stems from and is completely interchangeable with the virtual.

The totalitarian "simulacra" had nothing in common with that Western virtual society. In a sense they were just the opposite. The "virtual model" of our society (the communist bureaucratic utopia) had one characteristic—it could reproduce no reality but itself. As Vladislav Todorov wrote—factories produced ideological poems, but not commodities. The only thing that this nonproductive, and in that sense impotent, symbolic order was capable of doing was to control the other languages; to enforce a mandatory total world of appearance; to self-reproduce by means of terror.

The very "reality" was precipitated as an irrational, anti-utopian residue, as a dark, obscure remainder after the nonproductive ideological procedures of the totalitarian society. Being a function of an utopia that never came true, reality seemed utterly wretched, disgracefully failed, consisting mainly of **deficiencies**—of commodities, books, technologies, entertainment, authenticity . . . and most importantly of signs. This was an a-semiotic "pure reality" that could only demonstrate its own wretchedness. Reality could only speak in a **figurative way** since what constituted it was precisely the **deficiency of language**, and in order to be articulated it was forced into using the only legitimate form of expression—imitation of the reigning ideological language. Reality itself manifested as a painful absence that perpetually created simulations which problematized, picked on, perplexed, scandalized, and blocked the functioning of the totalitarian discourse.

Ideology masked reality and deprived it of its genuine voice. In order to speak up, reality employed (as counter-simulation) imitations of the ideological language. The virtual and the wretched reality struggled to outwit one another. Thus the totalitarian simulation failed to organize the Desire; it failed to unlock the luxurious games of temptations and lustful images. Since "reality" could demonstrate only a number of deficiencies, the totalitarian discourse was capable only of organizing the Disgust and Intolerance in symbolic models.

In this sence, the Art of Simulation practiced in the milieu I am trying to describe was not something invented in it. It was neither its fault nor its contribution. This art was "ontologically there." If we dare to parody Heidegger—simulations simulated. They were the Word of the very totalitarian Being.

Can explanations like these foresee or prevent, even to a small extent, the misunderstandings that stalk that book?

Some time ago a foreigner that had come across some texts of Todorov, Ditchev, Kristev, and Kiossev formulated his impressions in the following way: "I have never suspected that in Bulgaria I could find such a virtuoso reception of . . . " and, if I am not mistaken, here followed the names of Baudrillard, Derrida, Foucault, and Lyotard. I tried to explain the inadequacy of the term "reception" in cases like ours, and I think we finally did not understand each other. He was thinking in classical categories—great authors—great books—diligent readers. But the young intellectuals of Bulgaria (and probably these in Poland, Romania, Russia, etc.) were reading authors and books outside and beyond the structures of their Western institutionalized worship. They were reading them without a context and without a corrective: egoistically, abusively, conspiratively, and passionately as an alternative form of intellectual and political life (language), which was to overcome the deficiencies. And that is why the Western Medieval or postmodern, psychoanalytic or structuralist, hermeneutic or deconstructivist texts were not an object of a disciplined study and research by young scholars and artists. They were a focus of ecstatic energy. That is why these people were not "reading the classics" (were they from the Middle Ages or postmodern), they were searching for allegorical forms in order to express a different, silent, and painful experience. Through this process of allegorizing, the *ideologemes* of totalitarianism acquired some "conspiratorial" meaning. The voices were becoming hermetic, the communication was encapsulated. This again shrunk the circle, and this mute experience in the name of which people had started speaking became once again alienated and incomprehensible.

The reading came out to be not a reception and not a communication, but a mutation—a transformation of the genetic structure of texts and readers.

So, after the political changes there were reasons enough for the Diaspora of the circle, and for the different languages to start roaming the world, and the mutant symbolons to invade the West and the East. And probably this is well illustrated by the already swelling up difference between texts like *Political Aesthetics of Communism, The Post-paranoid Condition, An Essay on Terror,* and *An Essay on Political Terror.* Those fragments, broken off from the body of the "promiscuous closeness" had become already complete in themselves—locked up so as not to let the past in. Each one tells its own story. And while the former texts written in the style of "inflammations and disfiguring figures" reproduced the figure of repetition, the latter unconsciously reproduce the figure of dispersing ("of the galaxies"—wrote once Ivaylo Ditchev in a short story, but there is no need of such grand metaphors any more). It is just a dispersing of human beings, friends, texts.

And the "introduction" itself, a genre to be understood only within quotation marks, has only one chance left: to reproduce, by no means unconsciously, the figure of impossibility.

Part I

Ars Simulacri

The Transparent Book
Ivaylo Ditchev

The first meeting of the postmodernist society was at hand when Mr. Todorov and I suddenly looked at each other: "Shit, what are we going to analyse?" Our only advantage was that postmodernism did not exist in our country. That gave science the unique chance to create its own object. Here is how it happened: all of a sudden we invented the Transparent book.

It was a nylon-bound book made of photographic paper and sewn with fishing string. Apart from the 100 numerated copies, there existed the artist's negative matrix carefully kept away from sight, which, of course, was meaningful. Ten glass cover copies were presented on special occasions in cellophane wrapping. Do you see or are you seen? Rumor had it that some of the copies had mirrors on the bottom, so that in looking at them you were supposed to see yourself—but these are shallow metaphors. Our interpretations were far more ambiguous. Focus eyes on book—disappears world; focus eyes on word—disappears book. Yes, we were beginning to penetrate the profundity of our message: the world was transparent, the sign was the only opaque thing in it.

It seemed obvious that all artwork is self-referential; so the only possible title was "Title." Below it, the genre: "Transparent Book," followed by a note to the reader: "Characters are the only opaque thing in this book." Of course the book narrated the story of its sudden invention and explained what it was supposed to mean (cf. supra). The cultivated reader was expected to guess that he had to put his hand under the page so that the characters would appear in their syntagmatic relations against the one-dimensional background. At this moment he read:

> Dear reader, having inserted your hand between the transparent pages you have destructed the unity of the present work; you are seeing the page, but you cannot see the book. Reading it now, you understand what you have done, but if you hadn't done it, you would never have got aware. You have lost the work the minute you attained it. . . .

At this point we perceived new abysses of meaning. It was the work that was transparent, and interpretation—opaque. Add to this all allusions to utopian fantasy, think about the challenge of a political joke, consider the instantaneous disappearance of the Transparent book in murky rooms or in a bath full of water, the magnificent sparkling of meaning at the touch of jam drops or cigarette ashes. Already Byzantine theologians realized that image cannot hold eternity; image represents but its own incapacity to do so; in denying itself, it points to the beyond. Maybe the book is still somewhere around, the wind leafing through its pages on a secluded bench. But we do not want to thrust eager hands into its integrity. For it is the Transparent book, existing by not existing; the only opacity whatsoever is the story about it.

Literalisms
Ivaylo Ditchev

It's the most stunning thing: everything is quite literal. When a thing happens to someone else, it carries its "other" significance, but look at me—I am alone at last; I'm dying and it doesn't signify a thing.

His eyes are not completely shut, there remains a whitish stripe traversed by capillaries. The habit, going back many years, of using him as a mirror, makes me feel like my own eyes are closed (in that case how could I have been seeing him?).

No time left, the mutual blood, now mine only, is getting cold. I am writing for the first and last time—I mean really writing—the kind nobody reads.

Not only "metaphor" and "grotesque," but even a description like "nature's whim" seems to lend our condition an aesthetic repose. But this condition can only be expressed with a fraction: above the line one (that's us), below it—several million (births). Day after day, moment after moment—the thought of this fraction, the rage against it, and so on.

Of course—comparisons with other more or less probable fractions. Chang and Eng—bounded together shoulder-to-shoulder—what sort of curse could that be? Whenever you wish you can turn to the other, when you get sick of him you can feast your eyes on the different Chinese stuff surrounding you.

Or the two Americans, of whom testifies J. B.—bonded back to front (so that gradually, one of them turns into sort of rucksack for the other). Yet, is there any better separation between two privacies? One of them—always watched from behind, but free to look wherever he pleases; the other one—forced to look forever at his brother's nape, yet, at the same time—absolutely invisible to him. But these people, though by coercion, are simple free of each other!

And here we are in the middle—stuck together by the force of some fraction—forehead to forehead till the end of our days.

Just the opposite of the two-faced Janus, whose symbol is a door, the entrance and the exit; we are in an angular position, through which you can neither come or go—something like an anti-mythology, so to speak.

Is it possible at all to be in a more unnatural position? You open your eyes and he is always there—looking at you from a couple of inches away. You try to go, but he tries to go as well, so that due to the equivalent forward pressure you start moving in a circle. You eat under a mutual testing look, you sit on chamber pots relieving yourselves without letting each other out of sight, you both close your eyelids for sleep and in a moment open them simultaneously to check whether the other one is sleeping. And so on.

When we were born, the doctor told Mother that science could not detach us. One of us had to be sacrificed. But who? Mother was horrified by the necessity of choice. "Well ... this one," said the doctor, holding now my bottom, now my brother's; "No it'd better be this one ... no wait a second!" He reached under his apron and took out a coin.

"I have to think!" muttered out Mother, and grabbing us—one under each arm—she scurried home. If she is still alive, she's probably thinking even now, "I don't know." I guess this indecision of hers is the cause of it all; maybe other people owe their freedom to their mother's greater decisiveness.

In my childish tantrums, I have accused her, beat her knees furiously with a fist, and jumped, landing my heels on her feet. Mother stays still. She stands mysteriously staring through the dim wintry window and smoothes our hairs with her hand. There, where the two meeting forelocks form a wave, the hand disappears, only to be felt by me again after a steady moment, warm and insistent.

Really—how could I have known, that it would be I who remained—that fate, Mother, science, or whoever loves me more than one-half? Furthermore, even if I had remained—how could I be sure that it was I who remained? And so on.

Our happy days. Hop around the ring. The wrestling which necessarily ended in a mutual tumble. The obscene pet name which Mother called us, it is hard for me to write it down . . . Well, all right: "billy-goats." How moronically literal!

In fact, we generally didn't see Mother, we heard her. The field of vision of each of us, margined off by the other one's legs, included things like the carpet's design, lemonade bottle caps, unvacuumed dust mice, or a fly gone dizzy for some reason or other. Mother we can see with a help from little round mirrors that we always carried tied to a rubber band around our necks. (O, how flat and ugly seemed to us people's faces when we discovered photography for the first time!)

Of course, you could always blind the other one with a reflected sunbeam and such stuff. With the appearance of long, wavy hairs around our Adam's apples we began using the convenience of the mirrors for something more romantic as well; when, for example, we would wind up in a streetcar next to a pair of female legs. There followed a winking session: my left eye to his right, his left to my right, or left-left, right-right, or chain-like: my left, my right, his left, his right and—the mirrors crept up to the dress, so that the angle of reflection—and so on.

At night, we waited impatiently for Mother to turn off the lights and leave the room, so that we could get on what we then called "pencil with a rubber," and the eyes shining in the half-darkness winked with rising frequency: left-left, right-right, right-right, left-left . . .

So . . . What was I saying? Oh! right! Mother! The point was not only in that we saw her diminished, twinkling in our hands. We saw her whenever we wished (as if we made her); that is, when we decided to take the mirrors out of our shirts and to direct them, according to the respective law of physics.

Only her voice was real. More than real. It came from beyond our field of vision and each of us thought that it was directed at him. More than that—in speaking to the other one, each knew that he was actually speaking to her. "I feel like eating a carrot," you say to your brother. But if *she* doesn't hear you, why the hell say it? Since anything he could do—buy it, wash it, shred it—you would have to do with him anyway, quite literally. I don't feel like living any longer. What time is it? I have a headache. How could I fare such a moron for a twin! And so on. Even the winking I mentioned—it was a secret, but a secret from her.

What happened when the desired carrot, meaning, hour, aspirin, etc. didn't appear? You had to repeat it louder. Scream, stamp your feet, deafen your brother—until she hears and comes. Your brother is, so to speak, the material target for your voice—as you for his, by the way.

But, one day, Mother decided to get married—that's the way it went. He wore a spotlessly clean black suit; in the little mirrors the creases of his pants looked endless and sharp as knives and his face was lost high up somewhere.

"You've grown up," he said, twirling around his finger a key on a chain, which drew up menacingly near to the mirror, then receded into a dot. "Your mother has the right to be happy, just like anyone," and so on.

"Tell him to shut up," I said to my brother. "Tell him to shut up," he said to me. And once more and again—louder each time—reached a full-fledged scream. When we came to, the man was gone, and so was Mother.

Since that day on, it became useless to talk—there was no one to hear. We reached silently for the canned food, we walked in a circle around the center of the carpet, staring between our legs. Mounds of tin cans on the living room floor. Flies buzzing inside the tin caverns. The growing smell of an unwashed flesh, whether yours or the other's, there was no way to tell. Pencils with rubbers. Unemptied chamber pots.

Also: people holding their noses at queues. Comments that we are disgraces to the city, that we suggest false generalizations. That we are not typical.

Some service started leaving canned food at our doorstep, so at least we could stop going out. The days became identical, only the cans and the stench grew steadily.

. . . . until one day, most unexpectedly, I heard a voice:

"Look here, let's clean up a bit." Seconds passed before I realized that the movement of my brother's lips coincided with the spoken syllables.

He was talking to me; there were only two of us. But why the hell this thought has crossed his mind and not mine, when day and night everything that happened to us was exactly one and the same?

"Let's sweep up," I said and throw out the cans.

My brother watched me—as usually—from close up. I was already certain that the suspicion had infiltrated his mind, too. The suspicion, that things said are too literal to be just so. That since the other had no purpose in just saying it, then he must mean something more.

For a while we worked with the two pails and the two brooms, circling concentrically around the mounds of trash. When the last can has been dumped down the incinerator we dragged up the two chairs, one opposite to the other, and sat down. I tried smiling and he tried, too.

"How are you, what have you being doing?" I said. Of course, I was testing him—for I knew perfectly well how he was and what he's being doing since the day of our birth (he, in a sense, that's I!)

"I'm fine," he fell into the trap, but somehow spitefully. "Liar!" I screamed out at once and we both jumped to our feet—red-faced, the tendons at our necks athrob, pressing our foreheads together with all our might. Then, even more suddenly, he alleviated the pressure and said:

"I am very disappointed"—and *that* was so preposterous, that I had to contemplate whether it wasn't actually the truth.

Why couldn't we converse? This thought prevented me from sleeping the whole night through, and that means it prevented my brother from getting asleep also, because turning in the bed involved getting up, turning around and lying down on the other side.

Even the most insignificant matters caused insoluble problems: "Where is the salt-cellar?" Why doesn't he ask me; I think he knows just as much about the salt cellar's fate as I do. The question is obviously rhetorical—he could just as well have exclaimed: "Oh, there it is—under the sink!" But is it possible to live in a rhetorical world? In order for words to beget meaning (and thus the world built through them), he must have meant something more, for example: "You are so stupid that all I can discuss with you is the salt-cellar." Notice, that I myself profited from being insulted—it was a question of life and death for my reality.

Doomed to spend our lives forever in the same situation, we had to hate each other in order to exist. Everything turned into cause for a brutal strife. Who will turn off the light. Of course, we both have to get up, but even so who would do the actual "click"—who is younger, weaker, unworthier, who turned it off yesterday, and so on. Until it dawned outside, anyway.

Nothing more unbearable than looking someone in the eyes and talking to him precisely, I mean literally. Now when Mother's gone, the words themselves, seemed to make you do things to the other one—forcing him to walk backwards to the bathroom, and suchlike. Why? I don't know myself. There was no one to judge, to understand, to spank us—from both sides it was just us, he and I.

In one of these power-struggles, I screamed out: "I'll kill you!" "That's impossible because you'll die too," said he and that was the very truth, and I knew it perfectly well. But exactly because of that, it suddenly turned untrue; I don't know how to phrase it—it simply had to say the opposite immediately: "That's not true!," he: "It is true," I: "you'll see," he: "I won't see"—and thus—with the greasy fork in one hand and the can opener in the other—and so on.

My legs are going numb, the cold seeps from him into my head. I have never produced so many words by myself; it seems to me that I am speaking to the paper, so that he would hear me. Or maybe, all this is just another joke played on me by words? New words. Quickly, more words, in the short interval when he is no longer here, but still isn't gone.

Angulus:
The Figure of Sameness
Vladislav Todorov

1. Two rules concerning the principle of interpretation:
—Any interpretation begins when I, the reader, discover in the work something that I recognize as a frozen form of my own vision.

—Any interpretation considers the work "as if" written after it was read.

In order to set correctly the relation author/reader, after reading the short story *Literalisms,* I demanded from the author to insert in it a paragraph which would certify my specific interpretation. He agreed. That is why I am writing now. This paragraph is italicized and anyone can easily find it.

2. The major problem this story reveals is: How to express Sameness?

—and it finds the way: Angle is the proper figure of Sameness. Angle makes Sameness manifested.

The message of *Literalisms* is implied in an opposition between two figures—Door and Angle. Let's examine it more closely:

The Door is both exit and entrance. It bears the ambivalent sign of the threshold. The Door divides space in two heterogeneous zones—Here and Beyond. The Door marks an ontological split and figures the encounter of the two faces of being—the external and the internal mode of existence. The Door testifies to a heterogeneous world.

In the classical age the whole set of twin-myths is based on the function of Door. Any mythological twin-couple represents a mysterious joint of being which puts together the "creator" and the "destroyer," the "profane" and the "divine" force of life, etc. There existed a common certainty that everyone has his/her own demon, genius, double, who communicates human life Here with that Beyond the Door of the world. For the world had a centaur-like construction.

The Centaur is a racing Door. God Janus has a Door-face.

The individual dimension of the common ancient representation for Persona is possible only as a special merger of the two faces of life. The uncanny appearance of a face makes it appear personal because the double nature of a Persona emerges on it.

Inversely, the essence of Sameness is not heterogeneous and thus non-transferable from Here—There. What remains after death is Sameness—a foul reality. Thus sameness becomes appalling. It cannot be contemplated for it radiates repugnance. Nausea is a symptom for a growing Sameness.

The Angle, contrary to the Door, is not a threshold that splits up space. The Angle is bifurcation—for instance a bifurcated vector or a bifurcated circumference:

The Angle is a broken threshold—a broken line or a broken plane. The Angle divides—an obtuse and an acute division:

There is no ontological difference between an acute and an obtuse angle. One of them is simply smaller. The space that a circumference closes is quantitative and the obtuse angle has just more space-quanta then the acute one. It contains more Sameness.

The Angle is a dethroned Door. It does not engender heterogeneous world but simply divides, enlarges, and diminishes Sameness.

3. Throughout this short story speaks a twin-couple whose heads are congenitally grown together. So it bears the congenital figure of an Angle, not a Door. An Angle is born whose two vectors prone on the ideal geometric surface are totally identical.

Certainly it does not make any difference which one of the twins speaks. As far as the ancient twin-figure is concerned, there always were signs by means of which you were able to recognize who spoke and who was who—the tokens of heterogeneity. In our story the voice of the one springs from the same source as the voice of the other does. What actually speaks is a point at which the line of silence was broken because the twins were born. The two bodies are two membranes of one voice. They are identical organs of One and the Same being. Sameness.

The classical Persona simultaneously reverberates two incompatible voices. It is a Gordian knot. It is a mystery.

The modernized Persona is an acoustic organ of Sameness. It is a tube. It is a hollow.

Angle's birthday:

A point begins to speak when it opens up an angle and pins down a center of a circumference. It shuts up when the vectors complete a full circle and disappear into it.

Let's configure it in this way:

Given—a stolidly silent plane. Suddenly a point appears which emanates a vector. It bifurcates and begins drawing a circumference. The speech originates right here—in the bifurcation and sounds until everything vanishes into the same plane. The speech does nothing but dash through Sameness and quantify it differently in different places. It does exactly the same thing in all its phases.

Phases:

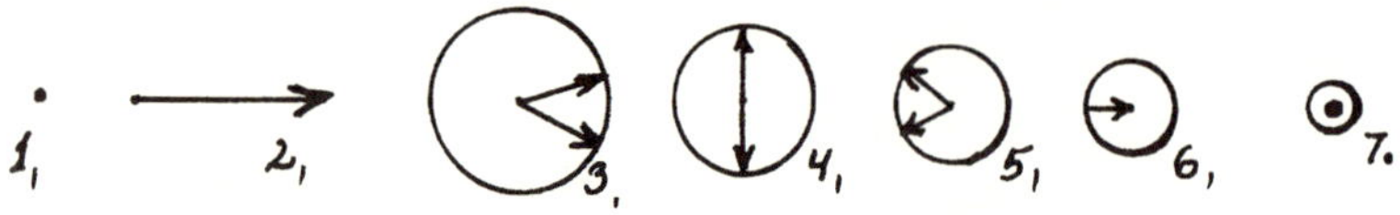

[figure: phases 1–7, dot → arrow → circle with inward arrow → circle with vertical diameter → smaller circle with inward arrow → small circle with arrow → dot in circle]

Thus human life could be configured as a geometry that progresses from birth to death. There is no mystery, no teleological development, no sacred path, no proved uniqueness either.

The riddle of the Sphinx was solved not because it was de-riddled but because it became irrelevant. Man dropped it and turned it into an Angle.

Man is no more a brave and wise Centaur. He dropped his Other and became what he literary is—an Angle which emerges in space and quantifies certain Sameness.

Sameness is a gaping Angle.

4. The conceptualism of the story could be minimized in this way:

I AM THE DOOR   VS.   I AM THE ANGLE

    CHRIST   X

The Four Luxembourgs, Civitas Peregrina

From the diary of a traveler
Pseudo-Vladislav Todorov

Vladislav Todorov

The explorers of Luxembourg usually designate its four stages according to the four possible etymologies of its name. The first three: the Luminous one, the Dissipated one, and the Twisted one stem from the Latin: Lux, Luxuriosus, Luxus. The fourth is usually derived from the name of the legendary revolutionary Rose Luxembourg. The present exploration shall adhere to these interpretations of the name thus established through tradition.

I. The Luminous City of Luxembourg

Some travelers also refer to it as the City of the Sun. This city encloses an enormous hill. Seen from afar its architecture resembles a gigantic mesh that has caught and subdued the upheaval of the mighty masses of earth, which had inflated with gas and lava the earth's crust and left behind the mountains as monuments of their provocative erections towards the sun. The city is segmented into seven circles or rings that grip the hill in concentric circles towards the top. It resembles a formidable crinoline that repulses any rascal who might crawl up the hill. A grandiose temple is erected at that very top. To be precise, the temple itself is the top. It springs up into an extraordinarily large dome on the top of which rises another smaller dome in whose center gapes an orifice that looks straight on the middle of the temple where the altar is placed. The dome is painted inside with the map of the celestial constellations, as if the sky repeats itself only lower down and smaller than itself. It has stooped down to the temple like a mystical constellation, a cipher that locks the meaning of the earthly events. The orifice is the threshold at which the maximal cosmic space is turned over into the minimal symbolic space of the temple. It is precisely through this orifice that the cosmos discharges its own superfluity for it to descend as the sacred order of the temple. Thus, the temple resembles a Cyclops's skull turned towards the sun that has scorched his eye in order to illumine him from inside. In this sense the illuminated (the internally luminous) city is blind. Thus built, the temple manifests through its figure the original sin of man towards the sun. Because before he stood on two legs, before his forehead bulged out like a church dome, before his eyes turned radiant, before he became sunlike, man was turning up towards the sky and its luminaries, his back scarlet and cracked like an enormous sore ape's ass. It is precisely this original anal openness of man towards the sun that some travelers saw manifested in the architecture of the shrines. The radiant—the seeing eye, the organ of light that bathes in rays—will always drag after itself like a tin can the embarrassment of being once an anus. Thus the central aperture of the temple, respectively the city expresses the ambivalent openness of the citizens towards their ruler— the Sun. Anyone entering the temple seems to cave in an ass through whose anus the Sun downcasts its stern and all-pervasive gaze. It is the source of the total illumination of the city. In general, the whole city is arranged in such a way that it culminates spatially in the aperture. Thus the whole city bathes its guilt in light. That is an all-encompassing luminescence in which you cannot help but wallow. This is the city of the total vertical transparency emanated by its center (the aperture). An all-pervasive solar gaze descends downwards as a guillotine. Man who stares against this gaze glows completely illumined from inside. Man stops casting a shadow. The city corpus is, in fact, the terrestrial figure of this superterrestrial gaze. The very body and structure of the city are the terrestrial incorporation of the downward gaze of a superpower. The city itself represents the total exteriorization and exhibition of life before this gaze. The descending transparency of the world manifests the epiphany of the Eye of the supreme supervisor—the Sun. Any kind of opaque negativity is usurped by the center. It is located there beyond and above the aperture of the city. Inside and below the aperture all is positive-transparent. The people are neighbors for they are totally illumined and all-pervaded by the selfsame luminous substance. They bathe in this totality and thus they prosper. Completely transparent and weightless they seem to lack bodies with tunnels flatulent with heavy slops. This is the city of the completely erect and utterly projected outwards and upwards man who bathes in the descending divine gaze. The emblem of the city is the Obelisk. Its erecting corpus is the spiritual gaze enacted in the matter of the world: The Eye-Sun as phallus.

▓ II. The Dissipated City of Luxembourg

This city rises not completely built and not completely demolished. A grand bust happened and the crowd bustles around the city somewhat rowdy, somewhat corrupted, somewhat raped, somewhat exhausted, promiscuously fornicating, having once transformed plummets into maces. The demolished city gapes like a cold volcano resounding from time to time with damnation. Once the people had grown defiant and started erecting a Tower City in order to reach God. They tried to look upwards and see God. They wanted to erect the vertical (upwards) transparency of the world. It was an attempt to establish surveillance over God. To catch God on the spot. So God got furious and segmented, that is demolished, their language. He dismantled it into a multitude of mutually impenetrable languages. A total incongruity set in that demolished the corpus of the city. The demolished Tower City stands for the demolished human look advancing upwards to make transparent the world space. The fragmentation of language manifested an opaqueness that descended from above. This figured the absence of God, i.e., the absence of a center in the space of the City that could fully absorb all negativity in itself and thus make the people neighbors. God abandoned the Babel. The Godforsaken city developed an exclusively horizontal vision and strategy. The neighbor turned stranger. The space between people hollowed out. When God desolated the city, He, so to speak, distributed the negativity among the citizens. He turned everyone into something partial, strange, alien, something "other" than everyone else, into a capsulated particularity. The only possible interest became the horizontal interest between the incompatible particularities. Everyone lusted after power, strove to achieve self-made and self-fashioned Deiformity. The space of the city became a space of internecine strife. Thus the negativity discarded by God burst forth and desolation occurred.

Each desired the other in order to possess and abuse him, to subdue and master him. The space between thee and me was reduced. The city life demonstrates the desolation as a common condition. The corpus of the city that had started threatening erection towards God was castrated and went limp as a gut—the cesspit. God forced man to bend over. He twisted his bold gaze downwards. Thus God reinstated man's guilty position. Bent over in guilt man, met the eyes of his fellow man and desired him. He desired his neighbor. The Cross became the emblem of the castrated city corpus: The broken-up obelisk.

III. The Twisted City of Luxembourg

Before they lived in their city, the people were engulfed in the intestines of a Bull. The Bull was God. And then one day the Hero appeared and led them out by killing the Bull-God. Before this happened, the world was split in two chambers, into allegorical and physical space. The allegorical space was the Labyrinth, whose tunnels always led towards the mouth of the Bull. The physical space was the Bull himself. The Labyrinth allegorically represented and exhibited the Bull's intestines. The mouth of the Bull was the aperture that connected the two spaces. Exactly there "the one" began and ended in "the other."

The mouth was the threshold. The world was set up as a two-chambered device engulfing the people from one space into the other. The allegorical space (the Labyrinth) continually collapsed into the physical one (the Bull's mouth). This way the procession of Death was performed. The physical space was God himself. The allegorical one—His phony presence outside His own natura. In order to succeed, the Hero had to walk back this same lethal path, to do an act opposite to the engulfing. It was precisely for this reason that the Hero did not appear among the living ones in the allegorical space in front of the mouth of the Bull-God. He appeared in the rear of the physical space or at the aperture opposite to the mouth—the anus of the Bull-God. From there he entered the physique of the intestines and led the people engulfed there back to the mouth. He led them out. Thus the Hero liquidated the Bull-God. He abolished the physique of the God and as a consequence of this he found himself together with his people in the allegorical space of the Labyrinth which survived as the One space. This turned out to be the virtual City of their liberation. The liquidation of God reduced the world to the omnipresence of the allegorical space. Nothing could exist beyond it. The tunnels of the figurative reality did not lead to any apertures. They were blind. The liquidation of God came as a radical denaturalization of existence. The Labyrinth is by itself a twisted construction. The corpus of the Labyrinth City does not resemble any bold exalted erection. It can never be straight, nor can it be broken. Its natural joints are twisted so that it cannot stand up. It drags its spreading horizontality. The transparency is reduced to the direct visibility in the convolutions of the tunnel. The global allegorical space could be recognized in the fact that the Labyrinth is exactly the same in all its cells and can be surveyed without moving about. It is a self-duplicating sameness. The citizens live in one and the same allegory without being able to see each other because of the vertebral-like structure of the Labyrinth. The physical space was absolutely shredded up and so busted. The allegorical one opened unlimited space and thus became omnipresent. There was no power able to justify this endless allegorical order. The Labyrinth has no center. Every place in it is absolutely identical to every other place. In each cell of it emerge exactly the same things as in every other one. There are no heroically privileged places. When the Hero led his people into the Labyrinth, he himself disappeared. He took a place in it and became like everyone else. He acquired the anonymous existence of everyone else. The Labyrinth as an emblem signifies nothing but the torso of the world after God was wrested off it. Nothing is present to testify to the sense of life, nothing exists to justify the order of the world but it is total. The Absurd. It is conspicuous by the final degradation of the phallus into a colon. The erection is supplanted by constipation.

IV. Luxembourg—the Phantom City

Comrade Luxembourg—this is a woman
—Platonov

Most travelers describe it like this: a gigantic corpus, slowly augmenting, because it inflates and at the same time blackens. Having reached the point of bursting, exactly when its crust is ripping frightfully, threatening to let out slops and gases, the corpus starts slowly to soften and lighten up until it turns into a pulp. It is a necrotized womb stuffed up by dead substances: A womb turning into a vampire. This is the city of the most incredible metamorphose, mutation, and vicissitude.

This city is organized according to the grammar of an instructive language. In contrast to the Tower City, here the language has not been demolished, but nevertheless, no tower has been built, no "Common Home." This language propagates and agitates people to perform the sublime act—to claw the earth in exaltation. It was necessary to dig harder and more cunningly in order to transform the earth interior into a "Common Home." The main effort of the subjects was to dig out a colossal pit, a gigantic aperture—sanctuary, an organized subterranean eternal sun-trap.

The total language projected reality of the Phantom City. In the space of the City reverberated thunder like proclamations. The people became heralds of stunning proclamations, of verbal maltreatment because the proclaimed reality was a bruised piece. Reality dispersed in panic chased away by its own proclamations.

Language was the virtual reality and all things real peek out of it as phantoms. The Last Judgment was proclaimed real in order for a phantom to be punished—the bourgeoisie. Communism was proclaimed real in order for the other phantom to be immortalized—the proletariat. It was realized by being proclaimed. Do you recollect the story of the madman who believed he was a hen, so they fed him with raw corn? He did not stop being insane, but he stopped pretending to be a hen so that he wouldn't have to gnash his teeth on the raw corncobs. Someone proclaimed himself God and proceeded to feed on soil. The sun was proclaimed to be the Universal proletarian. Language. In the language there was no center nor horizontal or vertical coordination. It performed twisted parables according to the rules of its grammar. Language was a radioactive instrument that caused monstrous mutations in the City. Uncanny, melancholic longing engulfs the souls of the citizens: A longing for reality. And only through longing could reality open itself in the minds. Through this longing did the unnamed reality rush into the phantom figure of the City. The longing became the aperture through which reality made known its own presence. One thing sustained the population and the militants of the City—the fact that there had to be a super point of view, one might say a central herald of the proclamations, for whom everything that happened was observable, manageable, and goal-oriented. There existed the certainty that the life of the City is performed before the gaze of one centralized Eye-Mind. A certainty, that one surveyor observes and supervises the correct goings on of the grandiose ceremony called Proletarian Revolution. Otherwise to every glance from inside, life passed as an arbitrary dispersal or merging of phantoms and names. The despair came with the suspicion that this super Eye-Mind was also a phantom: A high density phantom arbitrarily authorized with a centralized ontological presence. The certainty that the transparency of the City descended from above was a sham. This "see-through-all" Eye was also proclaimed. Through renaming its realities, the Phantom City assembled and disassembled itself like an animated toy puzzle before the amazed eyes of the greatest Dadaist of the world (proclaimed to be such in Zurich). Like a real hero, this Dadaist succeeded in getting to the bottle and letting loose the genie of the most imbecile Hocus-pocus. And with an exalted babble it penetrated the City and proclaimed it. Another Dadaist of the same rank constructed a machine for executions with quite artistic and precise functions. Then he himself jumped into it and thus became the requisite matter for its function in order to demonstrate its exquisite perfection. At night, tired by the excessive work of the Hocus-pocuses, the citizens of the Phantom City sulked and listened to the lamp fuse sucking in the kerosene. And in order to stifle the rumbling of their empty stomachs, they nibbled the wall plaster. This city had no special emblem. It was emblem itself. For there existed no sign that could stand for it. Everything got proclaimed—interned into the City.

The Four Luxembourgs, Civitas Peregrina

All travelers observe a strict tendency towards denaturalization of Luxembourg during its four stages: passing from a vertical into a horizontal symbolism and its vanishing into crooked parabolas; an ever more irreversible dislocation of the natural joints and apertures of the city corpus; presence, then absence, then abolishing, and at the end turning into a vampire of the city center; from emblem representing the essence of the city—to a city emblem of itself.

Usually the travelers evade the teleological interpretations, because they lead life unto a certain destination and in this sense to certain utopia or anti-utopia. Others speak of the cyclic recurrence of the herein described stages. Still others to whom we pertain are convinced of the principle of the back and forth momentum. According to this principle the City of the Sun and the Phantom City are respectively the upper and lower deadpoint between which historically acts the piston of Luxembourg.

IMPLETA CERNE! IMPLENDA COLLIGE!

Pierre Menard, the Author of Don Quixote
Ivan Kristev

> *Why are we confused by the fact that Don Quixote is a reader of **Don Quixote**? I think I have find out the reason: turns of the kind implies that if the invented characters could be readers, then we—their readers—could be invented.*
>
> Pierre Menard

It took me seven years to examine Pierre Menard's personal archives. After the death of their owner—Baroness de Bacourt—and after the retirement of Countess de Bagnorregio into a monastery (to the great amazement of the public) the archives have reached one of those library depositories with Pierre Menard's immortal verse above the entrance. Damp and dirty, constant victim of flood and rats, these depositories are the last refuge for thousands of long forgotten books, and for the ambitions of their authors that nobody knows of. It still remains a mystery how it happened that the Pierre Menard's archives were in those lamentable surroundings. And yet another mystery is the document bearing a seal from the town council in Nimes that I happened to find. It was shoved in with the last letters of the poet and it made my seven-year-long painstaking work pointless. The document was written on a ordinary form and it certified that Pierre Menard and Pierre Menard were identical. The date *August 1st, 1939* was written in the right corner and the authenticity of the signature was doubtless.

I have no other choice as to quit the library forever and to by a little farm.

I am leaving this brief letter, together with my unfinished theses-metaphors in the archives of Pierre Menard.

▦ Theses-Metaphors

1. According to Pierre Menard **Don Quixote** is a protagonist of identity; with his longish and weakly silhouette resembling a letter, he looks as if he has just stepped out of the open pages of a book. Don Quixote reads the world incessantly and by his perusal he proves the verity of the book. He is the ideal reader: reading is the modus of his existence. Nonreading disfigures the world and makes it contingent. Cervantes was reported to read even "the paper bits on the street." In a curious way reading precedes living (being), constituting it. Reading as an act of intercoursing (coming into contact with letters) is transcending; it is the path of a descending beyondness. Reading as an existence is rereading; it is translation, translocation in this very beyondness.

The father of the Carolingian Renaissance, Charles the Great, could read but not write. The advent of Alkuin—the Librarian—is connected with his rule. The librarian is a stranger, actually from the absolute outside. The librarian is the image of the descending beyondness. Library plus reading king—this is already the condition for the emerging of an empire. The empire presupposes integrity and completeness, and integrity and completeness cannot be created by man, they could be only pre-given.

Thus the Library is another Utopia: it constitutes the world, always remaining out of it. There is no place for the Library in the world and, at the same time, the Library constitutes its being as the condition for its possibility. But there is no place for the library outside the world either, because it is the Library which constitutes that Outside.

The Library-Utopia has double existence; on the one hand it exists in the modus of reading and is read as be-

Pierre Menard, the Author of Don Quixote

Ivan Kristev

> *Why are we confused by the fact that Don Quixote is a reader of **Don Quixote?** I think I have find out the reason: turns of the kind implies that if the invented characters could be readers, then we—their readers—could be invented.*
>
> Pierre Menard

It took me seven years to examine Pierre Menard's personal archives. After the death of their owner—Baroness de Bacourt—and after the retirement of Countess de Bagnorregio into a monastery (to the great amazement of the public) the archives have reached one of those library depositories with Pierre Menard's immortal verse above the entrance. Damp and dirty, constant victim of flood and rats, these depositories are the last refuge for thousands of long forgotten books, and for the ambitions of their authors that nobody knows of. It still remains a mystery how it happened that the Pierre Menard's archives were in those lamentable surroundings. And yet another mystery is the document bearing a seal from the town council in Nimes that I happened to find. It was shoved in with the last letters of the poet and it made my seven-year-long painstaking work pointless. The document was written on a ordinary form and it certified that Pierre Menard and Pierre Menard were identical. The date *August 1st, 1939* was written in the right corner and the authenticity of the signature was doubtless.

I have no other choice as to quit the library forever and to by a little farm.

I am leaving this brief letter, together with my unfinished theses-metaphors in the archives of Pierre Menard.

Theses-Metaphors

1. According to Pierre Menard **Don Quixote** is a protagonist of identity; with his longish and weakly silhouette resembling a letter, he looks as if he has just stepped out of the open pages of a book. Don Quixote reads the world incessantly and by his perusal he proves the verity of the book. He is the ideal reader: reading is the modus of his existence. Nonreading disfigures the world and makes it contingent. Cervantes was reported to read even "the paper bits on the street." In a curious way reading precedes living (being), constituting it. Reading as an act of intercoursing (coming into contact with letters) is transcending; it is the path of a descending beyondness. Reading as an existence is rereading; it is translation, translocation in this very beyondness.

The father of the Carolingian Renaissance, Charles the Great, could read but not write. The advent of Alkuin—the Librarian—is connected with his rule. The librarian is a stranger, actually from the absolute outside. The librarian is the image of the descending beyondness. Library plus reading king—this is already the condition for the emerging of an empire. The empire presupposes integrity and completeness, and integrity and completeness cannot be created by man, they could be only pre-given.

Thus the Library is another Utopia: it constitutes the world, always remaining out of it. There is no place for the Library in the world and, at the same time, the Library constitutes its being as the condition for its possibility. But there is no place for the library outside the world either, because it is the Library which constitutes that Outside.

The Library-Utopia has double existence; on the one hand it exists in the modus of reading and is read as be-

longing to the beyondness and to the constitutive possibilities; on the other hand, its second existence is the modus of writing—it is being written as belonging to "hereness" and as reconstructing the constitutive completeness and integrity. The image of its beyondness is the burned library—for example, the Alexandrine library—put on fire by Pierre Menard (according to his novel **The Name of the Rose**). The image of the "hereness" is the writer, the creator of books. In an empirical aspect writing precedes reading, in a metaphysical aspect reading precedes writing. Within a personal biography reading and writing can be hardly differentiated. In the personal-biographical dimension a particular place is given to copying.

The copyist is inseparable from the being of the Library. His bent figure, drawing letter after letter in a mystic excitement, is the image of expansion. The copyist multiplies and at the same time his personality implies reading and writing; he is guarantee for their unity in the eyes of the Library. Book printing deprives him of this function and gives birth to the plagiarist. The plagiarist is the fraudulent copyist, he is the Scandal. With the origination of book printing, the Library archives its infinity and its imperial completeness. The plagiarist is the figure through which the order of the Library-Empire is actualized. Existing as a scandal, the plagiarist allows the expression of the basic principles of the Library. Achieving its imperial completeness, the Library reaches its exhaustion and gives birth to the Catalog. The Catalog is the sharpened spear of expansion. The plagiarist is the point where the Library and the Catalog meet. He is the fist of the Catalog and the solar plexus of the Library. The Catalog is the secret police of the Library, it is to know the places of things. The plagiarist is the scoundrel who undermines the foundations of that knowledge. Owing to the Catalog, the Library need not read itself.

Pierre Menard is not a Scandal, he is not a copyist or a plagiarist. Pierre Menard doesn't aim at expansion and therefore he is invisible for the Library: he doesn't leave any traces on the dusty shelves. He exists in the dimension of reading. Pierre Menard deprives us of the certainty that the **Don Quixote** we are holding in our hands is the **Don Quixote** of Cervantes and not Pierre Menard's. The Library turns out to be useless. We can reach out for a book as in the past but we no longer know whose book it is.

2. Reading, writing, quoting, collecting—these are the keywords of these theses. They are used like metaphors indicating different stages and strategies in the book-world relationship; they are the tentacles of the Library. But reading, writing, quoting, and collecting are used in a non-metaphoric sense as well; they must give life to a differentiation which Pierre Menard draws between book and text (in his article **From Work to Text**). According to Pierre Menard, the differentiation of work and text is the result of a certain change—the fact that something has happened in modern culture. The ambition is to catch this "something," this change, and if this is not possible, to catch the "catching" itself.

The work is a material fragment occupying a portion of the space of the books (in a library, for example). The text on the other hand is a methodological field. The work can be seen (in bookshops, in catalogs), the text is a process of demonstration and self-identification. The work can be held in hand, the text is held in language. The text is not the decomposition of the work, it is the work that is the imaginary tail of the text. If the text is experienced only in an activity of production, it follows that the text cannot stop.

This definitions of Pierre Menard will not be subjected to critical analysis here; they will be acknowledged not because of their unquestionable truth but because of the presupposition that trying to explain the modern situation they create it; they conceive it in the modus of existence. The "something" and the "catching" turn out to be identical. The cultural reality described by Menard is Menard's descriptions as real.

3. Don Quixote is the ideal reader (but not the ideal reader as a silly abstraction). Don Quixote is the ideal reader of Cervantes's **Don Quixote.** The ideal reader of the traditional work of literature is the protagonist of this work *Writing is always constructing its ideal reader through the text itself"* (P. Menard). Moreover, it constructs him as a protagonist of this text.

Don Quixote is intended for Don Quixote; it is written for him and this is the first level of "ideallity," of Don Quixote's reading. To read a book in tradition means to be changed by this book and live in its reality in a curious way. Living is the only privileged interpretation. The aim of the book is to mold the world. The idea of the author as the best reader of his own works cannot be understood if another classical axiom is not made explicit—the axiom clearly expressed in Flaubert's dictum *Madame Bovary—c'est moi.* The author is the ideal reader as far as he is a protagonist in his own work and as far he is produced by it. Cervantes himself is the author of his protagonist in two different ways. In the prologue to the second part he polemically defends his rights over the character, proving that Cervantes himself is the author of **Don Quixote** and that he has written it. But Cervantes is an author of **Don Quixote** in another, often unnoticed way as well. His **Galatea** happens to be among the books that the barber and the priest find in the bookcase of the knight-errant. Cervantes simultaneously constructs and constitutes his protagonist. Reality is only a narrow slit between two books.

There is no boundary between world and book for Don Quixote. The visibility of this boundary (visible to us) is an optical illusion, caused by the spellbinding nonreading.

The tragic, the comic, and the inadequate in Don Quixote's behavior in the first part of the book are a direct consequence of the fact that the rest of the characters have not read enough chivalrous romances.

In his famous essay **Don Quixote and the Problem of Reality,** Menard poses the fundamental question: *How* *is possible that Don Quixote's intimate world should not be solipsistic; how is it possible that this world be inhabited by the minds of other people as well who are not just objects of Don Quixote's mind but also that they share with him, at least to a certain extent, the belief in the potential or actual reality of his world?* The answer to this question could be found in the Library, in the understanding of Don Quixote as constituted as a projected conscience. The Library is Berkley's God LTD.

In the second part the world has already entered the book: almost all characters have read the first part and though this entrance happens by way of a game and a parody, it is constituted as well. The Library motivates the behavior of all the characters. The invading world is, in fact, conquered by reading. And unlike Cervantes, Pierre Menard doesn't constitute his Don Quixote. The priest and the barber will never find one of his (Menard's) books in the bookcase of the knight-errant. Pierre Menard doesn't even write a book about its protagonist—Cervantes has already created it. Pierre Menard substitutes it.

4. Pierre Menard is the author of the Identical. He is the identifier. His ambition is to write **Don Quixote**, and what is more, he doesn't want to invent another **Don Quixote**—that would be easy—but **Don Quixote** itself. Needless to say, he has never aimed at mechanically copying the original. His extraordinary ambition is to create several pages which coincide verbatim with the ones written by Miguel de Cervantes. Pierre Menard is the ideal reader as well. Like Don Quixote, he also read **Don Quixote**. But Pierre Menard is the ideal reader in a cultural situation where reading and writing have become dead metaphors. The text cannot be written and finished; it can only be read through. My overall idea of **Don Quixote**—as Pierre Menard writes in a letter of his simplified by indifference and oblivion, can be fully identified with the vague prototype of the still unwritten book. For Pierre Menard **Don Quixote** has failed out of his reality and become merely a potentiality, become a text. As Menard points out, work and text cannot be differentiated in a purely chronological sense; an ancient text could be a text while many products of modern literature are in no ways texts. The modern cultural situation has not created the text, it has identified it. The work is conceived as the imaginary end of the text—its tail. For Pierre Menard, **Don Quixote** is a text that tries to catch its tail.

5. The microscopic smallness of handwriting, thought of metaphorically, is one of the essential characteristic features of the text and his author. *I remembered his notebook with chequered pages*—Pierre Menard wrote about Pierre Menard—*there were places crossed out in black ink, and peculiar proofreading and signs and letters, as tiny as midges.* The text intentionally tries to be invisible; the miniature letters cannot actually be read, they could only be invented and supposed. The only way to read the text is to accept the responsibility of becoming its author. Pierre Menard's **Don Quixote** is the final, the borderline of variant of a text. It is unreadable but not in the same way as the vanguard literature: Pierre Menard's text cannot be read, it is invisible for us. We are blind for it.

6. In its essay about collection **Unpacking Library** (wrongly attributed to Walter Benjamin) Pierre Menard mentions a Wutz, Jean Paul's teacher, who leafed through catalogs—not with the intention of choosing the book he would read—but the ones he would write (and a title that attracted his interest became a title of a new book he actually wrote). The substitution Wutz made was insignificant, unimportant, and invisible for the collector. Collecting in pure sense is not connected with reading. The Collector doesn't read, he acquires. The book is having, possessing, touching, it is an event. The Library has lost its constitutive beyondness. The biography of the collector has turned out utopian as is his effort to collect it and provide a history for himself.

Collecting is constituting the past; the collector experiences the present by delving into the past, providing a past. The future is completed past. If the empire of Charles the Great falls down after his death, the collector's death is what makes an empire of his biography.

7. Wutz is a reversed Pierre Menard. Collecting is the inverted face of quoting. These are the two halves of a disintegrated whole—the catalog. The Catalog is the materialized notion of authorship in Modern Times. It carries the unity of author-and-book (understood as a configuration of signs), and meaning of the book. The catalog guarantees the privileged position of the author's interpretation. Pierre Menard is invisible for the Catalog. His insane deed—his **Don Quixote**—makes the existence of the catalog senseless. As a result of Menard's insanity **Don Quixote** disappears. It can no longer be quoted, as there are no guarantees that we face Cervantes's work, and not Menard's. The author cannot prove his paternity to the work. Pierre Menard is the collector of perusals. Similar to Wutz his **Don Quixote** belongs to him; Pierre Menard makes his biography an object of an incessant reading. Pierre Menard transcends his own biography: he quotes **Don Quixote** in an invisible work and this invisible work is Pierre Menard's reading of **Don Quixote**. Quoting confronts itself. Quotation marks become impossible: their function is to set somebody else's text apart and guarantee a strictly defined meaning behind it. Pierre Menard tears this link apart—thus killing the quotation marks—this is Pierre Menard's peculiar method. The history of this quoting is a possibility for the modern cultural situation to be grasped as unique.

PS.
I think that everybody who happens to read these remnants of my seven-years-long efforts will understand the horror and despair on discovering the confounded document. Pierre Menard and Pierre Menard were identical. Therefore there were books which Pierre Menard could not write—Pierre Menard's books.

Goethe's Indigo
Alexander Kiossev, etc.

It is only modesty to prevent us from dedicating this text to J. L. B. Therefore we dedicate it to Goethe.

Last year the prestigious literary-historical magazine for German literature **Philemon and Baucis** carried a text whose scandalous nature went beyond the academic circles and justifiably roused the indignation of both the collaborators of Goethe Institute and the broad public, which, nevertheless, dearly treasure the classical figures of Goethe, Schiller, Eckermann, and Zeitler. Before that, as if the wave of jokes connected with the name and work of Goethe had being brought to a head by the claim of the eccentric contemporary writer that the last phrase uttered by the Weimar Hellene "Licht, mehr Licht!" had actually being wrongly overheard by those around Goethe's deathbed—in actual fact it allegedly ran like this: "Nicht mehr, nicht!" However, the excerpt **Goethe's Indigo**, whose discoverer and publisher (or perhaps author?), signed with the provocative pseudonym of Roland Macpherson, presented (and later juridically defended it by means of a chemical analysis of the composition of paper and ink) as a fragment, deliberately covered up and not included by Eckermann in his **Conversations with Goethe in the Last Years of His Life**, amounted to something more than a mere joke—it was a scandal, a flagrant mockery of the very idea of classics. The fact that contrary to his own interests and the decision of experts, in the written answers in the numerous interviews in the German press (given with the mediation of a secretary), the mysterious Macpherson dropped some broad hints to the effect that all that was only a mystification, a hypothetical structure on which modern semiotics could expand some paradoxical comments (which did not impede his winning the official case and turning the fragment's authenticity into a juridical fact) added more fuel to the scandal.

At any rate, the pose and the comments of Roland Macpherson shocked, and not only for the lack of respect for the great names in German literature, but also for the negligent manner in which he had sketched his semiotical comment, which resembled a semiotic exercise, a variation, even play rather than serious science. On top of all that, as if they showed through the prototype of **The Name of the Rose** which divested **Goethe's Indigo** from originality: just like Umberto Eco built the subject matter of his novel around the missing part of the classical European book, Aristotle's **Poetics**, Macpherson sought another such "missing" classical text—and from this point of view, the choice of the classical figure of Johann Wolfgang von Goethe and of Eckermann's **Conversations** was more than predictable.

Of course, the above is true, given that the fragment is indeed, a mystification of Macpherson—because, in any event the other alternative exists—it may well be Eckermann's text. Trying to keep up the good academic tone and scientific objectivity, we shall reproduce here the fragment itself, as well as Macpherson's comments accompanying it—and we shall leave it to readers to judge whether the text is an authentic testimony to Goethe's life, or an illustration of an abstract and play-like semiotic concept. In conclusion, we shall say again a couple of words.

Alexander Kiossev

Good old Johann Peter Eckermann wished to conceal from the eye of time a tiny fragment of his **Conversations**

with Goethe, and yet, in all probability, the eye of time preferred the opposite, because this excerpt come to my hands and I publish it for the broad world public and in front of the excited eyes of the German philistines. I prefer to pass over in silence the circumstances under which I got hold of this text; I shall only mention that it is an intricate story over the past 150 years. The text seems to have been preserved and kept in the societies of Freemasons, because in 1860 a secret Masonic writing mentioned **Goethe's Indigo** twice. Later on, the likely fate of the manuscript might be traced back to the Swiss theosophical circles—there is ground to believe that some of their esoteric interpretations would have been impossible without their being aware of Goethe's outlook concerning the indigo, expounded by him before Eckermann. A huge archive of German texts from where the fragment—again secretly—has been transferred back to Europe, was discovered in a southern American country in the sixties of our century. All that mysteriousness is rather funny—after all, there is not too much to conceal in this excerpt. Behind the motive of the pathetic Eckermann to cover it up probably stood the understanding that it was a "great key" to a classical and mystical devotion, a key that does not unlock the "doors of eternity" to the uninitiated. Actually, everyone who took the pains to read the voluminous ennui of the "German Hellene" could not but become aware that the concepts expounded by Goethe by that conversation could be easy enough reconstructed from other statements of his, with the exotic symbol of the indigo being the sole novelty. What Eckermann (and permanently great Goethe too) could not see, is that their conversation about the indigo proved a possibility for several substantial paradoxes from the sphere of the philosophy of language to be deduced. Their dedication has, of course, become possible only today when the very idea of classics has been reduced to no more than some dust, and after the works of some epoch-making names in the development of semiotics, the philosophy of language, and the theory of communications. So the genuine secret of the indigo remained invisible to both Goethe and Eckermann.

Here is the authentic text of the fragment itself.

Thursday, January 20th, 1831

I shall probably remember this day as the luckiest in my life. I heard and saw things that make me feel initiated into a sublime secret, which I shall keep till my last gasp.

I had been invited and went to see Goethe in the evening. Expecting to see cheerful company there, I saw him alone in the Urbino room, with the blinds pulled down. There were two lit candles, a bottle of Reims wine and some delicious biscuits on the table. He was scrutinizing a drawing and the concentrated noblesse his face was emanating made me feel excited. His big, beautiful hand rested calmly on a red file.

The conversation focused on my project to edit and publish Goethe's letters. He again commented on my notes, stressing that I had already learnt those tiny and insignificant, at first sight, fragments and notes according to their genuine value, like pieces of an internally complete life.

"Once, many years ago, I burnt all the letters that I had received since 1772 by that time—Goethe said—now I don't think I did the right thing. You know, I ordered that my letters and even the tiniest note I wrote be copied, and usually I give the rough copies to be clipped together—in this way they start bearing the completeness of a spontaneous book. And what else is life, but a book! And the deeper and more versatile is life, the better each of its details enters the thorough composition of this invisible work. Genuine life requires a talent, similar to that of the creator of a great work."

Our conversation switched to the passion for collecting and preserving various, and at first sight, insignificant relics of the past. Goethe mentioned his collection of minerals, handwritings, busts, and drawings, saying that they had brought him big worries, though he could neither give them up nor deny his ambition to collect the traces of every experience and instant. Then he fixed his eyes on the flame of the candles and for a while he was deep in thought. The drawing he was scrutinizing was on the table in front of him. He held it against the light and gave it to me.

"Is this plant familiar to you?" Goethe asked me. I answered in the negative—looking at me from the drawing was a medium-sized bush with its twigs and leaves slightly resembling those of the acacia tree, but having deep pink petals.

"Actually, you could hardly know it"—Goethe smiled—"Although some time ago I gave you the Bashkirian bow, and your knowledge of the ash-, maple-, nut-tree varieties and the processing of their wood amazed me. This is an indigo plant. It grows only in India, China, and Ceylon. I heard attempts are being made of late to grow it in America, too."

"Is the dye produced from this bush?" I asked. Goethe nodded pensively.

"Yes, that's right. Although that is by far the most interesting thing about it."

He rose and started walking about the room, while I remained seated the way he liked it.

"Young man, today I shall impart to you a profound idea, because, following your own way, you have proved worthy of and ripe to know it. In this plant I discovered a genuine symbol, a symbol in which the majestic simplicity of the ever-changing, divine nature and the predestination of the human spirit are equally well shown. I wonder why the ancient people felt reverences for the mandragora; in my view the indigo is a much more mysterious and sublime plant. It was already familiar to people in Babylon, in Egypt, in ancient Judah.

As early as 2000 years ago the part of the Talmud called the **Mishna Book** mentioned of a ban of the destruction of the indigo bush until it is three years old.

And the Arabs made an attempt to grow it in the warm parts of Western Asia, because its transportation from India made it too expensive. It is the best and the fastest blue dye ever. Despite Marco Polo's information, its production was not familiar in Europe, and it was brought to the continent only after the sea route to India became possible. You know, in the seventeenth century the indigo was under a ban in Germany, because in all probability it displaced the local plant-based dyes and farmers protested. But it is likely that the law against it is also connected with its mysterious qualities, with the fact that some witches and sorcerers used it as a cure and the people called it *Teufelfarbe*. However, I shall be hardly able to tell you everything today—the indigo is one of the symbols we usually call universal—and for years now I have been studying it in my literary and scientific works. When, dear Eckermann, you take to the compendium of my **Teaching on Colors** as you have promised me, I shall tell you of the connection I see between the basic color regularities in nature and the change in the indigo colors (from the pale yellow juice of the just-picked plant; through the deep yellow infusion which, when exposed to air, gradually turns dark green; to the dark blue indigo powder, which, to become a dye, should have passed through the "indigo white," while when heated it releases copper-red crystals). And at the moment I am occupied with the life of the indigo plant in connections with my **Metamorphosis of Plants**, which has already greatly grown in volume. I'll be telling you of this another time. I would now like to tell you of something more important."

Goethe took the red file and opened it. Contrary to my anticipations that there would be another drawing or engraving there, from the file he took a strange, dark blue sheet and handed it to me. One side of the sheet was matte, but the other one had had a glistening dark blue layer which stained my finger a little. After I had examined it, Goethe took it back and placed it between two blank, clean sheet of paper. Then he wrote on the upper sheet: *Salve,*

Eckermann, sub specie aeternitatis! When he separated the sheets I saw the Latin inscription printed on the lower sheet: with a single movement of the hand he had created two inscriptions.

"Perhaps in this you can see no more than an ordinary copying" Goethe said and again smiled rather inscrutably at that "but it is something much, much more. One should penetrate into the symbolical meaning of this doubling, it takes a long time and requires great concentration. It took me fully thirty years to get to the bottom of this phenomenon. The symbol has many layers and I shall reveal them to you one by one.

We are on Earth to learn to turn the transient into eternal. But it is only one who is able to really appreciate both—the transient and the intransient things, the instant and eternity, to attain this. One of the most substantial human concerns, particularly so of the one who has taken to literary work, is the preservation and conservation of literary monuments. What pitiful remnants of the great works of Aeschylus and Euripides, of Plautus, and of my favorite, Menander, have come to the present day! The written works are the fruit of a transitory and fragile experience, although people have resorted to various means to preserve and conserve them. Some people wonder at my passion for collecting all kinds of most diverse and insignificant texts, at my writing even the most trivial notes and rough copies, which I later preserve. But I have nearly physical perception of the disintegration of paper, of the way bad people falsify what has already been said or written. In this respect the sheet of the indigo paper[1] is a miraculous object: doubling what has been written, it preserves and conserves it in a peculiar way. If one of the texts happen to disappear, the other one will remain; if someone else's insertion has been added to one of them, the second one will certify the truth; if part of one of them and part of the second are destroyed, placing them one on the other will probably save the better part of the work itself. You may well say however, that both copies may be as equally and fully destroyed as only one of them, consequently the indigo should preserve nothing and shall conserve nothing. The magic key is just in this, young man."

Goethe sat and looked in a friendly way at me.

"Truly, the indigo creates the *symbol* of preservation of what has been written along with the very process of writing rather, than preserves what has been written. You send a note to someone, carelessly written in pencil, inviting him to have a glass of wine with you this evening. The note is connected with the empiricism of the situation and as if it should be fully confined to it to disappear with it; the indigo, however, reproduces another copy of the note, completely useless with regard to empirical circumstances. Through it you don't invite your friend to visit you, you send your word to another time, to future people; in a nutshell—you send it directly to eternity. To think of the future, or of the eternity when you are doing something concrete, is the worst kind of vanity—and here again, the indigo relieves us of it. It helps us fully dedicate ourselves to the instant, to really appreciate the present and commit ourselves to it; and besides, it directly clips a copy of our thoughts and words, without our being aware of it, together with the certificate of eternity. The instant is invisibly doubled and preserved; in this way the indigo teaches us that every state, even the instant, are extremely precious because they are representatives of entire eternity! You know me to be the most spontaneous man who, just like a child, is capable of living with the instant, of dedicating, with passion and to the full, to the new feeling. Along with this, however, I am a citizen of millennia and statues seem to me ridiculously transient: I cannot imagine a monument in tribute to any worthy man before I have seen it knocked down and battered and the stone eaten up with erosion. For me the symbol of the indigo has proved to be the miraculous bridge which spand the transient with eternity— it seems to me, I am living as if doubled by the indigo, that I am writing my life not only in the concrete circumstances of our century and of our poor Germany, but directly on the golden sheet of Time!"

Enraptured with what he was saying I was breathless. On his last words, his verses whose meaning I could grasp only now, suddenly came to my mind:

> Die Zeit ist mein Besitz,
> Mein Acker ist die Zeit!

Goethe drew his big face closer to the candle and the multitude of wrinkles stood out more prominently.

"The indigo has also another symbolic meaning which I call "collective." Because no matter what we present us to be, all of us are collective beings. How little we possess of what we can refer to, in the purest sense of the word, as our property!

Writing is born of the instant, by some concrete, transitory experience. However, the instant itself is collective. The instant is the public! Every expression of our subjectivity (on which romanticists have been wasting their words) is intended for the eyes of the public, the posterity which expects no accidental or too odd confessions from us, but a revelation of the universal human nature. You, I suppose, remember that I have written about Winckelmann's letters to Berendis..."

Goethe rose, and from a regales by the wall he took in his hand the volume of **Winckelmann and His Century**, turned over its pages, found the passage he was looking for and read it out:

"Letters should be regarded as one of the major documents an individual leaves behind. People of lively imagination, even when talking with themselves imagine at times, as though an absent friend is by their side, a friend to whom they are imparting their inmost thoughts. Likewise, the letter is a kind of conversation with oneself, because the friend to whom we are writing is often the occasion rather than the subject of the letter. Everything that pleases or injures us, that depresses or occupies us comes from the bottom of our hearts, and similar letters—the lasting traces of an experience, of a state, are the more important for posterity, the stronger the writer is possessed by the moment and the less he thinks of the future."

He closed the book and looked at me, a serene, noble fire in his deep-set eyes.

"You see—herein I have tried to express this contradictory interweaving of loneliness and transience on the one hand, and the collective and eternity on the other, which are both present in the act of writing. And it is again the symbol of the indigo to express in the best way this contradictory knot. Writing is imparting to a close friend, and yet, the indigo leaves a copy of the writing in the primary loneliness of the writer, thus lending a character not of any concrete, but of universal imparting, to it—not to the concrete friend who will destroy what has been written, but to posterity, to other people, to the whole of mankind.

Therefore, the one who uses indigo while writing needs, it goes without saying, a self-imposed, noble discipline. The indigo takes him away from the instant and loneliness and sends him to eternity and mankind—therefore, he should rid himself of everything accidental, of everything which is too peculiar and individual within him. The writer is to render everything private within and around him, general and universal. If the one using indigo while writing is negligent and allows mistakes to slip in, the latter starts looking deliberate, they grow into a stylization of mistakes and negligence and lose their chaotic nature. Therefore, while writing, he should be very careful not to make any mistakes or display any negligence—doubled by the indigo it might, in a sinister way, present itself as something universal and try to place itself among the universal symbols of mankind.

It is exactly for this reason that the indigo is used in recording only what is worthwhile, to have it preserved for eternity, and the writer himself feels evaluated and in high spirit, divested from the empirical within him. Only noble, vehement, and sound thoughts cross his mind; the eternity the indigo is emanating penetrates his instants as a serene, calm, and divine exuberance. The spirit of the indigo rejects everything which is weak, feeble, ailing or too subjective: it is an objective classical spirit, contrary to today's romantic vogues. If you have indeed grasped the spirit and the symbol of the indigo, you will become aware that writing with it bears something divine: on the sheet of eternity the writer's hand again records universal and eternal values, divinity has embraced the writing man as a noble receptacle, it has allowed him to achieve the otherwise inaccessible universality and objectivity.

And there is something else to it . . . "

Goethe was again standing and walking about the room. Listening to him speak in this way an enormous and unknown joy filled me, but along with it, I felt somewhat nervous. It seemed he considered the question of the indigo so important, and he had taken it so to heart that he got excited to a measure which rarely happened, when bearing in mind his enormous placidity.

"The documents, young man, the documents the magic blue, sheet leave behind, are the documents of your own life on which you can look back again in order to attain the greatest grandeur and heroism—to be always who you are, to preserve who you are. Napoleon's particular grandeur was actually this—all the time, before battles and after them, after victories and defeats, **he was always one and the same.** Through the documents left by the indigo, a man who lacks the life talent of Napoleon—this compendium of the world!—can make an attempt to discover himself, the internal low of his development, it stages and epochs, the identical, invariable entelechea (or monad as Leibniz calls it). The documents of his own life left by the indigo provide him a sublime, divine possibility—he can *objectively* look at himself, trace back the composition of his life book, get in touch with the mysterious—for him—principle of his own unity!"

Goethe turned to me, his eyes burning.

"Having perceived this classical, balancing role of the indigo, I got ready to understand one more thing. Indigo is not only the blue sheet of paper. I watched pictures and engravings on subjects of my verses and poems, I admired the marvellous Delacroix, who, in his illustrations of my "Faust" had gone beyond my own ideas, I had printed myself on the indigo of someone else's art. I had many enemies and adversaries and no less friends and people who really understood what I was doing. The literature of Germany, and I think of Europe as well, had become unthinkable without me—the signs my hand left had been engraved and printed in an invisible wealth we call culture.

However, I got really excited on perceiving that the dearest creatures that surround me are also a metamorphosis of the indigo. My beloved women, the friends, the spiritual companions... Lilly Schönemann... we are used to calling our beloved "mirror of our soul," but this comparison conveys almost nothing! And how could the transient mirror reflection, which cannot but be connected with illusion and vanity, with the altering play of light, with the limited *hic at nunc,* be compared to the perception of eternity the magic sheet emanates, the sensation that we are printing, engraving, encrusting ourselves in someone else! Lilly... this angelic indigo!..."

Goethe stood silent with his back to me. Then his deep voice came to me:

"Yet, no one of the beloved women for whom I have felt genuine infatuation can be compared to a great indigo I had the luck to possess. If you could only imagine, Eckermann, the way his noble soul accepted and turned into objective, eternal form every incidental flicker of my thoughts and feelings! I also mirrored and copied him; through me, he also shed the accidental within himself and the restrictions inherent of his talent. If it were not for me, he would have not created. **Wilhelm Tell** and **Wallenstein** so cleansed and great. How I loved his letters! In them I discovered the imprints of my soul, I came to know myself through an objectivity which was God's gift. I remembered some passages of these letters to this very day—and to this very day they are for me the noblest and genuine self-cognition... Listen: 'For a long time, and always with amazement, I have been following the development of Your spirit, though from considerable distance, to discover the path you had been predestined to follow. You are seeking the necessary in nature, but seeking it, you choose the most difficult way, which every mediocre talent would have evaded. To shed light on the single phenomenon, you have, indeed, spread to the entire nature. In the integrity of his forms of manifestation you discover the basis for explanation of the individual. From the materials of the entire universe you are rising, step-by-step, from the simple organism to the more developed, to build, at long last the most complex of all—man. A great and valiant idea indeed, showing well enough the way your spirit maintains the rich entity of human ideas in a beautiful unity. Everything that analysis has been painstakingly seeking, is in your intuition... This is how I approximately assess the development of your spirit and it is you to judge whether I have been right...'

Whether he had been right... Eckermann, he was more than right—like a great indigo he showed the path of my own mission, he was discovering the divine imprint in me of which I had only vague premonitions! He was seeking the eternal in me in a way which had been inaccessible to me.

You know, Eckermann, I have to confess something to you. When I invited you to edit my manuscripts and take care of my books, I also thought of something else. To put in order my archives was, of course, extremely necessary. But I had something else on my mind—the wish to be followed daily, at any time and moment, by the eyes of an intelligent and dedicated young man. I shall imprint myself on the indigo of his admiration. But this is not exactly what attracts me, it is not that superfluous vanity that appeals to me. These eyes will lend the noble discipline I need and without which I have the feeling I am dissipating my efforts in an insipid empiricism to my life. It was he who taught me this—that another one, a loving and intelligent man is needed, a man who through himself, through his attention and love, would judge me for the accidental within me, extract and constantly imprint my general form on himself, so that I may have it for myself—have it constantly before my eyes as a noble example. You are my indigo, Eckermann! ... "

Goethe stopped with emotion and instantly turned to the window. When he again turned his face to me his eyes were again serenely calm and kind.

"This evening I would tell you one more thing concerning our indigo, the mysterious **Indigoferia tinctoria** and the divine sheets produced from it.

Perhaps their deepest and most symbolical essence is the simple fact of repetition. The indigo *repeats,* it repeats what cannot repeat itself—the passing time. It has thus proved to be the missing bridge between the realm of freedom, the human realm, and the realm of the divine nature, in which there is nothing new, in which everything repeats itself in one, two, thousands of dimensions and be nevertheless one and the same. There is nothing in the world to have existed only once, because everything contains in itself the general, the thing that repeats itself. And the thing that repeats itself is perfect. Those great prephenomena which prepare and sanction any deviation through an internal law, are nature's indigo before which we hold our breath."

I do not remember exactly how I got home that evening.

Friday, January 21st, 1831

Yesterday was one of the happiest days in my life; today is the most wretched. Never before have I been closer to desperation and only my Christian faith in providence and the faith that every human being, modest and insignificant as he may be, has his place on earth, stopped me from doing the fatal thing.

This morning I sat at the writing desk in high spirits. I took the indigo sheet Goethe had presented to me out of the red file and held it with reverence for an instant as if it were the philosopher's stone. Then I took some blank, white paper and placed the indigo between two sheets. I prepared to write. Although it was January, mild light was penetrating my humble lodging through the windows, as if the countless invisible eyes of nature were serenely and gently observing me. I had decided to make a clean copy of a poem of mine, the idea of which had been born on the anxious night when, having learnt of the sudden death of Goethe's son, I was traveling from Gotha to Weimar and the moon had come out of the thick clouds for a few seconds; the poem was about the waft of befriending and unruffled calm, woven into the moonlight, with which Goethe had later welcomed me without uttering a single syllable about his deceased son.

My writing went smoothly, one line coming after the other. I stopped for a moment only when the initial arrangement of the motif or the atmosphere needed some more objectivity. Having finished it, I had the feeling that at last I have created something really significant, which might even match some of Goethe's poems. While writing I was deep in thought and fully oblivious of the indigo, but now that I again remembered it, I was seized with the previous agitation. I unfolded the sheets with trembling hands and looked at the lower sheet—where I was supposed to see the same text written in the signs of eternity.

It was blank!

Its clean, virgin surface emanated a kind of soft and antique radiance and unattainability, as if no writings ever created by man could touch it.

For a few seconds I stared at it unbelieving, then tears streamed from my eyes and my head sank in despair. With the first wave of my pain over, I came to know what had happened. I had reversed the indigo. Now, on the reversed side of the upper sheet there was a kind of incomprehensible interlacing of nonexisting signs, diabolical scrawls, with no trace left on the second one.

The vehemence of this omen overwhelmed me. God was giving me a sign that only the chosen writing hands could get in touch with the calm sheet of millennia, that God's finger wrote only through the pen of the man of genius and only through it, do pre-phenomena and universal living forms glimmer forth in the ordinary motives taken from an empirical life. While the presumptuous writes only incomprehensible scrawls on himself, a demoniac nail is scrawling, like a mirror gleam opposite his pen, distorting and turning incomprehensible his signs as a symbol of vanity and self-destruction. And the radiant white paper of eternity remains for ever untouched by the dilettante's hands.

Several hours of despair and pain passed in which I slowly came to know how heavy the burden of the indigo symbol for the uninitiated was. At dusk I had already decided not to include the notes of today and yesterday in my future **Conversations . . .**"

Peter Johann Eckermann
January 21st, 1831.

It is irony of fate that after its 150 years wandering, Eckermann's problematic fragment fell into mine and not someone else's hands. Honestly speaking I have never been able to read a text by Goethe to the end, while in his "Olympian" pose I have always seen a kind of histrionics: I share the irony of Walter Benjamin, who in his well known fragment on **Kinship by Choice** mocks at Goethe for his "self-cult" and for his passion to collect rubbish from his own life.

The very text Eckermann tried to cover up seems to me to be rather pompous, so that at point I wondered whether Eckermann himself had not invented the whole story and then covered it up rather unskillfully—so that it may one day fall into the hands of "posterity" . . . It seems to me that there are some style differences (though difficult to grasp) between the fragment in question and the prevailing tone of the narrative in the **Conversations with Goethe**—particularly so when Eckermann describes the second day of his adventures with the indigo. But even if the case with the indigo had been invented, this can hardly be of any importance—I wonder whether more of our images of Goethe haven't actually been invented by Eckermann—by the filter of his pathetic **Conversations**?

It is said that a comment accompanying a discovered and just published classical fragment doesn't do to contain any assessments, as reserved as they may be, much less to express any personal preferences, or to manipulate, in an interpretative way, the text just unearthed from the ancient remnants. In one way or another I have already taken liberties to make some assessments, so I shall take the risk to go further (I shall take even the risk of my comments being denounced with indignation by the idyllic taste of the editors from the German literary-historical magazines[2]).

The awareness of being a contemporary makes me get irritated with almost everything in that text. Everything around Goethe and Eckermann is always "serene," "calm," "bright," "full of friendliness and innate noblesse," of "sublime simplicity," "sincerity," and "kindness." Every line of the fragment (as well as of Eckermann's **Conversations with Goethe**) is meant to suggest that everything in their daily routine is "classical," that they are two Hellenes who only accidentally landed in the Weimar situation. Goethe looks through the window, Goethe drinks a glass of wine, Goethe buttons his trousers—all that is intended to show through: a kind of mixture of spontaneity and such an unruffled internal dignity, as if at that moment at least fifteen generations were contemplating the "divine body" and the "immortal spirit" of that "perfect man." But our contemporary cannot but start suspecting that the metaphoric order of the "serene," "calm," "classical" and so on and so forth, amounts to no more than an iron-governing discourse which does not only set Goethe and Eckermann the norm and filter of writing ("missing" thus all not too classical details of their life[3]), but does something more essential—it really governs and sets the form and the range of values of their spiritual world, making it freeze into pious, worthy, and . . . prescribed forms.

The present reality (the world we live in) is an ambiguous reversion of all similar "Goethean" values: the "indigo-doubled life" already seems to us a monstrous idea, which lends an absurd museum shade to the most elementary, free, and chaotic actions. Goethe pathetically claims that at the root, all of us are "collective beings," that "the instant is a representative of the eternity," and for this reason one should write objectively, with the writer ridding himself of everything which is, more or less peculiar and subjective, and letting the universal and the general flash forth. Nowadays, in the time when everything entered in the "Zeitalter der technischen Reproduzierbarkeit" (Walter Benjamin), the universal and the general are totalitarian and postindustrial facts: their name is the printed and multiplied human anonymity, the dispensable people of no "peculiar fate" and "ohne Eigenschaften" at all; according to Adorno, the claim that the individual is still autonomous (that he can still rise with his impulses and feelings to the Fate), that he still can do something spontaneously, is nothing else but an ideology: every "individual" is born out of a perfect repetition (which cannot be attained by an indigo sheet, magical as it can be) and has become "more general," than Goethe could ever dream of.

Goethe's meditations about the "noble discipline" induced by the indigo are most amusing of all. A long way prior to Freud, Goethe's super-indigo has turned into a exteriorized super-(ind)Ego whose philistine eyes monitored whether every thought was "worthy enough," so that only "noble, strong, sound thoughts" may occur to people.

Generally speaking, listening to the classical succession of indigo metaphors, other words, so specific of the twentieth century, which oddly enough, duplicate the "Goethean"—Dossier, Censorship, Receipt, Museum, Pose, Mass media, Order, Power... occur to the contemporary.

But I've already gone too far, even for a "nonclassical" comment. As a matter of fact, my initial idea for which I took to the publication of Eckermann's fragment was to try to translate the indigo situation into a contemporary semiotic language. I shall not conceal the fact that I take some pleasure in this. It could be said that Goethe's concepts of the symbolic value of the indigo are a Saussurian construction. Indigo's doubled life establishes a sign relation between the instant and eternity (after all, "everything visible is only a symbol"); every empirical fact grows to a signifier of something signified, accessible to the "great time." We could differentiate between "Goethe"—the signifier, and /Goethe/—the signified. The accidental in classical man has proved to be in a signifying connection with the substantial in him. On the other hand, the accidental and the substantial, the instant and eternity are as inseparable as the two sides of the sheet through which Saussure compares the indivisibility of the signifier and signified. Besides, there are other analogies which delight the eye—the concrete instants attain their significance in their linear correlation in biographical time, which can be referred to as a life integrity, life work: just in the same way the Saussurean signifiers are stretched, they are realized in linear time along with this, they form a structured entity of a message. The peculiarity of this message is realized on the basis of universal laws which normatively govern the system of language; just in the same way the peculiarity of an individual human destiny is invisibly governed by the perfection of Goethe's "eternal repetitions" and "universal, general laws." Nature and the language system are in the same conformity as the individual life and the individual message: therefore human life is a message against the background of eternity—if it occurs to us to contaminate Goethe and Saussure. In Saussure the signifier-signified relation is arbitrary and yet is invariable owing to its sociohistorical existence; it governs not only the individual who cannot alter it but the collective as well.

In Goethe an instant is a motivated signifier of the eternity only in terms of incognizable, divine will which is cast in complete human destinies. In this sense, from a human point of view, the instant-symbol should be regarded as arbitrary, nonmotivated. But it also involves a supraindividual and supracollective "classical" norm because it is necessarily "worthily" and "sensibly" lived through; and it is this internal invariability of its form (this public validity of the instant), that enables it to perform its sign function.

All similar analogies show not only that the classical idea of the indigo contains a more or less implicit semiotics of Saussurean type, as well as the opposite—that there is something "Goethean" in Saussure's ideas.

What happened with Eckermann on January 21st, 1831 can be described only from the viewpoint of entirely nonclassical semiotics.

The mirror indigo imprint on the reverse side of the sheet (the diabolical scrawls which Eckermann refers to in horror), cannot be described as a signifier-signified relation; the signifier does not "shine through," it does not turn into semantic clarity. As a whole, the sign is not transparent and does not involve automatic comprehensibility. Along with this, the reversal imprint is not arbitrary—on the contrary, its essential form is in motivation. Every point and stroke of the scrawls is a mirror reproduction of the characteristics of the "signifiers" and are in an iron-strong dependence and motivation by the right layer of the sheet.

Naturally, to go ahead with the game, we must necessarily stress that the signifier-signified relation, in the case in point, has been substituted for the signifier-signifier relation—provided we assume that in a space which is mirror-reversed with regard to Eckermann's, a diabolical hand is also writing down signifiers with Eckermann's writings being the signified, but they are, for their part, also signifiers whose signified are the reversed indigo (diabolical?) traces and so on and so forth to *ad infinitum*. The classical Goethean-Saussurean sign is an image (an acoustic image of an instant, a concrete life situation), which transcend into a concept. The nonclassical Eckermann's sign is absurdly self-concentrated; the signifying function cannot leave the sign's own hermetic micro space; it is incessantly "shuttling" between the written traces and their indigo reflections.

So that, to our joy, writing with reversed indigo has not turned out to be a symbolical image of the "eternal repetitions" as universal law: or rather the opposite—the very act of writing in itself give rise to a primary differentiation. Every sign is, at the very moment of its birth, doubled with its diabolic Otherness which reduces it to an anti-sign and to the evil will of pure Chance. In comparison to Derrida's *differance*, the reversed indigo is rather a sinister variant of differentiation. It doesn't open the space (the necessary Derridian "espacement," "spacing and temporalizing"!) for an endless play of *"les grammes"*—the infinite chain of traces, of "presence of the absences," the structurally controlled transformations and the richness of this "bottomless chess-board"—language-world-textuallity. The hermetic and obsessive microspace between sign and its reversed indigo double is rather a closure: an annihilation of every *"espacement"*; it is not the "absence" as "trace of the Other" in every presence, but rather the absence in a form of absolute, evil, destructive, and mocking Nothingness, which—without any "deferment"—annihilates every will to signify. The reversed indigo is a Supplement which is Death itself.

In this sense, writing with reversed indigo turns out to be, unexpectedly, a universal law again—but a very strange one. Death is a low to which one should obey only once: a universal rule which bears no repetitions.[4]

Was this the reason for Eckermann to cover up the indigo fragment? Was he frightened by the thought that **every single text,** even the most "classical" one, could be rewritten on the reversed, sinister blue sheet in order to inscribe Death in its every single signifying monad? And that

"everything visible" could reveal itself as a dark, dying side of a symbol?

By the way, is this so bad an idea? Why not do that deliberately—to re-read the whole classical universe of texts and men through the reversed indigo sheet.

And I find it the best thing to do, to start with Johann Wolfgang von Goethe and his prophet.

Roland Macpherson
Weimar, January 21st, 1988

In the beginning we mentioned that this translation of the **Philemon and Baucis** magazine aims to inform Bulgarian readers of a much talked literary scandal, and that in the superficial notes which accompany Eckermann's texts and Macpherson's comments, we will do our best to keep the academic tone and the scientific objectivity intact. However, the reader has already become aware of the redundant provocativeness contained in both the claim and the very pose of Macpherson, and that they somehow urge a going out of academic goodwill atmosphere and induce the response irony. As a whole, "anti-classical" gesticulations before a broad public were known as early as the time of Marinetti and Dada for their flippancy and the lack of sufficient self-reflection. The first question to be put to Macpherson (or pseudo-Macpherson) is, whether, when he wrote his comments, he had not, nonetheless, accidentally placed an indigo between the sheets of his typewriter? Doesn't he, when personally writing his "nonclassical" works, all the same, keep a copy for his own archives? We could express the fear that similar "nonclassical" authors have become a frequent phenomenon—authors, demonstrating in a rather scandalous and noisy manner, innovations in the public space and sharing, otherwise, the quite "classical" everyday life of all writers: a well-arranged indexcase, well arranged (and why not clipped together?) manuscripts, quite a "museum" attitude to every line which has been created by their hands (The "personal computer case" makes things even worse—the "indigo function" being on and so forth to *ad infinitum.* The classical Goethean-Saussurean sign is an image (an acoustic image of an instant, a concrete life situation), which transcend into a concept. The nonclassical Eckermann's sign is absurdly self-concentrated; the signifying function cannot leave the sign's own hermetic micro space; it is incessantly "shuttling" between the written traces and their indigo reflections.

So that, to our joy, writing with reversed indigo has not turned out to be a symbolical image of the "eternal repetitions" as universal law: or rather the opposite—the very act of writing in itself give rise to a primary differentiation. Every sign is, at the very moment of its birth, doubled with its diabolic Otherness which reduces it to an anti-sign and to the evil will of pure Chance. In comparison to Derrida's *difference,* the reversed indigo is rather a sinister variant of differentiation. It doesn't open the space (the necessary Derridian "espacement," "spacing and temporalizing"!) for an endless play of *"les grammes"*—the infinite chain of traces, of "presence of the absences," the structurally controlled transformations and the richness of this "bottomless chess-board"—language-world-textuallity. The hermetic and obsessive microspace between sign and its reversed indigo double is rather a closure: an annihilation of every *"espacement";* it is not the "absence" as "trace of the Other" in every presence, but rather the absence in a form of absolute, evil, destructive, and mocking Nothingness, which—without any "deferment"—annihilates every will to signify. The reversed indigo is a Supplement which is Death itself.

In this sense, writing with reversed indigo turns out to be, unexpectedly, a universal law again—but a very strange one. Death is a low to which one should obey only once: a universal rule which bears no repetitions.[4]

Was this the reason for Eckermann to cover up the indigo fragment? Was he frightened by the thought that **every single text,** even the most "classical" one, could be rewritten on the reversed, sinister blue sheet in order to inscribe Death in its every single signifying monad? And that

"everything visible" could reveal itself as a dark, dying side of a symbol?

By the way, is this so bad an idea? Why not do that deliberately—to re-read the whole classical universe of texts and men through the reversed indigo sheet.

And I find it the best thing to do, to start with Johann Wolfgang von Goethe and his prophet.

Roland Macpherson
Weimar, January 21st, 1988

In the beginning we mentioned that this translation of the **Philemon and Baucis** magazine aims to inform Bulgarian readers of a much talked literary scandal, and that in the superficial notes which accompany Eckermann's texts and Macpherson's comments, we will do our best to keep the academic tone and the scientific objectivity intact. However, the reader has already become aware of the redundant provocativeness contained in both the claim and the very pose of Macpherson, and that they somehow urge a going out of academic goodwill atmosphere and induce the response irony. As a whole, "anti-classical" gesticulations before a broad public were known as early as the time of Marinetti and Dada for their flippancy and the lack of sufficient self-reflection. The first question to be put to Macpherson (or pseudo-Macpherson) is, whether, when he wrote his comments, he had not, nonetheless, accidentally placed an indigo between the sheets of his typewriter? Doesn't he, when personally writing his "nonclassical" works, all the same, keep a copy for his own archives? We could express the fear that similar "nonclassical" authors have become a frequent phenomenon—authors, demonstrating in a rather scandalous and noisy manner, innovations in the public space and sharing, otherwise, the quite "classical" everyday life of all writers: a well-arranged index-case, well arranged (and why not clipped together?) manuscripts, quite a "museum" attitude to every line which has been created by their hands (The "personal computer case" makes things even worse—the "indigo function" being automatized). Generally speaking, parasitizing on classical habits, classical forms of producing texts, classical institutions (what else a German literary-historical magazine could be?) is an apparent precondition for similar "nonclassical" demonstrations and had people like Macpherson boasted a little more self-reflection, they could not but perceive this.

In 1909 Marinetti, too, wanted to set fire to the libraries and let the waters of the Tiber in the museums, but the fact that all the same we know of this, is due to the "preserved" museums and libraries. So that with good reason, Macpherson is right in being grateful for the tolerance displayed by the editors of the **Philemon and Baucis** magazine—but his mistake consists in his failure to perceive the cultural meaning of this tolerance.

The lack of self-reflection is connected with another, still more apparent and irritating "characteristic" of his comment—the negligence with which they have been written, in terms of both style and intellectual construction. We could ask ourselves whether the rush and the negligence with which they were written is not actually typical for similar postmodernist texts; as a semiotics claimed, as if what counts more today is to be eccentric and not truthful, thorough, or perfect. Because how could we otherwise explain the not-too-good-a-taste in the stylistic combination of Macpherson's comments—between the destructive pathos with which he denounces all those "discourses of power," the totalitarian and the posttotalitarian multiplied anonymity of man, and the ironic and provocative, purely play-like "semiotic" end of his notes?

Naturally, there is no denying that Macpherson has got some ideas, and yet he somehow fails to develop them to the full, to make use of an idea's own possibilities, so that the wish occurs to his reader to "write them to the end." With good reason, the reader anticipates some indigo variation on the famous **Licht, mehr Licht!**, but Macpherson obviously did not take the pains to elaborate well his own play-like construction. Why, for instance, while reasoning about the fact that in the classical consciousness of Goethe and Eckermann life is always referred to as biographical time taken in its wholeness, and referring to Death as the indigo's *ultima ratio,* he missed the marvelous opportunities to play with some of the most famous of Goethe's verses? *Verweile doch, du bist so schön* . . . wouldn't it be an excellent idea to interpret the indigo as the very essence of the "Faustian man" of the contemporary epoch? Or to use some of Goethe's maxims like **He who can connect the end of his life with the beginning is the luckiest man of earth.**" A critic, more diligent than Macpherson, could have naturally associated such maxims with "classical" examples as well—with the assertion of the ancient that a lucky life is one which is crowned with lucky death or with the following remarkable thought of Goethe himself: **On the scaffold Madame Roland wish to be given paper and something to write with, to write down the peculiar thoughts which hounted her in her death hour. It is a pity that she was refused this, because at the end of life a reconciled spirit is dominated by thoughts, otherwise impermissible. They are blissful demons which sit in radiance on the peaks of the past.**"

The indigo—a blissful demon sitting in radiance on the peaks of the past! What potential associations, what semiotic and philosophical variations Macpherson missed! Elaborating this dimension of the indigo symbol, he could also rid himself from the annoying and airy ironic-apocalyptic tone of his last remarks—because the indigo teaches us that Death, the connection of the Beginning with the End, could be also Bliss and Happiness and not only a mocking nothingness caused by the fact that 150 years ago somebody had occasionally reversed a sheet of carbon paper.

However, herein we have no intention of finishing what Macpherson was to do. His negligence is not at all accidental, it results from the statute of writing in his text. It is careless in its very essence—it lacks exactly that "self-imposed noble discipline," Goethe was speaking about. Such strategy of writing runs counter to the classical precision of elaboration—a self-conscious procedure of getting rid of all the random and chaotic elements, of attaining such kind of complexity and harmony, necessity and completeness which could transform the text into a Work. The essence of this classical procedure is, of course, the ***repetition*** again; the self-mirroring into a universal, perfect form. And here we are able to transform a little the remarkable words Goethe said to Eckermann and add "***Only*** things that repeat themselves are perfect"—only texts which have interiorized the "noble discipline" of the indigo could become *good* texts. And the bad text of Macpherson is just another proof for that. Maybe he didn't forget to put an indigo sheet in his typewriter—but, metaphorically speaking, he was negligent enough to reverse it.

Because—and this is valid for the poor, unfortunate Eckermann as well—the reversal of the indigo is the figure of the Negligence itself, which imprints itself as a quality of a text.

As for Macpherson's attitude to Goethe, it borders on hooliganism. The reference made here is not only to direct disrespectful qualifications which he is not sparing, but also to the unsubstantiated, drastic substitution of the metaphoric paradigm of classical thinking for its ironic duplicate. The epoch of Goethe and Eckermann is not studied in terms of its specifics and differences from the present day (of its "otherness"), while its values transfigure in a kind of monstrous ghost of theirs. Manipulated like this, noblesse turns, naturally, into a pose; mankind—into a printed and multiplied crowd of anonymous, manipulated beings; excitement—into a false pathos; self-restraint—into a control of a somewhat fascizoid super-ego. It is as though Macpherson does not at all assume that "sincerity," "simplicity," "serenity," and "calm" are possible to have! He aggressively claims that there are quite different cultural preconditions in the present epoch, that the contemporary man lives with another "existential aesthetics," and for this reason he regards everything classical as ideology. However, the way the word "contemporary" is used herein, is rather frivolous. Every "contemporary" man has the fragment of his everyday routine in which he lives according to absolutely classical milestones; even the most ever multiplied being has something individual about it, and every one of us has experienced moments of serenity and calm, simplicity and sincerity even amid the social neurosis of the postindustrial society. And, as a whole, it is hardly justifiable to speak of a single and universal "existential aesthetics" of the present reality, because there are many different perceptions of reality; man nowadays lives in a pluralism of many similar kinds of "aesthetics," and the latter are very frequently dated to various periods of their historical origin and have different values.

And yet the crucial negligence and lack of criticism in Macpherson's comments is neither in the impure stylistics, nor in the missed intellectual opportunities. They are not in the reversal of values and metaphors of the classical thinking either. The way in which he slides over the question of authorship and authenticity of this particular fragment by Eckermann (?), is so inadvertent that we may well suspect him of some forethoughts.

Being the discoverer of the fragment Macpherson **must** ask himself, for a very good reason, certain questions which, he, for some inexplicable reasons, doesn't do. Given, that this is indeed a conversation written down by Eckermann, why doesn't Goethe meditate on the indigo in other places of his voluminous creative work? Goethe's huge literary heritage provides no support for his assertion that he deals with the indigo problem in a multitude of scientific and literary works. And though the fragment was invented by Eckermann—has Eckermann any motives to write against himself? If he, through himself, symbolized in general, the figure of the initiated, why then didn't he include it in **Conversations with Goethe** to lend more prestige to it, to "canonize" it as a Goethean idea which supports the contrast between the man of genius and a dilettante?

We may, as well, ask ourselves several questions which Macpherson already could hardly have any reason to do. If the fragment was invented by Macpherson, what then is the function of the mystification? Why is it, indeed—and what does a mystification in a system of semiotic ideas described by Macpherson himself mean? Given that the fragment is a mystification, how should the question of the virtuosity of mystifying (which even experts haven't managed to cope with) on a semiotic plane—how should we interpret the hint dropped by Macpherson that as a whole, Goethe himself was perhaps invented by Eckermann, by his living indigo? The copy, the secondary text, the mystification, etc. (i.e., the indigo), quite paradoxically turn out to be the "primary" text, copies engender their originals, the self-propelled indigo are the reasons for written text to emerge, the artificiality and the secondary element always transcend into a kind of "authenticity." However, isn't the reverse possible too?—if Macpherson invented this text about Eckermann, and "Goethe" stylized a way of writing different from his own, both Goethe and Eckermann are "alive" in him—they are authentic alternatives of the pluralistic discourse Macpherson himself is capable of producing; and from this point of view, Macpherson turns out to be no more than the indigo imprints of a multitude of similar authentic voices, while his own authenticity assumes problematic meta-dimensions. The truth about authorship in similar questions resembles, ever more, a strange play between interwoven texts and discourses, in which the sheet turns indiscernible from the indigo and the indigo—from the "antique white," untouched paper.

We could go on with the questions.

What, exactly, should the strange pseudonym "Roland Macpherson" mean? The meaning, which is clear enough at first sight—that "Macpherson" is a hint of the famous mystification with **Ossian's Songs** (an in this sense it is an apparent signal that the fragment is not authentic), while "Roland" is the real first name of a famous contemporary semiotician—this obvious meaning does not suffice. Because the name "Roland" corresponds with, the not mentioned by Macpherson but otherwise well known, Madame Roland (of whom Goethe, as already mentioned, also speaks), who wishes to double, by means of the indigo scaffold **Sein zum Tode** itself. However, the names "Macpherson," "Ossian," and "Goethe" are, apart from this, in another peculiar relation. As is known **Die Leiden des jungen Werters** includes entire passages from the **Songs of Ossian**, which Goethe extols for their great natural sincerity and purity (at that time he considered them to be authentic songs by the folklore bard). The texts of these songs are an authentic part of Goethe's novel—but the very texts are Macpherson's mystification. It turns out that Macpherson came, so to say, before Goethe; the mystification is "condition of possibility" of an "authentic" work—the mystified text has engendered a whole range of text reactions, cues, and allusions which, built it in Goethe's novel in an irreversible way, turning **Werter** into a great work (which, as is well known, at the time provoked a wave of most authentic suicides) built on fraud. But this Macpherson is not the Macpherson of the eighteenth century: the contemporary Macpherson relies on Goethe's authentic works, which are not authentic, because they are built on the mystification of that Macpherson, and they are not merely mystifications, because . . . An interpretation of the pseudonym would lead to a paradoxical and superintricate set of contradictory assertions concerning the authenticity or nonauthenticity of Goethe's authorship (and along with it, of any possible authorship, of the authenticity of the "monuments," the "certificates," the "preservations," the "indigo copies" and . . . eternity.

Of course, all this is possible, given that the reader is as kind and as good intentioned to Macpherson's "nonclassical" comments as not to stop interpreting them halfway. The very interpretation, however, as we very well know, is a classical philological institution (a precise, repeating, disciplined reading, which avoids every negligence), and it would be impudence "nonclassical" authors who deny its terror to demand that it be applied to them. So that, the

best way to approach texts of the kind of Macpherson's comments, is probably to leave them to themselves. Their impudence will, anyway, fade away with time. The best attitude to them is a classical indifference.

Alexander Kiossev

▓ Notes

1. Initially carbon paper was produced from the indigo plant and for this reason the word "indigo" in the Bulgarian language is still a metonymy of "carbon paper." In the present translation, the word indigo shall be referred as a synonym of "carbon paper."

2. With my comment already published together with Eckermann's fragment, I am left nothing else but express my gratitude for the tolerance displayed by the editors of the *Philemon and Baucis* magazine.

3. In this connection, it would be in the nature of things to recall Goethe's telling maxim "Everyone has something of his character, which, if express publicly, would provoke disapproval."

4. I am not going to introduce the reader in all the paradoxes following from the expression "a universal rule which bears no repetitions." Here just a quotation from Wittgenstein's **Pilosophical Investigations**: "199. Ist was wir" ein Regel folgen" nennen, etwas, was ein Mensch, nur einmal im Leben, tun Könnte?—Und das ist natürlich eine Anmerkung zur Grammatik des Ausdrucks "ein Regel folgen." . . . . Es kann nicht ein einziges Mal nur ein Mensch einer Regel gefolgt sein es kann nicht ein einziges mal nur eine Mitteilung gemacht, eine Befehl gegeben, oder verstanden worden sein, etc.—Einer Regel folgen, eine Mitteilung machen, einen Befehl geben, eine Schachpartie spielen sind Gepflogenheiten (Gebräuche, Institutionen)." Should we interpret Wittgenstein in a following manner—"Death is the single rule which is no institution?"

best way to approach texts of the kind of Macpherson's comments, is probably to leave them to themselves. Their impudence will, anyway, fade away with time. The best attitude to them is a classical indifference.

Alexander Kiossev

Notes

1. Initially carbon paper was produced from the indigo plant and for this reason the word "indigo" in the Bulgarian language is still a metonymy of "carbon paper." In the present translation, the word indigo shall be referred as a synonym of "carbon paper."

2. With my comment already published together with Eckermann's fragment, I am left nothing else but express my gratitude for the tolerance displayed by the editors of the *Philemon and Baucis* magazine.

3. In this connection, it would be in the nature of things to recall Goethe's telling maxim "Everyone has something of his character, which, if express publicly, would provoke disapproval."

4. I am not going to introduce the reader in all the paradoxes following from the expression "a universal rule which bears no repetitions." Here just a quotation from Wittgenstein's **Pilosophical Investigations**: "199. Ist was wir" ein Regel folgen" nennen, etwas, was ein Mensch, nur einmal im Leben, tun Könnte?—Und das ist natürlich eine Anmerkung zur Grammatik des Ausdrucks "ein Regel folgen." . . . . Es kann nicht ein einziges Mal nur ein Mensch einer Regel gefolgt sein es kann nicht ein einziges mal nur eine Mitteilung gemacht, eine Befehl gegeben, oder verstanden worden sein, etc.—Einer Regel folgen, eine Mitteilung machen, einen Befehl geben, eine Schachpartie spielen sind Gepflogenheiten (Gebräuche, Institutionen)." Should we interpret Wittgenstein in a following manner—"Death is the single rule which is no institution?"

Part II

Political Aesthetics of Communism

Introduction to the Political Aesthetics of Communism
Vladislav Todorov

Everything has happened in a figurative sense
                                                  Pascal

▨ Beginning

Communism created ultimately effective aesthetic structures and ultimately defective economic ones. That is what empowers its strong presence and durability in the world. That is what fortifies it.

Factories are not built to produce commodities. They produce the united-working-class-body. They are allegorical figures of industrialization. Industry represents the leading metaphor of party ideology and factories are the works of this ideology. They result in a deficit of goods, but an overproduction of symbolic meanings. Their essence is aesthetic, not economic. They are the poems of communist ideology. The work process creates just these factory poems, not commodities. Labor is a ceremony begetting the communal body of the working class. The worker labors for the sake of the factory poem, not for the sake of the market. The aim of labor in the factory is the poetic completeness of the factory itself.

Originally published in *Textual Practice* 3(1991): 363–382. Revised for this collection.

A campaign of mass social engineering took place. A definition of the social engineering could be—Power forms the people whom to represent. Party power, according to a certain ideologically justified vision, designs and materializes its own social basis. The Party imagines its constituency and proceeds with its creation. It consolidates and disciplines the historical object summoned to fulfill the party project. The Party has to provide itself with constituency holding the majority of the society which is automatically recruited to build up the Future.

The large-scale industrialization was a political action with the only goal—to produce the Party constituency. Labor was designed to (re)produce the working-class body as the social basis of the Party. Thus, Party power provided itself with historical legitimacy.

The reality of communism is poetically worked out. Society is a poetic work, which reproduces metaphors, not capital. The speech figures of party ideology are the building blocks of the mind. The key metaphors and symbols, the productive means of language, are worked out by the supreme organ of the party-politburo. It is crucial to own not the machines, but the metaphors, the means of production of symbolic meanings, but commodities. Labor forges symbols. The labor force cannot be a commodity, because it is the creator itself.

The fundamental academic field of communism lies in its political aesthetics. The political economy is a simulative one. It generates an initial appearance of an economically motivated society. Actually, it produces the symptoms of such a society, not the causes for it. The working out of metaphors and figures of speech is what generates life forms. The identity of communism reveals itself in the overproduction of words and symbols. The political economy falsifies the genuine character of communism.

The idea has become quite popular that we have lived in an actually fulfilled utopia. The common idea that communism was impending prevented us from seeing that we were actually in it. All the key metaphors of communist

Introduction to the Political Aesthetics of Communism
Vladislav Todorov

> *Everything has happened in a figurative sense*
>
> *Pascal*

▇ Beginning

Communism created ultimately effective aesthetic structures and ultimately defective economic ones. That is what empowers its strong presence and durability in the world. That is what fortifies it.

Factories are not built to produce commodities. They produce the united-working-class-body. They are allegorical figures of industrialization. Industry represents the leading metaphor of party ideology and factories are the works of this ideology. They result in a deficit of goods, but an overproduction of symbolic meanings. Their essence is aesthetic, not economic. They are the poems of communist ideology. The work process creates just these factory poems, not commodities. Labor is a ceremony begetting the communal body of the working class. The worker labors for the sake of the factory poem, not for the sake of the market. The aim of labor in the factory is the poetic completeness of the factory itself.

Originally published in *Textual Practice* 3(1991): 363–382. Revised for this collection.

A campaign of mass social engineering took place. A definition of the social engineering could be—Power forms the people whom to represent. Party power, according to a certain ideologically justified vision, designs and materializes its own social basis. The Party imagines its constituency and proceeds with its creation. It consolidates and disciplines the historical object summoned to fulfill the party project. The Party has to provide itself with constituency holding the majority of the society which is automatically recruited to build up the Future.

The large-scale industrialization was a political action with the only goal—to produce the Party constituency. Labor was designed to (re)produce the working-class body as the social basis of the Party. Thus, Party power provided itself with historical legitimacy.

The reality of communism is poetically worked out. Society is a poetic work, which reproduces metaphors, not capital. The speech figures of party ideology are the building blocks of the mind. The key metaphors and symbols, the productive means of language, are worked out by the supreme organ of the party-politburo. It is crucial to own not the machines, but the metaphors, the means of production of symbolic meanings, but commodities. Labor forges symbols. The labor force cannot be a commodity, because it is the creator itself.

The fundamental academic field of communism lies in its political aesthetics. The political economy is a simulative one. It generates an initial appearance of an economically motivated society. Actually, it produces the symptoms of such a society, not the causes for it. The working out of metaphors and figures of speech is what generates life forms. The identity of communism reveals itself in the overproduction of words and symbols. The political economy falsifies the genuine character of communism.

The idea has become quite popular that we have lived in an actually fulfilled utopia. The common idea that communism was impending prevented us from seeing that we were actually in it. All the key metaphors of communist

utopia have turned into reality, something which will be discussed further on. We made it through fraternity, equality, the liquidation of money, the disappearance of the state, of property, of economic structures. We experienced the conjuration of communism. We attempted to build it and to live in it. We survived in it.

Utopia is a certain poetic, a certain political genre. It is just that, a genre which has its own structure and generates its own metaphors. Utopia compensates for the displeasure of the overimposed power structure by inventing a fictional perspective of life: an impossible perspective, which helps us to bear the actual order of life and to criticize it from the standpoint of another, nonactual but cherished order of life. The transformation of utopian structures into genuinely political structures creates a society based on political aesthetic and political rhetorical principles and not on economic ones. In such a society, power immediately reigns over bodies with words. It reigns over the social processes through the conjuring of language. It spellbinds.

The final objective that justifies this reality is not the legal order, but the mummy of the leader. The mummy objectivizes political power. It is the superior body. The party power finds its radical representation in the mummy. The political aesthetics of society reaches its sublime terms in the spectacle of the mummified Leader.

Political economy deals with idealized economic models; Political aesthetics with corporeality made eternal. Political aesthetics deals with mummified bodies, objects, and spaces which eternalize the strong presence of communism on earth.

At home, everyone has a measure, which he or she uses to ascertain the real dimensions in space. But somewhere out there, kept in special conditions, is the ideal measure. Its length is a convention. It is the original only by virtue of a social agreement.

Everyone has, at home, images and words of Lenin. They are signs, they are allegorical instruments, which testify to the existence of the original. The original Lenin is kept in a mausoleum and is a unique, not a conventional, body. A mummified uniqueness spellbinds the space embracing it. His images and his words, spread everywhere, is the radiation which imbues minds with communism.

The reality of the communist experiment is guaranteed by the magic reality of the body, stuck to the magic words of the primordial experimenter. Lenin is the author of communism. His immortalized body perpetually authorizes and legitimizes the Party. That is why the mummy must immediately be appropriated and registered in the party inventory.

The problem of the political aesthetics of society is far more general than the problem of communism. In a historical perspective, the merging of the political and aesthetic projects for creation of a purely novel society-poem has existed as a process even before its actual accomplishment in 1917 in Russia. One of the characteristics of modernist culture at the beginning of this century was the idea of radical liquidation of the inherited structures and the generation of a bold phantasm for the organizing of an unprecedented society.

This radical phantasm creates its own genre: the manifesto. The manifesto is the verbal radicalization of the modernist vision and immediately builds the political aesthetics of the modernist endeavor. With a closer look into the different political and aesthetic manifestos, we could reconstruct a global Modernist project for unprecedented corporal integrity of society and for the daring act of building it.

In respect to this global project, political Dadaism in Berlin and the Proletcult in Russia during the 20s have quite decisive roles. The programs and projects of these two movements present to us a decisive merger of political and aesthetic ideas, of the concepts of artistic and civil action.

The 1920s saw the birth of a powerful political art both in Russia and Germany, an art which deliberately scrapped the border between artistic and political action. This political art was subsequently repressed by "Party" art. Nazi and Bolshevik partisanship in the arts, imposed through administrative channels by Hitler in Germany and by Stalin in Russia, liquidated political art. It is symptomatic that Nazis in Germany repressed political Dadaism, whilst the same happened to the Proletcult in Russia, liquidated by Lenin. Party policy abolished political art, especially Proletarian art. This will be discussed in more detail later. For the moment I will say only that identifying the principles of political art with the principles of party art is a gross error. Of course Nazis, as well as Bolsheviks, turned into reality many of the radical metaphors and visions of Modernism, of Futurism, of Constructivism, of Political Dadaism. The political aesthetics of communism manifests the most terrorist recurrence of the modernist phantasms.

My point is that the principles of party art arrested the principles of modernist art, that is, that art in which visions and metaphors of future radical change arise. In short, totalitarianism as a kind of realization of the political aesthetics of Modernism arrested Modernist Art.

In this respect, Lenin is an interesting case. He is the man whom the Dadaists in Zurich pointed out as the greatest Dada on Earth. Political Dadaism in Berlin embraces the ideas of Lenin and gradually melts into the radical communist movement. Lenin is directly involved in the Proletarian modernization of the political ideas of that time. That same Lenin carries out the Bolshevization (read as Modernization) of life through a radical act: the Revolution. After performing it that same Lenin devised party policy as the rule of the starving Bolshevik lands. Party policy liquidated the processes of Modernization.

Lenin's mummy blocks any further modernization. In it, the political and the aesthetic merge as the ultimate party body. The mummy of Lenin is the point at which modernization is terminated and the omnipresence of the Party is imposed. This is the very point at which the idea of a political modernization of society terminates in a totalitarian mummified communism. Communism realized a radical aesthetic, noneconomic modernization of society.

▥ Merger of the Political and the Aesthetic

Dada emerges as an international movement in Zurich in 1916, in reaction to World War I and as a reactive concerted action of radical leftist and anarchist intellectuals of different nationalities and styles who were in Zurich at that time.

Dada is a reaction against bourgeois culture. Dada modernizes the world in an insolent anti-bourgeois style. The motives of artistic action are far wider than the territory of art. Dada presents itself as a daring intervention, which will cure humanity of bourgeois dementia, such as politics, art, and morality. Dada will chase away the monsters which have crawled out on the earth's surface, such as Imperialism, Victorian morals, and prejudices, together with the chef d'oeuvres of classical art. Dada acts, it doesn't produce works of art. Dada shakes up the stiff corpse of European culture. It tramples sanctimonious bourgeois morality. It seethes in the cells of the healthy bourgeois brain. Dada blocks the logical train of thought and thus frees the human being from its importunate training in common sense.

Dada stripped tabooed organs, objects, and actions naked, introducing a new material in art which was base and depressing by bourgeois moral standards. Through blatant musculature of expression, Dada brought to the limit the unrestrained collective will to mock the bourgeois individual cocooned in his morality.

The demand for political efficiency in artistic action leads Dadaist techniques to decisive public operations and offensives which undermine the bourgeois political system, the bourgeois moral imperative, and the phantoms of bourgeois art. All of this helps adapt the project to the radical modernization of society. The will that modernizes society is syncretic in its nature. In it, the aesthetic and the political are inseparable. The chief materialization of this will are photo montage, propaganda posters, allegorical constructions, and assemblages of machinery which disturb the bourgeois order of things. Industry, art, and politics are three heads of a single body, in the throes of one and the same will to modernization.

An exhibition of Soviet avant-garde art was held in Berlin in 1922. Arriving with the exhibition, constructivist Lisitskii started publishing, along with Yerenburg, the magazine *Veshch* (Object), which introduced the West to modern art in Soviet Russia. The spirit of Constructivism, new objectivity, and new materiality promoted by *Veshch* was already popular among Berlin Dadaists. Russian constructivist Tatlin was a dominant influence on the first Dada Fair in Berlin in 1920.

Political Dadaism is infected by the ideas of Machinism and the organizational theories of the Russian Constructivists, obviously mixed with the organizational theories of the Proletcult and its ideologist Bogdanov. Constructivist are neither embellishes life nor creates works beyond it. It organizes life completely. In its aesthetics, the geometrical and the political mind coincide. Constructivism is a syncretic state of science and politics. The modernization of society is guaranteed by such mergers of science, art, and politics.

If Constructivism is called the Socialism of vision, then Dadaism could be called the Bolshevism of action. In Germany Dada is taken over by Bolshevik visions of a "laboroid" space assembled of flesh and metal, of bodies and aggregates, of scaffolds and machines, of clenched fists and chanting mouths. In Berlin, Dada organizes political attractions, mounts centaurs of bodies and machines, in order to make a show of the magic of the endless Proletarian feats of labor.

Contrary to Left Political Expressionism, Dada is remarkably sinuous. After the trampling of the revolutionary movement in Germany, some of the Expressionists retire, others commit suicide, still others sink into a deep mysticism. Dada, on the contrary, experiences exasperation. It accuses Expressionism of consecration of the sick inside of man, of whimpering over its Gothic structures. Dada has no illusions. Dada does not suffer from any prophetic spirit. Dada is a saboteur and is oriented externally, towards expansion. During these years of social shock, the ontology of the world changes for the Expressionists—which destroys them. For Dada, the only thing that changes is the direction of the Proletarian strike, and that doesn't in the least make them turn off the engines. Because the noise of the engines manifests the (idio)syncrasies of the political, industrial, and aesthetic modernization of the world.

The athletic Proletarian body molds details from metal and with a geometrical precision puts together machines with which to attack the complacency of the senile world. Dada amplifies to the limit ideology and practice of the Creator-Machinist.

The Political Aesthetics of the Modernization

The Magic of the Apparatuses

Dada appears in an age already proclaimed modernistic. It extols the beauty of war; Mass-Man's athleticism; synthetic materials; mechanized voice—radio and megaphones; the machine-eye—photo and movie cameras. The legacy of Modernism, has been also absorbed by parties' and organizations' political programs on setting the world straight and replacing it by a radically new, a Brave New World. Marinetti extols war as a natural excess of the senses, of the machinism and communal athleticism of bodies. War is the remarkable transgression through which politics is wholly transformed into aesthetics, and political passion into immediately aesthetic passion. Political interest contorts in a sublime military convulsion and spews forth the charred images of the new world.

The Machine

In it the human is overcome. The organic is surpassed by the mechanical. In the machine, life reaches its ultimate organization. The human body is merely an organ of the machine. The organic element is one of the nodes of a mechanic totality. Only now, and now at last, is the Mind freed from the pathetic body and moves into a dwelling organized and invented by itself—the machine.

The Machinist is Superman. The Machinist is not subjected to subconscious repression, or sense guilt, he is not infected by individuality or sensitivity. The Machinist is the creator of the modernized age, who has decisively overthrown the yoke of the sniffling sentimentality of his perverse body, its ugly organs bandaged with the outfits of culture—clothing. The Creator Machinist represents the mass superorganization of bodies. In this sense, he himself is not a separate body. He is the radically organized state of the laboring bodies with a machine-like principle of common action.

The creative body attains a communal machine-like physiognomy never seen before. In it, the political and the aesthetic are one.

Oculus ex Machina

Eyeglasses are a prosthesis to the eye. They help it see. The snapshot and movie cameras are the superprostheses of the eye. Through them, the eye overcomes its human principle of seeing and becomes a machine. The eye itself becomes Machinist. In this sense, it becomes collective, because it overcomes its individual being, its pathetic partiality and lachrymal. The eye begins to see objectively.

The camera's objective lens overcomes the eye's organic optics. The objective lens is a crystal absolute. It is a superindividual organization of sight. It is the unified being of all possible eyes. The object-glass is the new communal constructivism of sight. It is the ultimately modernized liturgical eye. The Cyclops.

The camera is a prosthesis which has reached its perfection. Its superhuman inventiveness has radically supplanted the function of the organ. The principle of this self-activating prosthesis manifests the essence of the new agent of modernization. The new communal medium. The mass-medium.

On the contrary, according to the classical bourgeois intuition "the subjective genius of art" cannot be political, in that it opens and guards the eternal, age-old order of things. In principle, it transcends the political and the eye opens itself to eternity. "Subjective genius" does not rest on montages and collages, on cutting out and patching up shocking sights, on attractions. It rests on the internal integrity of the chef d'oeuvres. It could not stand prostheses.

Inversely, the political art represents an ultimately focused objective genius, driven by the performance of wonderful aggregates, contraptions and joints, by the vision of unseen laboring automata, which modernize the procession of life. In general, the idea of world modernization is of inordinate political relevance.

The eye becomes agent of the objective lens. The organ appropriates the principle of action of the prosthesis. The natural is overcome. Objective vision marks a decisive victory of the unified automatic mass principle, which stems not from the integrity of bourgeois genius, but from the rhythmic action of the apparatuses.

Objectivity originates in the Machine, which has radically overthrown the Human. Thus, the objective world is always produced and never found. The modernization of the world is represented as mass production of objectivity.

Political Dada does not merely make collages of things and baubles. The world in which Dada raves is not the mercantile world of things, it is not the space of the bourgeois and of things soaked into a small private world. The world is industrial, labor communal, objective; things are uniform, not unique. They refract mass industrial relations. This is a world in which the uniformity reigns. Dada attacks the production of linear uniformity. It attacks common standards of vision. It takes over objective eye, takes over the forms of mass consciousness. It accomplishes wild patching of details and documents, of pieces and industrial wastes. This is a circus of industrially produced uniformity, a sudden breakdown of the prostheses which stimulates an erotic shivering in the organs supported by them.

Introduction to the Political Aesthetics of Communism 75

The camera's objective lens forms a joint between the eye and the view. The change in the optics of the objective lens makes the joint move. The objective lens is an Eye-Centaur who gallops.

The view, as well as the eye, is an agent of the optic structure of the objective lens. Political Dadaism does not merely pick in your eyes and break objects. It attacks the objective structure of vision—the conjuncture formed by the eye and the object in the photograph. It attacks the photograph, that is, the joining of eye with view. Dada is a decisive intervention in the joint. It dismantles it by a kick.

Photo montages, splicing and gluing, the retailoring of ready-made reality—this is the new artistic technique. Objectively snapped reality can only be recut, it cannot be recreated. The reality that appears through the action of the machine reactivates the action of the scissors and the saw, not of the brush and carver. Cutting and fracturing, bandaging and plastering, affixing prostheses—this is the political orthopedics of modernism.

The Cuts of the Collage

The eye armed with scissors and saw insolently crosses the spaces of objective reality by endowing objects with impressive fractures, and then proceeds with plasters, bandages, and prostheses. The scissors, this tireless guillotine, is the magical instrument of modernization. For example, the diaphragm of the photo camera is an eye turned into scissors. It cuts off like a guillotine pieces of vision—frames, snapshots. The diaphragm performs spasm and contracts the vision. This contracted and cut-off view must be bandaged and fortified with prostheses. Then comes the magic of pasting, which reassembles the view chopped up in the camera.

The vision of the artist cannot be embodied in a picture. It can be rejoined after it has been fractured and dismembered by the diaphragm. In this political surgery of sight, the look acquires a distorted body. From this comes the feeling of a disparate and then indecently rejoined defective vision of the artist in political art. It is this principle of vision that Nazism attacks later from its party position, in order to liquidate political art of modernism.

Political Merger of Science and Art

Radical left Modernism feels a strong trust in constructive rationality, which has overcome bourgeois prejudices and developed its own bold visions in the industrial spaces. The political geometric mind is the genius of Modernization and finds its final justification in science. Each action of the new agent of history, the Proletariat, is constructively and scientifically guaranteed in advance in the clear spaces of political Geometrism. It is here that the Utopia of Modernism arises. When the concepts of each scientific field are deliberately generalized and made to solve global problems they turn into metaphors. They turn into crevices, through which gapes the wonderful view of a brand new world. Such an amplification of the scientific concept into a world-building metaphor, into a mythical poetic figure is a political manipulation. To be precise, it is a propaganda manipulation of a political plot for a total and radical world modernization.

The concept as an instrument of a scientific theory is usurped by the actual political design and comes to be used as a metaphor. It becomes pregnant with revolution. That is exactly what was done to the critical spirit of Marxism, to the racial theories, to the organizational theories. That is what was done to the scientific laboratories, whose poetic glorification made possible the mass experiments over immense areas of the Earth.

Science justifies all. The politically perfect world is the one which can be scientifically justified. Modern art builds just such a world. In this sense, Modern art is science turned into a work-world. That is the pinnacle of Modernization.

▦ The Red Geometrist

Man invents and produce ever finer and more perfect implements. Man constantly lowers their weight and thus achieves great technological and social results. These implements make man move ever faster and more precisely. They enable man to master the world and push man to the congenital limits of his corporal being. Propped up by these miraculous prostheses, man surpasses his earthly limitations and enters the spheres of the omnipotent inventive rationality. Art is a sublime organizational condition of those prostheses.

Russian Proletarian art, that is, political art, is in a decisive struggle with the irrational Russian soul, with the forces of its sobbing sentimentality. Proletarian political Constructivism introduces the Nordic spirit of the geometrical mind.

The red Specter of Communism becomes the Geometrist of the new age, the greatest Constructivist and political Dadaist. This Geometrist invented and produced unprecedented prostheses, which would release the laboring body and would throw it into the community of radiant comradeship.

▦ The Body-Aggregate

The modernized commune does not come together on a congregational basis, that is, on the principle of religious faith and initiation. It is built up on "aggregational" basis. The future collective body is represented as an electrified machine-like aggregate. This body, as any aggregate, cannot be described. The descriptive line (discourse) is helpless in this case. That is why the Constructivists and the Dadaists repudiate descriptive lines (discourses), because they have no political constructivist potentialities and power. Such a power has only planning, designing lines. Because of that, the body of the new political agent, the Proletariat, can be neither drawn, nor described. It can only be designed, tailored, and assembled. The red Geometrist designs and cuts out the body-aggregate of the Proletariat using special kind of tailoring machine like film camera and scissors.

▦ Disciplining of the Mass Man

If we attempt to reconstruct the modernist project from the start of this century, we will see that it owes its political aesthetic radicalism to the imperative—"Here and now replace this world with a new one!"—to exchange the old exhausted bourgeois world for a new, differently ordered world. That presupposes two things—invention, design of the new unity of the world, and the disciplining of an agent, or rather an actor, who would erect it. The new Unity of the world and the athletic capability of the Erector—these are prerequisites for the project. What remains to be done is for the action itself to happen to us here, now, immediately. This action is the Modernist act of genius, which will be achieved not by that degraded bourgeois personage the Artist, or by a senile, exhausted God. The decisive act of genius is achieved by the Mass Man. His communal body accomplishes a radical feat of labor by erecting the final work—the New World.

Apparently, the political order of this New World is designed as a work ultimately open, encompassing in its space the body of its creator. The creator moves into his creation. This waste-free act of creation leaves nothing behind itself or outside itself with which its sick body could inflame the new flesh of the world.

The suitability of the Modernist project to life is guaranteed by an already completed rational act, which aspires to the high status of being scientific. The project is scientifically thought out and proven. The designing of the new world is based on the cool minded Geometrist—the predecessor of Scientific Communism. The heat arises only later in the communal body of the Mass Man, who will make the effort of the construction itself. The Modernist Manifesto calls for an immediate mass action. In this sense, behind the manifesto lies the cool mind of the Modernist designer, and after it must be brought out the creative Mass Body. The Manifesto is framed by a scientific Mind and an artistic Creation. Before is the political design, after is the new political order of the world. It might be said that the manifesto is the third position, which stands between the scientifically worked out normative poetics and the concrete work created in accordance with it. In the manifesto, the scientific and the artistic, the political and the aesthetic discourses fuse. The scientific concept and the poetical metaphor merge in the imperative form of Manifesto. And began the Grand construction of scientifically proven metaphors, that is, the imperatives were realized.

The only thing that has been accomplished after the calls of Dada and of Scientific Communism is the party procedure of disciplining Mass Man. The creation of a new world did not take place, because the body refused to accept the communal state as its own creative state. The totalitarian State came to discipline a Mass Body, but it failed and it could not "wither away" as predicted by Scientific Communism.

When speaking of the "old world" one may say that bourgeois society has transformed the social bodies into organs of the personal, the one-sided, and the peculiar. Bourgeois space rests on the principle of heterogenia, because by virtue of its definitions every body is alien to all others. Bourgeois democracy creates a political order capable of governing the segmented social space and enabling the communication of the alien bodies. Bourgeois law regulates the possible concord, accordance, and togetherness of the heterogeneous bodies. It organizes into a community the individuals that occupy a different place in society. According to this juridical principle, no physical body may exist outside the law or above it. The law acts equally both on the body of the President and the Dadaist. In contrast to this, the bodies are entitled to differ with respect to their property, interests, physiognomy, and choice. Equivalent social relations are introduced and ruled by mediators, such as money, alienated from the bodies. Precisely, money enables the expression and realization of the actual differences between the separate bodies and their peculiar intercourse in the common space of the market.

And conversely, in order to create a Mass Man, it is necessary to liquidate all attributes, procedures, and principles which identify the bodies as particular and one-sided, as personal entities in a common space. In this case, equivalence will not be ensured by alienated mediators such as money, but by the physical bodies of the subjects of the new communal world. Thus they become equal and Homo-genius, which makes possible the act of a great Construction that involves a maximum of mass participation and ultimately welds the bodies together. The communal body consists of fragments that have an equal stake in the common entity and an equal interest in everything beyond their physical limits. Thus money is rendered superfluous, and so is the right to be different, and so is the state as an institution which protects the differences. What remains is the body of the Mass Man, left alone with his own will which draws strength from his primal natural drives: to eat, to copulate, to be in a well-lit and warm place.

An interesting example of Mass Man Utopia are the ideas of Bogdanov, that vigorous ideologist of the most outspoken political art in Russia—the Proletcult. This art was suffocated by Lenin because it did not give in to Bolshevization and did not conform to party interests. The political Modernism of Bogdanov became harmful because Lenin had already turned the political idea into a party idea and the Proletariat had to build not a world, but a party.

Bogdanov charged the Proletariat with ontological interests. Lenin charged it with ideological ones. Modernization as the meaning of political art manifests intuitions of a World. Ideology as the meaning of party art manifests intuitions of a Power.

▦ The Center that Unites the Class

It was Bogdanov, the author of the "organizational theory" of society, who worked out various visions and metaphors for the role and place of the new Proletarian art, which captivate the mass conscience even now. Art, he said, is the higher organization of the social experience, the most powerful means for the concentration of the collective forces of the new class. Art is a perfect organization of the class struggle. It is a radically collectivized labor. In it the notion of private property and personality cannot exist. It is a supreme stage of mass Proletarian labor.

Modern grand scale industry is turned into a gymnastic platform with futuristic apparatus assembled on it where Proletarian art demonstrates its stunning "attractions" (Eisenstein), its grotesque "bio-mechanics" (Meyerhold). All of this rests on the scientific justification of modern technology and automation. Here originates the principle of the creative mass force engaged in this process: *Comradeship.* The collectivism of the Proletarians homogenizes their social interest. It unifies them and sensitizes them to all things alien, to all things bourgeois. Comradeship does not arise from religious love, but from the technological togetherness of bodies in the process of labor. Comradeship springs from the new geometrical mode of life. The human corporality must become the immediate substance of comradeship. That is why the Proletarian body of the new class must be united through a common substance.

For Bogdanov, blood is the very substance that should be exchanged between comrades and thus comradeship will flow directly into the bodies of the Proletarians. He founded the first blood transfusion clinic, only not with a medical but with an immediately political purpose. Science thus directly begins serving politics, or to be more exact, directly grows into politics. Blood transfusion as the subject of science becomes a means for homogenizing a united collective political agent: the Proletariat.

Brotherhood solidified through blood fusion is an ancient ritual that is charged with enormous symbolic power. This sacred act, which has its cause in the poetic-mythical constitution of the world, becomes an instrument of science and is conducted through sheer medical procedures ideologically justified and practiced on a mass scale.

This took the life of Bogdanov, himself. He exchanged blood with a man with whom he was totally incompatible. He failed to survive through the antagonism of the alien blood and died. The attempt to produce a purely communal body ended with death.

The Party Modernizes Society by Condensation and Concentration of the Population

The Modernist visions for a Mass Man, inhabiting Sun Cities and Garden Cities find quite a decisive incarnation in the wide Communist land of the Soviets. First of all, because Modernism was directly tied there to Russian universal messianism and thus became a mystery; second, because the party uses of such visions were rather ingenious. Projects for Linear Cities were practically accomplished through the building of gigantic highways and canals. Cities were designed in the form of a grand scale assembly line, or of a linear transmission for the transfer of large masses of live flesh and soil.

The working out of such dynamic communal spaces turned out to be much harder than the building of stationary communal spaces, so-called communal flats. Professional architects take it upon themselves to design and build such stationary spaces called, at that time, the "new social condensers." Such a space condenses the social body in order to make it communal. At the same time, inspired by modern political technology of communism, there arises the idea of concentrating the communal body—the concentration camps.

Now there is a tendency to see the communal flat as a civic place, and the concentration camp as devoid of civil rights. In both cases the communal space is repressive, but it differs in its technology. Besides, in the total absence of civil rights and in the hitherto unseen mass inhabitation of such spaces, the practices of condensation and the practices of concentration become analogous. The condensation and the concentration of the population are two completely equivalent technologies for modernizing society.

One of the spaces, through a simple procedure, fed the other. The subjects concentrated in the camps had already been condensed in the communal flats. The communal flat is something like the entrance to a concentration camp, something like a preparatory chamber. Thus, the process of communization (read as modernization) of society is two-chambered: first condensation, then concentration. Behind this whole process there is no hidden right, no law and order, no legally empowered and constitutionally legitimized procedure. This is a pure case of modernized social technology for the production of a supreme ideological party article—the communal body, or the Mass Man.

Now, let us examine what the space of the condenser is and how exactly are the bodies transferred into the concentration camera. The condenser represents a long row of cell-rooms, connected by a common corridor. At the end of the corridor are the common toilet-bathroom and the common kitchen-dining room. In the projects of official architects, such as Moses Ginsburg, for example, there is also a common library. The library, however, was rarely bothered with.

The cell-room is the place for sleep. There, an individual can be alone with his or her body. The room is the only possible erotically intimate space. But that was not quite so, because the erotically intimate body presupposes a different order of society and its common public spaces. The erotically intimate body can be solely the civic one / but not the communal one / because it has a particular private presence in the social space which excites the "other" bodies. In this sense, the communal homogeneity of the bodies cannot presuppose eroticism. The communal body of the subject is forced to be intimate, for to reproduce itself it must copulate.

In the communal flat, all initiatives of the body are centralized in common public cameras and timetables. There they are trapped and sanctioned as impersonal: eating, cooking, hygiene, etc. The common space presupposes a centralized order in which everything becomes visible except for the sexual act, which is accomplished in the dark of the room.

Fear and Famine

Now let us examine the transfer of bodies from one camera into the other. As the beginning of concentration we can see deadly fear and famine, which is suffered by the bodies in the condensers. Famine stems from the fact that the political economy of communism and all economic laws lead to famine and sustain famine on purpose. Famine is an initial organizational condition of communism. Famine, compared to the plague, is not a calamity, but a social technology for the collectivization and concentration of the population. Famine welds bodies together.

Fear stems from the inexorable course of the transmissions of modern society which rhythmically feeds the concentration camps with bodies. Fear is produced by an already experienced concentration. It welds yet again by causing trembling.

The transferring of bodies from one chamber into another happened at night, when people were withdrawn into acts of forced intimacy. There was a knock on the door and They took them away. The bodies in the adjacent cells used to hear noises of the apprehension and expect every night to be visited by the same knock. At that time demographers registered a sudden lowering of the birth rate. Fear decisively prevented intimacy. The knocking on the door

Introduction to the Political Aesthetics of Communism 85

caused an acute castration complex, just as the statue of Commander knocked on the door of Don Juan, in order to punish him with a granite fist.

The concentration of bodies begins already in the condensation camera through a repressive centralization by means of *fear and famine* of the two strongest urges of zoomorphous man: eating and copulating. Thus, the communal body is deprived of all of its natural initiative. It possesses only the party designed initiative.

Thus happened Communism.

Party vs. Political Art

A. The Racial-party Approach. The Racial Eye.

Among the pictures submitted I have observed a number of works which actually lead one to assume that certain people's eyes show them things differently from the way they really are. In other words, there really are men who see today's Germans simply as degenerate cretins and who perceive—or as they would doubtless say "experience"—the meadows as blue, the sky as green, the clouds as sulfurous yellow, and so on. I do not want to enter into an argument as to whether or not these people actually do see and perceive things this way, but in the name of the German people I wish to prohibit such unfortunates, who clearly suffer from defective vision, from trying to foist the products of their faulty observation on to their fellow men as though they were realities, or indeed from dishing them up as "art." No, there are only two possibilities. Either these so-called artists really do see things in this way and so believe in what they are representing—if so one would have to investigate whether their eye defects have arisen by mechanical means or through heredity: in the former case these unfortunate people are profoundly to be pitied; in the latter it would be a matter of great concern for the Reich Ministry of the Interior, which would then have to consider ways of putting a stop to further transmission of such appalling defects of vision—or perhaps, on the other hand, they themselves believe in the reality of such impressions, but have other reasons for inflicting this humbug on the nation, in which case it would constitute an offense falling within the area of criminal law . . .

Hitler, Adolf. quoted in *German Art in the 20th Century. Painting and Sculpture 1905–1985.* Eds. Ch. Joachimides, and N. Rosenthal, and W. Schmied, Munich: Prastel-Verlag, 1985.

The artists discussed here are the Modernists. In 1937 in Munich, the Nazis organized two parallel exhibitions. One of "degenerative art," in which the Modernist artists are deliberately shown to be total idiots, especially in their particularly imbecile category, Dada. The second offered "healthy" German art, a manifestation of athleticism, of muscular eroticism, of the blue-eyed perspicacity of the German national spirit.

Undoubtedly, the problem of sight and vision is of great importance. How is it solved in this case? Since the artist paints not what is seen by the "healthy" eye, there are three possibilities: first, the damage is mechanical and this induces pity and is a medical case. Second, the damage is genetic or hereditary, and this case is delegated by Hitler not to medicine, but to the Ministry of internal affairs. Third, the damage is mostly simulated and can be directly prosecuted under criminal law. The first two cases suggest pathology, the third suggests sabotage. Or, from another point of view, the first is physical, the latter two are ideological.

The Nazi party ideology penalizes the case of the genetic malformation as an assault against the race. The race-party criterion is the criterion of the "healthy" and the sensible, the one of common sense. Common sense is something typical of party art, because the party is the ideologically organized interest of a homogeneous mass of people, with their own common sense for the order of things, with their own organ for uniform vision, *sensus communis.* In contrast, eccentricity is typical of political, not of party art, because the political act demonstrates and identifies a particular agent with his own acute partial social interest. The fighting political agent publishes his own interest differently from the party agent. From the standpoint of common sense of the party agent, the publications of the political agent are always subversive. In this case even genetic malformation is treated as subversive, that is, as a political phenomenon, because genetics is loaded by National Socialism with a party sense.

Let us get back to defective vision. We have spoken already of the machine eye, of machinism in general, and of the collage principle of modernizing normal sight. The Modernist principle of representation is just such a machine for reorganizing vision. In this sense, Modernism does not represent, but reorganizes the organic principle of sight into a mechanic, technological, geometric one. The Modernist eye invents the view. Of course, from the point of view of normal vision, and the more so when it is loaded with ultimate party sense, this eye is faulty. The spectator looking at the canvas does not find a recreated reality there but a set of prostheses belonging to the handicapped eye of the painter.

The racial-party approach elevates the organic into an ultimate value and considers as an assault against it any attempt at attaching prostheses. This same Nazism deifies the machine, but only as a means of exhibiting the will of the organic. The mechanic as a willful extrapolation of the organic.

The Modernist idea of radical replacement of the naturally organic with the machine is a sabotage. In this sense, the party ideology of National Socialism is the opposite of the Modernist one. Hitler attacks Modernism as a phenomenon that is political in its nature.

Nazi art is open to the *sensus comunis*. And common sense dictates the following: art organizes the vision and virtually represents the organics of the visualized. A painting does not represent merely some object or body, but the principle of its natural organics. If the object-prototype is slightly marred, then its image brings back its organics. In this sense, defective images are not possible in art, because art itself is a regenerative, not a degenerative activity.

The problem of party censorship lies in the depiction of the "representable," because party truth is connected to it. The image is neither an actual empirical prototype, nor the thing immediately represented on the canvas. The representable offers the ideal integrity of the image. The representable cannot pose technical problems, but only ideological ones. In it resides a Truth lying beyond any empirical manifestation. Artistic mastery lies in the act of making the image ultimately transparent, so that the representable can stand before the eye clearly and fully.

Such censorship is a party institution, not a political one. It does not come from any concrete political agent who is in power and who says what can and what cannot be published. This censorship is not a political institution, defined as a state structure. The censorship which guards party truth works by giving form to thought and imagination.

Party censorship is not a separate institution, which permits one type of thought and prohibits others. It acts as the structure of thought or sight. It poses the organically fundamental state of things, and not their politically defined state. Such a censorship does not censure the phenomenon, but the person who gives birth to it. It does not outlaw the painting, but the person who has seen the real that way. On the contrary, political censorship prosecutes the phenomenon, the thing born. Ideological party censorship prosecutes the nature of the birth. Because it prosecutes persons, and not phenomena, it is not defined as a state institution, but acts through the organs of security.

Party truth liquidates political art, because it liquidates the political personality in general: either everybody in the party or everybody in the camps!

B. The Class Party Approach. Party Replaces Class.

Now let us discuss the class party approach as similar to and different from the racial party approach. The one liquidated political art in Germany, the other in Russia. And everything began with Dada and the Proletcult.

The racial party approach stems from the organic unity of "blood and soil" as a genetic source of national purity and the historical mission of the race. Things are not so simple with the class party approach, because the communist party claims to be one thing, but is, in fact, quite another. But let us begin elsewhere.

> Literature must become party literature. Down with non-party writers. Down with the writer-supermen.
>
> The literary work must become a building block of the organized, planned, united. . . . party work.
>
> Writers must necessarily enter the party organizations. Publishing houses, reading rooms, libraries—all of these must come under party control.
>
> In defining the borders between party and anti-party writing, the criterion must be the party program. . . . its statute. . . .
>
> Lenin, Vladimir. "Partiinaia organizatsiia i partiinaia literatura." *Iz istorii Sovetskoi esteticheskoi mysli; 1917–1932*. Eds. G. A. Belaia, and A. E. Gorpenko. Moscow: Iskusstvo, 1980.

It is evident from Lenin's thought, cited above, that the Communist party idea, even as far back as its prerevolutionary state, has been developing as an imperial idea. The new emperor is the party.

What Lenin wanted in 1905 was actually accomplished in 1932 at the writers' conference, where Formalism (read as Modernism) was totally liquidated and the omnipotence of the new party truth in art was proclaimed. Thus the writers enter the party. Those who do not go to the camps. Thus the political person in art is liquidated. Party truth flourishes and recruits its shamans and priests. Party truth or Party justice *(Pravda)*, becomes the basis of the new Inquisition. True art is justified by Party art.

In 1920, Lenin devises an attack against the Proletcult. The motives are that in its ideas and practices the Proletcult is decisively independent of the party line and party interests. And that is true, because the Proletcult is the actual political Proletarian art of that time with its ideology and action program, with its own organizational structure independent from the party. Not party literature, but Proletcult is the politically representative art of the Proletariat. The ideologists of Proletcult are people, all of whom have been trampled by Lenin and thrown out of the party. We are not discussing here the extremism of this art and this idea in general. We have already discussed that in relation to Dada. Here, the important thing is that a structure is being built independent of the party, which represents the Proletariat itself. But the party liquidates all this, because it subverts and competes with its political representativeness. Everything which might undermine the political representativeness of the party comes under the knife. The peasant for example, a political person, whom the party does not represent, is totally stripped of rights, if not physically exterminated with administrative executions and deliberately caused mass famine. The deprivation of rights goes as far as the peasant's lack of a passport, because of which he cannot leave his village. He is actually not a citizen and cannot represent even himself, because he is totally illegitimate from the party point of view.

Thus a new class is formed—the party oligarchy which holds the entire power. It is not the means of production, but the means of power, which organize the new communist social relations. Who holds and who reproduces political power through its own means? Not the Proletariat! The party interest has nothing in common with the Proletarian interest. The party represents the interests of those who are the immediate body of power—the so-called "nomenclature." The party membership mass organized on horizontal principle is a totally fabricated phenomenon. But party interest continues to fake a Proletarian class interest and constituency. Party art vigorously continues to express the workers' presence in the world. Why? The laboroid imagery in no way represents the virtual social interest of the party oligarchy.

Why doesn't it glorify itself? It remains hidden, invisible, and untouchable. It acts as a lizard, which tears off its tail as soon as it is stepped on. Because, from the point of view of civil law and order, from the point of view of the politically public agent this oligarchy is illegal. So Party art represents a fabricated political agent: the Proletariat.

The question of the legality of the party and party policy in art is central. In his article about party literature Lenin elaborates this question. At that time, before 1917, the party and all its publications are illegal. Legal publications are nonparty. But there comes a time when the party begins functioning legally and then all possible publications have to become party ones. Coming out of illegality, the party usurps the whole press and there is no need of any law for the press (because law is necessary where there are different political interests, i.e., different political agents). In a state of all-encompassing party policy, a law is unnecessary because the only differentiation is party/anti-party, and that differentiation is ruled upon by the program and statute of the party. The statute of the party is the very law which constitutes the possible relations. In this case, the state actually does begin dying off, because the party takes up its functions and gradually replaces it.

Not until now have there been preparations for legislating a law of the press and not only of the press. Only now has the possibility of the existence of political agents outside the party been admitted.

Inter-party life is conspiratorially closed from the point of view of the state and the few laws there are in it. But it is legal, nevertheless. Lenin begins, but does not develop his thoughts on the legality of the party. That the party is legal does not prevent it from developing an internally conspiratorial life, with its own structure, discipline, and secrets. Any change in the power structure happens in the form of a conspiratorial plot.

Through Revolution, Party conspiracy seized the whole power and became legal. We make the difference between the concepts of **legal** and **legitimate**. Something is legal if it does not contradict the law and justifies its existence through the law. The law may not contain explicit provisions for the existence of any such particular phenomenon. For example, the law does not say whether a workers' party should or should not exist. It comes under the competence of the law only after such party has appeared by itself. On the other hand, a phenomenon is **legitimate** if: (1) It has been categorically enacted and regulated by the law. In this sense, Parliament is a legitimate division of power. A legitimate entity cannot be regarded as legal or illegal insofar as it is made by the law and do not depend on someone's will expressed in accordance with the law or in spite of the law. (2) Besides, legitimacy insists on the representative character of the political phenomena, delegated through a due legislative process. From this point of view the Communist Party by its conspiratorial principle may be "legal" if it does not break any existing law, but it is not legitimate as the only party on power, at least for two reasons: its party leadership that has merged with the State power has been elected through party vote and discipline rather than by general elections. Thus Party imposes the interests of the conspiracy onto the structures of the State. Moreover, its exclusively leading role is decreed by the Constitution. Its first article reads that the only party—the communist one—has the leading role in the Socialist State and that the communist party turned into an all-national representative. That automatically undermines the very essence of a constitution as fundamental law of the State, which ought to decree the possible forms of political life, not the specific entities involved in it. Legitimacy concerns the procedure of authorization. There is a difference between the legal existence and the legitimate power of a party.

The existence of the party is legal, but it is illegitimate in holding and executing the whole power, which it has actually usurped through conspiracy. It actually represents the interests of the party oligarchy and no one else; it is not sheathed in a law, voted for by free citizens. It does not possess delegated rights from a multitude of citizens; it endows itself with power through its program, the State constitution is only a repetition of this program. The territories, where party interests act most strongly, are not regulated by law, because there no other political agent can exist, or have a legal status. The law is possible only where there are relations between independent political agents.

The party suffers from a chronic insufficiency of representativeness, that is, of legitimacy. From here on it begins to liquidate and take away the rights of anything which might compete with it, or subvert it, or sabotage its representativeness. It liquidates Modern political art, precisely because it competes with its right to represent the Proletariat. The Party collects a great mass of members, and creates its own simulated social-political interests, which only it can represent. It invents a class party approach, which should define good and evil and other tricks, so that the real class, the real interest should sink into conspiratorial darkness, since it cannot have public forms, because it is illegitimate, and rules over the public, visible world through ghosts. The Proletariat as a class, as an actual political agent has long ago disappeared, because the structure of social relations is ruled not through ownership of the means of production but through possession of power and by the degree of initiation into the party conspiracy.

The phantom of Proletarian class interest continues to exist as a means, not as an end. The class party approach is the means of production of power.

The trick with the party policy of art is in the following—that which is given to us as party criterion, that which we have caught and hold on to as a party truth is only the tail of the lizard. The lizard has long ago escaped unharmed. We hold on to words, phrases, slogans, hammers, tanks, images of laboring hands and brave blood donors, of bridges and golden wheat, with the ontological certainty that we are holding on to the whole new and daring

Communist reality. But this is only the lizard's tail. Whoever does not wish to hold on to the lizard's tail and pretend to be holding the Proletarian hammer in hand, is liquidated. The lizard comes back to feed itself.

The racial party approach of Nazism is clear. National Socialism comes to Germany through a legal procedure and for a short while it really begins to express and represent the German national mind which is inspired by it. The party is legal and its structures are not conspiratorial. The power which it holds becomes legitimate organ of highly organized national interest.

The class party approach of Bolshevism, the internally conspiratorial structures of party life, the publicly simulated structures of party truth—this drenches the whole physical space of society with permanent revolution.

The mummy of the Leader! Why does a civic legal political power need mummies?

The class struggle and the dictatorship of the Proletariat become the main ideological alibi for the liquidation, which the party carries on against all evidence and witnesses of its own illegitimacy.

The class motive and the racial motive of the totalitarian parties liquidated Modern political art. The two motives are completely different, as I have attempted to explain. The link between them is that both have worked out their own technologies and ideologies for the liquidation of possible political agents, who by definition represent nonparty interests.

Presently, when the serious work on the analysis and criticism of the Class Party Empire—in art and public forms of life in general—is forthcoming, we have to take into account what Dada virtually is, what a scandal this crocodile is, what a saboteur it is, that Party truth did crush it in panic with a ferro-concrete fist.

From Anatomy of the Political Body
Ivan Kristev

Even when Ilyich is no more, we still have Lenin.

I. A Political Anatomy of Communism

The autopsy took four hours and forty minutes. The press release was a triumph of materialism. It described Lenin's body in minute detail, with a special emphasis on his brains—1,340 g of them. One is left with the impression that the main purpose of the press release was to show that LENIN HAD A BODY, which had functioned through all physiological processes typical of the human body. LENIN'S BODY WAS A HUMAN BODY.

Such a statement is plain as plain—to the point of absurdity. However, this absurdity is logical. The monstrous minuteness of the press release was actually directly linked with "the principal question," "the question of power"—a total political power which was ubiquitous and "expropriated" medical authority. Health turned into a political, rather than a medical problem.

In 1922, Lenin wrote to Molotov: "I have two letters from Chicherin. He wonders whether, at the Genoa Conference, we shouldn't concede—if we get reasonable compensation (supplies, etc.)—to minor amendments in our Constitution, namely the participation of other parties in the Soviets.

"This suggestion shows, I believe, that Chicherin needs treatment, send him to a sanatorium at once."

Had Lenin written "send him to prison at once," the idea would have sounded perfectly alright. A similar resolution was fully justified when one was accused of pluralism. But why send one to a sanatorium? Nor was Chicherin's case an exception. Krassin, for instance, was one of dozens of people who were ordered to undergo psychiatric treatment. Lenin behaved like a GP, rather than a government leader.

The dividing line between medicine and politics was obliterated. A closer analysis of Lenin's political medicalism shows that "sending Chicherin to a sanatorium" exemplifies certain theoretical attitudes.

Bolshevik metaphor makes abundant use of medical imagery to express the idea of social reform. The old bourgeois world is malignant and decaying, and it is in agony. Headed by its vanguard—the communist party, the working class has no choice but to "excise" the bourgeois tumour from society like an expert surgeon. Strangely enough, this places the very political act in an entirely new light. Executing "the enemies of the revolution" becomes a medication, rather than the killing of people.

Total political power proved possible insofar as it constantly posed as medical, intellectual, or any other power.

The blurred line between politics and medicine also blurred the line between sanatoriums and prison. Sanatoriums and prison were just two different asylums for the political body. Physiology was thoroughly politicized. Lenin himself fell victim to political medicine. Lenin was not treated by doctors—he was treated by the Politburo. Politburo sessions approved Lenin's regimen by vote and prescribed his daily walks, diet, etc.

The problem of the political body and the problem of mortality clashed.

The doctors who autopsied Lenin tried to show that Lenin's body was human—but failed.

The commission in charge of Lenin's funeral was renamed a Commission for the Immortalization of Lenin's Memory. A government resolution recognized Lenin's body as a political body. A mausoleum was built. Earlier, at the Soviets' Second Congress, Stalin "spilt the beans," making the crucial admission: we, Bolsheviks, are made from special stuff.[1]

Exactly what sort of stuff Bolsheviks are made of has remained unclear.

The mausoleum is the true home of totalitarian power.

II. The Guillotine and Acid

This wasn't waxwork.

Is there a wax figure of Lenin at Madame Tussaud's? Is the fire which destroyed Madame Tussaud's in 1925 in any way connected with Western press allegations of the period that what was displayed at the Mausoleum was a wax figure, not Lenin's embalmed body?

Lewis Fischer's book *The Life of Lenin* does not answer these questions, but it does cite facts relevant to one possible answer.

To dispel doubts about the mummy's authenticity, a group of journalists, Fischer included, were invited to inspect the relics. Professor Zbarsky, the world famous biochemist (who took part in Lenin's embalming) delivered a short lecture. Claiming that the body would keep for about a century, the professor opened the hermetically sealed glass case, caught Lenin's nose and turned his head to the left and to the right. "This wasn't waxwork," wrote Fischer. "This was Lenin."

This statement of paramount importance in 20th century history dispelled a dangerous illusion. Faced with the ultimate Bolshevik objectification—the mummy, the West suddenly realized that the Bolshevik revolution was not a 1917 version of the storming of the Bastille. Having "interpreted" events in Russia behind Western intellectuals' backs for years, Jacobean metaphor started having fits of claustrophobia. Lenin could have no wax figure—his body symbolically ruled out the creation of one.

The parallel between the wax figure and the mummy, between Madame Tussaud's and the Mausoleum, completely objectifies the polar notions of power, and hence, the different anatomy of the political bodies at the heart of the two revolutions: in France in 1789 and in Russia in October 1917.

This excerpt deals with the execution of Louis XVI and the liquidation of Nicholas II. The murders of the king and the emperor, the symbolic aspect of the murder techniques, are treated as a code which can be applied to decode the programmes of the French and Russian revolutions.

The idea of the new revolutionary corporeality, the "new political Adam," is not inferred from the ideologues' utopian works, but from the method used to execute the symbols of the old world.

The Guillotine

"The execution of Louis XVI was a political act." The trial against the king was a trial against justice. Today, similar statements are generally accepted. To a large extent, the decline of French Marxism has proven to be the end of "the notion of the French Revolution as fateful." It is now clear that the French Revolution solved one basic problem: the king's physical elimination. The king's body proved to be the insoluble contradiction in a changing French society. For 18th century French society saw the king's body as a political reality rather than a metaphor. To function, the monarchy needed the corporeal presence of the king. The revolution had to metaphorize the king's body. In a certain sense, the guillotine was a workshop for metaphors.

The revolution had to execute the body of the existing power, the divine right, and constitutional inviolability of the monarchy. To strip someone or something of their inviolability is one way of producing political metaphors. But the monarch's constitutional inviolability was guaranteed by the revolution itself. The 1791 Constitution ruled out the possibility of executing the king. Since royal authority was divine, the king was inviolable as long as he was king; deprived of his sanctity, he could be tried only for crimes which he had committed as an ordinary citizen, as non-king.

To execute the king, the revolution had to execute its own legitimacy. The guillotine thus became a workshop for the illegal production of metaphors.

On November 13, 1792, Saint-Just addressed the National Convention in a speech which should have cut the Gordian knot: "I have taken the floor, citizens," said he, "to prove that the king may be tried because both the opinion upholding royal inviolability and that of the Committee, which wants to try the king as an ordinary citizen, are equally wrong." The important point for Saint-Just was to try the king in his capacity as king, so he accused him of a metaphysical crime—"the crime of being a king."

The symbolic separation of powers proved possible only as a physical severance of the king's two bodies: the political body of Louis XVI and the body of Louis Capet, father and husband. Figuratively speaking, in this case the guillotine did not kill—it separated the one from the other. Having failed to survive this separation, the innocent Louis Capet was buried, while Louis XVI's body was displayed in its metaphoric integrity at Madame Tussaud's. On the orders of the revolutionary authorities, Madame Tussaud moulded Louis XVI's portrait before his execution.

The body of power was amputated from the body of the king. The king's head was moulded in wax, yet wax was the body of seals. Having embodied absolute power, Louis XVI also embodied the absolute seal. The revolution separated the bodies of Louis and the seal. Madame Tussaud put them together again in a parody.

Acid

The meaning of the Bolshevik revolution is to be found in the symbolic interpretation of two biochemical processes. The first process took place in July 1918 and may be described as decomposition of a base through acid; the second was in January 1924 and may be defined as the transformation of death into eternal life—in a certain sense, this biochemical process was a miracle.

This paper will discuss the decomposition of a base through acid only. Or it will examine the murder of the Russian Emperor Nicholas Romanoff as one stage in the process of turning society into a conspiracy. The emperor's murder was itself part of this conspiracy. It was no different from the murder of any petty bourgeois. There were no trial, dramatic speeches, charges, or crimes. One night the Romanoffs were shot dead; their bodies were then loaded on a truck, driven out of town (Yekaterinburg), and buried. We do not even know who ordered the execution. Paradoxically, the murder of the Russian emperor lacked a symbolic dimension. Louis XVI's head rolled in the heart of Paris, at the heart of the French Revolution. Nicholas Romanoff was killed as a dog "at the back of the beyond." The emperor's crime was covered up. If in killing Louis the French Revolution executed its own legitimacy, the murder of Nicholas was tantamount to rejecting legality. The problem facing the Bolshevik revolution had nothing to do with the legalization of a purely political act like the execution of Louis XVI. The problem of the Bolshevik revolution was that of any criminal: how to hide the corpse so as to avoid discovery. The emperor's corpse—not his body—actually foiled Bolshevik plans. After burial, the royal corpses were exhumed and drenched with acid. Later, the building where the Romanoffs had been imprisoned was destroyed as well. If the execution of Louis XVI was a political crime, the murder of Nicholas II was a criminal offence, depriving a person of his life with the purpose of robbery.

The idea of destroying the old power and abolishing classes automatically placed Bolshevism beyond politics and the political. Liquidating power proved possible only as an infinite exhaustion of a total and unlimited power. The idea itself lent an absolute value to this very power. In this sense the body of Nicholas II was no longer different from the millions of other bodies that populated the underground.

The very act of going underground practically stripped the emperor of his power, for the strength of his power lay in its legitimacy—yet this legitimacy was outlawed. Nicholas II posed a threat in time only, therefore his corpse alone constituted a threat.

The public and the underground reversed roles once and for all. The guillotine was absolutely useless. The only power which the emperor's body had was the power of history, of time. The emperor's body lost its organic essence, becoming dangerous only as a geological formation.

The acid poured over Romanoff was the real weapon of the revolution. The new government did not execute—it wiped people out. Socialism proved to be the end of sociality.

Certain hypotheses claim that the acid used on the emperor's corpse was the main component of the stuff with which Lenin was mummified.

Note

1. "We are such stuff / As dreams are made on" (William Shakespeare, *The Tempest,* IV. i. 148).

Part III

The Post-Paranoid Condition

The Post-Paranoid Condition
Ivaylo Ditchev

In the times of allegory I had imagined a fantastic country that had decided to base its politics on science, rather than irrational values. Unlike communism, it was not political economy, but genetic engineering which was supposed to make it possible to improve human nature at any moment. The result was not exactly predictable. To begin with, the geneticians themselves seized the opportunity to make their own genitals several times bigger, which resulted in massive shortage of blood supply to the brain, fainting-fits, and bad government. Metabolism had to be speeded up, and consequently more food was needed, so geneticians devised supplementary elephant trunks for the fruit-pickers in order to raise the productivity of labor (realizing thus Fourier's dream of what he called the "archy-hand"). This necessitated the reduction of feet and the introduction of new means of transportation like wings, the latter implying a diminuation of the fruit-picker's body and, respectively, a decrease of productivity.

The revolutionary process went on and on even after gradual discontent began to spread among the creatures, who had lost all resemblance to the human race. But who else, if not the geneticians again, could find the way back to the natural state? Genetics was now largely taught at school and the best engineers, chosen in the most democratic way, were asked to increase their brains to such an extent that they could no longer do anything but lie in bed, like the famous philosopher, and invent clever traps for nature to show up on its own; but any time someone pretended to have got hold of it, there burst out a terrible quarrel, for you couldn't be sure whether this was Nature at last, or whether the engineer in question was not furthering a self-interested project, and he was remodelled, and someone else took his place, and the political struggle had no end.

There is no transcendence about capitalism, no eternal truth, no image or example (from Mirandola to Marx and Sartre). What does it mean, then, to return to capitalism? Return to shapelessness, to the void of freedom? But was communism really a shape for man, transcending him? All constraints imposed upon him were but "political decisions," that is, based on the struggle for power between forces in a historical situation; they were not real in the way a taboo or the obligations of honor are. (The Berlin wall was never anything but an act of political force, for both sides—unlike the Chinese wall, for instance.)

That's why the villain disappeared miraculously, like a computer-game-enemy, who leaves no trace behind. The irrational thing about the fall of communism is due to the fact that in itself it was but an act of force, but off from eternity: the moment it is defeated, it seems to have never been there at all. Like the ghost in a bad dream it has no other reality outside the fact of struggling with you; it was you, in opposing it, who made it exist (you = the democratic world, common reason, the dissidents, etc.).

In a way, politicizing the world leads naturally to paranoia: everything and everybody is turned into a pawn of the great mortal struggle; things have no value in themselves outside the interpretation with respect to the big stratagem. Unlike its medical counterpart, political paranoia presupposes a certain control of the process, that is, you may interpret everything in the political perspective, but then you go home and read a book or kiss your wife without planning these as moves in the final destruction of imperialism. In his *Meditationes* Descartes seems to suggest something like controlled paranoia to be the ultimate foundation of reason (the extreme example of doubt). What if

a *malin génie* were tricking me and all my sensations were false? There is no way to prove that everything around me is not the product of someone's wicked will; one thing is nevertheless certain: my doubt, my ability to evoke this possibility, to imagine my total defeat and the irreality of the world I am familiar with. Is it **me** who controls the situation—even to the point of self-negation?—I have the upper hand over the demon, I create him, not he me.

Descartes, however, did not envisage the case when doubt could be imposed upon the subject by the alleged demon himself by the means of terror, propaganda, ideology, etc. "I doubt, therefore I am" turns into "he forces me into doubt, therefore **he** is." Now there is no way out: both certitude and doubt are at the side of the demon, he asserts at the same time that he does and that he doesn't exist; that everything is and is not manipulated. Getting rid of the demon then actually means having him back on your shoulders, as it was he who constantly wanted you to do away with him... In other words, the question of post-communism is: how do you get rid of a **revolutionary** power, aiming to abolish all power in the world?

The Department of Rumors

There is a rumor that the department for spreading rumors among the population at the State security still exists. You can't even say that it has gone underground, for departments like that are underground in principle. It may have spread the rumor of its own dissolution, but also, and this is even worse, of its existence (which is perhaps its only form of being!). After some reflection, you come to the conclusion that there is no way to get rid of the rumor-department: it will be there the moment you think of it.

Rumors were indispensable in the great communist deconstruction of the subject. "Department for disinformation," as we used to call such institutions, is incorrect, as it implies that rumors are definitely false. Rumors may be true, but not necessarily. Usually there is the eroticism of eavesdropping, of getting more than you should, but it

might be just a piece of useful information that is nowhere to find. For instance, during the Chernobyl catastrophe while the media went on and on repeating there was no danger whatsoever, an elderly lady from the local party headquarters in Sofia rang at people's doors, saying confidentially to everyone that she had some friend at the Ministry who told her it might be better for the children not to drink milk.

The essential about a rumor is the subjective way it represents reality—it is a *doxa* needing to be proved by public procedures (i.e., to be universalized in some way). The central paradox of communist culture lies in the fact that public representations were no less subjective than rumors themselves: they were not intended to be true, but to help the victory of communism (the preservation of power), that is, open and frank ideology. Note the obscene character of the very notion of ideology in a Marxist-oriented type of discourse: what does it mean if I call my ideas "false consciousness," if I consider them to be but a means for something else? It means I'm not ready to **die** for them; I will die even more readily for bread, for a better life, for power, but never for truth, as stupid people did for ages. Thus, when you neighbor tells you she heard a rumor and when a party chief says he adopted an ideology, there is not much of a difference: neither **is** what she or he says.

Deficiency of the official ideological information presupposes rumor and the subjectivity of rumors presupposes official confirmation—this is a vicious circle. In such a system of total relativity, man can no longer be an identical, responsible social subject: he acts according the fluxes and refluxes of desire, of hope, and despair (accordingly, you believe or disbelieve radiation).

The class struggle of representations—socialist versus capitalist, official versus unofficial, tactic versus strategic—is aimed not at imposing the true one, but at maintaining the struggle, at undermining the principle of truth in itself and reducing man to a series of situations of desire. The most amazing thing is that class struggle begins the mo-

a *malin génie* were tricking me and all my sensations were false? There is no way to prove that everything around me is not the product of someone's wicked will; one thing is nevertheless certain: my doubt, my ability to evoke this possibility, to imagine my total defeat and the irreality of the world I am familiar with. Is it **me** who controls the situation—even to the point of self-negation?—I have the upper hand over the demon, I create him, not he me.

Descartes, however, did not envisage the case when doubt could be imposed upon the subject by the alleged demon himself by the means of terror, propaganda, ideology, etc. "I doubt, therefore I am" turns into "he forces me into doubt, therefore **he** is." Now there is no way out: both certitude and doubt are at the side of the demon, he asserts at the same time that he does and that he doesn't exist; that everything is and is not manipulated. Getting rid of the demon then actually means having him back on your shoulders, as it was he who constantly wanted you to do away with him... In other words, the question of post-communism is: how do you get rid of a **revolutionary** power, aiming to abolish all power in the world?

The Department of Rumors

There is a rumor that the department for spreading rumors among the population at the State security still exists. You can't even say that it has gone underground, for departments like that are underground in principle. It may have spread the rumor of its own dissolution, but also, and this is even worse, of its existence (which is perhaps its only form of being!). After some reflection, you come to the conclusion that there is no way to get rid of the rumor-department: it will be there the moment you think of it.

Rumors were indispensable in the great communist deconstruction of the subject. "Department for disinformation," as we used to call such institutions, is incorrect, as it implies that rumors are definitely false. Rumors may be true, but not necessarily. Usually there is the eroticism of eavesdropping, of getting more than you should, but it

might be just a piece of useful information that is nowhere to find. For instance, during the Chernobyl catastrophe while the media went on and on repeating there was no danger whatsoever, an elderly lady from the local party headquarters in Sofia rang at people's doors, saying confidentially to everyone that she had some friend at the Ministry who told her it might be better for the children not to drink milk.

The essential about a rumor is the subjective way it represents reality—it is a *doxa* needing to be proved by public procedures (i.e., to be universalized in some way). The central paradox of communist culture lies in the fact that public representations were no less subjective than rumors themselves: they were not intended to be true, but to help the victory of communism (the preservation of power), that is, open and frank ideology. Note the obscene character of the very notion of ideology in a Marxist-oriented type of discourse: what does it mean if I call my ideas "false consciousness," if I consider them to be but a means for something else? It means I'm not ready to **die** for them; I will die even more readily for bread, for a better life, for power, but never for truth, as stupid people did for ages. Thus, when you neighbor tells you she heard a rumor and when a party chief says he adopted an ideology, there is not much of a difference: neither **is** what she or he says.

Deficiency of the official ideological information presupposes rumor and the subjectivity of rumors presupposes official confirmation—this is a vicious circle. In such a system of total relativity, man can no longer be an identical, responsible social subject: he acts according the fluxes and refluxes of desire, of hope, and despair (accordingly, you believe or disbelieve radiation).

The class struggle of representations—socialist versus capitalist, official versus unofficial, tactic versus strategic—is aimed not at imposing the true one, but at maintaining the struggle, at undermining the principle of truth in itself and reducing man to a series of situations of desire. The most amazing thing is that class struggle begins the mo-

ment you want it to begin. Between the point of view of the theoretician, stating that there is such a thing as class struggle and the ideologue, who produces purposeful theories that would serve one side of the struggle there lies nothing more and nothing less but readiness to die—asceticism, sacrifice, self-negation, whatever we will call it. Eternity, as a transcending point of reference, attained through the irreversible, is the most forbidden thing under communism, as it undermines the principle of the mass, which should be in constant movement (H. Arendt); the masses are life, whereas the individual begins with the awareness that he or she is mortal. Communism abolished death just like the Russian utopia dreamt of (the result was the *evaporization* (Orwell) of millions and millions, deprived of their own death). We can't deny a certain gratification in this new erotic structure: total uncertainty implies the immortality of timelessness.

Now let us make one more step. In a world of all-embracing (class) struggle man could at least *engage* himself, take sides, that is, the side of he, who is going to win in the course of history. This was obviously the case with many western leftists, having nothing to do with the *real socialism*. But what happens if you begin to think that both conflicting representations are produced by the same author, that is, that power produces its own enemies (as in "1984")? The heroic choice itself becomes dubious. Who would sacrifice his life fighting a fictitious enemy?

In telling the story of Andropov, Vosslensky relates the fact that in the beginning of the eighties there were quite a number of accidents with high-ranking officials. This, he says, might have been:

1. just a coincidence;
2. the elimination of rivals by the KGB;
3. an elimination of some rivals, done to intimidate other rivals;
4. just a rumor, spread by the KGB on the occasion of an accidental fact in order to intimidate rivals; or

5. a rumor, spread to intimidate rivals, having no relation to reality.

We have arranged these gradual steps of collapse into class struggle paranoia in an order, quite similar to Baudrillard's *precession of simulacra*. You have:

1. event; no power
2. power over event
3. power over event and power over man
4. power over man; no power over event
5. power; no event.

The beginning resembles dogmatic metaphysics; at the end Nietzsche's thesis is realized: there are no facts but only interpretations, which are acts of will to power. The problem is you have no fixed place on the scale; your own position in the process of collapse is not a fact but an interpretation again. The very moment you start suspecting the world, it yields political phantoms and disintegrates; the stronger your interpretation, the greater the collapse. It seems that the subject was all of a sudden forced into a state of unexpected and ill-timed freedom (as he or she was detached from death and eternity), and this deconstructed him or her into a series of paranoid situations.

There was no total control under communism,[1] there was the rumor of total control; but how do you get rid of a rumor?

The Nomenclatura of Dissidents

It has often been said that anti-Communists form a sort of new nomenclatura: the origin of their movement is conspiracy; the principle of nomination, at least in the first days after the victory, is personal loyalty. Anyway, you can always suspect people in a classless society of representing no one but themselves, as there are no articulated interests of the different social groups. Except for a few outspoken dissidents, the new political elite is totally unknown to the population; they are accepted as a team in thanks to the general (eschatological) wish for change.

Nomenclatura comes from *nomen* + *clamo,* "to call names," that is, an enumeration of names, a **list**. In the linguistic intuition of a Bulgarian or Russian, they form an arbitrary group (like the items present in a storehouse). Now let us imagine what it would mean to replace a traditional class by a nomenclatura. There would no longer be any content, economic, cultural, symbolic or whatsoever behind the constellation of people designed; nothing transcendent to the (political) situation would motivate the adherence to it—a name is either present on the list or it is not, and that is all. To be present on the list does not necessarily imply that you occupy a certain post or share some privilege: it only makes these probable, as the list is not a description, but an act of power. And when we ask "whose power?," we get a circular definition: the power, acquired thanks to the list.

Once social differences are abolished society is about to collapse into chaos, and this was precisely the case of the Soviet union under the modernist rule of Lenin. In an act of postmodern genius Stalin succeeded in both preserving the modernist deconstruction of hierarchies and the social functioning: by introducing the system of lists, he made social differences **arbitrary.** He knew that the other name of equality is arbitrary inequality. The masses don't just need to have no superiors, they need superiors who have their own superiors, and feel guilty; superiors who are constantly sacrificed. The masses need to feel that the rule over them is not eternal, that there is a basic **reversibility** of roles (like in the carnival). In tradition there was always the transcending principle of death (eternity, God, the ancestors), which legitimated power by undermining it at the same time; because the beyond not only gives the ruler his power, but also puts limits to it. The Bolsheviks carried this to the extreme: for the first time in history power undermined itself, affirming that it was no longer based on eternity, but just on the political situation—power stated "I am but a situation of power, my main goal is to abolish all power in the world including myself." It was constantly moving, reforming, purging itself, being thus even harder with its own people than with the population.²

The western use of "nomenclatura" to design what Jillas called the *new class* ignores the amplitude of the phenomenon. Here are some other examples. The list of all who live in Moscow (or: of those, who have to live in Magadan). The list of *kulaks*, that is not of the rich peasants, but of those who have been interpreted as such (sometimes in order to cover a percentage, required "from above"—the abstract figure makes the process even more arbitrary). The list of party members, percentage again according to sex, occupation, nationality, etc. The list of those who should no be seen on TV, but are allowed to publish in the press. The list of those who are not allowed to publish anywhere, but are not to be fired. The list of potential collaborators (of the police, of local authorities). The list of people who might (or might not) be shown to foreigners. The list of writers, composers (the "unions"). The list of Hungarians, Tatars, Turks. The list of the persons allowed to buy a flat of more than 120 square meters . . . We could go on like this until we have described the whole of the communist society. The ideal, thus, would be a state where **all** the relations are alienated in such (public) lists and **all** the efforts of the individual are directed towards moving from list to list³—that is, of being interpreted in such a way as to become a member of the desired nomenclatura group or to escape from the undesired one. At that point, man has no "inside" and is entirely public, as everything in him is language. Thus factories produce signs instead of goods (to use V. Todorov's expression). Boss X does not manufacture shoes for shoes' sake, he manufactures shoes in order to be interpreted by boss Y as "manufacturing shoes"; it is no longer consumption by the buyer that motivates him (or rather its representation in the field of exchange), but interpretation by the superior (or rather the interpretation pattern, that is "ideology"). The mode of production (public property, application of the Marxist-Leninist formula, etc.), becomes more important than the product itself and this has become possible thanks to the new social mediator, power without content, alienated in the bureaucratic list. By it, an age-long ambiguity of culture seems to be resolved: the project for the control of man over nature (the utopian limit of which is consumption) has been entirely engulfed by the one for the control of man over man (implying a potentially endless struggle for power). The various "triumphs" over nature, from agriculture to space travel, are nothing but *simulacra:* they have no value outside the great struggle (of classes, of systems, of gangs).

And yet, real communist societies differ from the ideal one in an important aspect: not all lists are public, they form a sort of conspirative hierarchy. For instance, a common man knows the list of party members, but the list of district-committee nomenclatura remains in principle a secret (a party member has more chances to know who participates at level No. 2). Ordinary police collaborators know nothing of the collaborators of the KGB. And maybe still less people know the list of those allowed to buy U.S. dollars or to grow mushrooms in their cellar. All this bears the traces of the underground period, when communists had to rely on pure secrecy with no properties. To found structures on the existing values (such as personal honor, truth, morals, etc.) would mean to accept the old world, which was supposed to be *demolished to the foundations*. The proletariat was supposed to be the radical negation of capitalist society and its avant-garde, communist party, could not base his activity on immediate positive values (the positive side of it should come afterwards, that is, it was **mediated** through the bright-future image). This is how Brecht puts it in **The Measure:**

> He who fights for Communism should be ready to fight and not to fight; to say the truth and not to say the truth; to do favours and not to do favours; to hold promises and not to hold promises; to seek danger and not to seek danger; to be seen and not to be seen. He who fights for Communism has only one of all the possible virtues: that he is fighting for Communism.

Today we perceive a macabre note in what Brecht thought to be an eulogy, although the description is quite right. The radical revolutionary, the communist, has only one trait, which amounts to tautology: that he is a revolutionary. Thus, the only way for him to be identified by his collaborators is the interplay of presence and absence—the secret list (absence from the public field, presence to conspiracy). When the underground revolutionary turns into an anonymous *aparatchick* the conspirative link becomes bureaucratic, but does not change in principle. All "depth" of the individual is but an artefact, the result of political decisions with no transcendence; all his or her traditional "contents" like competence, responsibility, morality, are reduced to the surface of pure presence or absence from the list. Even the will of those who interpret his behavior, as to range him or her into a given list, is not transcendental to the situation, as power is assumed in a collective way; for the first time in history the ruler has renounced to the essence of power—to have a face, an identity, a name, an opinion, a sense of pride or honor. Power is **anonymous** and consequently completely irresponsible, as there is no individual to assume personal responsibility. The mythical figure of the Leader carries this to the extreme—standing for the masses and for History itself, he is always right and never guilty, he won't die for anything, he personifies the masses' immortality (as a mummy, if necessary).

As a new type of social mediator, replacing money, laws, knowledge, etc., the nomenclatura list brings about a real revolution in human relations. It is the rationalization of the situation itself, making it possible to think and calculate the bare power-constellations without reference to anything else; thanks to it power can be from now on thought of in terms of being or not being there. (A similar revolution was, in its time, the invention of money, representing the bare value of a thing with no relation to its essence.[4]) In traditional representations of power, we are always "distracted" by something transcending it: a king makes us think of ancestors, blood, tradition, ritual; a president evokes the principle of representation; even a conqueror is associated with something other than pure presence like force or cruelty. The nomenclatura-member is the man without qualities, the relation between him and his place in society is mediated through the anonymous interpretative process.

All people living in such a society become members of **some** nomenclatura list, whether they wish it or not. In the course of the decencies this has a strange effect: little by little the seriousness of life disappears; instead of being interested by the depth of things, you turn more and more to the surface of language; instead of living, you represent yourself as somebody living. On the surface of simulation there is no place for the tragic essence of life, this is the kingdom of fiction, that is, of immortality. It is maybe the feeling of this tragic seriousness that makes the changes so difficult, almost impossible: how could a fiction become reality?

Storming the TV

The building of television was in the center of the Romanian revolution. In Sofia it was under siege for months, first by the one, then by the other, finally by both groups shouting at each other across the police cordon.[5] Unlike the riots in '68, no students demanded broadcasting time; it was *das Man* itself that attacked the media.

In the days of the French revolution, clocks are said to be shot at by the armed crowds; new religions burn the sacred books and destroy the temples of the old ones—in short, man fights not only with a body, but with a symbolic reality as well. But what does TV stand for? Its aim is no longer to represent some event or value: in its principle television is a substitute for reality, it is reality-as-artifact.

This makes storming the TV paradoxical: there is no longer any wax-enemy to be stabbed, nothing to be burnt, no symbols to be replaced; there simply is nothing but television as all aother representation can be televised. Thus the revolutionary masses don't seem to have much to communicate. It is as if Vladimir and Estragon had taken the stage by storm in order to find out there is nothing to do but be present there. And we saw them in Bucharest, crowding by dozens in front of the camera, pressing into the frame without a word. These were the revolutions of pure presence: no stratagem, no project for a better world was motivating them, as all that smells of transcendence had been discredited long ago.

Totalitarian culture once had largely been a culture of cinema. A film, being a closed system, produces both its text and its context (you watch it silently in the dark, as any other point of reference may disturb your perception). This creates a world of total relativity—Laurel & Hardy are small when the furniture around them is big; the voice of the commentator denotes the item shown on the screen as one does in real life, but in the film both voice and thing are man made. The Russian montage-school founded its whole theory on this; the experiments of Kuleshov showed that the whole meaning of a sequence may be changed; prisoner's face followed by window suggests longing for freedom, but that very same face, followed by a plate of soup, all of a sudden begins to express simple hunger. And yet we are persuaded that this is reality itself, as we identify the events and objects of life, being transcribed faithfully by the machine. Reality itself seems to be totally manipulated by a new, completely different type of author: not the one that speaks, writes, plays, but someone who mounts all these, a meta-author, placed above reality as a whole, he is born by our paranoid suspicion. The meta-author is often personalized in the person of the director of the film, but in fact "he" is a semiotic function, not less than the Leader in the fictionalized communist reality. You need a stratagem, a focus of some invisible interest behind in order to understand the mutilated—by scissors or by decrees—reality.

Totalitarianism went on and on with this film-editing *montage* principle: left in the dark with no outside points of reference, man was caught in a system of absolute relativity where life was lived to be represented and representations had to be acted out—take a 5-year plan, a party congress,[6] a brigade, a space rocket: was this fiction or reality? The edited reality produced, as in cinema, the figure of the "He who manipulates all this"—the Party and its Leader. You could prove or refute the existence of the meta-author no more than the existence of God; though He was badly needed to understand what had been deprived of sense.

The boredom of TV suddenly interrupts this paranoid process. There couldn't be an author behind televised reality as there couldn't be one behind the clock. As a form of synchronization of social life, as a measure of the public, TV seems to go back to what Weber called *formal rationality*. It is the becoming of the world itself—day after day things happen, information piles up, images seduce us, and there is no sense, no end, no transcendent meaning. No final touch, no summing up, no sacrifice is thinkable in this new medium: TV is life itself, it never stops, never leaves a trace upon eternity—as it is eternity itself. This makes it the ideal medium of post-communism (and maybe a determining factor of the changes, as well). By storming into the frame of TV, the masses destroyed not only the function of the meta-author, but with him the very possibility of history, which, as they have learnt from Hegel, begins with negativity, with death. And this seems to be the ultimate sense of this new, postmodern, postparanoid democracy: no power, no walls and borders, no progress, nothing—just being there, forever.

Dubrovnik, November 1990

Notes

1. It is ridiculous to talk about total control in underdeveloped countries, where a train can never leave on time. H. Arendt and others have explained the phenomenon by the principle of terror.

2. The priviledges of the elite (before the Briejnev era, which was of course the time of decay) cannot be compared to the

insecurity they lived. No one would risk his or her life just for a *datcha*; some quite different type of mivation was obviously moving people.

3. This can be clearly seen in the classic utopias: social regulations take the form of bureaucracy as it is the case with More's permissions to travel, Plato's—to have children, etc.

4. Could we go on with the parallel and speak of use-power and exchange-power?

5. Moscow putsch and counter-putsch were no less centered round the TV screen.

6. It's interesting how S. Krakauer relates the shooting of "The Triumph of Will": the Nazi congress in Nuremberg was apparently the event to be filmed, but actually the congress itself was prepared in such a way as to be filmed.

Epitaph for Sacrifice, Epitaph for the Left
Ivaylo Ditchev

▩ No Misery

The most significant trait of the times we live through: no one is willing to die for whatsoever. Their emblem: the delirious Gulf war, having as main objective to avoid casualties in the first place, a war, carried out to demonstrate that "all is under control" and thus negate death and loss.

"All that is not given is lost," says an Indian proverb; but in our contemporary world nothing is ever given and all seems lost. Unhappiness itself has been deprived of its Christian attraction: being poor and ill today provokes but repulsion, mixed with a 19th-century-styled philanthropic attempt to buy oneself out, to have no longer misery before one's eyes. Unhappiness frightens to death modern man, who, in plunging into a world of boundless positivity, has been left without defense against evil. Suffering no longer makes sense, therefore suffering is unbearable.

The name for it is decadence. Samuel Butler's witty anti-utopia "Erewhon" (= nowhere) was an introduction to the decadence of the last century. In his imaginary land, people are despised, sentenced, or even punished as criminals for the bare fact of being unhappy. Society has placed itself entirely on the side of fortune and order, and all of a sudden misery has become a much greater menace than crime: it has to be banned. The Malta talks can be seen as an introduction to the 20th *fin-de-siècle:* evil was suddenly ordered out of the world. In this way, an essentially tragic vision of duel between two superpowers, the outcome of which tended to apocalypse, was replaced by the comic one of a world where minor villains menace peace and happiness, but the centralized forces of good quickly teach them a lesson without really risking anything. Thus suffering, hardships, endurance, victims are from now on, denied legitimate right to exist; it is but a complication, a peripeteia before the burst of laughter. The miracle of fraternization is everywhere—East and West, then Jews and Arabs, who'll be the next? What's the use to fight, to defend interests, to try and return universal tendencies; the world is what it is, there are the rich countries and the poor ones, experience has shown that it is better for the poor to let themselves be guided by the rich. Every problem can be resolved by peaceful means under the new pax americana. Opposing, confronting, politicizing—these are remnants of a delirious sado-masochist past, when man thought he was concerned with power. Today power seems to disappear behind technicians, journalists, opinion polls, and currency rates and man seek his identity at home.

In such a tender decadent world, the Iraqi occupation of Kuwait or the Serbian aggression are but dead ends of history wherefrom nothing could follow: they are to be simply skipped (Kant defined the comic as an intensive expectation that dissolves suddenly into nothing). All local suffering, denied access to history, becomes an act of terrorism; instead of being defeated, it is to be punished. In the good old times of duel between good and evil, you sympathized with one party taking, if he had the courage to do so, the risk to engage oneself on his side. In the times when good is a sort of police for evil, one no longer fights evil or wishes to do so, he or she simply wants to do away with the center of infection, as wars and conflicts terrorize with the very fact that they exist. No one wishes to knows who is to blame for the horrors in Somalia or Bosnia, first comes "stop the war," and only after that "may the just cause win, if possible." The West has, so to say, assumed the role of a parent for the rest of the world. In between small local terrorists, children have quickly learnt to cheat on the police of good: they know perfectly well that they will never be defeated, as they are but the shadow of the New World Order, that is, they are not fighting, but producing signs of evil that block the system of centralized good (as any signs these can be bargained at a profit).

In Erewhon, as in the New World (Dis)Order, the negative is no full-right enemy, defying the positive in dubious battle. If negative exists at all, it is but a lack of self-confidence, a neurotic tic of the positive. Suffering, violence, and death are no longer a necessary element in the development of society, as the forces of good and reason have things under control; Mephisto is discharged. But if we are already there, then progress itself is no longer real; if it can be effectuated in a reasonable way, the forces of reason themselves should have attained the ideal and wouldn't be supposed to develop any longer. No need for the future to extract itself from the present in tragic labor; it is the sweet memories of past happiness that have replaced the vision of a better future. What comes can only frighten in its irrationality and absurdity. The future terrorizes exactly like the Somalian skeletons, the Yugoslav concentration camps, or the German burnt Turks. What will happen? Why should anything happen at all? What, if not final catastrophe and death, could bring us the future? The police of good and reason tries to keep, here as well, things under hand, to make believe that nothing will happen, or, as this is somewhat difficult a task, at least to play the Malta trick and turn tragedy into comedy, affirming that whatever happens will be of no importance. All great notions are back out of the cupboard, all eternal values, all fashions, all nostalgias to assure us magically that the world has always been the same, nothing ever changes, nothing really important is at stake.

This seems to be the real end to two millennia of Christian civilization. Because, paradoxically, the *laic* (people) fight for a better future, from the French revolution to the fight against fascism or against the Vietnam war, was the final crescendo of this civilization. In fact, the deepest motive force of the European left movements has neither been the striving for the public (at the expense of the private), nor for equality (at the expense of liberty), but the readiness to assume the tragic break between present and future, that is the willingness to sacrifice. It may be objected that many other political currents call on selflessness as well (in *Mein Kampf,* for instance, the Aryan is presented as superior to the Jew, in that he is able to sacrifice himself, the latter being condemned to die like a beast). However, there is a world of difference between the self-affirming sacrifice on the right, through which the "master" (in Hegel's terms) imposes his name, his will, his passions, his race, his masculinity, and the radical sacrifice on the left, experienced in the name of the oppressed as self-effacement of an anonymous, if not androgynous comrade in the "class," the "cause," the "historical necessity." (Or, if you wish, between phallus and castration.)

This explains why communism never won in the West: the East offers a better milieu for self-effacement. To take away private property or to erase the differences of class, knowledge, or sex is in its essence a sacrificial act, for he who does fight for such erasement, in expropriating the "phallus" of the ruling class, cancels the very possibility to acquire it himself, that is to be male, master, proprietor, etc. Envy destroys not only the other but oneself, as it undermines the very ideal of the ego (the "good object" of M. Klein). Nazism, if it had survived, would have ended up in liquidating all others; communism, after destroying all the ideal projects of the I (ancestors, tradition, identity, truth, dignity, law, wealth, science, and party members themselves) went as far as destroying itself in the supreme gesture of the Perestroika. The ultimate sacrifice of communism was the sacrificing of communism itself. (Is then communism dead or does it still live: here you are a logical paradox similar to the one of the liar saying "I am a liar.")

Communism's Guilt Machine

It is not by chance that the fall of the Berlin wall brought about such unaccountable despair, and that, on both sides. It seems that the communist bloc played a greater role than people inside and outside it would be willing to admit. Today we could argue that the whole thing was a tasteless combination of Schlaraffenland and Gulag. And yet, in another perspective, the essential was not what communists were ready to die and kill for, but that they were ready to do so in a world of positivity, that had no defense against death: it was they who assumed to be the agent of the destruction of the old and the birth of the new, to be the ecstasy of rupture itself as scapegoats and hangmen at the same time.

The notion of sacrifice has been banalized by Stalinist propaganda, as well as by the anti-Communist folklore, but this should not mislead us. We simply have to get rid of its positive connotation: sacrificial exchange was but a type of social relation. In fact, being transformed into a state policy, manipulated, perverted, it became a terrible burden for the "liberated" populations. This side of communism is rarely analyzed; normally one is tempted to see the utilitarian side of the thing—the regime confiscates, the envious populations rob the individual of rights and property. But in fact the interaction had a deeper symbolic dimension. To make of the "proletarian"—by definition being deprived of property, power, knowledge, sex[1]—the basis of society means to incriminate all "phallic" attributes of man (power, property), and to impose symbolic castration as a moral (and even a juridical) norm: any form of existence above the imaginary zero-point called "proletarian" was branded with guilt. This has certainly been the utmost radicalization of Christian culture.

According to the official doctrine of the Stalin-era, the present generation had to be sacrificed for the one to come (this seems to be a "cosmization" of the convictions in the Slav-orthodox family that parents should "sacrifice" themselves for their children). Agriculture had to be sacrificed to industry, consumer-good production to the production of means of production. We could analyze the whole (pseudo-) Marxist economic theology in terms of what is due to what. Besides, children had to sacrifice their parents (Pavlik Morosov), party officials, accused by mistake, had to sacrifice their honor for the honor of the Party, etc.

Or take the example of the communist party, this strange structure that was supposed to govern the Soviet-style countries and that, according to Stalinist norms, covered up to 14 percent of the population. The Party was based neither on property, nor on birth, nor even on some special function or knowledge (the 14 percent pierced through all levels of society). What united its members, motivated by the normal human wish for social success, was the readiness to sacrifice themselves and feel guilty for what they would not sacrifice. A party member was supposed to work more than the rest; I do not say that he or she in fact did work, what matters is that they were expected to, both by official discourse of propaganda and by private grumble. He or she had to be at the disposal of the Party, because the Party had given them everything (work, house, life) and had thus infinitely indebted them: the member had to be ready, in return, at any moment to organize, to put into practice, to rouse enthusiasm, to be the avant-garde model for the rest. What observers rarely notice is that other stranger "moral" expectations were attached to those: for instance, the party member was supposed not only to be modest in his or her private life (initially: poor, of "proletarian background"), but also sociable, that is a "collectivist," transparent. There was a typical story of the party secretary who lived with no curtains. Privacy and selfishness was supposed to be sacrificed: the first step upwards in the social hierarchy (Komsomol, Party) implied an amount of self-denial or at least its simulacrum (the latter was obviously more often the case). But even then, imagine the identity of a person who is constantly torn between pretention and intention, imagine the lack of freedom that person would have to live with. What is more, the sacrifice/guilt pattern was linked to a monstrous apparatus of secrecy. Vague rumors of crimes, tortures and murders, racist and imperialist phantasms behind closed doors, secret, semicriminal advantages and benefits: this is what made the strange conspiratory organization in power stick together. It makes no sense to compare the privileges of the elites of "real socialism" with those in the developed countries or in Africa; the essential problem is that everything these elites possessed was outlawed and nevertheless tolerated, if not secretly encouraged; that the overall incrimination of social differences, opposed to the practice of such differences, created a situation of general indebtedness. One should not be astonished that ex-communist parties do not dissolve after the fall of the regimes: they are more than a political structure.

Power reposes on symbolic exchange; in order to rule you have to give. And yet, there seems to be no other example in history of such a systematic culpabilization of a ruling group.[2] One may think of early Islam, a culture imposing severe self-restrictions of those in power and equally tending towards military and ideological expansion; although Islamic culture guaranteed—at least to men—the superiority over women, providing thus the "natural" basis on which a minimum of power could be built up. Under communism all power had to be reconquered again and again by acts of sacrifice, as it had been deprived of "substance" (property, blood, sex). On the top of the pyramid there was the image of the sacrifice as such: Stalin, in his plain "stalinka," who didn't sleep at night, thinking so much of the well-being of the people and who even sacrificed his only son ("I don't exchange a soldier for a general"). He represented the perfekt I, the sublime effacement of individuality, melting into the anonymous masses. If we know today that despite his outward modesty and impersonality there was the perverse eroticism (or paranoia) of unlimited power, symbolic exchange remains the same: Stalin sacrifices his personal life to the people, the people ought to return the gift, in offering their freedom.

Thus communism, as designed by the Stalin era, transformed the purest essence of human nature: that is the faculty of giving, sacrificing, and owing into a monstrous technology of domination. The guilt machine it engendered seems perfect today, none the less it was—the result of a chaotic mixture of traditional Russian cultural structures, revolutionary ideas imported from the West, and a concurrence of circumstances. In fact, it was not giving, but taking away that came first historically: the Party had confiscated the whole of social reality, and thus everything, even life itself, became a gift and the object of symbolic exchange. Such relations with power were obviously an anachronism in the 20th century, for gifts are the exact opposite of rights. For instance, if travelling abroad were a right, you wouldn't have to feel grateful for being "let" abroad or guilty for having "fled." If there were public procedures of applying for a post and legal guarantees against being thrown out at any moment, the employee would not be indebted to the Party and could act as a free person according to his moral conscience. If you could buy all you need on the market using your own money, you would not be indebted to the seller, etc. Rights break the links and liberate the individual, symbolic exchange binds them to produce a community.

The greatest discovery of the system was the combining of the gift-and-sacrifice mode with bureaucratic anonymity. The unprecedented centralization of all that touched to representation aimed, primarily, at dissociating humans from their bodies. The physical, sexual, passionate subject, who in the traditional societies exchanged gifts and acts of generosity, were now replaced by an abstract bureaucratic file; humans were reduced to a point in the topography of nomenclatura. It was not the glorious chief X who was indebted to the notorious warrior Y, but an abstract bureaucratic position, defined in abstract terms (did he or she own a cow before the revolution? join the Komsomol? celebrate Lenin's anniversary?). Imagine that the glorious chief is not a desiring body, but a construction, a collage: some clerk registers a great victory he won, another sticks to him the glorious phallus, yet another makes the inventory of his ancestors. The file completed, he can be situated on nomenclatura level "chief" and effectuate a great, generous potlatch. Then some clerk (for some quite personal reason) inserts into the file the observation that the chief was telling political jokes, offending another chief: he is immediately placed into another level, and becomes, say, "foreigner" or "woman."

For the West, modernization implied the destruction of the symbolic exchange between social positions and persons, in introducing rights, mediators, neutral (Wertfreie-Weber) spheres of transaction and thought where the subject doesn't oblige and isn't obliged to anyone. Marx, one of the most radical thinkers of western modernity, as well as Nietzsche and Freud, concentrated their fire in the first place on the symbolic debt that mystified the relations between man and power. They were obviously working in the right direction; by the end of modernization, not only the notion of morals and guilt, but the overall system of giving and sacrificing was eliminated from culture. Thus loss, misery, and death loosed all their sense and became an object of dumb horror for the individual.

The East, and Slav orthodoxy in particular, lived the shock of modernization in quite another way: it radicalized and globalized the sacrifice/guilt pattern, extending it to cosmic, eschatological dimensions. No single spot of reality was left untouched by owing-and-being-owed, no indifferent nature or rational, pragmatic interaction sphere outside the splitting into friends and enemies, progressive and reactionary, good and evil. The heroic movement forward to industrialization seemed to be but the ideological facade for its opposite—the radicalization of the symbolic exchange pattern; and it is Dostoievsky rather than Marx who can explain to us this universe, attempting to jump over modernity: "Everyone is guilty before everyone for everything and this is paradise."[3]

Seduction International

The symbolic exchange had its international dimension. On one side you had countries that kept their habits, brands of whiskey, names of the streets; on the other, the five-year-period is the maximum that reality can hold out. Apart from the heroic side of suffering, representing the great socialist experiment as the guiding star of humanity, in everyday life the East developed a strange discursive masochism, a morbid delight to dwell in misery under the gaze of the prosperous West, horrified by unhappiness. It was as if division of labor was effectuated throughout Christian civilization: one half had undertaken to be happy and enjoy itself, the other to sacrifice and suffer. (As far as the facts it was the contrary, for it was the West that worked harder, but I am considering images, not economy). There exists an ancient archetype: some renounce to life, that is, to pleasures, sex, freedom, power, success, and wealth and submit of their own free will to discipline and privations by going to a monastery/convent. Monasteries are miniworlds, situated by the side of the real one, they have social structures, culture, laws, power relations, and even economic production of their own—only life is supposed to be harder than outside. They are worlds of permanent sacrifice, especially concerning the sexual side of the human being,[4] worlds that take onto themselves suffering in order to liberate the "real" one from it.

We can see the communist bloc as a planet-scale monastery, where suffering and misery is assumed to liberate the rest of the world from the anxiety before it. Symbolic exchange was globalized through the massmedial unification of the world. Note the strange fight carried out of communist and Stalinist ideology against all that might be pleasant: fashion, dancing, chewing gum, entertainment, "art for art's sake," infidelity, and all hints of eroticism. How does this fit into a "materialist" ideology? In a strange way the phantasms as Slav (Russian) soul, communist martyrdom, and postcommunist "miserabilism" merge. One somehow expects suffering to take place in this part of the world, that is, voluntary suffering (and this is why the third world can hardly play the role of monastery). It seems—or seemed for some time—quite natural that whole postcommunist populations bombard the West with victimary discourses, saying that everything of the life "before" was awful, absurd, ugly, terrible, every single minute of it.

Leave aside the question whether it was really that awful and if it could have been much better without communism. Just imagine, say, a well-bred healthy engineer, head of a family, coming up to you and saying: "I was a slave, all my life they humiliated me, you cannot understand." What noble ideals of personal freedom he must have, if he feels like this. Even if the man had really been a slave during the whole of his life, why should he tell it with so much excitement? Why should he draw an almost masochistic pleasure in the idea of his real or imaginary sufferings? Moreover, the real martyrs of the regime, for example, survivors from the camps, are much more reluctant to complain, trying to save their dignity in some way or another. Miserabilism is the cultural norm, a sort of perverted identity and you should not be surprised to hear the victimary discourse even from high-ranking communist officials. Living under the conditions of chronic indebtedness has evoked chronic self-hatred.

The self-hatred discourse became a genre of communication long before the fall of communism, and in some of the countries long before its establishment: standing in queues or having a dull time in an office, people amused each other with facts or jokes showing "how normal everything is abroad and how absurd it is at home." Here is a real one: a Japanese literary scholar was said to have expressed astonishment at the bold imagination of a bulgarian poet having written: "if suddenly there were a power cut." Whereas to the Japanese the image of electricity being cut off all of a sudden is a metaphor, similar to the one of the sun being extinguished, no Bulgarian will ever suspect it to be a figure of speech. In fact metaphor was the chief strategy of the genre, that is, the comic jump from "here" onto "there": everything "here" is a metaphor of the original "there." And if propaganda projected this original onto the communist future, whereas everyday life discourse projected onto the consumer paradise, it boils down to the same (in fact by the end of the '70s this difference began to disappear, as the regimes looked more and more westwards). What persists is self-hatred.

Here is one more sample of the genre, this time a fiction. A Russian specialist falls among man-eaters, who capture him and prepare the cauldron. "Comrades"—he addresses them—"Have you ever heard of the Great Socialist October Revolution?" "No."—the tribe answers. "Do you know what in means to built socialism?" "No." "Have you ever celebrated the centenary of the great Lenin?" "No." "Then why have you become man-eaters?" The joke obviously attacks the communist thing; note however the masochist axis on which it has been built: the "we" is degraded to savagery. This is not the irony that every "normal" (non-monastic) nation has for its shortcomings. Pretending to boast that the USSR is the best (the sacrificial avant-garde of humanity), it effectuates an about-turn in order to present them as being the worst (cannibals). Curiously, however, the two extremes merge, because to confess you are bad, sacrificing your pride and identity, means that you become even better then those who have lead a normal virtuous life. (This paradox used to be the kernel of Christianity: you cannot be virtuous, affirm it, remain it without committing the "sin of pride"; you have to sin and repent.) The "we-are-the-worst" genre is running higher and higher these days; the whole of life "before," that is economy, politics, art, is not only rejected, but bluntly destroyed, sacrificed before the fascinated eye of the West. (What noble ideals of economy and social life they must have to act like this.)

Certainly there has much to be changed, and certainly it has to be done quickly. There is, however, something suspect in the readiness and euphoria with which whole populations engage, for the second time in less than a century, in the making *tabula rasa* of the past, sacrificing the totality of social reality before the altar of modernity. It is this belief in miracles, more typical of the countries of orthodox culture, and particularly of Russia, that combine in a strange way with the armchair theories now of Marx, now of the Monetary Fund. The economic miracle, as any other one, is to be paid for by suffering; although, unlike the individual everyday sacrifice, required by the "protestant ethic" (M. Weber), the orthodox ethic exalts unrealistic hope, cataclysm, fusion in the community, Easter.

No one has the right to judge a whole culture; the problem consists in the fact that today this (as any other) culture is no longer isolated, being involved in the worldwide seduction game with the West. In destroying itself, the East tries to capture, once more, the love of the West, to impose an obligation on it. In fact, the two central figures in the transition period discourse are the debt of the respective country towards the West (no one ever bothers to specify who the creditors are and whether the western countries themselves are not even more indebted) and the duty of the West towards the East (you have let us suffer in signing the Yalta agreement, in not declaring us war). The West has, so to say, given credit to the communist fathers, then indebted them, now it ought to give new credit to the sons. The fathers won over the West by sacrificing themselves in the fight against fascism; the sons have to win their heart by equal selflessness in fighting communism. All around the ex-soviet bloc there is the rumor of a new Marshall plan, which the West is somehow obliged to launch, and this makes one think of the Bolsheviks, who awaited the general proletarian revolution as help, reward, and recognition. What will happen when the "masochistic" peoples realize that misery is banned and that the wealthy democracies are not involved in symbolic exchange with them, but only in selling images?

Towards Ecophilanthropy

Today it seems that Soviet communism, in making perverse usage of sacrifice and generosity, compromised the very possibility of left-wing ethics. But then why did the Brezhnev universe itself decay in introducing hereditary principles of power, open privileges, security, cynicism?

Demographers would tell us that along about the '70s the massive processes of migration were stabilized, the flux of rural populations to the industrial zones diminished parallel with the slowing down of extensive growth of production. All desired liberations were, if not fulfilled, at least accepted by public discourse. In fact the Fourierist revolution of '68, based not on sacrifice and misery, but on sex and happiness, was a sort of suicide for the European left and it was not by chance that the aging communist parties were instinctively against it. Pleasure was enthroned, nothing in principle was any longer opposed to desire: it remained just to devise technologies to fulfill it. Somehow the world need no longer change. Even the scientific euphoria seemed over, after man had marched on the moon: a dream had come true and what of it? If television had not existed, this epoch would have invented it. Wasn't it in fact TV that killed the left, as well as real socialism? Its pan-aesthetic mode of life was a perfect shield against sacrifice and generosity. Even the fall of communism turned out to be but a media scoop, implying neither risk nor engagement. There is nothing to take or give to the picture-world; being situated outside it, you cannot even answer by a picture of your own, as this, unlike using normal language, is technically impossible. The only thing you are supposed to do is contemplate it motionless in the dark.

Trying to do without the ordeal of change, a happiness-bound world replaces the tragic figure of the revolutionary by the comic one of the philanthropist. Neither left-wing nor right-wing, he is a protagonist of decadence. In the imaginary world of the 19th century, he never risks his life, nor even seriously damages his wealth; he gives without really losing, resolving thus miraculously the fundamental problem of human existence. If today the good-natured uncle with the top hat has been replaced by televised humanitarian missions, the desire they express is still the same. So to say, the "master," the former colonialist, the postindustrial capitalist has suspended the give-and-take exchange with the "slave," he will give, although, seemingly not in order to bind and subject the latter to his will, but to get rid of him! The gift draws lines of demarcation: we rich are here, you poor stay there. The ideology of this new status quo is a sort of racist, cultural or other ecology, aiming at preserving everything as it is. The industrialized West accepts to pay ransom in order to get rid of the suffering, straining in all over the world.

According to psychoanalysis, the repressed never does disappear, at one time or another it re-emerges in an irrational form; similarly, repressed misery and suffering shall certainly be back one day, the whole problem is under what a monstrous shape they will manifest themselves. I wonder whether the western TV-watcher realizes what humiliating, degrading effect this sort of "ecological" aid has on the population, denied forever access to the community of their benefactors? And that what the wretches on the far side of TV really need is someone to fight shoulder to shoulder with them, moved by the project of unification for mankind.

The world seems never to get wiser. If you want to know about today, look back at post-Fourierist 19th century decadence with its horror of death and the future, with its obsession with beauty and well-being. If you want to know about tomorrow, think of what followed.

▨ Notes

1. In the *Manifesto* capitalist machine production is accused of effacing the differences between men and women, which was, in fact, another culpabilizing phantasm (if so, why should spinning factories be reserved for women?)

2. The communist party was obviously not a ruling class: not all members had power, though all in power had to be members. It was a virtual identity, a promise of power, provoking shared crime and shared guilt.

3. This is the sublime revelation of the future saga Zossima after having renounced the idea of duel, that is, of personal masculine honour ("The Karamazov Brothers").

4. Note the equation that Freud establishes between the fear of death and the fear of castration. Assuming castration would equal assuming death. Note the Puritan obsession of Soviet-style communism after the 20s.

An Essay on Terror
Alexander Kiossev

To Vladislav Todorov (by whom this text has doubtless been influenced)

1. The Ultimate Revolution

In a sense, all revolutions have been a failure. Not that they failed to achieve their ends (although this is also true): they were not truly revolutionary—they were no radical utopias.

All utopias dream of a future fairer order, which presupposes that the current order will be destroyed. However, all interpretations of social systems or orders to date have been rather narrow minded: changes have affected the political, economic, or class order alone, overlooking the global symbolic order of which the affected order is a part. Total power, which revolution craves to seize and change, belongs to neither politicians nor the rich, nor to any classes—for they all must conform to realities. "Realities" are nothing but symbolic products, effects of the symbolic order, of its infinite mesh of symbolic games generating its own referents within itself.

What could the idea of an ultimate revolution possibly be? To replace the symbolic order by another, juster one. This is tantamount to replacing realities by other, juster ones.

Of course, empirical revolutions destroy and replace certain old symbolic subsystems—they rename streets and months, change the spelling, rewrite history, or introduce a new chronology. As all things empirical, however, this is far from the eidos of total revolution which will replace everything—from the structure of social groups to the structure of dreams, from comprehensible everyday vocabulary to the cultural and physiological mechanisms of erection—by something else which is juster. Something juster will also replace the very notion of justice, for this notion also belongs to the old symbolic order, along with that of change. And with the notion of a notion.

The ultimate revolution will not materialize when everything written by poets and philosophers comes true, but when something more—all they have not written—comes true, too (for writings and inventions are also captives of the old, unjust social order). The ultimate revolution dissolves into its own infinity (which is paradoxical?, vicious?—we cannot know since the laws of logic have been replaced by other, juster ones).

The only thing that cannot be conceived of as changed is the instrument which will effect "the change." Terror.

In this sense the "velvet revolutions" that swept across Eastern Europe are revolutions without a specific quality. Their lack of a reign of terror is a problem. It can be formulated in two ways: 1. Why was there no reign of terror? Now this is a theoretical problem. 2. When will there be a reign of terror? This is a practical problem.

Because of his innate, irrational optimism, this writer opts for the theoretical problem.

2. Symbol and Blood

It is an ancient truth written in blood that major values, standards, and norms are imposed by force. Violence, however, should not be regarded as limited and localized in those high levels of symbolic order only. It is not to be found within "the values" only—violence is all-pervasive.

From Plato's *Cratylus* to Ferdinand de Saussure's and Benvenist's courses in general linguistics, all projects on semiotics have focused on one problem: is the relation between signifier and signified arbitrary? The answer depends on the type of mediating "third term," which is in-between the signifier and the signified. It could be a "natural rightness" of the relationship—or again, it could be a "pure convention." The signifier could be related to the signified by the very nature of the latter, by the reality of the signified. The polar view holds that they are bound by the conventional reality of social habits.

A view which invalidates the "natural"-vs.-"conventional" opposition eliminates this pointless alternative. Realities are symbolic conventions which are forgotten to have been conventions. Far more force has been used and far more blood shed to strike THEM out from memory, than for "the values" and "models." Conventions are the result of ultimate violence—a violence which does not concentrate on a visible bursting point, but drains through an infinite network of invisible channels: violence so stark that it suppresses its own terror by turning it into a habit, into naturalness, naturality, reality.

Realities are conventions which are forgotten to have been conventions; conventions are violence forgotten to have been violent.

Suppressed (from "suppression" or *Verdrängung*) violence is what welds the signifier and the signified together. To be born, "the world" was terrorized.

3. Tattooing and Articulation

The human body seems to be a reality. It seems to be the ultimate reality which will survive even when all others have crumbled. Everyone from Protagoras to modern philosophical anthropologists have seen this reality as a measure, a scale of all other realities. The reality of the human body seems to be the foundation that makes possible all other symbolic-system-realities (even the Lord bows before it during the Last Judgement—and obeys the need to raise the dead in flesh and bone in order to administer divine justice).

Yet as a transcendent signified, the human body cannot survive the infinite symbolic dynamics, the game of signifiers. The symbolic order(s) scars the body with social labels of sex, status, age, ethnicity. These, however—clothes, colors, accessories—are just the body's outermost semiotic crust.

On a more inward plane, the symbolic order of a certain culture is tattooed on the body irreversibly: it pricks a pattern into the skin, cuts the breasts into shape, moulds Chinese feet, stretches the native's lip to the ground, or circumcises the Muslim.

On an even deeper level, the symbolic order may interfere with the so-called physiology of the body itself—it could make the body vomit in disgust, infect or heal it, change its sex, delimit it from (or merge it with) other bodies. This is a kind of deeper tattoo: a deep engraving which determines the form of the body's very "reality." The ultimate in this tattoo is articulation: the body is articulated in parts, zones, members.

Lacan claims that the subconscious is structured like language, or more precisely, like a multitude of superseding vertical levels of signifiers: the prototypal text of the subconscious is the unattainable point at which the symbolic order has clashed with nonarticulated biologism over what ought to be called the proto-body. This is where it was tattooed, engraved in this proto-body, sinking ever deeper, shaping its amorphousness, articulating within it differentiated parts, coherent forms, erogenous zones for the first time... Only thanks to articulation did amorphousness evolve into a body, into a reality identical to itself.

The constitution of the body's reality is an act of violence doomed to oblivion. At the same time, it is a mystery (since all violence is, among other things, a mystery phenomenon). In ancient rituals, the human sacrifice objectified this mystery violence: one could see the axe of symbolic order drop and dismember the body. Mysteries are not just violence. They are also a revelation: one can see the dismembered becoming articulate, categorical, definite.

In his short story "The Penal Colony," Franz Kafka invented a machine for ultimate revolutions. This machine radically engraves the new symbolic order straight onto the body of the condemned, which for an instant flutters on the verge between life and death, in the domain of revelation. At first the uninitiated take the engraved body for a terrorized body—but terror in the colony follows rigid rules and conventions. From the colony's perspective, the body is conventionalized so as to be transformed into a new, changed body—into a new reality. The new body's passage unto death is more than a matter of pure biology. A reversal is still possible until this moment: the body can revert to its old reality, the new reality proving to be pure convention, pure arbitrariness, pure violence. Death rules out the possibility of a reversal as the new reality evolves into something which seems to escape the symbolic order and pass into a beyond of sorts: it becomes super-reality. The referent becomes a Transcendent Referent. Nothing can provide a more efficient foundation for the new symbolic order than the guarantee of death—death provides the fixed point which transcends all structures and avoids the endless game of signifiers. At the same time this game, which *per se* would build a network of equally arbitrary terrorist conventions, gets a chance to produce reliable, resistant realities guaranteed by superreality: death.

A revolution which does not terrorize, tattoo, engrave and/or articulate the body, which does not bring it to the verge of death, is an unstable revolution. The enforcement of its symbolic order is reversible. It lacks a foundation. That is why this revolution could always crumble back into laughter: uncemented by terror, its symbolic constructs could always rebound; they could always be denounced as being entirely arbitrary, brazen. It is constantly threatened by its own (latent) comic metamorphosis: to become an unfounded claim.

Lyotard recounts how the King of Ou ordered his general, Sun Tze, to make fine soldiers out of 180 of the his favorite wives. The general started drilling them to turn "right!," "left!," and "about face!" to the drumbeat. The women giggled, chatted, and refused to obey. The general drew his sword and chopped off the heads of two of the king's best-loved wives. He got perfect discipline. The new symbolic order promptly triumphed: the women started behaving as soldiers. The lapse into laughter was no longer possible. Death stabilized the new realities.

4. Nonspecific Revolutions

The velvet revolutions have been velvet until now. They have not exploded into a mass reign of terror so far (at the time of this writing, 20 August 1991). Perhaps there will be no reign of terror, and this will set a precedent in history.

The velvet revolutions did not make a terrorist attempt to engrave a new symbolic order onto the biological body of the individual or group social bodies. They presupposed that, in fact, nothing new needed to be imposed—it was enough to simply clear the way for the old order, a "natural" order, which had always existed and had merely been subjected to terrorist repression under totalitarianism. Therefore, many people declared the velvet revolutions to be restorations or counter-revolutions rather than revolutions. However, something was wrong, and this was obvious in the paradoxical names tagged on to them: "velvet revolution," "counter-revolution of normality." Something "natural" and "normal" needed to be restored—but the restoration itself had to be effected through a paradoxical gesture which went beyond a simple establishment of normalcy. It was not necessary to resort to terror since the "normal" and "natural" symbolic order was conceived of as the hitherto suppressed reality itself, which now had a right to free expression. However, this reality had been suppressed too hard too long—it could no longer merely set in, it had to triumph. This was possible in only one way—which was radically different from terror—as a festival.

In festivals, reality is manifested as joy. The problem velvet revolutions seemed to face was not the forcible installation of a new symbolic order, but an ecstatic expression of the old one. Imbued with humanistic and liberal values, the "natural" bodies emerged in the menacing public space of totalitarianism and started eliminating its external limitations. They broke all public rules, reshuffled present perspectives of totalitarian architectural space, pronounced tabooed words and sang tabooed songs, used an inconceivable language, proceeded from "eternal" symbols. The conflict seemed to be between "inward" naturalness and "outward" violence; reality vs. fear. The festival got in full swing when, identified in its arbitrariness, terror (seen as a purely external limitation, a threat external to the free "natural" will) seemed to have vanished—the totalitarian world collapsed as a house of cards: a world without a foundation.

In fact, this was just underrating totalitarianism and totalitarian terror.

In the wake of the radical festival, the bodies, which had gotten an opportunity for expression, were expected to remain in the everyday world and face their "normalcy" and "naturalness." This did not happen. After the symbolic order of totalitarianism was denounced, the signifiers—declared "old" and "normal"—of democracy, freedom, and perennial values refused to meld with the available signified: mutants, mute chthonic creatures for which there were no symbols, crawled out of the crack between the symbolic orders. The "normal" became a post-totalitarian utopia—the average "das Man" was crowned with a transcendent nimbus in the West.

5. The Post-totalitarian Mutant

The mutant metaphor is important here. A mutant is any articulation with an error, an aberration in the programming code. Of course, "error" and "aberration" are other, already obsolete metaphors. They are figures of the suppression of a "rightness" whose model has been imposed by violence. That is why we will take a different approach to mutation: a mutant is an articulation which results from the interbreeding of two (or more) codes; a mutant is any articulation in which the symbolic order is engraved incompletely, any misprint: its "incompletion" and "misprinting" are the result of another code in action.

In a mutant, the violence of symbolism could never settle completely—in oblivion. The two intersecting symbolic orders mutually demonstrate their arbitrariness. Mutant articulations cannot petrify in "naturalness"; they are the eternal burning memory of the fact that every reality is semiotically (i.e., violently) articulated.

Totalitarianism did its best to articulate correct, non-deformed totalitarian bodies. Both the theory and practice of terror were radicalized precisely under totalitarianism: dozens of millions were liquidated and as many were concentrated: the collective bodies were subjected to new discipline in camps, the construction of motorways, sun cities, inter-sea canals, and tenements (Vladislav Todorov). All former spaces, institutions whose mazes and channels used to traditionally discipline the bodies, were transformed.

Still, communist totalitarianism suffered from a rashness and incompleteness. It was rash because it wanted to achieve in dozens of years what other civilizations had done in centuries; it wanted to carry out too quickly the terror-convention-reality transition. In earlier civilizations, the violent engraving of symbolic order spanned dozens of generations, it ramified and scattered into myriad small centers of violence (family, informal communities, professional groups, school, hospital, army . . .). Communist totalitarianism set out to radically centralize all violence—and to do it fast on an industrial scale. This, however, triggered local resistance—micro-institutions of the former symbolic reality conspired against the new symbolic order and cocooned a series of old symbolic chains: the radical centralization project proved to be a utopia.

The other flaw of communist totalitarianism was that it failed to achieve the radical expansion which would have left it without competition as regards the criteria of "reality." It coexisted with another reality-producing system of a relatively traditional type (Western society, "realized" through the symbolic order of the Modern Age). Thus conspiratorial foci, which produced alternative reality within the totalitarian society, acquired an external verification of their symbolic production: alternative reality existed out there somewhere as "normal" reality.

This prevented totalitarian terror from becoming total terror: it remained a "reality" in *statu nascendi,* heterogeneous and at war with former traditional forms of "reality."

The body of totalitarian man was in a constant process of double, militant engraving: it was articulated as a mutant of the incomplete and ongoing war between two incompatible symbolic orders. Totalitarian man proper thus remained incomplete. His body wavered between two conflicting engravings—it was a traumatic body as an experience of an unachieved terrorist-conventional identity. However, it was also a mutant body due to the impossibility of such an achievement—because of the interference of incompatible symbolic models.

6. Velvet Revolutions as a Festival; Festivals as Tics of the Schizoid Body

Minimal revolutions could not have resorted to terror because of the utopia of normalcy—this would have run counter to the immanent meaning of the utopia. As mentioned above, they acquired their purely symbolic expression in the festival—the wild revelry and abandonment of liberated "natural" bodies expressing the "perennial" articulations of democracy, freedom, humane justice, etc.

Festivals radically changed these bodies' habitat—but could not interfere in their tattoos and engravings as radically. Bodies remained mutants with a traumatic self-awareness of being "abnormal" (which, in fact, was only a memory of the terror).

Presumably, festivals could not solve this problem. They are conservative in their very function—their task is to disperse maturing destructive energies in an established symbolic reality so as to reproduce this same reality, stabilizing its referents. The festival is a ritual act for the purge-innovation-reproduction of the everyday world—the ruling symbolic order. Revolutions are catastrophically providential, whereas festivals are cyclic; revolutions change the ruling order, while festivals reproduce and consolidate it. Revolutions are followed by a totally new everyday life, and festivals—by an old, traditional everyday life.

The revolution-presented-as-restoration called to life street festivals—they were only to purge and establish "the order of normalcy." These festivals were to have expressed "living in truth" and restored the cycle of a normal everyday life. This meant that the body had to carry out procedures and acts intended to purge and peel former symbolic cumuli—cumuli of the totalitarian "unnatural" symbolic order. Unlike terror, however, festivals did not rearticulate the body once and for all (bringing it near death), but merely masked, disguised it. Terror engraves the body; festivals paint on the body—they paint on it, hyperbolically doubling this body's own members. Terror engraves and articulates a new body. Festivals only explicate and celebrate the old body's traditional symbolic elements.

Totalitarian engravings had to be cast aside, shed through festive cries, grimaces, and dances. This, of course, was impossible. The festivals of velvet revolutions painted on bodies their own normalcy—but under the surface, their distorted, nonfocused, mutant members struggled to break out. In the upended public and architectural space, the bodies danced, grimaced, and twisted in an effort to shed their tattoos and tear their own monstrous members engraved by totalitarian terror.

This was impossible. More and more festivals were held. The street gestures and grimaces of mutant bodies struggling to break free and purge themselves, froze in tics.

Tics are the festivals of mutants turned into a fixation. Tic-festivals were to have made up for the lack of a reign of terror—that is why conventionally enacted mystery forms of terror could be made out in the motions of the feting bodies. There was a universal yearning for some kind of grand Orgasm-Catharsis-Repentance, some beyond-Terror, which would have made a new life possible.

7. The Unbearable Everyday World

Traditional festivals impose and establish a cosmic order—an everyday world. Festivals present forgotten (conventionalized and suppressed) terror as harmony and meaning which permeate the everyday world.

The post-totalitarian everyday world could not produce the order and meaning yearned for by the festivals of velvet revolutions. It was a somber space of hunger and futurelessness. In the everyday world, mutation affected not only bodies, but also all foci of the socium: there was no bread in the bakeries which sold shirts, tons of meat were dumped during the worst famine, writers and cops turned businessmen, decaying animals floated in the Black Sea and fish died, streets were littered all over, leaders of the opposition proved to be liars, mutant communists increased their mutant electorate.

In this sense, the post-totalitarian everyday world was a reign of terror—but a peculiar kind of terror. It was in the bodies themselves: social space terrorized itself through an immanent terror. A traditional reign of terror imposes an order-and-meaning. Post-totalitarian terror ensued from the painful experience of the absence of order and meaning: a chaotic machine which inscribes a set of meaningless letters and pseudo-signs on bodies—it tattoos them with scribbles, with disgusting drawings, and articulates them in line with the forms of chaos. Unlike all other kinds of violence, which transcended into a conventional order and meaning (and were therefore bearable), this terror was unbearable. It did not lead to the realm of revelation.

There is only one salvation from unbearable terror: flight. Some people took flight to the space west, which blinded them with its radiant "Normalcy" (a geographical utopia).

Others sought refuge in religion—the meaninglessness of the post-totalitarian everyday world was declared to be an excruciating Trial on the way to the future Revelation.

Still others took to flight in a recurrent Tic-festival which enabled them to scream "Down with communism" until breathless, and went on and on as a permanent street promise of the Great Catharsis.

All fugitives bore along their mutant bodies—which in fact generated the meaningless terror.

8. Instead of an End

This text stops at this point—at the point where history has stopped. It will not mutate into forecasts and optimistic versions. This makes it meaningless; an essay with neither a future nor a hope—a text which emanates the violence it describes.

August, 1991

An Essay on Theoretical Terror
Ivan Kristev

The 1694 *Dictionnaire of the Academie Francaise* already distinguishes the political meaning of the word "revolution": "a vicissitude, a major change in the destiny and in the things of the world." Furthermore, the *Dictionnaire* recommends six appropriate adjectives qualifying the revolution: "great, timely, surprising, strange, wonderful, amazing."

In "An Essay on Terror," Alexander Kiossev is also faced with the need to define the revolution and to specify it through adjectives. In a mystic way, he likewise ends up with six adjectives: "ultimate, empirical, total, velvet, unstable, minimal."

The discrepancy is full and symptomatic. The fate of the word "revolution" has undergone a great change. What characterizes the concept vested in the Academie Francaise *Dictionnaire* is that "it (the revolution) is a category of historical awareness, an event which could be identified only *ex post facto*." The intuition of the *Dictionnaire's* authors is that revolutions are not made—they happen. This intuition stems from a definite historical reality: The Glorious English Revolution. Until the mid-18th century, the word "Revolution" was capitalized only when referring to the events in England in 1688.

On hindsight, however, this first European revolution strikes one with its unspecificness. It was not brought to life by a radical utopia nor based on a project which was to be fulfilled. It seems as though the sole purpose of this revolution was for it to be forgotten. Nor is this accidental. The Glorious English Revolution problemizes the "apparent" connection between utopia and revolution. For unlike Alexander Kiossev, this writer could hardly assume that utopia can boil down to the "dream of a future fairer order, which presupposes that the current order will be destroyed." Utopia or, to be precise, the utopia of the Modern Age is an alternative world not in the sense of an idyllic picture but as a rational construct, a project which is fulfillable under certain circumstances. That is why utopia is first and foremost a text or a family of texts: a text which precedes revolution and should be substantiated.

"The Glorious Revolution" of 1688 lacked such a text. It was, rather, mottoed by the restoration of an erstwhile political order as a new interpretation of an already substantiated text: the Holy Bible. The English Revolution was conceived at that time as a rejection of political anarchy and rampant instability—events which were known at that time as "revolutions." It was a Revolution-Restoration, a restoration of fundamental political laws; a Revolution bracketed off by modernity. Much later, in 1790, Edmund Burke was to admit that what attracted him in the "Glorious Revolution" was its nonrevolutionariness. This admission was made possible by the storming of the Bastille on 14 July 1789.

The Invisible Geography

In Kiossev's concept—a concept wholly in the spirit of the modern age—the revolution presupposes a radical utopia, the making of a world, the creation of a new political Adam. Kiossev's intuition with regard to revolutions is based entirely on the experience of the French Revolution, which became a model in the mid-19th century and was "repeated" as such in 1917. Imposing the French Revolution as a model was closely related to the intellectual dominance of radical ideologies (and Marxism in particular), which elaborated the doctrine of typical (the French) and untypical (the English) revolutions. The utopia-revolution-Terror relation also emerges within the thus imposed "typicality"; in Kiossev's view, this relation acquires the dimension of universality. This makes it possible to construe "the ultimate revolution"—a revolution which is not confined to political change but "replaces realities by other, juster ones." The ultimate revolution may be triggered only by an ultimate utopia. It cannot have conscious agents; it is a text which cannot be interpreted because all interpretations are locked within existing realities. The ultimate revolution changes EVERYTHING: "the only thing that cannot be conceived of as changed," writes Kiossev, "is the instrument which will effect 'the change.' Terror." Terror is the *differencia specifica* of all revolutions. In talking of revolutions, we talk of Terror. That is why the study is entitled "An Essay on Terror." An essay provoked by the complex reality of "gentle revolutions," of their "abnormality," "misconstrued modernity." An essay provoked by the fact that the theoretical reflections on these revolutions resign themselves to the absence of a Reign of Terror, to the disruption of the link between Terror and revolution. Kiossev regards his own text as radical (a text "beyond good and evil") precisely because he refuses to accept the apparent naturalness of this absence.

The ultimate revolution, the universal Terror-convention-reality transition, the Terror-festival opposition: radicalized, Kiossev needs all those fundamental "prostheses" (to quote Vladislav Todorov) so as to regard the Eastern European change as a revolution, as the making of a world.

Yet isn't "An Essay on Terror" an attempt at Terror? How should one interpret the stance of Kiossev, perched on the Danton-Derrida line and engulfed by the hysterical chaos or chaotic hysteria of a political situation which counters any attempt at being rationalized? A public inquiry into Alexander Kiossev's eroticized metaphors presupposes applying historicism (this is the only way they can be made comprehensible and responsible). In this case, historicism is an instrument for deradicalization, for decoding the aforementioned text in its preconception, in its ultimate gesticulation.

The primary metaphor is the Reign of Terror. It is branded with a metaphysical metaphoricalness. The Reign of Terror is taken out of all context whatsoever and stripped of its traditional content. It stands for terror, fear, a premonition of terror, and something else, plus other things. It creates the world (visions the world); forgetting Terror makes it possible for the world to exist. Terror is forgotten in its excess. Applying historicism presupposes treating the Reign of Terror not as spontaneous violence but as an instrument for the creation of a "juster world" which is, at the same time, like this selfsame world. If in Kiossev's radical concept Terror and violence are synonymous, this writer's stance is radically different. The very idea of regarding them as two words with the same meaning seems to me ultimately suspicious, terrorist.

The French Connection

The Reign of Terror is no spontaneous violence. It must be organized and motivated. In his brilliant study "Revolutionary Terror," French philosopher Claude Leforte upholds the thesis that the debates on Terror which flared up in the Convent in Year II were part of the Terror itself. The Reign of Terror is unthinkable without a constant self-quotation of motives or an incessant emphasis on its mystic association with Liberty and Equality. Terror talks—it talks about itself—and this makes it different from the mute violence against tyrants. Terror is theatricalized and performed before an audience in the squares of the Republic. It is not accidental that the main points motivating every Reign of Terror are: first, the idea of the latter's inevitability and second, the creation of a polar space where revolutionary Terror is opposed to counter-revolutionary Terror, red to white Terror. "What constitutes the Republic," says Saint-Just, "is the total annihilation of everything that opposes it." Terror visualizes the relation of death to Liberty and Equality. The world of the dead is symmetrical to the utopian world which is to be imposed. Rousseau's prerevolutionary view that man is born free was enhanced by the idea, born in the years of revolutionary practice, that people are equal in death.

Precisely this disposition was the mechanism which set in motion the first utopian machine of the Modern Age: the guillotine. As Dr. Guillotin himself noted in the project he submitted to the Constitutional Assembly, "the means of punishment ought to be identical for all sentenced by the law to death regardless of the crime they are charged with. Criminals should be beheaded. The beheading should be achieved by a simple mechanism." Unlike the executioner's axe, the guillotine does not deprive of life but restores Liberty and Equality in the form of death. The guillotine symbolizes a type of violence which is radically different from that known in the premodern age; it symbolizes Terror—the Terror which replaces the life-death opposition by the ideological oppositions of freedom-nonfreedom, equality-inequality. Death is instrumentalized. It is not a border we are faced with nor is it truly important. From an instrument, Terror itself has turned into a world. Terror is not synonymous with violence—it is synonymous with a new world.

The Body

Kiossev's essay asks how is Terror possible. It associates the possibility of tattooing new symbolic orders with the ideology that "the reality of the human body seems to be the foundation which makes possible all other realities." The revolution does not destroy this "appearance." In the domain of Terror, "we have no bodies, we are bodies" (Reich). The annihilation of corporeality, pain, death are so irrefutably real that they transfer the quality of "irrefutable reality" onto the power that breeds them. The deprivation of Terror is a deprivation of reality. This is one of the existential insights of the case in point. What upsets the writer is that the "velvet revolutions" produce societies suffering from a chronic shortage of reality. The "gentle revolutions" themselves are unreal, unspecifically gentle.

Alexander Kiossev's basic intuition is that Terror alone makes us real, enabling us to experience the reality of the world. This intuition is reproduced in our political situation in a spontaneous and very strange manner. The body is present in the "velvet revolutions" in a peculiar way. It builds "live chains" and merges in marches to push itself to the limit in the act of a hunger strike. The hunger strike expresses the impossibility of forgetting a Terror that was. Revolutionaries do not terrorize but relive the terrorization of their own bodies over and over again. The body of the Other, of the enemy, proves incorporated into our own body. The hunger strike expresses the impossibility of forgetting the old Terror, as well as the impossibility of having a new one.

The Impossible Terror

Alexander Kiossev's "An Essay on Terror" raises two fateful questions, a theoretical: "why was there no reign of terror?" and a practical one: "when will there be a reign of terror?"

In regard to the latter, the practical question, the writer confines himself to a humanistic ἐποχή (refraining from judgment). The entire essay is meant to motivate the legitimacy of these two questions. Questions which legitimize the study of "velvet revolutions" in their "defectiveness," their deviation from the model. Strange as it might be, Kiossev falls prey to the idea of a "normal revolution," of the universalization of specific features of modernity. The question which Kiossev will not ask is: "is Terror possible in a post-utopian situation?" As he himself notes, the Eastern European revolutions are deprived of a radical utopia.

They lack a text which is to be substantiated. The end of communism marks the exhaustion of modernity, of its projectionism. The ideological basis of the Eastern European revolutions were not utopias but anti-utopias. Modernity has thus proved to be in a hall of mirrors—it cannot simultaneously escape from the hall and from its own image. It is the lack of radical utopias, the rejection of utopias that makes the Reign of Terror impossible. Violence, monstrous violence is possible, but it will not be legitimized as ensuing from Liberty and Truth. The prerequisite for this legitimacy is destroyed—the conviction that a "juster world" can be imposed; furthermore, that a "juster world" can be invented. The "utopia of normalcy," and Kiossev perceives this, is de facto a rejection of utopia—it does not vision the world but displays it. It displays the world not in its naturalness but in its conventionality. The future lies several hundred miles away, the aspiration for liberty is replaced by the demand for democracy, no one cares about the materialization of the human essence. Churchill loved saying that democracy is not the perfect but the best of familiar forms of government. Something in the world has changed radically.

A Short Anti-Kiossev Manifesto

The Reign of Terror did not nor will it take place. It is over. The violence which might erupt is stripped of its ideological motives and doomed to muteness. The "brave new world" in which we have ended up is also doomed to muteness or nonarticulation. This muteness spawns a desire for radical gestures, radical theoretical gestures. The theoretical intuition of modernity tries to terrorize the world which does not fit into its patterns. In this sense, one can say that Kiossev's essay "stinks of guts": the guts of the gutted classical viewpoint.

Kiossev's text resembles Spielberg's world: a world enamoured of its own mutation. Kiossev's stance also laments the radically new stance of the intellectual, the fact that it is no longer possible for men of letters to build worlds and create pedagogical dictatorships. A lament which cannot hear itself.

The End[1]

Note

1. The present text has doubtless been influenced by Vladislav Todorov—not by his radical mode of thinking and metaphor but by his Departure.

Epilogue:
Health Takes the Power
Alexander Kiossev

This book happens to end with Ivan Kristev's essay—a fact which, of course, is accidental and yet could hardly be more symptomatic. For it quite unequivocally demonstrates that the texts included in the book do not end on their own but have been **forced** to end.

They were, one could say, suppressed: placed beyond the Symbolic Law of the post-totalitarian world. The suppression did not, of course, take the form of a direct administrative sanction—it did not deprive individual persons of their public voice, did not overtly taboo one or another topic which these texts dealt with (and, therefore, had nothing to do with totalitarian censorship). In fact, after the change of 1989 in Bulgaria, as in the other Eastern European countries, such overt suppressions, sanctions, and acts of censorship did not seem to be possible at all: for a short period of time the Bulgarian public domain seemed to enjoy the greatest degree of freedom, if not of frivolity, in the world.

Still, a kind of suppression existed: in the Bulgarian public domain a consensus was being established that such mode of writing was "out of date." The rationalized hostility against it took various forms (the accusations ranged from the claim that it was unforgivably irresponsible to the charge that it was terrorist, from the reproach that it was incoherent and intellectually undisciplined, to the attack that it was perverse and sacrilegious); its effect, however, was all of a pattern: it manifested itself in a kind of idiosyncratic hostility to that type of discourse—to its mechanisms of meaning-generation and its significant practices.

At least one of the reasons for this "suppression" seemed comparatively clear. It consisted in the effort to quickly and efficiently forget one's own past. This mode of writing, by virtue of being bound up with a particular human group (with the hermetic nature of the intertextual games of the "intellectual oasis" referred to in the introduction), was pregnant with far too many shameful memories. The most important of those was not at all the fact that, in the long run, the group never got beyond the state of half-resistance and never overtly challenged the totalitarian institutions, thus making it impossible for any one of its members to morally capitalize on it in the post-totalitarian situation. It seems to me that for each one of the members the shame actually bore a purely personal aspect—the identities that the group allowed room for were amorphous, uncompleted, compensatory identities. Given the lack of creditable models of social behaviour to be followed, every one was doomed to an ex-centric existence: the young intellectuals in this group existed in too great a measure **through one another**—they existed through mutually inspired ambitions, rivalries, friendships, dialogues, quarrels; they projected their personalities into and developed them by means of the intellectual-erotic togetherness which was supposed to make up not only for the lack of authoritative figures but also for the lack of a broad public, intellectual, and political horizon. In the post-totalitarian period the craving for such well-defined, solid models of authority became particularly acute: after so many years of a dependent, inarticulate life, a huge number of people came to need the belief that such well-defined, "mature" identities really existed. Thus, the members of the group became even more acutely aware of the compensatory and amorphous character of their former undefined positions. Their awareness seemed to reach a kind of breaking point when, in the eyes of many, those positions began to appear as solely defined by their amorphousness and unautonomousness, when they began to be seen as anchored in the safe haven of a well-protected, promiscuous, and game-playing minority, that is, to be seen as some intellectual and political puberty from the past when the human identity and the human choice are still shamefully incompleted. A puberty which was once and for all outgrown. The narrative about how everybody had moved from an unautonomous "then" to a self-autonomous "now" came to wield tremendous power—all of a sudden in post-totalitarian Bulgaria everybody felt grown-up. The ironically transgressive discourse of the former intellectual group, playing not only with the context of the group but also with the global symbolic mechanisms of totalitarianism, suddenly lost its chances of survival: for the Bulgarian public domain as well as for many of the exponents of this discourse it came to represent only the shameful and infantile aspects of their own past. It was, therefore, to be forgotten as soon as possible.

In a sense, despite all its attempts at *Vergangenheitsbewältigung* (public debates about the guilt, mutual accusations of dishonour, revelations about the victims of totalitarianism, and the coercive pressures upon intellectual life in communist times, acts of repentance and pseudo-repentance), the post-totalitarian world represented—and still represents—a typical example of *Vergangenheitsverdrängung*. The case in point proved to be no exception. Stripping down the simulative and play-acting intellectual discourse to bare shameful puberty was a typical attempt to repress the past. The hostile idiosyncrasy towards this puberty aspect blocked the hermeneutic access to other dimensions of the discourse: its intellectual and political potential was declared nonexistent, its complex rhetoric began to irritate, its dialogue with certain Western postmodern and poststructuralist thought-strategies was seen as an empty fashion. Public consensus prevented its being carried across into the "new" post-totalitarian age as specific intellectual experience. Its reduction to figures of shame and amorphous identity constituted, in fact, an attempt to lose the key to its understanding—the reduction was part of the wholesale process of the oversimplified rewriting of the totalitarian past.

It was also part of something else, however—what engendered it was yet another important context without which the above mentioned "suppression" would have been hard to imagine or comprehend: the context of the general discursive situation of post-totalitarianism. In other words, the attempt to confine the respective discourse to only one of its aspects was part and parcel of the struggle of dominant rival discourses; it was indicative of the disposition of the rhetorical forces and interpretative strategies defining the post-totalitarian *Öffentlichkeit*.

This discursive situation characteristic of Eastern Europe after the fall of its totalitarian rules can, of course, be described in much greater detail, yet it is beyond the scope of this brief epilogue to do so. I will, therefore, allow myself to define it from a rather general and one-sided perspective—it was simply a **blockage of all critical discourses.** The situation which actually arose in the East has been termed by me in my *Essay on Terror* "the utopia of normalcy." In this process, the repression of the totalitarian past was, in fact, mirrored upside down by an opposite process—the repressed was now being replaced by new, "grown-up," one-dimensional identification models invading with imperialist aggressiveness the vacant space—now cleansed of shame—in their self-appointed guises of final Freedom, Democracy, Free Market, Truth, Faith, Maturity, and National Sentiment. This urge to restore traditional social models of Modernity (which in post-totalitarian Eastern Europe were perceived as the only "natural," "organic" patterns of social behavior) made virtually impossible any criticism of the fundamental conditions of post-totalitarian society despite the unceasing discussions and debates, the public scandals, and the mutual attacks on political and cultural party-programmes. The traditional social models (predominantly of a right-conservative type) came to life again carrying a transcendental aura round their empirical substance: in the East one could, for instance, quite seriously claim that private ownership was **sacred**, that communism was **demonic**, that in the moral human being, public and private behaviour fully coincided, that it was bad if "homosexuals," "Turks," "gypsies," and other "deviants" ruled the country. In the post-totalitarian world new taboos revived—in Poland it became difficult to utter public critiques of Catholicism, in Bulgaria the same applied to free-market economy, Eastern Orthodox religion or patriotic sentiments. This was determined by the specific normative horizon of the post-totalitarian public domain: on the one hand, it was characterized by the taken-for-granted Western models in which the West functioned as utopia for the East (the so called *zapadniki,* the programmes seeking "a way to Europe," "a place among the civilized nations of the world," etc.); on the other hand, it was marked by an equally strong reaction against such models, the *ressentiment of potchveniki,* seeking the West as anti-utopia and identity-loss, the homegrown doctrines of "native originality," of metaphysical superiority of the East over the West, etc. The overall effect, however, was that the critical potential of Eastern Europe diminished in a socially dangerous measure. All this found concentrated expression in the specific post-totalitarian "economy of truth" (in the Foucauldian meaning of the term—an ensemble of institutionalized mechanisms for the production, legitimation, distribution, circulation, and impact of "truth-telling" discourses.)

Here I will confine these institutionalized mechanisms—despite their multiple variants—to two basic rival discourses. The two dominant truth-telling Modes of Rhetoric—two matrices for the production and distribution of "truths" which blocked the access to intellectually informed critique—were exemplified by and embodied in two public figures representing the two Authors of Truth which post-totalitarian society recognized as the only legitimate ones. These were the Intellectual-Parrhesiast and the Expert.

The antique term *parrhesia* (studied by Michel Foucault), denoting "free utterance," "freedom of speech," "the risk of openly speaking the truth in the tyrant's face," can give us an idea of the first type of the "political economy of truth." This type can be regarded as hypertrophied dissident discourse, which in totalitarian times—heroically, putting at stake its own body and social position—categorically denounced "the world of the lie": that is, the self-reproducing totalitarian ideology. In post-totalitarian time this discourse paradoxically came to occupy a position of power, undergoing quite unexpected transformations. Irrespective of its actual substance, the parrhesiastic utterance (the scandalizingly transgressive, outright, and uncompromising pronouncement of the "truth" in everybody's face) began to be seen as produced by a taken-for-granted moral position: it carried a preconceptional form of truth and could not be refuted by facts. Its traditional form—the form of a simple and direct negation of a *whole* order of symbolic representation—prevented this utterance from entering into dialogue with **any** localized, **detailed**, specialized truths; it inevitably proved hostile to all other "expert truths" (which were morally neutral as such and did not preclude being integrated into a potential "world of the lie"). Thus, in Bulgaria the parrhesiastic mode of rhetoric at a certain moment generated a series of militant arguments crusading against sociology, demoscopy, and the political studies. The image of the individual sacrificing himself in the name of Truth (there were "cities of truth" in which those sacrificing themselves tried to start a new life; there were also hunger strikes against the lie) was radically opposed to that of the individual who did not live "globally" but was content to perform a certain professional role. The expert, the administrator, the politician, the man of science or business were paranoidly suspected of belonging to the communist Mafia and conniving at the grandiose secret Conspiracy of the Lie meant to prevent the regeneration of Eastern Europe. This was another of the unexpected transformations of the dissident parrhesiastic mode—in order to be able to reproduce its globally negative form it, at the same time, had to proclaim again and again that the world of the lie had not yet come to an end; it had to evoke transcendental-paranoid representations of the communist Enemy and to produce unending images of its metaphysical battle with this enemy (a Bulgarian writer was quite in earnest when he declared that the failed coup in Moscow of August 1991 had been "an astral battle between the Armies of Good and Evil"). Post-totalitarian parrhesia turned into a cult of the literal, plain word which shook society to its very foundations. It consequently demanded from the parrhesiasts a constant perpetuation of the tumultuously scandalizing attack upon those foundations and endowed the word with a specifically nonempirical and sacred aura.

Thus, most paradoxically, the parrhesiastic mode of rhetoric produced two diametrically opposed results: on the one hand, it subjected the post-totalitarian public sphere to tumultuous scandal, making brutality and the dismissal of every convention the be-all and end-all of the discursive space; on the other hand, it revealed its unsuspected kinship with resurgent fundamentalist and religious movements which also felt the need to publicly proclaim unquestionable, sacred, shattering, and global metaphysical truths.

The figure of the Expert—agent of specialized languages, disciplined techniques, and professionally acquired stratagems for solving problems—was the other important figure in the post-totalitarian space. This figure, typical of every modern society in which there exist autonomous institutionalized fields with a "rationality" of their own (sciences, law, religion, art, media, sport, etc.) took on quite a different aspect in post-totalitarian Eastern Europe. For, after the end of the "Great Historical Experiment" the Eastern European societies turned out to be in a unique nonexpert state for which no precedent was available and no "specialists" existed. As the professionally acquired stratagems for solving the various distressing problems were simply not available and as these problems arose not in the well-articulated disciplinary fields but in the chaotic society as a whole (i.e., they were not of a local and professional but of a constitutive and global nature), the above-mentioned societies were, in actual fact, characterized by "a crisis of the Expert Reason": the numerous groups of both Eastern and Western "specialists" unceasingly and noisily turned out projects for improving the situation which were then as noiselessly abandoned for having been proven totally inadequate. As, however, the expert discourses constituted one of the main attributes of the utopia of "a normal society" (in it, of course, there **had** to be specialists and specialized practices capable of dealing with every problem; there **had** to be experts producing the illusion that all was under control) this actual crisis had hardly any effect upon the public position of authority occupied by the expert discourse—it represented one of those solid identificational models of the New World Order which couldn't be subjected to questioning and critical reappraisal (only the parrhesiast's paranoid attack was to have validity against this discourse). In fact, the basic social function of this type of discourse was to offer models of social behaviour alternative to the parrhesiastic ones. In contrast to the "global" historical identity of the parrhesiast, craving to resolve the problems with one single gesture of soul and body, desiring to "begin to live in the truth," both individually and collectively, privately, and publicly, those models were to offer the alternative of a normalized averaged "identity," preserving such "normal" distinctions as professional function-existential position, ethics-politics, individual identity-social role, private-public, etc., and creating the illusion that these distinctions really existed in the mutated Bulgarian society. In other words, the "expert" represented merely one discursive possibility for producing utterances which **did not insist** that the public role of an individual should become identical with his self-sacrificing body; unlike parrhesia, they **did not insist** that the biographical dilemma of totalitarian man should sublimate into a scandalizing verbal act—they would rather repress it into a value-indifferent, detached social role. This was to be the **alienated** and **neutral** mirror-discourse opposing the parrhesiastic one: it consisted in stratagems of action, which were at least seemingly effective, in detailed and specialized rational practices which were at least seemingly verifiable. Prevented, however, from functioning effectively in the warped social space of post-totalitarianism, the expert discourse turned out in many cases to be mere Rhetoric, that is, a mirror-discourse, the marked member in the opposition of expert vs. parrhesiastic rhetoric. Consequently, the Expert—despite the potential of this social role (a real specialist solving particular problems in a localized professional field) turned out to be in much greater measure a political and public figure—a "politologist," a political "expert," an antagonist of the Intellectual-Parrhesiast. The paranoid, scandalizing version of Truth was contrasted with a self-confident and alienated technological version of it whose main function was to induce the sense of peace and social stability at all costs.

Bearing in mind the discursive situation described above, the ironic, game-playing, transgressive language of the former "intellectual oasis" was, in fact, left with no choice but to be suppressed. In its essence, the suppression was not direct (although there were instances of direct and vicious open attacks against this language)—rather, the suppression consisted in such retrospective interpretation of the merits and demerits of the language that it was bound—much in keeping with the supply and demand of new voices on the discursive market—to turn mute.

One of the objectives of the present book was to prevent the occurrence of this muteness. Refusing to conform to the newly established discursive *conjunctura*, it sought to preserve and protect from repression and oblivion the intellectual and political experience of this language. So, let us at this point—at the very end of the book—try to make explicit some of its dimensions which, in totalitarian times, were obliquely referred to, even its exponents not being entirely aware of them, let alone developing an ideology about them.

If the shameful memories were the first reason for "suppressing" the ironical, game-playing discourse of the "intellectual oasis," it was its rather specific "critical" potential which constituted the second reason for doing so. Clenched between the pressures of the "truth-telling discourses" of post-totalitarian time, silenced by shattering, global, paranoid-metaphysical truths on the one hand, and by mutated theoretic-expert languages on the other, it was given no chance to carry across its ability (an ability which failed to realize its own full potential anyway, which failed to fully shake off its infantilism and aesthetic narcissism) with active political irony to **transgress**, **promiscualize**, and **madden** orders of discourse which appeared grown-up and preconceptional, eternal and natural. We mean, in short—to use Vladislav Todorov's key metaphor—its ability to **inflame**.

In some of its aspects the mode of discourse called "inflammation" was an attempt at "writing as experience of limit" (in the sense that so many different scholars as George Battaille, Michel Foucault, Julia Kristeva attach to it). In this sense the phrase "critical potential" is not adequately chosen: the "inflammation" was not criticizing totalitarianism—it was trying to aggressively interfere with it, disruptively testing the limits of its Symbolic Order.

The inflammation-mode aimed at scandalizing the totalitarian public domain. But the scandal engendered by it was to also have political and philosophic dimensions. Along with its social and political task it was to be a philosophic act as well (or rather "action" as the intellectual group used to call it). In a not too complicated a manner the mode was to attempt practical solutions to some well-known philosophic and social problems: the first of those being contained in Wittgenstein's dictum that the function cannot be its own argument—that is, that a social system cannot evolve a final and objective self-reflexivity focused upon its structural framework, as such self-reflexivity will inevitably be **a part which seeks to encompass the whole.** In political terms, this was an attempt to overcome the above antinomy inherent in any social criticism of totalitarianism: such criticism not only invariably proved intrinsic to the totalitarian whole (i.e., it posited as a premise for its existence what it actually criticized) but also—in terms of its conceptual apparatus—already actualized the opposition of "ideological appearance vs. truth" and thus fell back into the "power of truth" and the "will to knowledge" of modern instrumental reason.

The "inflammation" attempted to solve these problems simply and by force: its aim was to demonstrate that in the totalitarian symbolic order there were central joints of symbolic representation that could be attacked (i.e., acts of intervention could be carried out against what has been termed by some the "Master signifier" of a symbolic order), and that it was possible for these joints to become "inflamed" so that their "non-naturalness," their morbidity could be revealed. The inflammation did not criticize—it simulatively replaced: it subverted the very constitutive metaphors of the Great Discourse of the Left, transformed by totalitarianism into a bureaucracy-police machine. It spawned their doubles in such a way that, instead of seeming the glorious projects conceived by reason, they turned out to be those awful monsters born from its sleep. Thus, in contrast to the situation in the West, the inflammation was a discourse of the anti-Left (without being, however, a discourse of the Right). After they had been inflamed, the key utopian metaphors and visions of the totalitarian world were not to be seen any longer as this world's natural foundations but rather as constitutive distortions in its very generative grammar.

To put it metaphorically: what had seemed the root of this world was now to be perceived—through an abrupt change of the *Gestalt*—as an inflamed wound, as a root-wound, which made the texture of this world (its Symbolic

Order) "radiate" with a nauseatingly non-natural, morbid light. In other words, this was to be the reverse of mystical revelation where one contemplates in a state of sublime ecstasy the very foundations of the world—as in Canto XXIX and XXX of his *Paradise,* Dante contemplates the Divine Center of the circle in which all time and space, all energy and force, all wisdom and love converge. A paraphrase of a famous Shakespearean line would more suitably describe this kind of operation: the inflammation made one feel that "the world is out of joint." It was thus to be perceived neither as "theoretical activity" nor as "theoretical criticism" in the exact sense of these words. Its gesture was far more excessive: it constituted a political transgression which—unlike the direct dissident challenge—was to be an "ontological" transgression too. What was being transgressed were not some specific coercive regulations and laws of totalitarian rule but the very constitutive principle of the totalitarian world—the inflammation sought to transform "the center," the sacrosanct "joint" of this world into a sacrilegious mutant. Rendered into the inflammation-mode the communist and avantgardist utopian visions revealed themselves as prostheses of the world's organics: Lenin's sacrosanct mummy which—according to Todorov—should be the focal point of the totalitarian symbolic order, is transformed by the inflammation into a monstrous stub; "terror" is perceived as the constitutive code of a profoundly "inauthentic" reality. The inflammation was to be an inverted act of the mystical *contemplatio* invoking not exultation but horror—causing a revulsion which, in its negative energy, was to be compared only to ecstasy.

To put it in more theoretical terms—this aggressive mode of discourse transgressively transformed the constitutive metaphors of a symbolic universe so that they lost their self-evidence and naturalness; it not only actually and violently inverted the "normal" value-oppositions and hierarchies of this world but also—through sacrilegious transfigurative acts—activated the whole "dark" potential of what Freud termed *Das Unheimliche.* The inflammation—

as it was introduced by Vladislav Todorov—was not a descriptive or argumentative mode (consequently, no theoretical counterarguments, no parrhesiastic or expert strategies, can deal with it) but an aggressive mode of discourse: it was an intervention, an attempt at a semantic scandal directed against the Master Signifier in order to set the dislocated joint of the totalitarian world: it was writing as experience of the utopian limit which was to have provocative and therapeutic functions. It strove to render the most glorious—the utopian vision—as disgusting cosmic voluntarism, sought to reveal the most horrible—terror—as the necessary solder of every "natural reality"; it represented an analysis in the mode of apocalyptic hypothesis. Its strategy was anti-Baudrillardian—not seduction but anti-seduction; an aggression against the cultural schematisms governing the economy of Desire; it was the strategy of invoking an almost hypnotic revulsion and horror by revealing the existent symbolic-institutional jointure of the world. This mode demanded from the reader that he should feel his own body as a totalitarian prosthesis; it called for a style which pricked the skin under the reader's ideological nails making it smart and sting; it did not exert actual terror upon the reader but forced him to become aware of the **already having happened**, the **already existent** terrorized totalitarian constitution of his social body.

The inflammation-mode, which I have described as anti-utopian, bore in itself, however (as does every anti-utopia), an empty utopian structure inherent in the belief that there existed such a thing as totality, that there **was** a "center" that could be inflamed. This structure embodied a longing which was the Other of the terror and claustrophobia instilled by totalitarianism. The political danger for this mode was that its global "discursive-ontological" ambitions cut it off from any open and "naive" political resistance. They risked to turn it into a self-contained stylistic curiosity unintelligible to the mass agent of political activity—a curiosity to be used in a purely "disinterested," aesthetic manner (in the Kantian sense of this term). The inflammation intertwined in a curious way with the other discursive strategy of the intellectual group referred to in the introduction to this book—the strategy of simulating, of producing subversive doubles, of anonymity and dissemination; the strategy which revealed itself in the impossibility of identification, in the play with quotations, authorships, and identities allowing no location of a "center" to be inflamed, no clear definition of "protagonists" and "antagonists," in short—no Minotaur to be slain by the hero. The implicit heroism of the inflammation mode was systematically parodied and deflatingly doubled by its own imitations—it transformed itself into laughter and play, into frivolity, into hermetic aestheticism, and even snobbery. Being subversively doubled, ironized, quoted out of context, this heroism underwent strange transformations: young people appropriated without asking Vladislav Todorov's authorship and used his inflammations for their own purposes. Todorov wanted to be a "virus" in the totalitarian discourse—yet the virus mutated into new races with different biological parameters: again and again the inflammation encountered Pierre Menard's paradoxes. The quoting simulations and games disrupted the "heroic centralism" of the inflammation-mode yet, at the same time, they made impossible that global politico-ontological action which constituted the structural utopianism of this mode.

In this context, it was perhaps exactly the "reversed indigo"—the image of the "inflamed quotation," of the scandalous and impossible duplication—which was the limit-point of all writing strategies available to the intellectual group: a limit point of incomprehensibility and pain.

The debate between *Essay on Terror* and *Essay on Theoretical Terror,* with which the present book ends, must be seen exactly in terms of this context—as part of the general process of "deradicalizing" and marginalizing these limit-texts (and as part of the specific process of Ivan Kristev's own "deradicalization"). Here operated the already mentioned regularity: the marginalization of the texts which sought to be "writing as experience of limit." Ivan Kristev's text attacked the discourse of the group rather than the actual *Essay on Terror*. The suppression discussed above is implicitly at work throughout the whole text: it represents, in fact, a hermeneutic blockade, a refusal to understand the strategy of the inflammation-mode. In short, *Essay on Terror* has been read in an arrogant manner—as something which it is not: as an avantgardist leftist manifesto which dreams of world engineering. Without much hesitation Ivan Kristev has turned the empty utopian structure of inflammation into its opposite: into a dream of an utopian project and of terror(?). Consequently, the laments caused by the lack of terror are laments uttered by a belated agent of Modernity (destroyer or constructor of worlds) against the new, ironic, and mute Postmodernity. The postmodern reality allows no destructions/constructions: its future has geographical dimensions—"it lies several hundred miles away"—and, therefore, the intellectual has to give up his pedagogical dictatorships.

However, Kristev is not content to be postmodern himself while the others are confined to the past of Modernity. He undertakes to do something different, quite incompatible with his postmodern pose: to correct the "branded metaphors" of the *Essay on Terror* (revolution, utopia, terror, etc.) by making them historically responsible and reducing them to the concepts of political science and history. (Let us here ignore the fact that such an act does not recognize the intention of inflammation to intervene not in the field of the expert, "sane" concepts, theoretically controlled and specified, but in a quite different semantic sphere—the sphere of nontheoretical mass intuitions which are in power in the post-totalitarian society.) *Essay on Theoretical Terror* insists upon a "normal" theoretical use of concepts, imagining it as meticulous historical specifying and terminological disciplining of concepts: demands which are attributes of a traditional figure of Modernity—the Expert. Kristev wants to examine, consult dictionaries and encyclopedias, to quote voices of authority, correct and analyse, to specify and "apply historicism." Read through an alien interpretative grid, the aggressive metaphors of inflammation are tamed into convenient concepts inscribed in a traditional disciplinary field. (This field, i.e., political science, has gained new authority from the radiance of the New World Order: the "politologists" were one of the most sought after scholarly commodities in post-totalitarian Eastern Europe.)

At the same time, however, in *Essay on Theoretical Terror* (and it is at this point that the repressed past rather than the "glorious postmodern future" reveals itself in the form of a stylistic symptom) the pose of the expert proves to be a merely simulated one. It is a quotation from the expert discourse which, however, is still punctuated by other nonexpert rhetorics. Ivan Kristev's text is characterized by a succinctness, swiftness, and even frivolousness of its logical enthymemes its proofs and conclusions are often premature, it contains jokes and teasing remarks, produces undisciplined, wild metaphors—"laments," "guts," "Danton-Derrida lines"—which as a stylistic approach and terminological apparatus are quite incompatible with the pedantic, neutral, and positivistically scrupulous expert discourse. They can be regarded as one thing only—as a trace of the free, scandalizing game playing of the "oasis." Ivan Kristev is simply trying to forget that there was a time when he, too, played Pierre-Menard-games. He now longs to assume the stable professional identity of a politologist and historian. And he almost seems to be taking the game seriously (somehow, among other things, he had become the head of a certain foundation as well as adviser of the president). The problem he faces is that, no matter how hard he tries to shake off his former inflammation, it breaks through the surface of his expert style in the form of a discursive subconscious undermining his serious professional pose of an Author of Truth.

In spite of all that, however—and quite independently of the stylistic symptoms of the repressed past visible to only a few observers—"expert texts" such as Kristev's performed a clear function in the discursive struggle of post-totalitarianism. The "serious," "professional" voices of such texts counterbalanced the parrhesiastic Truth and marginalized other discourse possibilities doing, no doubt, their share in establishing the new discursive status quo. This is a function which comes surprisingly close to the one described by Foucault: the "great confinement" of the respective "mad" discourses and symbolic formations; the appropriation of their voices and their alternative position by virtue of which they can be the Other of modern instrumental rationality; the introduction of the norms of "power/knowledge" regarding the deviant voices as mute objects, describing and classifying them in its conceptual grids in order to confine them at last to theoretical and political silence. Deep down, beyond the flirtation with words like "modern" and "postmodern" Ivan Kristev's text reveals the hostility of every neutral expert position towards any attempt to make the **individual biographical body of the expert himself part of the theoretical subject of his discipline** and to "**inflame**" the concepts of his value-neutral specialized language in such a way that they begin to appear as Dionysian metaphors branching out into trees of figurative exuberance.*

To summarize briefly—this was the hostility which a new, solid model of identity manifested towards the possibility of its own problematizing by the totalitarian past. Ivan Kristev's *Essay* exemplifies the position of the post-totalitarian expert—a position of which there have remained only the concern for its own preservation as well as its mass medial self-advertising. Not forgetting, of course, its sanctions against the other existing discourses. What it lacks, however, is something of crucial importance (something which alone justifies the existence of an expert discourse)—it lacks the theoretically detailed and practically operative formulation of what "velvet revolutions" are and how the problems which they left in their post-totalitarian wake are to be solved.

Some time after the publication of *Essay on Theoretical Terror* the transgressive-ironic discourse of "inflammations" and quotation-interplay was also attacked and mercilessly penalized by the other discursive position of authority—the parrhesiastic one. It received a few heavy religious (almost fundamentalist) blows from the newly established group of Orthodox-Christian philosophers. On the surface, the discourse and the group associated with it were accused in this religious attack of being infantile and immature and thus incapable of moral and political choice. However, the outburst of biblical fury and fierce abhorrence on the part of the young prophets spoke of deeper reasons. The discursive experience of the former intellectual group posed a threat to the very core of the new-old religiosity. This experience was still informed with the memory of how a "parasitic" existence could be led inside languages which proclaimed immutable values and postulated a nonverbal eidetic beyondness: "the Genuine Reality." This discourse was still able to inflame and incestuously transgress the indisputable hierarchies of Being which purport to be beyond any discourse (no matter what names they had been given—"historical necessity" or "Providence") perceiving them as invariably integrated in certain symbolic practices, and what is more—regarding them as constituted by such practices. For it was also able to recreate the genealogy of those "immutable values"—a genealogy which was in many respects intertwined with its own. Their profane, controversial, and noneidetic *Herkunft* could be traced back to the small proto-religious groups emerging from the same controversially simulative and not so radically subversive intellectual environment. The new religious variant of parrhesia was genealogically related to the collectively experienced, dark side of totalitarian discourse: it was no stranger to the dark, painfully devoid of language, agonizing and amorphous traumatic experience which now manifested itself in the impulse towards fundamental Truths and absolute forms of Eastern Orthodox philosophy. The transgressive discourse still carried within itself the memory of how such "fundamental" thinking could be hypothetically unfolded into its dark, anti-utopian variants. For years it had been carrying out—albeit not purposefully—an actual process of deconstructing the fundamental Christian opposition of word vs. Word. In terms of its experience, all symbolic practices, all names, in short—every verbal reality—were to be seen as a reality **of** this nonabsolute, empirical world; a reality which was ordinary and pregnant with conflicting potentials; a reality which could simultaneously liberate and enslave, invoke insight and blindness, be natural and unnatural. The possibility of "inflaming" the Word which claimed to possess eidetic values, of making transparent—as Roland Barthes would put it—its fascist dimension—all this was part of what the group had experienced and thought through. The insight it had gained spelt a whole range of possibilities which posed a threat to the new eastern-orthodox fundamentalism. This was a threat to any eidos, any Master signifier and thus also to the mystical contemplation of the Center: the transgressive discourse could inflame the existentials, the hierarchies, the ecstasy... Having outgrown the "puberty" of the intellectual group, having become "mature" and "wise"—possessors of an unshakeable identity—the religious-orthodox thinkers in Bulgaria could not allow this to go on with impunity. They could not remain indifferent in the face of the promiscuous, transgressive, travestive approach to the body which proved to be created not by God but by the totalitarian symbolic order, and thus deprived of all its "normal" and "natural" properties, divested of the "normal" periods of its aging or its "natural" sexual identity. This was the body which revealed itself in the unnaturalness of "its prostheses and bandages" (V. Todorov); the body which was terrorized and traumatized, marked by its morbidity, amorphousness, and plurality. Such an unnatural body could not have a "natural identity": a product of totalitarianism and branded in its very heart with totalitarian engravings, this body continued to feel the tragedy and physical distress of unfreedom being, thus unable to fulfill its fundamental

Christian mission, namely—to be the Body which fulfilled its own potential in the act of sacrifice. This act could be the dreamed-of release of dissemination, stabilizing the Word and thus realizing the economy of parrhesiastic Truth. Yet, in terms of the experience gained by the "oasis" every heroically sacrificial, "ontological" gesture deserved to be "inflamed" and thus stretched to the point where it revealed its conflicting disseminative potentials. This could no longer be infantile behavior—it represented a position of moral and political principle. In view of it, the wholesale religious crusade against the discourse of the group was to be expected—this discourse had to be discredited at all costs, it had to be stripped down to its unnatural, nauseating, shameful dimensions and seen as mere clownish posturing. According to the paranoid logic I have already described, it was, in the last analysis, labeled as communist (which to the representatives of the religious-orthodox variant of parrhesia was nothing else but a grimacing hypostasis of the satanic).

Must we now (and is such a procedure at all possible) assign heroic dimensions to both this simulative and inflaming discourse and the no longer existent intellectual group associated with it only because they did not hold out against the fierce discursive pressures and were forced to drop out of the social race? Is it possible to deny that the existence and the mode of this group represented in themselves a much too conspiratorial, esoteric, and "discursive" resistance which was unable to transcend the boundaries of its oasis and did not in any way predict the collapse of totalitarianism? Is it also possible to deny that the behavior of this group had a special erotic tinge? And that intrinsic to it was a certain self-contained and, no doubt, infantile narcissistic aestheticism, a certain self-delusion that scandalous verbal constructions represent the only creditable social action?

All this cannot be denied, of course. Yet, let others (and there is no shortage of them in the post-totalitarian world) fall into fits of rage over the above-mentioned features of this discourse, reducing it solely to them and thus coming to terms—in the easiest possible way—with their own past.

For, what proved fatal to this discourse were not the outside attacks and sanctions against it. Fatal to it was the "losing of the key" by its carriers themselves owing to the newly established political economy of truth. The members of the group yielded to the power of the new identificational models, assuming themselves the roles of parrhesiasts or experts and ceasing to understand **why**, in fact, they had been doing all this, **why** they had been seized by this insanity? They began to internalize the New Symbolic Order, themselves repressing their own past. In view of this we can say that the censorship against them was not of a bureaucratic-totalitarian but of a Freudian kind. Thanks to it, they began to forget quite effectively: to forget the political and philosophic charge of their own language and its mechanisms of resistance; to forget its intellectual and philosophic **potential**, the space of freedom which could be won by means of this language. Nobody wished to "test their own limits" any longer because they felt content within them. The members of the group had meanwhile also "grown-up," becoming members of parliament, ambassadors, advisers of the president, businessmen, and mass media stars in post-totalitarian Bulgaria. Others successfully stepped into similar well-established professional roles in the postmodern West, figuring there as paid experts on Eastern Europe. In their new environment they were, however, to encounter another sanction—this time imposed by the academic Left of the American and European universities which did not allow any excessive, libertarian acts of aggression against the Great Discourse of the Left, trying hard to preserve it from turning into a fossil. They were also to encounter the sanction of long-recognized experts who could not allow just anybody to undermine the authority of their professionally informed and strategic word.

The utopia of normalcy sought to represent the existing world as involved in the process of a global recovery to which any inflammatory process could only be detrimental.

In fact, in his text *Epitaph for Sacrifice, Epitaph for the Left* Ivaylo Ditchev deals with this very same situation, looking at it from a somewhat more general perspective: he sets out to examine that general atmosphere of the postmodern world which, in a way, naturally engenders such outlooks. This is a world where the great metaphysical struggle between Good and Evil, Reason and Madness has finally spent itself—nobody is seriously fighting for the negative cause any more, Mephisto has been fired; the sleep of reason no longer gives birth to monsters—it only produces small disagreeable insects. Even wars have become only local demonstrating that, in the long run, everything really is under control. The centralized forces of Good and Reason are quick to teach every aberrant act of frenzy a lesson. Local misery, suffering, madness—none of these, although encountered here and there, have a legitimate right to universal existence any more. In a sense, they are all improper for they no longer represent only one side of the metaphysical struggle and are thus merely regarded as a disgraceful incident which the police (in the old sense of this word—the institutional body entrusted with the duty of maintaining the harmony and well being of the world polis, including its good health) will quickly get out of the way.

And thus today, amidst the harmony of the New World Order, the inflammations gradually begin to disperse. One by one, the mad traumatic voices are falling into silence.

And if this book is not always behaving in a proper and healthy manner, the only choice left to it is to ask forgiveness.

And perhaps to come to an end?

Or to tell about all this in an act of muted resistance, in a style which can hardly inflame any one.

The style of an epilogue.

Note

* To quote just one example of this, *Revolutio* derives its origin from the field of astronomy where it referred to the cyclic movement of the planets and stars on the firmament. Experts argue that the original meaning of this word underwent a metaphorical change in the works of Seneca and Cicero where it came to denote "fateful" or "historic" processes. The meaning of cyclic movement was preserved as late as Shakespeare—in *Hamlet* "revolution" is said to refer to the turning of fortune's wheel. In Italian the use of the word *rivoluzione* in the sense of political unrest supposedly goes back to the beginning of the 13th century: Alexander Demand, from whose book *Metaphern für Geschichte, München 1978* these facts have been taken, argues that the use of the word "revolution" in this "inglorious" sense was already in existence at that early period. At this point we must ask ourselves by which of these meanings—the astronomical, the fateful, the Italian, the "glorious English" or the "modern French" one—we should be actually guided. And what, in reality, are we supposed to gain from being reminded of them? Which is the typical revolution (if this word does, indeed, mean anything beside will to power and politics of representation)—the French or the English one? Or maybe the astronomical one? Perhaps the "model-generating" ability of the French revolution has been exhausted to the extent that we could gain better insight into the next "revolutions" by turning to the stellar or fateful models. Traced in all its directions, the history of a word resembles not so much a tree with many branches as a tangled, madly chaotic bush which can disrupt the self-evidence of **all** of the word's sematic connotations, of **any one** of its modern uses: from the experimental to the "legitimate" theoretical one. Looking back into the abyss of its historical uses a concept can only become giddy. The vertigo is the only gain.

Contributors

Alexander Kiossev (born in 1953 in Sofia, Bulgaria) teaches cultural history of the Modernity at the university of Sofia. At the present moment he is a lecturer in Bulgarian language and literature at the University of Göttingen, Germany. His publications include a book in history of Bulgarian poetry, many theoretical essays (some of them translated in English, German, French, Hungarian, and Romanian) and a forthcoming book in Bulgarian about the discursive production of truth in totalitarianism and post-totalitarianism.

Ivaylo Ditchev (born in 1955 in Sofia, Bulgaria) teaches aesthetics at the University of Sofia. At the present moment he holds his Ph.D. at Paris 7 in France and participates at the French investigation group *The grey memory of the East.* He is author of several collections of short stories, a novel, and two collections of theoretical essays (some of them translated in English, German, French, and Hungarian).

Vladislav Todorov (born in 1956 in Sofia, Bulgaria) He was member of the Bulgarian Institute of Arts, the department of theater studies. At the present moment he holds his Ph.D. and teaches Russian literature at the University of Pennsylvania, Philadelphia, USA. His publications include a book in Bulgarian about the transformation of the utopian manifestos of avant-garde left art into a Symbolic Order ot totalitarianism and a forthcoming book in English (to be published by SUNY). Some of his theoretical essays are translated in English, German, French, Russian, and Hungarian.

Ivan Kristev (born in 1965 in Sofia, Bulgaria) He studied philosophy at the University of Sofia and specialized in political science at the University of Oxford. At the present moment he is director of the *Friedrich-Naumann foundation* in Sofia. His publications include a book of poetry and several theoretical essays (some of them translated in English, German, and Hungarian).

All four contributors were, in the period between 1987 and 1991, members of the intellectual group *Synthesis* in Sofia. The group published the semi-Samizdat collection of essays *Ars Simulacri (1989)* and the collection *Ars Erotica (1992)*. In 1993 the Hungarian publishing house *2000-Orpheus* published another collection in Hungarian: *A mutants egzotikuma. Bolgar postmodern essek (The Exotics of Mutants. Bulgarian Postmodern Essays)*.

Index

acid, 99–101
action, 66, 68, 70, 78, 164, 174; mass action, 79
aesthetic and economic structures, 65
aesthetics, political, 65–94
allegory, 105; allegorical, 65, 67
anatomy, political, 95–101
angle (Angulus), 10–14
archive, 25, 26, 35, 45, 54
Ars Simulacri, xvii, xviii
articulation, 137–140, 143; mutant as articulation with error, 141; nonarticulation, 153
assemblage, 71
author, 11, 25–32; author of Truth, 159, 170; Lenin as author of communism, 68; meta-author, 116–117. *See also* authorship, 25–32, 58–61, 168
avant-garde art, 71. *See also* Constructivism, Dadaism, Expressionism, Formalism, Futurism, Proletcult

blood, 81–82, 114, 125, 137; blood and soil, 89; blood transfusion as means for homogenizing, 81–82
Body, xi, 67, 68, 71, 75, 78–80, 84, 87, 95, 97, 100, 126, 127, 140, 142–146, 151, 152, 160, 173; biographical body, 171; bodies and aggregates, 71; body of the Other, 152; body's reality as act of violence, 138; collective body as aggregate, 77, 78, 142; communal body, 65, 78, 80–85; communal athleticism of the bodies, 72; conventionalized body, 139, engraved body, 139;erotically intimate body, 83; human body as reality, 137, 151; as transcendental signified, 138; king's body, 98; king's two bodies, 99; laboring body, 77; Lenin's body, 95, 96, 97; mass superorganization of bodies, 73; mutant body, 143, 145, 146 (*See* unnatural body, 173); party body, 69; political body, 96, 97, 98; Proletarian body, 81; proto-body, 138; reader's body as totalitarian prosthesis, 167; self-sacrificing Body, 162, 174; schizoid body, 143; social body, 82; superior body, 67; technological togetherness of the bodies, 81; totalitarian body, 142–143; traumatic body, 143; working class body, 65, 66, 140. *See also* corporeality, 67, 98; annihilation of corporeality, 151; corporeal being, 77
book, 26, 27, 28, 30, 155, 163; book-world, 28; life as a book. *See also* life-work, 51; transparent book, x, 1–2
Bull-God, 18–20

capitalism, 106
carbon paper, 61
castration, 17–18, 85, 122, 123, 134
catalog, 27, 28, 31, 32
censorship as political (party) institution, 88, 175
circle, x, xii, xiii, xiv, xvii, xx. *See also* community, group, milieu
city. *See* city of truth, 160; Garden cities; Linear cities; Sun cities, 82; The Luminous city of Luxembourg, 15–17; The Dissipated City of Luxembourg, 17–18; The Twisted City of Luxembourg, 18–20; The Phantom city, 20–23
classical, 34, 35, 43, 44, 49, 50, 51, 53, 54, 55, 56, 57, 58, 60, 61, 70, 74, 153; classics, 33, 35; nonclassical, 51, 53, 54, 55, 60
collage, 74, 75
collecting, 28, 30, 31, 32, 36
communism, 65–94, 95, 105, 106, 108, 109, 110, 113, 123, 125, 129, 131, 132, 146, 153, 159. *See also* communist bloc as planet scale monastery, 128
community, x, xi, xii, xiv, xv, xvi, xvii, 126, 131, 133. *See also* circle, group, milieu
comradeship, 81
concentration camp, 82, 83, 129, 142; Yugoslav concentration camps, 121
condensation and concentration of the population, 82–85
conspiracy, 92, 100, 110, 114; conspiracy of the Lie. *See* conspiratorial life, 91; meaning, xx; plot, 91; principle, 92; resistance, 174
Constructivism, 69, 71, 77; communal constructivism of sight, 73
convention, 67, 137, 139; convention as result of ultimate violence, 137; symbolic convention, 137; (terror-) convention-reality transition, 142, 149; conventionality, 153
coping, 28, 36, 39; copy, 36, 39, 40, 42, 54, 60; copyist, 27

Dada, 54, 69, 71, 72, 74, 86, 89, 90, 94. *See also,* Dadaism, 68, 69, 74; Dadaist, 22, 77
death, 100, 109, 111, 117, 119, 121, 123, 133, 134, 144, 151; death as supereality guaranteeing the symbolic order, 139–140; relation of Death to Liberty and Equality, 151
Desire, xix, 167
dialogue, x, xv, 157, 160
difference, 53
dilettantism, xv
discourse, xi, xiv, xix, 50, 77, 78, 79, 124, 156, 162, 175; blockage of all critical discourses, 159; discursive *conjunctura,* 163; discursive market, 163; discursive masochism, 128; discursive subconscious, 170; dissident discourse, 160–161. (*See* parrhesiastic discourse, 172); every day life discourse, 130; expert discourse, 162–163, 170; "great confinement" of the "mad" discourses, 171; Great Discourse of the Left, 165; mirror-discourse, 163; struggle of dominant rival discourses (discursive struggle), 158, 171; (suppression of) the ironically transgressive (play-acting) discourse, 156, 157, 163, 164, 172. (*See* discourse of the group, 169, 174); transition period discourse, 131; truth-telling discourse, 159, 163; "virus" in the totalitarian discourse, 168. (*See* parrhesiastic discourse, 163); victimary discourse, 129

disfiguring figures, xiii
Disgust, xix, *See* revulsion (negative ecstasy), 166–167
disintegrity, hermeneutic, xvi
dissemination, 168, 174
dissident, xii, xv, xvii, 106, 110
dissimulation, xv, xvi, xvii, *See also* imitation, xix; repetition; simulacrum, xviii, 110, 113, 124; simulation, xvii, xviii, xix, 115, 168; simulations simulate, xix.
door, 10–14

ecophilantropy, 132
ecstasy, 123, 166; ecstatic energy, expression of, xx, 141
empire, 26, 32; Library-Empire, 27
engineering, genetic, 105; social, 66, world engineering, 169
engraving, 44, 138–144. *See also* imprint, 44, 45, 46, 59
eroticism, xi, 84, 86, 107, 125, 128; erotics, xii, 74. *See also* Eros, claustrophobic, xi; intellectual-erotic togetherness, 156
evil, 119. *See* duel between good and evil
expert, 159, 161–163, 169, 171, 177; crisis of the expert reason, 162; expert discourse, 162–163
Expressionism, 71–72
eye. *See* look, oxulus, sight, vision, 73–76, 81–82, 86, 87, 88. *See also* fascinated eye of the West, 130; gaze of the prosperous West, 128; "healthy eye," 86; machine eye, 87; racial eye, 85
eye-sun. *See* all-pervasive gaze; illumination; organ of light, 15–17; eye-sun as phallus, 17

festival, 141, 143, 145; tic-festival, 143–145, 146
form of life, xi; alternative, xx
Formalism, 89
Futurism, 69

game, xii, xv, xvii, 30, 52, 168; game of signifiers, 138, 139; intertextual game, 155; Pierre-Menard games, 170; scandalizing game, 170; seduction game, 131, symbolic game, 135
generation, xiv
genetics, 105
genre, ix, xiii, xxi, 1, 67, 130; genre of self-hatred discourse, 129; we-are-the-worst genre, 130
good, 120; duel (battle, struggle) between good and evil, 120, 161, 176; good as police for evil, 120–121, 176
group, xiii, xiv, xv, 156, 168, 172. *See also* circle, community, milieu
guillotine, 98–99, 151
guilt, 123, 127, 157; guilt machine, 123, 126

happening, intellectual, x
health as political problem, 95, 155, 176
Herkunft, 172
hero, 19–20, 168
hunger strike, 152

identification, xv, 28, 168; one dimensional identification, 158, identification models of the New World Orders, 162
identity, xvii, 26, 120, 122, 124, 134, 162, 168, 170, 171; identity of communism, 66. *See also* sameness, 10–14; preserving who you are, be always one and the same, 43, 121; self-duplicating sameness, 20; uncompleted, compensatory, amorphous identity, 156, 158, 173; sexual identity, 173; terrorist-conventional identity, 143

ideology, x, xv, xix, 50, 57, 65, 72, 80, 86, 90, 94, 107, 112, 128, 129, 133, 148, 151, 160, 163; ideology of National Socialism, 87

indigo, x, 33–62, 168; indigo-scaffold, 60; living indigo, 59; reversed indigo as inflamed quotation, 168. *See also* symbol of the indigo, 35, 37, 38, 39, 40, 41, 42, 56. *See also* secret of the indigo, 36; super-indigo-super-Ego, 50

inflammation, xiii, xxi, 164–168, 169, 170, 172, 176; inflammation as empty utopian structure, 167. *See also* aggressive mode of discourse, 166–167

inter-disciplinary, xv

interpretation, xvii, 1, 11, 15, 23, 60, 106, 110, 112, 148, 163; as a classical philological institution, 60; living as the only privileged interpretation, 29

key hermeneutic, x, xii; "great key," 35; key metaphor, 66. *See also* key to understanding, 158; losing the key, 175

labor, 65–66, 71, 81, 105; division of labor between East and West, 128; tragic labor, 121

labyrinth, 19–20

language, total, 21; as virtual reality, 21; language-world-textuality, 53

Left, 119, 122, 132, 175, 176. *See also* leftist, 109, 169; Great Discourse of the Left, 165, 175

legality and illegality, 91

legitimacy, 92, 93, 98–101, 152; illegitimacy, 94

library, 26–32, 54; Alexandrine, 27; burned, 27, common, 83; Library-Empire, 27; library under party control, 89; library-utopia, 26. *See* librarian, 26

list, 110–115; list as a new social mediator, 114. *See also* catalogue

literal, 3, 7, 8

machine, 11, 72–75; chaotic machine, 145; guilt machine, 123, 126; machine for ultimate revolution, 139; utopian machine, 151. *See* Machinism, 71, 72. *See also* Creator-Machinist, 72, 73; Machinist as Superman, 73; Oculus ex Machina, 75

manifesto, 68, 78–79, 134, 153, 169

mask, xv, xvii,

Mass Man, 78–80, 82–83

Master signifier, 165, 167, 173

mausoleum, 68, 97, 98

merger of science, art and politics, 70–72, 73, 76–77

metaphor; 67, 69, 81, 97, 98, 99, 130, 142, 150, 154; aggressive metaphors, 170; Bolshevik's metaphors, 96; branded metaphors, 169; concepts turned to metaphors, 69, 76, 79; constitutive metaphors, 166; Dionisian metaphors, 71; eroticized metaphors, 149; Jacobean metaphors, 97; key metaphor, 66, 164, 165; metaphor as means of production, 66; political metaphors, 98; wild metaphors, 170. *See* metaphysical metaphoricalness, 50. *See also* Metaphern für Geschichte, 177

milieu, intellectual, xii, xiv, xv, xvi, xviii, xix; semi-academic-semi-artistic, xiii, structural ambiguity of, xvii. *See also* circle, community, group

modernization of society, 70, 71, 74, 76, 80, 83, 127; agent of modernization, 73. *See also* industrialization, 65, 127; production and overproduction, xviii
Modernism, 69, 72, 76, 82, 87, 89
Modernists, 86
montage, 70, 74, 75, 116
monument, 39, 40
mummy, 67–69, 94, 97, 98, 114, 166
mutant, post-totalitarian, 141–145; mutation, 153
mystification, xiii, 34, 59–60

narrative, ix, x, xi, 49, 157; narration, x
negligence, postmodern, 55–57, 58
nomenclatura, 90, 110–115, 129
normalcy, 140–141, 144, 146

opposition, xv, xvii. *See also* resistance
order, 51, 119, 145, 148, 160; actual, 67; bourgeois order of things, 71, 79; centralized, 84; conventional, 146; eternal, 74; legal, 67; metaphoric, 49; New World (Dis)Order, 121, 162, 170, 176; old order, 140; order-and-meaning, 145; order of discourse, 164; order of normalcy, 144; political order of the new world, 78; sacred, 16; symbolic order, xviii, 135–136, 138–144, 151, 164, 165, 166, 173, 175. *See also* space, bourgeois, 79; common, communal, 80, 82–83; physical and allegorical, 19–20, 94; public, 83; grammar of instructive language, 21
organics, 87; world's organics, 166. *See* organic, organ, 73, 89;

organic into mechanic, 87, organic patterns of social behavior, 158
Other, the, 14, 18; Otherness, 53. *See* body of the Other, 152; the Other of the modern instrumental rationality, 171; the Other of terror, 167

Paranoia, 106, 125; class struggle, 110; controlled, 106; political, 106; paranoid attack, 162; logic, 174; space, xvi, xvii; suspicion, 116. *See also* post-paranoid condition, 105–117; democracy, 117
parrhesia, 160; parrhesiast, 159, 162–163, 171, 175
Party, 66, 68, 80, 82, 89, 90, 91, 93, 94, 96, 112, 113, 117, 124, 126, 134; race-party criterion, 86
party art, 68, 86, 89, 90
phallus of the ruling class, 122
phantasm, 134; imperialist, 125; modernist, 68, 69; Slav, 129
philosophy of language, 35
plagiarist, xviii, 27
political, 74; action, 66; art, 68, 69, 76, 77, 86, 88, 89, 93, 94; attraction, 71; changes, xi; collective political agent, 81; force, 106; intuition, xv; puberty, 157; struggle, 106; political transgression as ontological transgression, 166; political unconscious, xviii
post-totalitarian age, 157; Bulgaria, 157, 175; Eastern Europe, 158, 161, 170; expert, 171; mutant, 141; Öffentlichkeit, 158. *See also* discursive situation of post-totalitarianism, 158; post-totalitarian public domain, 155, 159; 161; period, 156; society, 158, 169; world, xi, 145–146, 155, 157, 159, 174;

Post-totalitarian age *(continued)*
post-communism, 107, 117; post-utopian situation, 152
power, 66, 67, 80, 90, 92, 93, 95, 96–101, 107, 108, 111, 114, 117, 118, 120, 123, 126, 127, 128, 132, 134, 151, 155, 177; body of power, 99; essence of power, 114; games with the power, xv; minimum of power, 125; nomenclatura as the immediate body of power, 90; parliament as legitimate division of power, 92; power as reposing on symbolic exchange, 125; power/knowledge, 171; preservation of power, 39, 108; production of power, 93; reality as total power, 135; traditional representations of power, 114
Proletcult, 68, 69, 71, 80; Proletcult as the actual Proletarian art, 89–90

quoting, 28; quotation, 168, 170, 172

race, 86, 89
reading, xviii–xix, 1–2, 28, 31, 32; as act of intercoursing, 26; as conquering, 30; as modus of existence, 26; as proceeding writing, 27; as rereading, 27. *See* reader, 1–2, 26, 29, 55, ideal reader, 26, 29, 30
reality, xviii, xix, 69, 110, 115–117, 126, 128, 131, 143, 149, 151, 152; alternative, 143; a-semiotic, pure, xix; communist, 94; cultural, 28; Don Quixote and the Problem of Reality, 29; figurative reality, 19; Genuine Reality, 172; historical reality, 147; inauthentic reality, 166; political reality, 98; postmodern reality, 169; potential or actual, 30; ready-made, 75; reality as convention, 137; reality as a narrow slit between two books, 29; reality as suppressed violence, 137; reality as symbolic product (as semiotically articulated), 135, 142; reality in *statu nascendi*, 143; reality of communism, 67; reality producing system, 143; suppressed reality, 140; symbolic reality, 115, 144; utopia as reality, 67; verbal reality, 173; virtual reality, xviii–xix, 21. *See also* criterion of reality, 143; production of objectivity, 74
reception, xx
repetition, 3–9, 46, 50, 53, 60, 61, 93; eternal repetition, 53. *See also* copy, double, twin, xviii, xxi, 3–9, 12, 13, 26, 39, 40, 42, 143, 164, 168; indigo doubled life, 50; dissimulation
representation, ix, 12, 109, 112, 115, 117, 126, 160, 165, 177; class struggle of representations, 108; modernist principle of representation, 87; political representativeness, 90, 93; public representations and rumors, 108; representable, 88; transcendental paranoid representation, 161
repression, subconcious, 73
resistance, xiii, xvi, xvii, 175, 176; half resistance, 156; local resistance, 142; "naive" political resistance, 167. *See also* opposition
revolution, 69, 76, 92, 94, 96–101, 115, 116, 122, 127, 130, 131, 132, 135, 144, 145, 147–149, 169, 177; empirical vs. ultimate (total) revolution, 135–136,

147, 149; normal revolution, 139, 147; untypical revolution, 149; velvet (nonspecific, minimal) revolution, 136, 143–144, 147, 148, 149, 152, 171. *See also* counter-revolution, 140; restoration, 140; revolution-presented-as-restoration, 144; revolution-restoration, 148

rumor, 107–110, 125. *See also* doxa, 108

sacrifice, 109, 117, 119, 122, 123, 125, 128, 131, 132, 174, 175; sacrificing as a monstrous technology of domination, 126; sacrificial exchange, 123; sacrifice/guilt pattern, 125, 127; self-sacrificing body, 162; *See also* perestroika (sacrificing of the communism itself), 122; self-effacement, 122, 125

scandal, 27, 33, 34, 54, 94, 164; semantic scandal, 167

seduction, 128, 131, 167; anti-seduction, 167. *See also* tempting and luxurious reality, xviii

semiotics, 34, 35, 55; nonclassical semiotics, 52, 137; semiosphere, xii

sign, 44, 48, 51–53; anti-sign, 53; nonclassical sign, 53; sign function, signifying function, 52, 53. *See also* signifier-signified relation, 51–53, 137

suffering, 119, 121, 128, 129, 131, 133, 176. *See also* loss, 119; miserabilism as cultural norm, 129; misery, 128, 131; unhappiness, 119, 128

suppression, 155–158, 169

symbol, xiii, 4, 42, 48, 54, 98, 115, 136, 141; instant-symbol, 52; symbolic exchange, 123–132. *See also* violence of symbolism, 142, 146

tattooing, tattoo, 137–140, 144–146, 151. *See also* articulation, engraving, 138–144

television, 115–117, 132; television as a substitute for reality, 115

terror, xix, xxi, 107, 135–146, 147–154, 158, 166, 167, 168, 169, 170, 172; post-totalitarian terror as an immanent terror, 145. *See also* violence

text, 2, 28, 31, 33, 53, 54, 55, 56, 59, 60; limit-text, 168; prototypal text of the subconscious, 138; substantiated text, 148, 153; text and context, 116; text beyond good and evil, 149; sing/understanding, ix

theory of communication, 36

totalitarianism, xi, xiv, 116, 141–143, 155–177; as realization of the political aesthetics of Modernism, 69; totalitarianism as linguistic phenomenon, xiii. *See* totalitarian, age (times, past, world, etc.), 155–177; anonymity, 55; censorship, 155; culture, xi, xiii, 116; discourse, xix, 172; hierarchy, xvii; man, 143; institution, 156; mask, xv; mechanism, xvii; past, 158; power, 97; simulacra, xviii; situation, 156; system, xvi, writers, xvii

trace, 37, 42, 53, 170; trace of eternity, 117; trace of the Other, 53. *See also* deferment, 53; *les grammes,* 53; supplement, 53

truth, 28, 39, 59, 88, 106, 108, 113, 122, 136, 153; cities of truth, 160; deconstructivist "truth," ix; expert truths, 160; fundamental truths, 172; ideological appearance vs. truth, 165; living in truth, xiii, xvi, 143, 162; metaphysical

truth *(continued)*
 truths, 161; paranoid version of truth, 163, 164; (economy of) parrhesiastic truth, 171, 174, 175; party truth (pravda), 88, 89, 93, 94; post-totalitarian "economy of truth," 159–160; power of truth, 165; preconceptional form of truths, 160; production and distribution of "truths," 159; saying the truth in a tyrant's face, 160. *See* parrhesia; truth-telling discourse, 159; twin paradox, 8–9

utopia, xviii, 66–67, 74, 80, 118, 143, 148, 153, 169; anti-utopia, 119, 153; geographical utopia, 146. *See also* The West as (anti-)utopia of the East, 159; normalcy as post-totalitarian utopia, 141, 143, 153, 158, 162, 176; radical utopia, 135, 147, 148, 152, 153; utopia as reality, 67; utopia as text, 148; utopian project, 169; utopian vision as cosmic voluntarism, 167; anti-utopian, xix, 173; modernist project, 68, 78; party project, 66; Schlaraffenland and Gulag, 123

Vergangenheitsbewältigung und Vergangenheitsverdrängung, 157

violence, 136, 141, 142, 146, 150, 151, 153; suppressed violence, 137; violence and terror as synonymous, 150

war, 72, 176
will to power, 110
word vs. Word opposition, 173. *See* inflaming the Word, 173
work, 28, 29, 31, 32, 36, 39, 57, 58, 59, 60, 70, 84; life-work, 51; party work, 89; society as poetic work, 66; work-world, 76. *See also* chef d'oeuvre, 74
writing, 27, 28, 29, 40, 41, 42, 47, 52–53, 56, 59, 155; party and anti-party writing, 89; writing as experience of (utopian) limit, 164, 167, 169

zapadniki and potchveniki, 159

Index of Personal Names

Adorno, Theodor, 50
Aeschylus, 39
Andropov, Jurij, 109
Arendt, Hannah, 109, 117
Aristotle, 34

Barthes, Roland, 173
Battaille, George, 164
Baucis, 33, 54, 55, 61
Baudrillard, Jean, xviii–xix, xx, 110, 167
Benjamin, Walter, 31, 48, 50
Benvenist, Emil, 136
Berkley, George, 30
Bogdanov, Alexander, 71, 80, 81–82
Boyadjiev, Lutchezar, xvii
Brecht, Bertolt, 113–114
Brezhnev, Leonid, 117, 132
Burke, Samuel, 148
Butler, Samuel, 119

Cervantes, Miguel de, 25–30
Charles the Great, father of the Carolingian Renaissance, 26, 32
Chicherin, Georgi, 95, 96
Churchill, Winston, 153
Cicero, Marcus Tullius, 177
Cratylus, 136
Cyclops, 16, 73

Dante, Aligieri, 166
Danton, George Jacques, 149, 170
Delacroix, Eugene, 44
Demand, Alexander, 177
Derrida, Jacques, xx, 53, 149, 170

Descartes, Rene, 106, 107
Ditchev, Ivaylo, xii, xvii, xx
Dostoievsky, Fyodor, 127

Eckermann, Peter Johann, 33
Eco, Umberto, 34
Eisenstein, Sergei, 81
Euripides, 39

Fischer, Lewis, 97
Flaubert, Gustav, 29
Foucault, Michel, xx, 159, 160, 171
Fourier, Charles, 105
Freud, Sigmund, 50, 127, 134, 166, 175
Fyodorov, Nikolaj, xiv

Ginsburg, Moses, 83
Goethe, Johann Wolfgang, 33–62
Guillotin, Joseph Ignace, 151

Havel, Vaclav, xiii
Hegel, Georg Friedrich Wilhelm, 117, 122
Hitler, Adolf, 69

Janus, 4
Jean-Paul (Johann Paul Friedrich Richter), 31
Jillas, Milovan, 112

Kafka, Franz, 139
Kant, Immanuel, 120, 167
Karaliichev, Angel, xiii

Kiossev, Alexander, x, xii, xvii, xx, 147–154
Klein, Melanie, 122
Krakauer, S., 118
Krassin, Leonid, 96
Kristev, Ivan, xi, xii, xx, 155, 168–171
Kristeva, Julia, 164
Kuleshov, Lev, 116

Lacan, Jacques, 138
Leforte, Claude, 150
Lenin, Vladimir Ilitch, 67, 68, 69, 89, 94, 95, 96, 111, 127, 130, 166
Luis XVI, king of France (Luis Capet), 98, 99, 100
Luxembourg (city), 15–23
Luxembourg, Rose, 15
Lyotard, Jean-Francois, xiv, xx, 140

Macpherson, Roland, 33, 34, 54–62
Madam Tussaud, 97, 98, 99
Marinetti, Philippo, 54–55, 72
Marx, Karl, 106, 127, 131
Menard, Pierre, 25–32, 168, 170
Meyerhold, Vsevolod, 81
Mirandola, Giovanni Picco della, 106
Molotov, Vyacheslav, 95
More, Thomas, 118
Morosov, Pavlik, 124

Napoleon, Bonaparte, 43
Nicholas II, (Romanoff) emperor of Russia, 98, 100, 101
Nietzsche, Friedrich, 110, 127

Orwell, George, 109
Ossian, 59–60

Philemon, 33, 54, 55, 61
Plato, 118, 136

Plautus, T. Maccius, 39
Polo, Marco, 38
Protagoras from Abdera, 137
pseudo-Dionysius the Aeropagite, xiv

Quixote, don, 25–32

Reich, Wilhelm, 151
Roland, Marie Jeanne (Manon) Philipon, 56, 60
Rousseau, Jean-Jaques, 151

Sade, de, xiv
Saint Just, Luis Antoine Leon, 99, 150
Sartre, Jean-Paul, 106
Saussure, Ferdinand, 51–53
Schiller, Friedrich, 33
Schönemann, Lilly, 44
Seneca, Lucius Aenaeus, 177
Shakespeare, William, 166, 177
Spielberg, Steven, 153
Stalin, Joseph, 69, 97, 111, 123, 126
Synthesis, group, xiii

Tell, Wilhelm, 44
Todorov, Vladislav, xi, xii, xvii, xviii, xx, 112, 142, 149, 154, 164, 166, 167, 168, 173

Vatimo, xiv

Wallenstein, 44
Weber, Max, xiv, 127, 131
Winckelmann, Johann, 41
Wittgenstein, Ludwig, 61, 164
Wutz, 31

Zeitler, 33
Zossima, 134

Post-Theory,
Games, and
Discursive Resistance

SUNY Series, The Margins of Literature
Mihai I. Spariosu, Editor

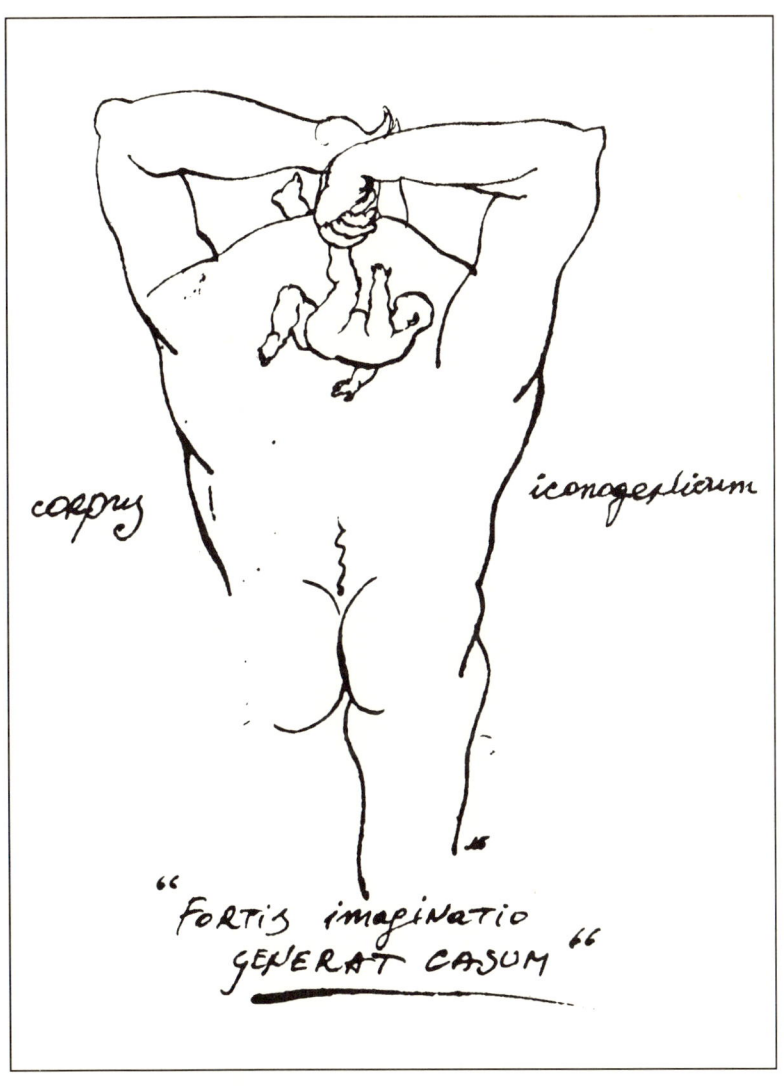

Luchezar Boyadjiev, b. 1957, Bulgaria
Cover for "ARS Simulacri," 1989, pen and ink on paper

Post-Theory, Games, and Discursive Resistance
The Bulgarian Case

Edited by
Alexander Kiossev

State University of New York Press

Production by Ruth Fisher
Marketing by Nancy Farrell

Published by
State University of New York Press, Albany

© 1995 State University of New York

All rights reserved

Printed in the United States of America

No part of this book may be used or reproduced
in any manner whatsoever without written permission
except in the case of brief quotations embodied in
critical articles and reviews.

For information, address the State University of New York Press,
State University Plaza, Albany, NY 12246

Library of Congress Cataloging-in-Publication Data

Post-theory, games, and discursive resistance : the Bulgarian case /
   edited by Alexander Kiossev.
     p.   cm. — (SUNY series, the margins of literature)
   Includes index.
   ISBN 0-7914-2357-3 (alk. paper). — ISBN 0-7914-2358-1 (pbk. :
alk. paper)
   1. Underground literature—Bulgaria—Translations into English.
2. Bulgaria—Intellectual life—1945–1990. I. K'osev, Aleksandŭr,
1953– . II. Series.
PG1145.E8P67   1995
891.8'108003—dc20   94-33220
                                                                                  CIP

10 9 8 7 6 5 4 3 2 1

Contents

Introduction: A Broken Promise   ix
Alexander Kiossev

Part I   Ars Simulacri

The Transparent Book   1
Ivaylo Ditchev

Literalisms   3
Ivaylo Ditchev

Angulus: The Figure of Sameness   11
Vladislav Todorov

The Four Luxembourgs, Civitas Peregrina   15
Vladislav Todorov

Pierre Menard, the Author of *Don Quixote*   25
Ivan Kristev

Goethe's Indigo   33
Alexander Kiossev, etc.

Part II   Political Aesthetics of Communism

Introduction to the Political Aesthetics of Communism   65
Vladislav Todorov

From Anatomy of the Political Body   95
    I.   A Political Anatomy of Communism   95
    II.   The Guillotine and Acid   97
Ivan Kristev

Part III The Post-Paranoid Condition

The Post-Paranoid Condition *Ivaylo Ditchev*	105
Epitaph for Sacrifice, Epitaph for the Left *Ivaylo Ditchev*	119
An Essay on Terror *Alexander Kiossev*	135
An Essay on Theoretical Terror *Ivan Kristev*	147
Epilogue: Health Takes the Power *Alexander Kiossev*	155
Contributors	179
Index	181

Introduction:
A Broken Promise
Alexander Kiossev

This text is an introduction. This means that its own genre makes it face problems that are insoluble. (In fact every introduction is impossible, but we will not elaborate on that now.)

The author made a promise to his American publishers to explain very clearly in this introduction the **context** of the whole collection: the chain of recurrent circumstances and events, the sharing of a common political and intellectual (besides a very private—that of close friends) milieu, and the particular plots of events that made the writing of the texts in this book possible. This would be a background which could make the texts, at least relatively, comprehensible.

As it happens, the promise, frivolously made, was impossible to keep.

And this is so not only because, as according to the general deconstructivist "truth," the context can never be described in a way that will guide and lead to a satisfactory and adequate understanding/using of the text. Every "representation" and "narrating" of a context always involves some totalizing procedures: politics of representation, control over the myths that set the semantic scale of an intellectual community, self-proclamation of the narrator (introductor) as the "legal" heir of this context, etc. The narrative about this context is impossible—and not because of the general reasons mentioned above, but because of some very specific ones.

In the first place this context does not exist anymore. The circle of friends, where "The Transparent Book," "Goethe's Indigo," or "Political Aesthetics of Communism" were born is gone. This could, of course, serve rather then disserve the narration: there is no easier way to take control of the mythology of a community than the act of retrospectively re-writing it, especially when nobody is there to contradict the narrator. But what actually happened to this community, to this intellectual circle, is something besides disintegration—it was a destruction of its potential to construct meaning, an effort to throw away and lose for good the hermeneutic key to it. In order to make possible its own disintegration it had to stop understanding itself: this was a necessary precondition for its destruction. Once the key is completely lost, the human and intellectual experience of this community begins to fade and escapes the totalizing mechanisms of the narration; today this experience seems to the author of the introduction himself somewhat unreal, and the effort to revive it—full of suspicious sentimentality and retrospective ideologies.

So the narrative has to narrate its own impossibility—to tell why this community cannot be told about.

Three of the four authors presented here were close friends for about ten years and the texts that they produced then bear the traces of this friendship: traces of discussions and arguments in pubs and streets of nighttime Sofia, of shared depressions and exaltations, of shared books—lived through together, of countless talks, dialogues and disputes, of reactions and reactions to the reactions, which nobody would manage to reconstruct now. This was as much discussing-things-together as it was living together, and everyone—under the influence of the other, under the influence of their own influences reflected in the other, etc.—was gradually losing (obliterating) his traditional, ideologically and professionally permissible profile, fixed by the totalitarian surroundings. And in the communal intellectual happenings Ivaylo Ditchev was less and less "a young writer," Alexander Kiossev—a "young literary critic," and Vladislav

Todorov—a "young theater critic" (that this was a natural process of shaping each other became clear later when Ivan Kristev joined the group and had to give up the perspective careers of a "young philosopher" and a "young poet" as well). These men not only ceased to be "young," but were also gradually turning into—for good or bad—something different, something for which the completely pieced-out-into-strict-categories totalitarian culture of Bulgaria simply had no name (nomenclature). The combination of studying the postmodern writers and leading a totalitarian/posttotalitarian existence created a common hybrid discourse and a community of obscure but passionate intellectual positions. From an orthodox-totalitarian point of view (including the totalitarian point of view of a narrative about them) they appeared like an intolerable monster. At the same time the new discourse they tried to create was not enough to explain everything. To slip away from professional nomenclatures did not suffice. This friendly debating circle was a "form of life"—vivid intertextuality, which the participants themselves experienced as an intellectual oasis. But in the cramped space of the oasis the bodies clutched at each other, the thoughts existed only in the ambivalent tension of aggression/erotics one towards the other. Thus the eroticism of the situation was paralleled by a claustrophobic feeling in a closed space: later Vladislav Todorov would call all this "promiscuous closeness." Like every oasis, this one would also at some point lose meaning and disintegrate (although at the time nobody was clearly aware of this)—and the disintegration would leave behind not only an intellectual but a corporeal void too.

Then came the political changes in Bulgaria: the "desert" of totalitarianism was taken over by a melancholic flora growing in the post-totalitarian chaos; the intuitions of space all of a sudden changed and the claustrophobic Eros of the oasis cooled down.

This introduction should try to hold the texts in a contextual unity and offer the reader the general form of their meaning. In addition, it is meant to perform this impossible hermeneutic operation at a point of time when the centrifugal energies of that very context dispersed the circle all over the world. Today Ivaylo Ditchev is in Paris, Vladislav Todorov in Philadelphia, Alexander Kiossev in Goettingen, and Ivan Kristev is on the way between Sofia, Oxford, Saarbruecken, and Boston. This suggests that the feeling of community the circle had created had been cracked and crumbling from the very beginning and probably had never been totally communal.

What is more, the "story" that each member of the group took away with them after the disintegration turns out to be quite different—not to say incompatible and hostile—from the other stories; denying the basic conceptual patterns of the rest, recalling different details and nuances of the relationship, continuing different (forgotten by the rest of the group) lines of former discussions. In this sense the hermeneutic key to the group was not lost, it was broken into pieces. And this introduction holds just one piece, one fragment of it. The rest, with which it could build up again the hermeneutic whole, the **symbol** ('symbolon'—the Hellenic piece, which the other carries to identify the community) are not only distant, but do not fit together. The elements of the hermeneutic puzzle were not simply transpositioned, they were transformed; the shape and contour of each fragment participates already in some other, completely different linguistic and human game; and joins together into other symbolons. The former fragments do not fit each other.

The impossibility of a proper introduction is increased as well by the fact that in a certain sense the texts published here owe something to a larger intellectual milieu, for which—*mutatis mutandis*—the above is also true. In the period between 1987 and 1990 the friendly circle of the authors existed amongst a crazy intellectual amalgamation of young university professors, graduate and undergraduate students—men and women of letters, philosophers, theater people, artists, sociologists, poets, and simply snobs—and this society sometimes perceived itself as involved in some act of resistance against totalitarianism still parasitizing inside its system of institutionalized languages and genres. The group "Synthesis," which gathered occasionally in the house-museum of the late Bulgarian writer Angel Karaliichev (this certainly with some effort could be interpreted symbolically—the group parasitized on the living space that had belonged to one of the numerous official Bulgarian authors, whom nobody read anymore) was not a dissident organization. It did not make the effort to "live in truth"—as "typical" dissidents like Vaclav Havel did (by the way, such people hardly existed in Bulgaria). Its strategy was to transgress the safeguarded totalitarian genres like fiction, philosophy, sociology, and theater which were ideologically limited and rigid. These genres had to be mixed and cross-fertilized to reach the point of appearing scandalous and becoming unregulated strategies of expression—"mystification," "inflammations," "disfiguring figures"—as the group itself defined the genres of its own writing and talking (indeed "Synthesis" existed mostly orally). For these "genres" the totalitarian state simply had no controlling mechanisms. The "radicalism" of that kind of intellectual-artistic behavior was certainly hyperbolized—and this hyperbolization was due to the fact that to the most part of the members of "Synthesis" totalitarianism itself, being in its late stage, was a purely linguistic phenomenon—a self-reproducing semiosphere with its own automatisms, which need to be broken.

The group "Synthesis" itself, was only a part of an even wider semi-academic, semi-artistic milieu without a common ideology. In this milieu "Synthesis" existed at times together, at times versus and against other different groups; in relations which ranged from overlapping and mixing of the groups to rivalry and open hostility. To this milieu belonged Marxist circles and secret Christian Orthodox communions, avant-guard theater groups, and students' research teams. These societies preserved their identity with an unerring instinct, drawing the line between themselves and totalitarian organizations like "Club of the Young

Writer" or "Council of the Young Scholar" that the official Communist power in Bulgaria carefully bred. In addition, they had the clear and sometimes condescending self-awareness of being a "generation" different from the preceding one of cultural clerks serving the totalitarianism.

All the groups and the loose communities referred to here were strange formations. They were naturally born as an inevitable intellectual alternative to the communist public code. They masked themselves as seminars and conferences, summer schools for young scholars—and workshops, philosophy salons, and poetic clubs. This was an attempt to outwit the system by simulative quoting of its own organizational-institutional and controlling forms (these were total, the whole life had to be "organized"—according to the totalitarian strategy).

In that kind of intellectual circle it was **possible** to mention the names of Max Weber, Vatimo, pseudo-Dionysius the Areopagite, de Sade, Fyodorov or Lyotard without the corresponding ritualistic Marxist formulas, which necessarily had to accompany them in other cases. Such an absurd list of names is not accidental. It reflects just how much this circle was productively lacking a single authority-center, that it did not have one and just one intellectual discourse—it was decisively *not* belonging to a common intellectual paradigm, a school. These authors could be mentioned, and their ideas passionately discussed without fear of sanctions. In this chaos of phenomenologists, structuralists, Orthodox believers, neo-Marxists and men of letters, postmodernists, sociologists, ethnologists, theater directors, and feminists, you could even expect that someone had read these authors. Actually the erudition was rather partial and very artistically fragmented—all these people were still semi-phenomenologists, not yet converted Christians, fresh and green postmodernists (the average age was between 25–30), the communities were organized "in pace"; this was an intellectual milieu in *status nascendi*, one that would never reach the point of being complete. In this respect the friendships, the rivalries, the discussions and the "dialogue," the latter brought to the status of an ideology (Bakhtin's ideas were in the air), were not just a form of communication but also a form of the self-generation of the intellectual communities. Dilettantism was both their sin and their vital atmosphere; it was though legitimated through the dream of "inter-disciplinarity"—another ideologeme important for the community—which hardly anyone was able to clearly formulate as an intellectual program. But on the other hand the feeling of being somehow in opposition was shared by everyone.

It is very hard to describe this intellectual milieu because of its ambiguity. Its inexplicitness was not only the characteristic feature of an intellectual puberty, it had some deeper dimensions—it could be defined as structural or even logical. None of the groups that it comprised could clearly state its ideas and did not even want to. Yearnings, biases, and feuds were not very much articulated. The amazing thing by this milieu was the very act of somehow managing to stand on the very edge of totalitarian permission and legality. It played games with the power (were they dangerous or harmless?), games of dissimulations and double dissimulations; this was a milieu where every intellectual had in one way or another masked in conspiracy his/her "true mission" so that even for the participants in this game was hard to identify the cultural or political roles of his fellows in the public space. A very refined political and cultural as well as psychological intuition was needed to be able to distinguish between a totalitarian mask and the cultural face of your neighbor; who is with you, who is against you, and what is actually your own position. The act of identifying "who is who" in this milieu built on defense strategies, conspiracy, and a problematic resistance to the all-controlling eye of the Big Brother resembled the endless process of opening a Russian doll. The identification was structurally impossible. If the distinctions could be easily made, if one could clearly and without doubt distinguish the conformist writer from the religious thinker, the potential dissident from the undercover informer, the radical community from the official institution, the postmodernist from the conservative Slavophil, this would be the end of the intellectual community. The ideological cops were always the first ones to make these distinctions. And this whole very ambiguous, but nevertheless fertile, intellectualism would be swept away in one single blow of repression by the created-for-that-very-purpose state services. Any clarity and perspicuity would actually fulfill their police ideal—total control. The ambiguity, the obscurity, the confusing and confused dissimulations, the blend of mimicry and resistance, all these were flaws of the milieu—but they were at the same time a condition for its existence, its constitutive basis. Its being in semiopposition, its nontransparent eclecticism (probably extremely repulsive for the current Western and Eastern lovers of historical *post factum* moralizing) were conditions necessary for its existence. And what is more—a prerequisite for its birth too.

In this sense the hermeneutic disintegrity of this milieu was not something that appeared later in time, it was a virus existing in in from the very beginning. As I have already said, for most of us this loosely woven network was an oasis: an intellectual island inhabited by friendly rivalry and sometimes hostile communities, which often stood at a different distance from the official ideology and official cultural institutions. This, parallel to the erotic tension, naturally created the feeling of solidarity and trust—they were not spoken about, but they were the oxygen, the condition for the existence of this milieu. But besides the solidarity—this was a paranoid space as well—a space of suspicion and distrust. Since the totalitarian system allowed for almost only impossible ways of resistance and "life in truth," nobody was completely certain, and could not be, that he/she had chosen the most correct position; everyone needed to fanaticize oneself—some procedure of self-persuasion and autohypnosis that he/she had made the "only possible choice." This inevitably caused great suspicion and distrust as far as other people's choices were different—and everyone secretly watched the conspiratorial games of the others surrounding him/her, drew their own lines between masks and faces, questioned the authenticity of the motivation of the others. Everybody wanted to know to what extent these games could be harmlessly integrated into the totalitarian mechanism, evaluated the behavior of the other not only as a covered-up resistance, but measured it against another scale too—as a probably successful strategy for an official career in the totalitarian hierarchy. In this respect, things were really getting worse due to the fact that Bulgarian science and literature of the 50s and 60s were an outstanding example of whole generations that had "started" on their way with an authentic cultural impulse and had wound up as a complacent mob of communist officials; informal circles had merged into official organizations like the "Union of Bulgarian Writers." "Dissidents" had wound up as secret agents of the ideological police or as belonging to the establishment totalitarian writers. So the structural ambiguity of the milieu had this dimension as well—from the very beginning of its existence the suspicion doubled the feeling of unity; different auto-interpretations haunted this milieu, the identities of its protagonists proliferated in number in a paranoid way, and the community itself managed to stay somehow on the edge between a solidarity of people in opposition and the secret hostile suspicion of everyone for everyone.

In the autumn of 1988, Vladislav Todorov and Alexander Kiossev—after knocking on door after door of the official institutions, after dissimulation, despair, and exaltation, after bottles of brandy for the printers and almost unbelievable luck—turned a semilegal manuscript with the title *Ars Simulacri* into 200 copies of a book. It was printed on an awful yellowish-gray paper with a flimsy binding. Later, in Ivaylo Ditchev's house, the four authors together with the illustrator Luchezar Boyadjiev, spouses and friends had to glue the illustrations, carbon sheets, etc. And, for the simulation to be complete, they put on the back cover of the book-simulation a stamp of the New York Bakers of 1913 (which somebody had accidentally come across), to parody the stamp of permission given by the official authorities.

Not by accident, in the first part of this book there is a recurrent trope. This is the trope of repetition: twins and carbon paper copies; doubling bodies, cities, and figures. The figure of Pierre Menar stands for this principle—a plagiarist of a greater genius than the author himself. This figure of the impossible identity is a symptomatic one. It bears the symptom of structural ambiguity which signifies the "recurrence of the suppressed." Thus the pattern of the Double was pervading the political unconscious of the milieu.

The authors were not aware then of how stable were the configurations of their communal political unconscious. What they wanted to do was to bring *Ars Simulacri* to the utmost because they had just made their first enthusiastic steps in reading Baudrillard.

But today it is easy to realize how little the totalitarian simulations had in common with the "precession of simulacra," that Baudrillard writes about. Because what he has in mind are virtual models whose only purpose is to produce reality—a tempting and luxurious one; the productivity (virtuality) of these models is not just a token of the disintegrating opposition between images and things, but also a sign for **potentiality** ("to produce means to materialize something by means of force," says Baudrillard) and for **potency.** To produce in Western society is not a problem. The problem is the overproduction. **Reality** is set aside just by a command on a computer because "the force" has acquired sheer informational dimensions. The real stems from and is completely interchangeable with the virtual.

The totalitarian "simulacra" had nothing in common with that Western virtual society. In a sense they were just the opposite. The "virtual model" of our society (the communist bureaucratic utopia) had one characteristic—it could reproduce no reality but itself. As Vladislav Todorov wrote—factories produced ideological poems, but not commodities. The only thing that this nonproductive, and in that sense impotent, symbolic order was capable of doing was to control the other languages; to enforce a mandatory total world of appearance; to self-reproduce by means of terror.

The very "reality" was precipitated as an irrational, anti-utopian residue, as a dark, obscure remainder after the nonproductive ideological procedures of the totalitarian society. Being a function of an utopia that never came true, reality seemed utterly wretched, disgracefully failed, consisting mainly of **deficiencies**—of commodities, books, technologies, entertainment, authenticity . . . and most importantly of signs. This was an a-semiotic "pure reality" that could only demonstrate its own wretchedness. Reality could only speak in a **figurative way** since what constituted it was precisely the **deficiency of language**, and in order to be articulated it was forced into using the only legitimate form of expression—imitation of the reigning ideological language. Reality itself manifested as a painful absence that perpetually created simulations which problematized, picked on, perplexed, scandalized, and blocked the functioning of the totalitarian discourse.

Ideology masked reality and deprived it of its genuine voice. In order to speak up, reality employed (as countersimulation) imitations of the ideological language. The virtual and the wretched reality struggled to outwit one another. Thus the totalitarian simulation failed to organize the Desire; it failed to unlock the luxurious games of temptations and lustful images. Since "reality" could demonstrate only a number of deficiencies, the totalitarian discourse was capable only of organizing the Disgust and Intolerance in symbolic models.

In this sence, the Art of Simulation practiced in the milieu I am trying to describe was not something invented in it. It was neither its fault nor its contribution. This art was "ontologically there." If we dare to parody Heidegger—simulations simulated. They were the Word of the very totalitarian Being.

Can explanations like these foresee or prevent, even to a small extent, the misunderstandings that stalk that book?

Some time ago a foreigner that had come across some texts of Todorov, Ditchev, Kristev, and Kiossev formulated his impressions in the following way: "I have never suspected that in Bulgaria I could find such a virtuoso reception of . . . " and, if I am not mistaken, here followed the names of Baudrillard, Derrida, Foucault, and Lyotard. I tried to explain the inadequacy of the term "reception" in cases like ours, and I think we finally did not understand each other. He was thinking in classical categories—great authors—great books—diligent readers. But the young intellectuals of Bulgaria (and probably these in Poland, Romania, Russia, etc.) were reading authors and books outside and beyond the structures of their Western institutionalized worship. They were reading them without a context and without a corrective: egoistically, abusively, conspiratively, and passionately as an alternative form of intellectual and political life (language), which was to overcome the deficiencies. And that is why the Western Medieval or postmodern, psychoanalytic or structuralist, hermeneutic or deconstructivist texts were not an object of a disciplined study and research by young scholars and artists. They were a focus of ecstatic energy. That is why these people were not "reading the classics" (were they from the Middle Ages or postmodern), they were searching for allegorical forms in order to express a different, silent, and painful experience. Through this process of allegorizing, the *ideologemes* of totalitarianism acquired some "conspiratorial" meaning. The voices were becoming hermetic, the communication was encapsulated. This again shrunk the circle, and this mute experience in the name of which people had started speaking became once again alienated and incomprehensible.

The reading came out to be not a reception and not a communication, but a mutation—a transformation of the genetic structure of texts and readers.

So, after the political changes there were reasons enough for the Diaspora of the circle, and for the different languages to start roaming the world, and the mutant symbolons to invade the West and the East. And probably this is well illustrated by the already swelling up difference between texts like *Political Aesthetics of Communism, The Post-paranoid Condition, An Essay on Terror,* and *An Essay on Political Terror.* Those fragments, broken off from the body of the "promiscuous closeness" had become already complete in themselves—locked up so as not to let the past in. Each one tells its own story. And while the former texts written in the style of "inflammations and disfiguring figures" reproduced the figure of repetition, the latter unconsciously reproduce the figure of dispersing ("of the galaxies"—wrote once Ivaylo Ditchev in a short story, but there is no need of such grand metaphors any more). It is just a dispersing of human beings, friends, texts.

And the "introduction" itself, a genre to be understood only within quotation marks, has only one chance left: to reproduce, by no means unconsciously, the figure of impossibility.

Part I

Ars Simulacri

The Transparent Book
Ivaylo Ditchev

The first meeting of the postmodernist society was at hand when Mr. Todorov and I suddenly looked at each other: "Shit, what are we going to analyse?" Our only advantage was that postmodernism did not exist in our country. That gave science the unique chance to create its own object. Here is how it happened: all of a sudden we invented the Transparent book.

It was a nylon-bound book made of photographic paper and sewn with fishing string. Apart from the 100 numerated copies, there existed the artist's negative matrix carefully kept away from sight, which, of course, was meaningful. Ten glass cover copies were presented on special occasions in cellophane wrapping. Do you see or are you seen? Rumor had it that some of the copies had mirrors on the bottom, so that in looking at them you were supposed to see yourself—but these are shallow metaphors. Our interpretations were far more ambiguous. Focus eyes on book—disappears world; focus eyes on word—disappears book. Yes, we were beginning to penetrate the profundity of our message: the world was transparent, the sign was the only opaque thing in it.

It seemed obvious that all artwork is self-referential; so the only possible title was "Title." Below it, the genre: "Transparent Book," followed by a note to the reader: "Characters are the only opaque thing in this book." Of course the book narrated the story of its sudden invention and explained what it was supposed to mean (cf. supra). The cultivated reader was expected to guess that he had to put his hand under the page so that the characters would appear in their syntagmatic relations against the one-dimensional background. At this moment he read:

> Dear reader, having inserted your hand between the transparent pages you have destructed the unity of the present work; you are seeing the page, but you cannot see the book. Reading it now, you understand what you have done, but if you hadn't done it, you would never have got aware. You have lost the work the minute you attained it. . . .

At this point we perceived new abysses of meaning. It was the work that was transparent, and interpretation—opaque. Add to this all allusions to utopian fantasy, think about the challenge of a political joke, consider the instantaneous disappearance of the Transparent book in murky rooms or in a bath full of water, the magnificent sparkling of meaning at the touch of jam drops or cigarette ashes. Already Byzantine theologians realized that image cannot hold eternity; image represents but its own incapacity to do so; in denying itself, it points to the beyond. Maybe the book is still somewhere around, the wind leafing through its pages on a secluded bench. But we do not want to thrust eager hands into its integrity. For it is the Transparent book, existing by not existing; the only opacity whatsoever is the story about it.

Literalisms
Ivaylo Ditchev

It's the most stunning thing: everything is quite literal. When a thing happens to someone else, it carries its "other" significance, but look at me—I am alone at last; I'm dying and it doesn't signify a thing.

His eyes are not completely shut, there remains a whitish stripe traversed by capillaries. The habit, going back many years, of using him as a mirror, makes me feel like my own eyes are closed (in that case how could I have been seeing him?).

No time left, the mutual blood, now mine only, is getting cold. I am writing for the first and last time—I mean really writing—the kind nobody reads.

Not only "metaphor" and "grotesque," but even a description like "nature's whim" seems to lend our condition an aesthetic repose. But this condition can only be expressed with a fraction: above the line one (that's us), below it—several million (births). Day after day, moment after moment—the thought of this fraction, the rage against it, and so on.

Of course—comparisons with other more or less probable fractions. Chang and Eng—bounded together shoulder-to-shoulder—what sort of curse could that be? Whenever you wish you can turn to the other, when you get sick of him you can feast your eyes on the different Chinese stuff surrounding you.

Or the two Americans, of whom testifies J. B.—bonded back to front (so that gradually, one of them turns into sort of rucksack for the other). Yet, is there any better separation between two privacies? One of them—always watched from behind, but free to look wherever he pleases; the other one—forced to look forever at his brother's nape, yet, at the same time—absolutely invisible to him. But these people, though by coercion, are simple free of each other!

And here we are in the middle—stuck together by the force of some fraction—forehead to forehead till the end of our days.

Just the opposite of the two-faced Janus, whose symbol is a door, the entrance and the exit; we are in an angular position, through which you can neither come or go—something like an anti-mythology, so to speak.

Is it possible at all to be in a more unnatural position? You open your eyes and he is always there—looking at you from a couple of inches away. You try to go, but he tries to go as well, so that due to the equivalent forward pressure you start moving in a circle. You eat under a mutual testing look, you sit on chamber pots relieving yourselves without letting each other out of sight, you both close your eyelids for sleep and in a moment open them simultaneously to check whether the other one is sleeping. And so on.

When we were born, the doctor told Mother that science could not detach us. One of us had to be sacrificed. But who? Mother was horrified by the necessity of choice. "Well . . . this one," said the doctor, holding now my bottom, now my brother's; "No it'd better be this one . . . no wait a second!" He reached under his apron and took out a coin.

"I have to think!" muttered out Mother, and grabbing us—one under each arm—she scurried home. If she is still alive, she's probably thinking even now, "I don't know." I guess this indecision of hers is the cause of it all; maybe other people owe their freedom to their mother's greater decisiveness.

In my childish tantrums, I have accused her, beat her knees furiously with a fist, and jumped, landing my heels on her feet. Mother stays still. She stands mysteriously staring through the dim wintry window and smoothes our hairs with her hand. There, where the two meeting forelocks form a wave, the hand disappears, only to be felt by me again after a steady moment, warm and insistent.

Really—how could I have known, that it would be I who remained—that fate, Mother, science, or whoever loves me more than one-half? Furthermore, even if I had remained—how could I be sure that it was I who remained? And so on.

Our happy days. Hop around the ring. The wrestling which necessarily ended in a mutual tumble. The obscene pet name which Mother called us, it is hard for me to write it down . . . Well, all right: "billy-goats." How moronically literal!

In fact, we generally didn't see Mother, we heard her. The field of vision of each of us, margined off by the other one's legs, included things like the carpet's design, lemonade bottle caps, unvacuumed dust mice, or a fly gone dizzy for some reason or other. Mother we can see with a help from little round mirrors that we always carried tied to a rubber band around our necks. (O, how flat and ugly seemed to us people's faces when we discovered photography for the first time!)

Of course, you could always blind the other one with a reflected sunbeam and such stuff. With the appearance of long, wavy hairs around our Adam's apples we began using the convenience of the mirrors for something more romantic as well; when, for example, we would wind up in a streetcar next to a pair of female legs. There followed a winking session: my left eye to his right, his left to my right, or left-left, right-right, or chain-like: my left, my right, his left, his right and—the mirrors crept up to the dress, so that the angle of reflection—and so on.

At night, we waited impatiently for Mother to turn off the lights and leave the room, so that we could get on what we then called "pencil with a rubber," and the eyes shining in the half-darkness winked with rising frequency: left-left, right-right, right-right, left-left . . .

So . . . What was I saying? Oh! right! Mother! The point was not only in that we saw her diminished, twinkling in our hands. We saw her whenever we wished (as if we made her); that is, when we decided to take the mirrors out of our shirts and to direct them, according to the respective law of physics.

Only her voice was real. More than real. It came from beyond our field of vision and each of us thought that it was directed at him. More than that—in speaking to the other one, each knew that he was actually speaking to her. "I feel like eating a carrot," you say to your brother. But if *she* doesn't hear you, why the hell say it? Since anything he could do—buy it, wash it, shred it—you would have to do with him anyway, quite literally. I don't feel like living any longer. What time is it? I have a headache. How could I fare such a moron for a twin! And so on. Even the winking I mentioned—it was a secret, but a secret from her.

What happened when the desired carrot, meaning, hour, aspirin, etc. didn't appear? You had to repeat it louder. Scream, stamp your feet, deafen your brother—until she hears and comes. Your brother is, so to speak, the material target for your voice—as you for his, by the way.

But, one day, Mother decided to get married—that's the way it went. He wore a spotlessly clean black suit; in the little mirrors the creases of his pants looked endless and sharp as knives and his face was lost high up somewhere.

"You've grown up," he said, twirling around his finger a key on a chain, which drew up menacingly near to the mirror, then receded into a dot. "Your mother has the right to be happy, just like anyone," and so on.

"Tell him to shut up," I said to my brother. "Tell him to shut up," he said to me. And once more and again— louder each time—reached a full-fledged scream. When we came to, the man was gone, and so was Mother.

Since that day on, it became useless to talk—there was no one to hear. We reached silently for the canned food, we walked in a circle around the center of the carpet, staring between our legs. Mounds of tin cans on the living room floor. Flies buzzing inside the tin caverns. The growing smell of an unwashed flesh, whether yours or the other's, there was no way to tell. Pencils with rubbers. Unemptied chamber pots.

Also: people holding their noses at queues. Comments that we are disgraces to the city, that we suggest false generalizations. That we are not typical.

Some service started leaving canned food at our doorstep, so at least we could stop going out. The days became identical, only the cans and the stench grew steadily.

.... until one day, most unexpectedly, I heard a voice:

"Look here, let's clean up a bit." Seconds passed before I realized that the movement of my brother's lips coincided with the spoken syllables.

He was talking to me; there were only two of us. But why the hell this thought has crossed his mind and not mine, when day and night everything that happened to us was exactly one and the same?

"Let's sweep up," I said and throw out the cans.

My brother watched me—as usually—from close up. I was already certain that the suspicion had infiltrated his mind, too. The suspicion, that things said are too literal to be just so. That since the other had no purpose in just saying it, then he must mean something more.

For a while we worked with the two pails and the two brooms, circling concentrically around the mounds of trash. When the last can has been dumped down the incinerator we dragged up the two chairs, one opposite to the other, and sat down. I tried smiling and he tried, too.

"How are you, what have you being doing?" I said. Of course, I was testing him—for I knew perfectly well how he was and what he's being doing since the day of our birth (he, in a sense, that's I!)

"I'm fine," he fell into the trap, but somehow spitefully. "Liar!" I screamed out at once and we both jumped to our feet—red-faced, the tendons at our necks athrob, pressing our foreheads together with all our might. Then, even more suddenly, he alleviated the pressure and said:

"I am very disappointed"—and *that* was so preposterous, that I had to contemplate whether it wasn't actually the truth.

Why couldn't we converse? This thought prevented me from sleeping the whole night through, and that means it prevented my brother from getting asleep also, because turning in the bed involved getting up, turning around and lying down on the other side.

Even the most insignificant matters caused insoluble problems: "Where is the salt-cellar?" Why doesn't he ask me; I think he knows just as much about the salt cellar's fate as I do. The question is obviously rhetorical—he could just as well have exclaimed: "Oh, there it is—under the sink!" But is it possible to live in a rhetorical world? In order for words to beget meaning (and thus the world built through them), he must have meant something more, for example: "You are so stupid that all I can discuss with you is the salt-cellar." Notice, that I myself profited from being insulted—it was a question of life and death for my reality.

Doomed to spend our lives forever in the same situation, we had to hate each other in order to exist. Everything turned into cause for a brutal strife. Who will turn off the light. Of course, we both have to get up, but even so who would do the actual "click"—who is younger, weaker, unworthier, who turned it off yesterday, and so on. Until it dawned outside, anyway.

Nothing more unbearable than looking someone in the eyes and talking to him precisely, I mean literally. Now when Mother's gone, the words themselves, seemed to make you do things to the other one—forcing him to walk backwards to the bathroom, and suchlike. Why? I don't know myself. There was no one to judge, to understand, to spank us—from both sides it was just us, he and I.

In one of these power-struggles, I screamed out: "I'll kill you!" "That's impossible because you'll die too," said he and that was the very truth, and I knew it perfectly well. But exactly because of that, it suddenly turned untrue; I don't know how to phrase it—it simply had to say the opposite immediately: "That's not true!," he: "It is true," I: "you'll see," he: "I won't see"—and thus—with the greasy fork in one hand and the can opener in the other—and so on.

My legs are going numb, the cold seeps from him into my head. I have never produced so many words by myself; it seems to me that I am speaking to the paper, so that he would hear me. Or maybe, all this is just another joke played on me by words? New words. Quickly, more words, in the short interval when he is no longer here, but still isn't gone.

Angulus:
The Figure of Sameness
Vladislav Todorov

1. Two rules concerning the principle of interpretation:
—Any interpretation begins when I, the reader, discover in the work something that I recognize as a frozen form of my own vision.

—Any interpretation considers the work "as if" written after it was read.

In order to set correctly the relation author/reader, after reading the short story *Literalisms,* I demanded from the author to insert in it a paragraph which would certify my specific interpretation. He agreed. That is why I am writing now. This paragraph is italicized and anyone can easily find it.

2. The major problem this story reveals is: How to express Sameness?

—and it finds the way: Angle is the proper figure of Sameness. Angle makes Sameness manifested.

The message of *Literalisms* is implied in an opposition between two figures—Door and Angle. Let's examine it more closely:

The Door is both exit and entrance. It bears the ambivalent sign of the threshold. The Door divides space in two heterogeneous zones—Here and Beyond. The Door marks an ontological split and figures the encounter of the two faces of being—the external and the internal mode of existence. The Door testifies to a heterogeneous world.

In the classical age the whole set of twin-myths is based on the function of Door. Any mythological twin-couple represents a mysterious joint of being which puts together the "creator" and the "destroyer," the "profane" and the "divine" force of life, etc. There existed a common certainty that everyone has his/her own demon, genius, double, who communicates human life Here with that Beyond the Door of the world. For the world had a centaur-like construction.

The Centaur is a racing Door. God Janus has a Door-face.

The individual dimension of the common ancient representation for Persona is possible only as a special merger of the two faces of life. The uncanny appearance of a face makes it appear personal because the double nature of a Persona emerges on it.

Inversely, the essence of Sameness is not heterogeneous and thus non-transferable from Here—There. What remains after death is Sameness—a foul reality. Thus sameness becomes appalling. It cannot be contemplated for it radiates repugnance. Nausea is a symptom for a growing Sameness.

The Angle, contrary to the Door, is not a threshold that splits up space. The Angle is bifurcation—for instance a bifurcated vector or a bifurcated circumference:

The Angle is a broken threshold—a broken line or a broken plane. The Angle divides—an obtuse and an acute division:

There is no ontological difference between an acute and an obtuse angle. One of them is simply smaller. The space that a circumference closes is quantitative and the obtuse angle has just more space-quanta then the acute one. It contains more Sameness.

The Angle is a dethroned Door. It does not engender heterogeneous world but simply divides, enlarges, and diminishes Sameness.

3. Throughout this short story speaks a twin-couple whose heads are congenitally grown together. So it bears the congenital figure of an Angle, not a Door. An Angle is born whose two vectors prone on the ideal geometric surface are totally identical.

Certainly it does not make any difference which one of the twins speaks. As far as the ancient twin-figure is concerned, there always were signs by means of which you were able to recognize who spoke and who was who—the tokens of heterogeneity. In our story the voice of the one springs from the same source as the voice of the other does. What actually speaks is a point at which the line of silence was broken because the twins were born. The two bodies are two membranes of one voice. They are identical organs of One and the Same being. Sameness.

The classical Persona simultaneously reverberates two incompatible voices. It is a Gordian knot. It is a mystery.

The modernized Persona is an acoustic organ of Sameness. It is a tube. It is a hollow.

Angle's birthday:

A point begins to speak when it opens up an angle and pins down a center of a circumference. It shuts up when the vectors complete a full circle and disappear into it.

Let's configure it in this way:

Given—a stolidly silent plane. Suddenly a point appears which emanates a vector. It bifurcates and begins drawing a circumference. The speech originates right here—in the bifurcation and sounds until everything vanishes into the same plane. The speech does nothing but dash through Sameness and quantify it differently in different places. It does exactly the same thing in all its phases.

Phases:

Thus human life could be configured as a geometry that progresses from birth to death. There is no mystery, no teleological development, no sacred path, no proved uniqueness either.

The riddle of the Sphinx was solved not because it was de-riddled but because it became irrelevant. Man dropped it and turned it into an Angle.

Man is no more a brave and wise Centaur. He dropped his Other and became what he literary is—an Angle which emerges in space and quantifies certain Sameness.

Sameness is a gaping Angle.

4. The conceptualism of the story could be minimized in this way:

I AM THE DOOR	VS.	I AM THE ANGLE
CHRIST		X

The Four Luxembourgs, Civitas Peregrina

From the diary of a traveler
Pseudo-Vladislav Todorov

Vladislav Todorov

The explorers of Luxembourg usually designate its four stages according to the four possible etymologies of its name. The first three: the Luminous one, the Dissipated one, and the Twisted one stem from the Latin: Lux, Luxuriosus, Luxus. The fourth is usually derived from the name of the legendary revolutionary Rose Luxembourg. The present exploration shall adhere to these interpretations of the name thus established through tradition.

▧ I. The Luminous City of Luxembourg

Some travelers also refer to it as the City of the Sun. This city encloses an enormous hill. Seen from afar its architecture resembles a gigantic mesh that has caught and subdued the upheaval of the mighty masses of earth, which had inflated with gas and lava the earth's crust and left behind the mountains as monuments of their provocative erections towards the sun. The city is segmented into seven circles or rings that grip the hill in concentric circles towards the top. It resembles a formidable crinoline that repulses any rascal who might crawl up the hill. A grandiose temple is erected at that very top. To be precise, the temple itself is the top. It springs up into an extraordinarily large dome on the top of which rises another smaller dome in whose center gapes an orifice that looks straight on the middle of the temple where the altar is placed. The dome is painted inside with the map of the celestial constellations, as if the sky repeats itself only lower down and smaller than itself. It has stooped down to the temple like a mystical constellation, a cipher that locks the meaning of the earthly events. The orifice is the threshold at which the maximal cosmic space is turned over into the minimal symbolic space of the temple. It is precisely through this orifice that the cosmos discharges its own superfluity for it to descend as the sacred order of the temple. Thus, the temple resembles a Cyclops's skull turned towards the sun that has scorched his eye in order to illumine him from inside. In this sense the illuminated (the internally luminous) city is blind. Thus built, the temple manifests through its figure the original sin of man towards the sun. Because before he stood on two legs, before his forehead bulged out like a church dome, before his eyes turned radiant, before he became sunlike, man was turning up towards the sky and its luminaries, his back scarlet and cracked like an enormous sore ape's ass. It is precisely this original anal openness of man towards the sun that some travelers saw manifested in the architecture of the shrines. The radiant—the seeing eye, the organ of light that bathes in rays—will always drag after itself like a tin can the embarrassment of being once an anus. Thus the central aperture of the temple, respectively the city expresses the ambivalent openness of the citizens towards their ruler—the Sun. Anyone entering the temple seems to cave in an ass through whose anus the Sun downcasts its stern and all-pervasive gaze. It is the source of the total illumination of the city. In general, the whole city is arranged in such a way that it culminates spatially in the aperture. Thus the whole city bathes its guilt in light. That is an all-encompassing luminescence in which you cannot help but wallow. This is the city of the total vertical transparency emanated by its center (the aperture). An all-pervasive solar gaze descends downwards as a guillotine. Man who stares against this gaze glows completely illumined from inside. Man stops casting a shadow. The city corpus is, in fact, the terrestrial figure of this superterrestrial gaze. The very body and structure of the city are the terrestrial incorporation of the downward gaze of a superpower. The city itself represents the total exteriorization and exhibition of life before this gaze. The descending transparency of the world manifests the epiphany of the Eye of the supreme supervisor—the Sun. Any kind of opaque negativity is usurped by the center. It is located there beyond and above the aperture of the city. Inside and below the aperture all is positive-transparent. The people are neighbors for they are totally illumined and all-pervaded by the selfsame luminous substance. They bathe in this totality and thus they prosper. Completely transparent and weightless they seem to lack bodies with tunnels flatulent with heavy slops. This is the city of the completely erect and utterly projected outwards and upwards man who bathes in the descending divine gaze. The emblem of the city is the Obelisk. Its erecting corpus is the spiritual gaze enacted in the matter of the world: The Eye-Sun as phallus.

II. The Dissipated City of Luxembourg

This city rises not completely built and not completely demolished. A grand bust happened and the crowd bustles around the city somewhat rowdy, somewhat corrupted, somewhat raped, somewhat exhausted, promiscuously fornicating, having once transformed plummets into maces. The demolished city gapes like a cold volcano resounding from time to time with damnation. Once the people had grown defiant and started erecting a Tower City in order to reach God. They tried to look upwards and see God. They wanted to erect the vertical (upwards) transparency of the world. It was an attempt to establish surveillance over God. To catch God on the spot. So God got furious and segmented, that is demolished, their language. He dismantled it into a multitude of mutually impenetrable languages. A total incongruity set in that demolished the corpus of the city. The demolished Tower City stands for the demolished human look advancing upwards to make transparent the world space. The fragmentation of language manifested an opaqueness that descended from above. This figured the absence of God, i.e., the absence of a center in the space of the City that could fully absorb all negativity in itself and thus make the people neighbors. God abandoned the Babel. The Godforsaken city developed an exclusively horizontal vision and strategy. The neighbor turned stranger. The space between people hollowed out. When God desolated the city, He, so to speak, distributed the negativity among the citizens. He turned everyone into something partial, strange, alien, something "other" than everyone else, into a capsulated particularity. The only possible interest became the horizontal interest between the incompatible particularities. Everyone lusted after power, strove to achieve self-made and self-fashioned Deiformity. The space of the city became a space of internecine strife. Thus the negativity discarded by God burst forth and desolation occurred.

Each desired the other in order to possess and abuse him, to subdue and master him. The space between thee and me was reduced. The city life demonstrates the desolation as a common condition. The corpus of the city that had started threatening erection towards God was castrated and went limp as a gut—the cesspit. God forced man to bend over. He twisted his bold gaze downwards. Thus God reinstated man's guilty position. Bent over in guilt man, met the eyes of his fellow man and desired him. He desired his neighbor. The Cross became the emblem of the castrated city corpus: The broken-up obelisk.

III. The Twisted City of Luxembourg

Before they lived in their city, the people were engulfed in the intestines of a Bull. The Bull was God. And then one day the Hero appeared and led them out by killing the Bull-God. Before this happened, the world was split in two chambers, into allegorical and physical space. The allegorical space was the Labyrinth, whose tunnels always led towards the mouth of the Bull. The physical space was the Bull himself. The Labyrinth allegorically represented and exhibited the Bull's intestines. The mouth of the Bull was the aperture that connected the two spaces. Exactly there "the one" began and ended in "the other."

The mouth was the threshold. The world was set up as a two-chambered device engulfing the people from one space into the other. The allegorical space (the Labyrinth) continually collapsed into the physical one (the Bull's mouth). This way the procession of Death was performed. The physical space was God himself. The allegorical one—His phony presence outside His own natura. In order to succeed, the Hero had to walk back this same lethal path, to do an act opposite to the engulfing. It was precisely for this reason that the Hero did not appear among the living ones in the allegorical space in front of the mouth of the Bull-God. He appeared in the rear of the physical space or at the aperture opposite to the mouth—the anus of the Bull-God. From there he entered the physique of the intestines and led the people engulfed there back to the mouth. He led them out. Thus the Hero liquidated the Bull-God. He abolished the physique of the God and as a consequence of this he found himself together with his people in the allegorical space of the Labyrinth which survived as the One space. This turned out to be the virtual City of their liberation. The liquidation of God reduced the world to the omnipresence of the allegorical space. Nothing could exist beyond it. The tunnels of the figurative reality did not lead to any apertures. They were blind. The liquidation of God came as a radical denaturalization of existence. The Labyrinth is by itself a twisted construction. The corpus of the Labyrinth City does not resemble any bold exalted erection. It can never be straight, nor can it be broken. Its natural joints are twisted so that it cannot stand up. It drags its spreading horizontality. The transparency is reduced to the direct visibility in the convolutions of the tunnel. The global allegorical space could be recognized in the fact that the Labyrinth is exactly the same in all its cells and can be surveyed without moving about. It is a self-duplicating sameness. The citizens live in one and the same allegory without being able to see each other because of the vertebral-like structure of the Labyrinth. The physical space was absolutely shredded up and so busted. The allegorical one opened unlimited space and thus became omnipresent. There was no power able to justify this endless allegorical order. The Labyrinth has no center. Every place in it is absolutely identical to every other place. In each cell of it emerge exactly the same things as in every other one. There are no heroically privileged places. When the Hero led his people into the Labyrinth, he himself disappeared. He took a place in it and became like everyone else. He acquired the anonymous existence of everyone else. The Labyrinth as an emblem signifies nothing but the torso of the world after God was wrested off it. Nothing is present to testify to the sense of life, nothing exists to justify the order of the world but it is total. The Absurd. It is conspicuous by the final degradation of the phallus into a colon. The erection is supplanted by constipation.

IV. Luxembourg—the Phantom City

Comrade Luxembourg—this is a woman
—Platonov

Most travelers describe it like this: a gigantic corpus, slowly augmenting, because it inflates and at the same time blackens. Having reached the point of bursting, exactly when its crust is ripping frightfully, threatening to let out slops and gases, the corpus starts slowly to soften and lighten up until it turns into a pulp. It is a necrotized womb stuffed up by dead substances: A womb turning into a vampire. This is the city of the most incredible metamorphose, mutation, and vicissitude.

This city is organized according to the grammar of an instructive language. In contrast to the Tower City, here the language has not been demolished, but nevertheless, no tower has been built, no "Common Home." This language propagates and agitates people to perform the sublime act—to claw the earth in exaltation. It was necessary to dig harder and more cunningly in order to transform the earth interior into a "Common Home." The main effort of the subjects was to dig out a colossal pit, a gigantic aperture—sanctuary, an organized subterranean eternal sun-trap.

The total language projected reality of the Phantom City. In the space of the City reverberated thunder like proclamations. The people became heralds of stunning proclamations, of verbal maltreatment because the proclaimed reality was a bruised piece. Reality dispersed in panic chased away by its own proclamations.

Language was the virtual reality and all things real peek out of it as phantoms. The Last Judgment was proclaimed real in order for a phantom to be punished—the bourgeoisie. Communism was proclaimed real in order for the other phantom to be immortalized—the proletariat. It was realized by being proclaimed. Do you recollect the story of the madman who believed he was a hen, so they fed him with raw corn? He did not stop being insane, but he stopped pretending to be a hen so that he wouldn't have to gnash his teeth on the raw corncobs. Someone proclaimed himself God and proceeded to feed on soil. The sun was proclaimed to be the Universal proletarian. Language. In the language there was no center nor horizontal or vertical coordination. It performed twisted parables according to the rules of its grammar. Language was a radioactive instrument that caused monstrous mutations in the City. Uncanny, melancholic longing engulfs the souls of the citizens: A longing for reality. And only through longing could reality open itself in the minds. Through this longing did the unnamed reality rush into the phantom figure of the City. The longing became the aperture through which reality made known its own presence. One thing sustained the population and the militants of the City—the fact that there had to be a super point of view, one might say a central herald of the proclamations, for whom everything that happened was observable, manageable, and goal-oriented. There existed the certainty that the life of the City is performed before the gaze of one centralized Eye-Mind. A certainty, that one surveyor observes and supervises the correct goings on of the grandiose ceremony called Proletarian Revolution. Otherwise to every glance from inside, life passed as an arbitrary dispersal or merging of phantoms and names. The despair came with the suspicion that this super Eye-Mind was also a phantom: A high density phantom arbitrarily authorized with a centralized ontological presence. The certainty that the transparency of the City descended from above was a sham. This "see-through-all" Eye was also proclaimed. Through renaming its realities, the Phantom City assembled and disassembled itself like an animated toy puzzle before the amazed eyes of the greatest Dadaist of the world (proclaimed to be such in Zurich). Like a real hero, this Dadaist succeeded in getting to the bottle and letting loose the genie of the most imbecile Hocus-pocus. And with an exalted babble it penetrated the City and proclaimed it. Another Dadaist of the same rank constructed a machine for executions with quite artistic and precise functions. Then he himself jumped into it and thus became the requisite matter for its function in order to demonstrate its exquisite perfection. At night, tired by the excessive work of the Hocus-pocuses, the citizens of the Phantom City sulked and listened to the lamp fuse sucking in the kerosene. And in order to stifle the rumbling of their empty stomachs, they nibbled the wall plaster. This city had no special emblem. It was emblem itself. For there existed no sign that could stand for it. Everything got proclaimed—interned into the City.

All travelers observe a strict tendency towards denaturalization of Luxembourg during its four stages: passing from a vertical into a horizontal symbolism and its vanishing into crooked parabolas; an ever more irreversible dislocation of the natural joints and apertures of the city corpus; presence, then absence, then abolishing, and at the end turning into a vampire of the city center; from emblem representing the essence of the city—to a city emblem of itself.

Usually the travelers evade the teleological interpretations, because they lead life unto a certain destination and in this sense to certain utopia or anti-utopia. Others speak of the cyclic recurrence of the herein described stages. Still others to whom we pertain are convinced of the principle of the back and forth momentum. According to this principle the City of the Sun and the Phantom City are respectively the upper and lower deadpoint between which historically acts the piston of Luxembourg.

IMPLETA CERNE! IMPLENDA COLLIGE!

Pierre Menard, the Author of Don Quixote
Ivan Kristev

> *Why are we confused by the fact that Don Quixote is a reader of* **Don Quixote***? I think I have find out the reason: turns of the kind implies that if the invented characters could be readers, then we—their readers—could be invented.*
>
> Pierre Menard

It took me seven years to examine Pierre Menard's personal archives. After the death of their owner—Baroness de Bacourt—and after the retirement of Countess de Bagnorregio into a monastery (to the great amazement of the public) the archives have reached one of those library depositories with Pierre Menard's immortal verse above the entrance. Damp and dirty, constant victim of flood and rats, these depositories are the last refuge for thousands of long forgotten books, and for the ambitions of their authors that nobody knows of. It still remains a mystery how it happened that the Pierre Menard's archives were in those lamentable surroundings. And yet another mystery is the document bearing a seal from the town council in Nimes that I happened to find. It was shoved in with the last letters of the poet and it made my seven-year-long painstaking work pointless. The document was written on a ordinary form and it certified that Pierre Menard and Pierre Menard were identical. The date *August 1st, 1939* was written in the right corner and the authenticity of the signature was doubtless.

I have no other choice as to quit the library forever and to by a little farm.

I am leaving this brief letter, together with my unfinished theses-metaphors in the archives of Pierre Menard.

Theses-Metaphors

1. According to Pierre Menard **Don Quixote** is a protagonist of identity; with his longish and weakly silhouette resembling a letter, he looks as if he has just stepped out of the open pages of a book. Don Quixote reads the world incessantly and by his perusal he proves the verity of the book. He is the ideal reader: reading is the modus of his existence. Nonreading disfigures the world and makes it contingent. Cervantes was reported to read even "the paper bits on the street." In a curious way reading precedes living (being), constituting it. Reading as an act of intercoursing (coming into contact with letters) is transcending; it is the path of a descending beyondness. Reading as an existence is rereading; it is translation, translocation in this very beyondness.

The father of the Carolingian Renaissance, Charles the Great, could read but not write. The advent of Alkuin—the Librarian—is connected with his rule. The librarian is a stranger, actually from the absolute outside. The librarian is the image of the descending beyondness. Library plus reading king—this is already the condition for the emerging of an empire. The empire presupposes integrity and completeness, and integrity and completeness cannot be created by man, they could be only pre-given.

Thus the Library is another Utopia: it constitutes the world, always remaining out of it. There is no place for the Library in the world and, at the same time, the Library constitutes its being as the condition for its possibility. But there is no place for the library outside the world either, because it is the Library which constitutes that Outside.

The Library-Utopia has double existence; on the one hand it exists in the modus of reading and is read as be-

longing to the beyondness and to the constitutive possibilities; on the other hand, its second existence is the modus of writing—it is being written as belonging to "hereness" and as reconstructing the constitutive completeness and integrity. The image of its beyondness is the burned library—for example, the Alexandrine library—put on fire by Pierre Menard (according to his novel **The Name of the Rose**). The image of the "hereness" is the writer, the creator of books. In an empirical aspect writing precedes reading, in a metaphysical aspect reading precedes writing. Within a personal biography reading and writing can be hardly differentiated. In the personal-biographical dimension a particular place is given to copying.

The copyist is inseparable from the being of the Library. His bent figure, drawing letter after letter in a mystic excitement, is the image of expansion. The copyist multiplies and at the same time his personality implies reading and writing; he is guarantee for their unity in the eyes of the Library. Book printing deprives him of this function and gives birth to the plagiarist. The plagiarist is the fraudulent copyist, he is the Scandal. With the origination of book printing, the Library archives its infinity and its imperial completeness. The plagiarist is the figure through which the order of the Library-Empire is actualized. Existing as a scandal, the plagiarist allows the expression of the basic principles of the Library. Achieving its imperial completeness, the Library reaches its exhaustion and gives birth to the Catalog. The Catalog is the sharpened spear of expansion. The plagiarist is the point where the Library and the Catalog meet. He is the fist of the Catalog and the solar plexus of the Library. The Catalog is the secret police of the Library, it is to know the places of things. The plagiarist is the scoundrel who undermines the foundations of that knowledge. Owing to the Catalog, the Library need not read itself.

Pierre Menard is not a Scandal, he is not a copyist or a plagiarist. Pierre Menard doesn't aim at expansion and therefore he is invisible for the Library: he doesn't leave any traces on the dusty shelves. He exists in the dimension of reading. Pierre Menard deprives us of the certainty that the **Don Quixote** we are holding in our hands is the **Don Quixote** of Cervantes and not Pierre Menard's. The Library turns out to be useless. We can reach out for a book as in the past but we no longer know whose book it is.

2. Reading, writing, quoting, collecting—these are the keywords of these theses. They are used like metaphors indicating different stages and strategies in the book-world relationship; they are the tentacles of the Library. But reading, writing, quoting, and collecting are used in a non-metaphoric sense as well; they must give life to a differentiation which Pierre Menard draws between book and text (in his article **From Work to Text**). According to Pierre Menard, the differentiation of work and text is the result of a certain change—the fact that something has happened in modern culture. The ambition is to catch this "something," this change, and if this is not possible, to catch the "catching" itself.

The work is a material fragment occupying a portion of the space of the books (in a library, for example). The text on the other hand is a methodological field. The work can be seen (in bookshops, in catalogs), the text is a process of demonstration and self-identification. The work can be held in hand, the text is held in language. The text is not the decomposition of the work, it is the work that is the imaginary tail of the text. If the text is experienced only in an activity of production, it follows that the text cannot stop.

This definitions of Pierre Menard will not be subjected to critical analysis here; they will be acknowledged not because of their unquestionable truth but because of the presupposition that trying to explain the modern situation they create it; they conceive it in the modus of existence. The "something" and the "catching" turn out to be identical. The cultural reality described by Menard is Menard's descriptions as real.

3. Don Quixote is the ideal reader (but not the ideal reader as a silly abstraction). Don Quixote is the ideal reader of Cervantes's **Don Quixote**. The ideal reader of the traditional work of literature is the protagonist of this work *Writing is always constructing its ideal reader through the text itself"* (P. Menard). Moreover, it constructs him as a protagonist of this text.

Don Quixote is intended for Don Quixote; it is written for him and this is the first level of "ideallity," of Don Quixote's reading. To read a book in tradition means to be changed by this book and live in its reality in a curious way. Living is the only privileged interpretation. The aim of the book is to mold the world. The idea of the author as the best reader of his own works cannot be understood if another classical axiom is not made explicit—the axiom clearly expressed in Flaubert's dictum *Madame Bovary—c'est moi.* The author is the ideal reader as far as he is a protagonist in his own work and as far he is produced by it. Cervantes himself is the author of his protagonist in two different ways. In the prologue to the second part he polemically defends his rights over the character, proving that Cervantes himself is the author of **Don Quixote** and that he has written it. But Cervantes is an author of **Don Quixote** in another, often unnoticed way as well. His **Galatea** happens to be among the books that the barber and the priest find in the bookcase of the knight-errant. Cervantes simultaneously constructs and constitutes his protagonist. Reality is only a narrow slit between two books.

There is no boundary between world and book for Don Quixote. The visibility of this boundary (visible to us) is an optical illusion, caused by the spellbinding nonreading.

The tragic, the comic, and the inadequate in Don Quixote's behavior in the first part of the book are a direct consequence of the fact that the rest of the characters have not read enough chivalrous romances.

In his famous essay **Don Quixote and the Problem of Reality,** Menard poses the fundamental question: *How* *is possible that Don Quixote's intimate world should not be solipsistic; how is it possible that this world be inhabited by the minds of other people as well who are not just objects of Don Quixote's mind but also that they share with him, at least to a certain extent, the belief in the potential or actual reality of his world?* The answer to this question could be found in the Library, in the understanding of Don Quixote as constituted as a projected conscience. The Library is Berkley's God LTD.

In the second part the world has already entered the book: almost all characters have read the first part and though this entrance happens by way of a game and a parody, it is constituted as well. The Library motivates the behavior of all the characters. The invading world is, in fact, conquered by reading. And unlike Cervantes, Pierre Menard doesn't constitute his Don Quixote. The priest and the barber will never find one of his (Menard's) books in the bookcase of the knight-errant. Pierre Menard doesn't even write a book about its protagonist—Cervantes has already created it. Pierre Menard substitutes it.

4. Pierre Menard is the author of the Identical. He is the identifier. His ambition is to write **Don Quixote**, and what is more, he doesn't want to invent another **Don Quixote**—that would be easy—but **Don Quixote** itself. Needless to say, he has never aimed at mechanically copying the original. His extraordinary ambition is to create several pages which coincide verbatim with the ones written by Miguel de Cervantes. Pierre Menard is the ideal reader as well. Like Don Quixote, he also read **Don Quixote.** But Pierre Menard is the ideal reader in a cultural situation where reading and writing have become dead metaphors. The text cannot be written and finished; it can only be read through. My overall idea of **Don Quixote**—as Pierre Menard writes in a letter of his simplified by indifference and oblivion, can be fully identified with the vague prototype of the still unwritten book. For Pierre Menard **Don Quixote** has failed out of his reality and become merely a potentiality, become a text. As Menard points out, work and text cannot be differentiated in a purely chronological sense; an ancient text could be a text while many products of modern literature are in no ways texts. The modern cultural situation has not created the text, it has identified it. The work is conceived as the imaginary end of the text—its tail. For Pierre Menard, **Don Quixote** is a text that tries to catch its tail.

5. The microscopic smallness of handwriting, thought of metaphorically, is one of the essential characteristic features of the text and his author. *I remembered his notebook with chequered pages*—Pierre Menard wrote about Pierre Menard—*there were places crossed out in black ink, and peculiar proofreading and signs and letters, as tiny as midges.* The text intentionally tries to be invisible; the miniature letters cannot actually be read, they could only be invented and supposed. The only way to read the text is to accept the responsibility of becoming its author. Pierre Menard's **Don Quixote** is the final, the borderline of variant of a text. It is unreadable but not in the same way as the vanguard literature: Pierre Menard's text cannot be read, it is invisible for us. We are blind for it.

6. In its essay about collection **Unpacking Library** (wrongly attributed to Walter Benjamin) Pierre Menard mentions a Wutz, Jean Paul's teacher, who leafed through catalogs—not with the intention of choosing the book he would read—but the ones he would write (and a title that attracted his interest became a title of a new book he actually wrote). The substitution Wutz made was insignificant, unimportant, and invisible for the collector. Collecting in pure sense is not connected with reading. The Collector doesn't read, he acquires. The book is having, possessing, touching, it is an event. The Library has lost its constitutive beyondness. The biography of the collector has turned out utopian as is his effort to collect it and provide a history for himself.

Collecting is constituting the past; the collector experiences the present by delving into the past, providing a past. The future is completed past. If the empire of Charles the Great falls down after his death, the collector's death is what makes an empire of his biography.

7. Wutz is a reversed Pierre Menard. Collecting is the inverted face of quoting. These are the two halves of a disintegrated whole—the catalog. The Catalog is the materialized notion of authorship in Modern Times. It carries the unity of author-and-book (understood as a configuration of signs), and meaning of the book. The catalog guarantees the privileged position of the author's interpretation. Pierre Menard is invisible for the Catalog. His insane deed—his **Don Quixote**—makes the existence of the catalog senseless. As a result of Menard's insanity **Don Quixote** disappears. It can no longer be quoted, as there are no guarantees that we face Cervantes's work, and not Menard's. The author cannot prove his paternity to the work. Pierre Menard is the collector of perusals. Similar to Wutz his **Don Quixote** belongs to him; Pierre Menard makes his biography an object of an incessant reading. Pierre Menard transcends his own biography: he quotes **Don Quixote** in an invisible work and this invisible work is Pierre Menard's reading of **Don Quixote**. Quoting confronts itself. Quotation marks become impossible: their function is to set somebody else's text apart and guarantee a strictly defined meaning behind it. Pierre Menard tears this link apart—thus killing the quotation marks—this is Pierre Menard's peculiar method. The history of this quoting is a possibility for the modern cultural situation to be grasped as unique.

PS.
I think that everybody who happens to read these remnants of my seven-years-long efforts will understand the horror and despair on discovering the confounded document. Pierre Menard and Pierre Menard were identical. Therefore there were books which Pierre Menard could not write—Pierre Menard's books.

Goethe's Indigo
Alexander Kiossev, etc.

It is only modesty to prevent us from dedicating this text to J. L. B. Therefore we dedicate it to Goethe.

Last year the prestigious literary-historical magazine for German literature ***Philemon and Baucis*** carried a text whose scandalous nature went beyond the academic circles and justifiably roused the indignation of both the collaborators of Goethe Institute and the broad public, which, nevertheless, dearly treasure the classical figures of Goethe, Schiller, Eckermann, and Zeitler. Before that, as if the wave of jokes connected with the name and work of Goethe had being brought to a head by the claim of the eccentric contemporary writer that the last phrase uttered by the Weimar Hellene "Licht, mehr Licht!" had actually being wrongly overheard by those around Goethe's deathbed—in actual fact it allegedly ran like this: "Nicht mehr, nicht!" However, the excerpt **Goethe's Indigo,** whose discoverer and publisher (or perhaps author?), signed with the provocative pseudonym of Roland Macpherson, presented (and later juridically defended it by means of a chemical analysis of the composition of paper and ink) as a fragment, deliberately covered up and not included by Eckermann in his **Conversations with Goethe in the Last Years of His Life**, amounted to something more than a mere joke—it was a scandal, a flagrant mockery of the very idea of classics. The fact that contrary to his own interests and the decision of experts, in the written answers in the numerous interviews in the German press (given with the mediation of a secretary), the mysterious Macpherson dropped some broad hints to the effect that all that was only a mystification, a hypothetical structure on which modern semiotics could expand some paradoxical comments (which did not impede his winning the official case and turning the fragment's authenticity into a juridical fact) added more fuel to the scandal.

At any rate, the pose and the comments of Roland Macpherson shocked, and not only for the lack of respect for the great names in German literature, but also for the negligent manner in which he had sketched his semiotical comment, which resembled a semiotic exercise, a variation, even play rather than serious science. On top of all that, as if they showed through the prototype of **The Name of the Rose** which divested **Goethe's Indigo** from originality: just like Umberto Eco built the subject matter of his novel around the missing part of the classical European book, Aristotle's **Poetics**, Macpherson sought another such "missing" classical text—and from this point of view, the choice of the classical figure of Johann Wolfgang von Goethe and of Eckermann's **Conversations** was more than predictable.

Of course, the above is true, given that the fragment is indeed, a mystification of Macpherson—because, in any event the other alternative exists—it may well be Eckermann's text. Trying to keep up the good academic tone and scientific objectivity, we shall reproduce here the fragment itself, as well as Macpherson's comments accompanying it—and we shall leave it to readers to judge whether the text is an authentic testimony to Goethe's life, or an illustration of an abstract and play-like semiotic concept. In conclusion, we shall say again a couple of words.

Alexander Kiossev

Good old Johann Peter Eckermann wished to conceal from the eye of time a tiny fragment of his **Conversations**

with Goethe, and yet, in all probability, the eye of time preferred the opposite, because this excerpt come to my hands and I publish it for the broad world public and in front of the excited eyes of the German philistines. I prefer to pass over in silence the circumstances under which I got hold of this text; I shall only mention that it is an intricate story over the past 150 years. The text seems to have been preserved and kept in the societies of Freemasons, because in 1860 a secret Masonic writing mentioned **Goethe's Indigo** twice. Later on, the likely fate of the manuscript might be traced back to the Swiss theosophical circles—there is ground to believe that some of their esoteric interpretations would have been impossible without their being aware of Goethe's outlook concerning the indigo, expounded by him before Eckermann. A huge archive of German texts from where the fragment—again secretly—has been transferred back to Europe, was discovered in a southern American country in the sixties of our century. All that mysteriousness is rather funny—after all, there is not too much to conceal in this excerpt. Behind the motive of the pathetic Eckermann to cover it up probably stood the understanding that it was a "great key" to a classical and mystical devotion, a key that does not unlock the "doors of eternity" to the uninitiated. Actually, everyone who took the pains to read the voluminous ennui of the "German Hellene" could not but become aware that the concepts expounded by Goethe by that conversation could be easy enough reconstructed from other statements of his, with the exotic symbol of the indigo being the sole novelty. What Eckermann (and permanently great Goethe too) could not see, is that their conversation about the indigo proved a possibility for several substantial paradoxes from the sphere of the philosophy of language to be deduced. Their dedication has, of course, become possible only today when the very idea of classics has been reduced to no more than some dust, and after the works of some epoch-making names in the development of semiotics, the philosophy of language, and the theory of communications. So the genuine secret of the indigo remained invisible to both Goethe and Eckermann.

Here is the authentic text of the fragment itself.

Thursday, January 20th, 1831

I shall probably remember this day as the luckiest in my life. I heard and saw things that make me feel initiated into a sublime secret, which I shall keep till my last gasp.

I had been invited and went to see Goethe in the evening. Expecting to see cheerful company there, I saw him alone in the Urbino room, with the blinds pulled down. There were two lit candles, a bottle of Reims wine and some delicious biscuits on the table. He was scrutinizing a drawing and the concentrated noblesse his face was emanating made me feel excited. His big, beautiful hand rested calmly on a red file.

The conversation focused on my project to edit and publish Goethe's letters. He again commented on my notes, stressing that I had already learnt those tiny and insignificant, at first sight, fragments and notes according to their genuine value, like pieces of an internally complete life.

"Once, many years ago, I burnt all the letters that I had received since 1772 by that time—Goethe said—now I don't think I did the right thing. You know, I ordered that my letters and even the tiniest note I wrote be copied, and usually I give the rough copies to be clipped together—in this way they start bearing the completeness of a spontaneous book. And what else is life, but a book! And the deeper and more versatile is life, the better each of its details enters the thorough composition of this invisible work. Genuine life requires a talent, similar to that of the creator of a great work."

Our conversation switched to the passion for collecting and preserving various, and at first sight, insignificant relics of the past. Goethe mentioned his collection of minerals, handwritings, busts, and drawings, saying that they had brought him big worries, though he could neither give them up nor deny his ambition to collect the traces of every experience and instant. Then he fixed his eyes on the flame of the candles and for a while he was deep in thought. The drawing he was scrutinizing was on the table in front of him. He held it against the light and gave it to me.

"Is this plant familiar to you?" Goethe asked me. I answered in the negative—looking at me from the drawing was a medium-sized bush with its twigs and leaves slightly resembling those of the acacia tree, but having deep pink petals.

"Actually, you could hardly know it"—Goethe smiled—"Although some time ago I gave you the Bashkirian bow, and your knowledge of the ash-, maple-, nut-tree varieties and the processing of their wood amazed me. This is an indigo plant. It grows only in India, China, and Ceylon. I heard attempts are being made of late to grow it in America, too."

"Is the dye produced from this bush?" I asked. Goethe nodded pensively.

"Yes, that's right. Although that is by far the most interesting thing about it."

He rose and started walking about the room, while I remained seated the way he liked it.

"Young man, today I shall impart to you a profound idea, because, following your own way, you have proved worthy of and ripe to know it. In this plant I discovered a genuine symbol, a symbol in which the majestic simplicity of the ever-changing, divine nature and the predestination of the human spirit are equally well shown. I wonder why the ancient people felt reverences for the mandragora; in my view the indigo is a much more mysterious and sublime plant. It was already familiar to people in Babylon, in Egypt, in ancient Judah.

As early as 2000 years ago the part of the Talmud called the **Mishna Book** mentioned of a ban of the destruction of the indigo bush until it is three years old.

And the Arabs made an attempt to grow it in the warm parts of Western Asia, because its transportation from India made it too expensive. It is the best and the fastest blue dye ever. Despite Marco Polo's information, its production was not familiar in Europe, and it was brought to the continent only after the sea route to India became possible. You know, in the seventeenth century the indigo was under a ban in Germany, because in all probability it displaced the local plant-based dyes and farmers protested. But it is likely that the law against it is also connected with its mysterious qualities, with the fact that some witches and sorcerers used it as a cure and the people called it *Teufelfarbe*. However, I shall be hardly able to tell you everything today—the indigo is one of the symbols we usually call universal—and for years now I have been studying it in my literary and scientific works. When, dear Eckermann, you take to the compendium of my **Teaching on Colors** as you have promised me, I shall tell you of the connection I see between the basic color regularities in nature and the change in the indigo colors (from the pale yellow juice of the just-picked plant; through the deep yellow infusion which, when exposed to air, gradually turns dark green; to the dark blue indigo powder, which, to become a dye, should have passed through the "indigo white," while when heated it releases copper-red crystals). And at the moment I am occupied with the life of the indigo plant in connections with my **Metamorphosis of Plants**, which has already greatly grown in volume. I'll be telling you of this another time. I would now like to tell you of something more important."

Goethe took the red file and opened it. Contrary to my anticipations that there would be another drawing or engraving there, from the file he took a strange, dark blue sheet and handed it to me. One side of the sheet was matte, but the other one had had a glistening dark blue layer which stained my finger a little. After I had examined it, Goethe took it back and placed it between two blank, clean sheet of paper. Then he wrote on the upper sheet: *Salve,*

Eckermann, sub specie aeternitatis! When he separated the sheets I saw the Latin inscription printed on the lower sheet: with a single movement of the hand he had created two inscriptions.

"Perhaps in this you can see no more than an ordinary copying" Goethe said and again smiled rather inscrutably at that "but it is something much, much more. One should penetrate into the symbolical meaning of this doubling, it takes a long time and requires great concentration. It took me fully thirty years to get to the bottom of this phenomenon. The symbol has many layers and I shall reveal them to you one by one.

We are on Earth to learn to turn the transient into eternal. But it is only one who is able to really appreciate both—the transient and the intransient things, the instant and eternity, to attain this. One of the most substantial human concerns, particularly so of the one who has taken to literary work, is the preservation and conservation of literary monuments. What pitiful remnants of the great works of Aeschylus and Euripides, of Plautus, and of my favorite, Menander, have come to the present day! The written works are the fruit of a transitory and fragile experience, although people have resorted to various means to preserve and conserve them. Some people wonder at my passion for collecting all kinds of most diverse and insignificant texts, at my writing even the most trivial notes and rough copies, which I later preserve. But I have nearly physical perception of the disintegration of paper, of the way bad people falsify what has already been said or written. In this respect the sheet of the indigo paper[1] is a miraculous object: doubling what has been written, it preserves and conserves it in a peculiar way. If one of the texts happen to disappear, the other one will remain; if someone else's insertion has been added to one of them, the second one will certify the truth; if part of one of them and part of the second are destroyed, placing them one on the other will probably save the better part of the work itself. You may well say however, that both copies may be as equally and fully destroyed as only one of them, consequently the indigo should preserve nothing and shall conserve nothing. The magic key is just in this, young man."

Goethe sat and looked in a friendly way at me.

"Truly, the indigo creates the *symbol* of preservation of what has been written along with the very process of writing rather, than preserves what has been written. You send a note to someone, carelessly written in pencil, inviting him to have a glass of wine with you this evening. The note is connected with the empiricism of the situation and as if it should be fully confined to it to disappear with it; the indigo, however, reproduces another copy of the note, completely useless with regard to empirical circumstances. Through it you don't invite your friend to visit you, you send your word to another time, to future people; in a nutshell—you send it directly to eternity. To think of the future, or of the eternity when you are doing something concrete, is the worst kind of vanity—and here again, the indigo relieves us of it. It helps us fully dedicate ourselves to the instant, to really appreciate the present and commit ourselves to it; and besides, it directly clips a copy of our thoughts and words, without our being aware of it, together with the certificate of eternity. The instant is invisibly doubled and preserved; in this way the indigo teaches us that every state, even the instant, are extremely precious because they are representatives of entire eternity! You know me to be the most spontaneous man who, just like a child, is capable of living with the instant, of dedicating, with passion and to the full, to the new feeling. Along with this, however, I am a citizen of millennia and statues seem to me ridiculously transient: I cannot imagine a monument in tribute to any worthy man before I have seen it knocked down and battered and the stone eaten up with erosion. For me the symbol of the indigo has proved to be the miraculous bridge which spand the transient with eternity—it seems to me, I am living as if doubled by the indigo, that I am writing my life not only in the concrete circumstances of our century and of our poor Germany, but directly on the golden sheet of Time!"

Enraptured with what he was saying I was breathless. On his last words, his verses whose meaning I could grasp only now, suddenly came to my mind:

> Die Zeit ist mein Besitz,
> Mein Acker ist die Zeit!

Goethe drew his big face closer to the candle and the multitude of wrinkles stood out more prominently.

"The indigo has also another symbolic meaning which I call "collective." Because no matter what we present us to be, all of us are collective beings. How little we possess of what we can refer to, in the purest sense of the word, as our property!

Writing is born of the instant, by some concrete, transitory experience. However, the instant itself is collective. The instant is the public! Every expression of our subjectivity (on which romanticists have been wasting their words) is intended for the eyes of the public, the posterity which expects no accidental or too odd confessions from us, but a revelation of the universal human nature. You, I suppose, remember that I have written about Winckelmann's letters to Berendis . . . "

Goethe rose, and from a regales by the wall he took in his hand the volume of **Winckelmann and His Century**, turned over its pages, found the passage he was looking for and read it out:

"Letters should be regarded as one of the major documents an individual leaves behind. People of lively imagination, even when talking with themselves imagine at times, as though an absent friend is by their side, a friend to whom they are imparting their inmost thoughts. Likewise, the letter is a kind of conversation with oneself, because the friend to whom we are writing is often the occasion rather than the subject of the letter. Everything that pleases or injures us, that depresses or occupies us comes from the bottom of our hearts, and similar letters—the lasting traces of an experience, of a state, are the more important for posterity, the stronger the writer is possessed by the moment and the less he thinks of the future."

He closed the book and looked at me, a serene, noble fire in his deep-set eyes.

"You see—herein I have tried to express this contradictory interweaving of loneliness and transience on the one hand, and the collective and eternity on the other, which are both present in the act of writing. And it is again the symbol of the indigo to express in the best way this contradictory knot. Writing is imparting to a close friend, and yet, the indigo leaves a copy of the writing in the primary loneliness of the writer, thus lending a character not of any concrete, but of universal imparting, to it—not to the concrete friend who will destroy what has been written, but to posterity, to other people, to the whole of mankind.

Therefore, the one who uses indigo while writing needs, it goes without saying, a self-imposed, noble discipline. The indigo takes him away from the instant and loneliness and sends him to eternity and mankind—therefore, he should rid himself of everything accidental, of everything which is too peculiar and individual within him. The writer is to render everything private within and around him, general and universal. If the one using indigo while writing is negligent and allows mistakes to slip in, the latter starts looking deliberate, they grow into a stylization of mistakes and negligence and lose their chaotic nature. Therefore, while writing, he should be very careful not to make any mistakes or display any negligence—doubled by the indigo it might, in a sinister way, present itself as something universal and try to place itself among the universal symbols of mankind.

It is exactly for this reason that the indigo is used in recording only what is worthwhile, to have it preserved for eternity, and the writer himself feels evaluated and in high spirit, divested from the empirical within him. Only noble, vehement, and sound thoughts cross his mind; the eternity the indigo is emanating penetrates his instants as a serene, calm, and divine exuberance. The spirit of the indigo rejects everything which is weak, feeble, ailing or too subjective: it is an objective classical spirit, contrary to today's romantic vogues. If you have indeed grasped the spirit and the symbol of the indigo, you will become aware that writing with it bears something divine: on the sheet of eternity the writer's hand again records universal and eternal values, divinity has embraced the writing man as a noble receptacle, it has allowed him to achieve the otherwise inaccessible universality and objectivity.

And there is something else to it . . . "

Goethe was again standing and walking about the room. Listening to him speak in this way an enormous and unknown joy filled me, but along with it, I felt somewhat nervous. It seemed he considered the question of the indigo so important, and he had taken it so to heart that he got excited to a measure which rarely happened, when bearing in mind his enormous placidity.

"The documents, young man, the documents the magic blue, sheet leave behind, are the documents of your own life on which you can look back again in order to attain the greatest grandeur and heroism—to be always who you are, to preserve who you are. Napoleon's particular grandeur was actually this—all the time, before battles and after them, after victories and defeats, **he was always one and the same.** Through the documents left by the indigo, a man who lacks the life talent of Napoleon—this compendium of the world!—can make an attempt to discover himself, the internal low of his development, it stages and epochs, the identical, invariable entelechea (or monad as Leibniz calls it). The documents of his own life left by the indigo provide him a sublime, divine possibility—he can *objectively* look at himself, trace back the composition of his life book, get in touch with the mysterious—for him—principle of his own unity!"

Goethe turned to me, his eyes burning.

"Having perceived this classical, balancing role of the indigo, I got ready to understand one more thing. Indigo is not only the blue sheet of paper. I watched pictures and engravings on subjects of my verses and poems, I admired the marvellous Delacroix, who, in his illustrations of my "Faust" had gone beyond my own ideas, I had printed myself on the indigo of someone else's art. I had many enemies and adversaries and no less friends and people who really understood what I was doing. The literature of Germany, and I think of Europe as well, had become unthinkable without me—the signs my hand left had been engraved and printed in an invisible wealth we call culture.

However, I got really excited on perceiving that the dearest creatures that surround me are also a metamorphosis of the indigo. My beloved women, the friends, the spiritual companions... Lilly Schönemann... we are used to calling our beloved "mirror of our soul," but this comparison conveys almost nothing! And how could the transient mirror reflection, which cannot but be connected with illusion and vanity, with the altering play of light, with the limited *hic at nunc,* be compared to the perception of eternity the magic sheet emanates, the sensation that we are printing, engraving, encrusting ourselves in someone else! Lilly... this angelic indigo!... "

Goethe stood silent with his back to me. Then his deep voice came to me:

"Yet, no one of the beloved women for whom I have felt genuine infatuation can be compared to a great indigo I had the luck to possess. If you could only imagine, Eckermann, the way his noble soul accepted and turned into objective, eternal form every incidental flicker of my thoughts and feelings! I also mirrored and copied him; through me, he also shed the accidental within himself and the restrictions inherent of his talent. If it were not for me, he would have not created. **Wilhelm Tell** and **Wallenstein** so cleansed and great. How I loved his letters! In them I discovered the imprints of my soul, I came to know myself through an objectivity which was God's gift. I remembered some passages of these letters to this very day—and to this very day they are for me the noblest and genuine self-cognition... Listen: 'For a long time, and always with amazement, I have been following the development of Your spirit, though from considerable distance, to discover the path you had been predestined to follow. You are seeking the necessary in nature, but seeking it, you choose the most difficult way, which every mediocre talent would have evaded. To shed light on the single phenomenon, you have, indeed, spread to the entire nature. In the integrity of his forms of manifestation you discover the basis for explanation of the individual. From the materials of the entire universe you are rising, step-by-step, from the simple organism to the more developed, to build, at long last the most complex of all—man. A great and valiant idea indeed, showing well enough the way your spirit maintains the rich entity of human ideas in a beautiful unity. Everything that analysis has been painstakingly seeking, is in your intuition... This is how I approximately assess the development of your spirit and it is you to judge whether I have been right...'

Whether he had been right... Eckermann, he was more than right—like a great indigo he showed the path of my own mission, he was discovering the divine imprint in me of which I had only vague premonitions! He was seeking the eternal in me in a way which had been inaccessible to me.

You know, Eckermann, I have to confess something to you. When I invited you to edit my manuscripts and take care of my books, I also thought of something else. To put in order my archives was, of course, extremely necessary. But I had something else on my mind—the wish to be followed daily, at any time and moment, by the eyes of an intelligent and dedicated young man. I shall imprint myself on the indigo of his admiration. But this is not exactly what attracts me, it is not that superfluous vanity that appeals to me. These eyes will lend the noble discipline I need and without which I have the feeling I am dissipating my efforts in an insipid empiricism to my life. It was he who taught me this—that another one, a loving and intelligent man is needed, a man who through himself, through his attention and love, would judge me for the accidental within me, extract and constantly imprint my general form on himself, so that I may have it for myself—have it constantly before my eyes as a noble example. You are my indigo, Eckermann!..."

Goethe stopped with emotion and instantly turned to the window. When he again turned his face to me his eyes were again serenely calm and kind.

"This evening I would tell you one more thing concerning our indigo, the mysterious *Indigoferia tinctoria* and the divine sheets produced from it.

Perhaps their deepest and most symbolical essence is the simple fact of repetition. The indigo *repeats,* it repeats what cannot repeat itself—the passing time. It has thus proved to be the missing bridge between the realm of freedom, the human realm, and the realm of the divine nature, in which there is nothing new, in which everything repeats itself in one, two, thousands of dimensions and be nevertheless one and the same. There is nothing in the world to have existed only once, because everything contains in itself the general, the thing that repeats itself. And the thing that repeats itself is perfect. Those great prephenomena which prepare and sanction any deviation through an internal law, are nature's indigo before which we hold our breath."

I do not remember exactly how I got home that evening.

Friday, January 21st, 1831

Yesterday was one of the happiest days in my life; today is the most wretched. Never before have I been closer to desperation and only my Christian faith in providence and the faith that every human being, modest and insignificant as he may be, has his place on earth, stopped me from doing the fatal thing.

This morning I sat at the writing desk in high spirits. I took the indigo sheet Goethe had presented to me out of the red file and held it with reverence for an instant as if it were the philosopher's stone. Then I took some blank, white paper and placed the indigo between two sheets. I prepared to write. Although it was January, mild light was penetrating my humble lodging through the windows, as if the countless invisible eyes of nature were serenely and gently observing me. I had decided to make a clean copy of a poem of mine, the idea of which had been born on the anxious night when, having learnt of the sudden death of Goethe's son, I was traveling from Gotha to Weimar and the moon had come out of the thick clouds for a few seconds; the poem was about the waft of befriending and unruffled calm, woven into the moonlight, with which Goethe had later welcomed me without uttering a single syllable about his deceased son.

My writing went smoothly, one line coming after the other. I stopped for a moment only when the initial arrangement of the motif or the atmosphere needed some more objectivity. Having finished it, I had the feeling that at last I have created something really significant, which might even match some of Goethe's poems. While writing I was deep in thought and fully oblivious of the indigo, but now that I again remembered it, I was seized with the previous agitation. I unfolded the sheets with trembling hands and looked at the lower sheet—where I was supposed to see the same text written in the signs of eternity.

It was blank!

Its clean, virgin surface emanated a kind of soft and antique radiance and unattainability, as if no writings ever created by man could touch it.

For a few seconds I stared at it unbelieving, then tears streamed from my eyes and my head sank in despair. With the first wave of my pain over, I came to know what had happened. I had reversed the indigo. Now, on the reversed side of the upper sheet there was a kind of incomprehensible interlacing of nonexisting signs, diabolical scrawls, with no trace left on the second one.

The vehemence of this omen overwhelmed me. God was giving me a sign that only the chosen writing hands could get in touch with the calm sheet of millennia, that God's finger wrote only through the pen of the man of genius and only through it, do pre-phenomena and universal living forms glimmer forth in the ordinary motives taken from an empirical life. While the presumptuous writes only incomprehensible scrawls on himself, a demoniac nail is scrawling, like a mirror gleam opposite his pen, distorting and turning incomprehensible his signs as a symbol of vanity and self-destruction. And the radiant white paper of eternity remains for ever untouched by the dilettante's hands.

Several hours of despair and pain passed in which I slowly came to know how heavy the burden of the indigo symbol for the uninitiated was. At dusk I had already decided not to include the notes of today and yesterday in my future **Conversations...**"

Peter Johann Eckermann
January 21st, 1831.

It is irony of fate that after its 150 years wandering, Eckermann's problematic fragment fell into mine and not someone else's hands. Honestly speaking I have never been able to read a text by Goethe to the end, while in his "Olympian" pose I have always seen a kind of histrionics: I share the irony of Walter Benjamin, who in his well known fragment on **Kinship by Choice** mocks at Goethe for his "self-cult" and for his passion to collect rubbish from his own life.

The very text Eckermann tried to cover up seems to me to be rather pompous, so that at point I wondered whether Eckermann himself had not invented the whole story and then covered it up rather unskillfully—so that it may one day fall into the hands of "posterity" . . . It seems to me that there are some style differences (though difficult to grasp) between the fragment in question and the prevailing tone of the narrative in the **Conversations with Goethe**—particularly so when Eckermann describes the second day of his adventures with the indigo. But even if the case with the indigo had been invented, this can hardly be of any importance—I wonder whether more of our images of Goethe haven't actually been invented by Eckermann—by the filter of his pathetic **Conversations**?

It is said that a comment accompanying a discovered and just published classical fragment doesn't do to contain any assessments, as reserved as they may be, much less to express any personal preferences, or to manipulate, in an interpretative way, the text just unearthed from the ancient remnants. In one way or another I have already taken liberties to make some assessments, so I shall take the risk to go further (I shall take even the risk of my comments being denounced with indignation by the idyllic taste of the editors from the German literary-historical magazines[2]).

The awareness of being a contemporary makes me get irritated with almost everything in that text. Everything around Goethe and Eckermann is always "serene," "calm," "bright," "full of friendliness and innate noblesse," of "sublime simplicity," "sincerity," and "kindness." Every line of the fragment (as well as of Eckermann's **Conversations with Goethe**) is meant to suggest that everything in their daily routine is "classical," that they are two Hellenes who only accidentally landed in the Weimar situation. Goethe looks through the window, Goethe drinks a glass of wine, Goethe buttons his trousers—all that is intended to show through: a kind of mixture of spontaneity and such an unruffled internal dignity, as if at that moment at least fifteen generations were contemplating the "divine body" and the "immortal spirit" of that "perfect man." But our contemporary cannot but start suspecting that the metaphoric order of the "serene," "calm," "classical" and so on and so forth, amounts to no more than an iron-governing discourse which does not only set Goethe and Eckermann the norm and filter of writing ("missing" thus all not too classical details of their life[3]), but does something more essential—it really governs and sets the form and the range of values of their spiritual world, making it freeze into pious, worthy, and ... prescribed forms.

The present reality (the world we live in) is an ambiguous reversion of all similar "Goethean" values: the "indigo-doubled life" already seems to us a monstrous idea, which lends an absurd museum shade to the most elementary, free, and chaotic actions. Goethe pathetically claims that at the root, all of us are "collective beings," that "the instant is a representative of the eternity," and for this reason one should write objectively, with the writer ridding himself of everything which is, more or less peculiar and subjective, and letting the universal and the general flash forth. Nowadays, in the time when everything entered in the "Zeitalter der technischen Reproduzierbarkeit" (Walter Benjamin), the universal and the general are totalitarian and postindustrial facts: their name is the printed and multiplied human anonymity, the dispensable people of no "peculiar fate" and "ohne Eigenschaften" at all; according to Adorno, the claim that the individual is still autonomous (that he can still rise with his impulses and feelings to the Fate), that he still can do something spontaneously, is nothing else but an ideology: every "individual" is born out of a perfect repetition (which cannot be attained by an indigo sheet, magical as it can be) and has become "more general," than Goethe could ever dream of.

Goethe's meditations about the "noble discipline" induced by the indigo are most amusing of all. A long way prior to Freud, Goethe's super-indigo has turned into a exteriorized super-(ind)Ego whose philistine eyes monitored whether every thought was "worthy enough," so that only "noble, strong, sound thoughts" may occur to people.

Generally speaking, listening to the classical succession of indigo metaphors, other words, so specific of the twentieth century, which oddly enough, duplicate the "Goethean"—Dossier, Censorship, Receipt, Museum, Pose, Mass media, Order, Power... occur to the contemporary.

But I've already gone too far, even for a "nonclassical" comment. As a matter of fact, my initial idea for which I took to the publication of Eckermann's fragment was to try to translate the indigo situation into a contemporary semiotic language. I shall not conceal the fact that I take some pleasure in this. It could be said that Goethe's concepts of the symbolic value of the indigo are a Saussurian construction. Indigo's doubled life establishes a sign relation between the instant and eternity (after all, "everything visible is only a symbol"); every empirical fact grows to a signifier of something signified, accessible to the "great time." We could differentiate between "Goethe"—the signifier, and /Goethe/—the signified. The accidental in classical man has proved to be in a signifying connection with the substantial in him. On the other hand, the accidental and the substantial, the instant and eternity are as inseparable as the two sides of the sheet through which Saussure compares the indivisibility of the signifier and signified. Besides, there are other analogies which delight the eye—the concrete instants attain their significance in their linear correlation in biographical time, which can be referred to as a life integrity, life work: just in the same way the Saussurean signifiers are stretched, they are realized in linear time along with this, they form a structured entity of a message. The peculiarity of this message is realized on the basis of universal laws which normatively govern the system of language; just in the same way the peculiarity of an individual human destiny is invisibly governed by the perfection of Goethe's "eternal repetitions" and "universal, general laws." Nature and the language system are in the same conformity as the individual life and the individual message: therefore human life is a message against the background of eternity—if it occurs to us to contaminate Goethe and Saussure. In Saussure the signifier-signified relation is arbitrary and yet is invariable owing to its sociohistorical existence; it governs not only the individual who cannot alter it but the collective as well.

In Goethe an instant is a motivated signifier of the eternity only in terms of incognizable, divine will which is cast in complete human destinies. In this sense, from a human point of view, the instant-symbol should be regarded as arbitrary, nonmotivated. But it also involves a supraindividual and supracollective "classical" norm because it is necessarily "worthily" and "sensibly" lived through; and it is this internal invariability of its form (this public validity of the instant), that enables it to perform its sign function.

All similar analogies show not only that the classical idea of the indigo contains a more or less implicit semiotics of Saussurean type, as well as the opposite—that there is something "Goethean" in Saussure's ideas.

What happened with Eckermann on January 21st, 1831 can be described only from the viewpoint of entirely nonclassical semiotics.

The mirror indigo imprint on the reverse side of the sheet (the diabolical scrawls which Eckermann refers to in horror), cannot be described as a signifier-signified relation; the signifier does not "shine through," it does not turn into semantic clarity. As a whole, the sign is not transparent and does not involve automatic comprehensibility. Along with this, the reversal imprint is not arbitrary—on the contrary, its essential form is in motivation. Every point and stroke of the scrawls is a mirror reproduction of the characteristics of the "signifiers" and are in an iron-strong dependence and motivation by the right layer of the sheet.

Naturally, to go ahead with the game, we must necessarily stress that the signifier-signified relation, in the case in point, has been substituted for the signifier-signifier relation—provided we assume that in a space which is mirror-reversed with regard to Eckermann's, a diabolical hand is also writing down signifiers with Eckermann's writings being the signified, but they are, for their part, also signifiers whose signified are the reversed indigo (diabolical?) traces and so on and so forth to *ad infinitum.* The classical Goethean-Saussurean sign is an image (an acoustic image of an instant, a concrete life situation), which transcend into a concept. The nonclassical Eckermann's sign is absurdly self-concentrated; the signifying function cannot leave the sign's own hermetic micro space; it is incessantly "shuttling" between the written traces and their indigo reflections.

So that, to our joy, writing with reversed indigo has not turned out to be a symbolical image of the "eternal repetitions" as universal law: or rather the opposite—the very act of writing in itself give rise to a primary differentiation. Every sign is, at the very moment of its birth, doubled with its diabolic Otherness which reduces it to an anti-sign and to the evil will of pure Chance. In comparison to Derrida's *differance,* the reversed indigo is rather a sinister variant of differentiation. It doesn't open the space (the necessary Derridian "espacement," "spacing and temporalizing"!) for an endless play of *"les grammes"*—the infinite chain of traces, of "presence of the absences," the structurally controlled transformations and the richness of this "bottomless chess-board"—language-world-textuallity. The hermetic and obsessive microspace between sign and its reversed indigo double is rather a closure: an annihilation of every *"espacement";* it is not the "absence" as "trace of the Other" in every presence, but rather the absence in a form of absolute, evil, destructive, and mocking Nothingness, which—without any "deferment"—annihilates every will to signify. The reversed indigo is a Supplement which is Death itself.

In this sense, writing with reversed indigo turns out to be, unexpectedly, a universal law again—but a very strange one. Death is a low to which one should obey only once: a universal rule which bears no repetitions.[4]

Was this the reason for Eckermann to cover up the indigo fragment? Was he frightened by the thought that **every single text,** even the most "classical" one, could be rewritten on the reversed, sinister blue sheet in order to inscribe Death in its every single signifying monad? And that

"everything visible" could reveal itself as a dark, dying side of a symbol?

By the way, is this so bad an idea? Why not do that deliberately—to re-read the whole classical universe of texts and men through the reversed indigo sheet.

And I find it the best thing to do, to start with Johann Wolfgang von Goethe and his prophet.

Roland Macpherson
Weimar, January 21st, 1988

In the beginning we mentioned that this translation of the ***Philemon and Baucis*** magazine aims to inform Bulgarian readers of a much talked literary scandal, and that in the superficial notes which accompany Eckermann's texts and Macpherson's comments, we will do our best to keep the academic tone and the scientific objectivity intact. However, the reader has already become aware of the redundant provocativeness contained in both the claim and the very pose of Macpherson, and that they somehow urge a going out of academic goodwill atmosphere and induce the response irony. As a whole, "anti-classical" gesticulations before a broad public were known as early as the time of Marinetti and Dada for their flippancy and the lack of sufficient self-reflection. The first question to be put to Macpherson (or pseudo-Macpherson) is, whether, when he wrote his comments, he had not, nonetheless, accidentally placed an indigo between the sheets of his typewriter? Doesn't he, when personally writing his "nonclassical" works, all the same, keep a copy for his own archives? We could express the fear that similar "nonclassical" authors have become a frequent phenomenon—authors, demonstrating in a rather scandalous and noisy manner, innovations in the public space and sharing, otherwise, the quite "classical" everyday life of all writers: a well-arranged indexcase, well arranged (and why not clipped together?) manuscripts, quite a "museum" attitude to every line which has been created by their hands (The "personal computer case" makes things even worse—the "indigo function" being automatized). Generally speaking, parasitizing on classical habits, classical forms of producing texts, classical institutions (what else a German literary-historical magazine could be?) is an apparent precondition for similar "nonclassical" demonstrations and had people like Macpherson boasted a little more self-reflection, they could not but perceive this.

In 1909 Marinetti, too, wanted to set fire to the libraries and let the waters of the Tiber in the museums, but the fact that all the same we know of this, is due to the "preserved" museums and libraries. So that with good reason, Macpherson is right in being grateful for the tolerance displayed by the editors of the **Philemon and Baucis** magazine—but his mistake consists in his failure to perceive the cultural meaning of this tolerance.

The lack of self-reflection is connected with another, still more apparent and irritating "characteristic" of his comment—the negligence with which they have been written, in terms of both style and intellectual construction. We could ask ourselves whether the rush and the negligence with which they were written is not actually typical for similar postmodernist texts; as a semiotics claimed, as if what counts more today is to be eccentric and not truthful, thorough, or perfect. Because how could we otherwise explain the not-too-good-a-taste in the stylistic combination of Macpherson's comments—between the destructive pathos with which he denounces all those "discourses of power," the totalitarian and the posttotalitarian multiplied anonymity of man, and the ironic and provocative, purely play-like "semiotic" end of his notes?

Naturally, there is no denying that Macpherson has got some ideas, and yet he somehow fails to develop them to the full, to make use of an idea's own possibilities, so that the wish occurs to his reader to "write them to the end." With good reason, the reader anticipates some indigo variation on the famous **Licht, mehr Licht!**, but Macpherson obviously did not take the pains to elaborate well his own play-like construction. Why, for instance, while reasoning about the fact that in the classical consciousness of Goethe and Eckermann life is always referred to as biographical time taken in its wholeness, and referring to Death as the indigo's *ultima ratio,* he missed the marvelous opportunities to play with some of the most famous of Goethe's verses? *Verweile doch, du bist so schön . . .* wouldn't it be an excellent idea to interpret the indigo as the very essence of the "Faustian man" of the contemporary epoch? Or to use some of Goethe's maxims like **He who can connect the end of his life with the beginning is the luckiest man of earth.**" A critic, more diligent than Macpherson, could have naturally associated such maxims with "classical" examples as well—with the assertion of the ancient that a lucky life is one which is crowned with lucky death or with the following remarkable thought of Goethe himself: **On the scaffold Madame Roland wish to be given paper and something to write with, to write down the peculiar thoughts which hounted her in her death hour. It is a pity that she was refused this, because at the end of life a reconciled spirit is dominated by thoughts, otherwise impermissible. They are blissful demons which sit in radiance on the peaks of the past.**"

The indigo—a blissful demon sitting in radiance on the peaks of the past! What potential associations, what semiotic and philosophical variations Macpherson missed! Elaborating this dimension of the indigo symbol, he could also rid himself from the annoying and airy ironic-apocalyptic tone of his last remarks—because the indigo teaches us that Death, the connection of the Beginning with the End, could be also Bliss and Happiness and not only a mocking nothingness caused by the fact that 150 years ago somebody had occasionally reversed a sheet of carbon paper.

However, herein we have no intention of finishing what Macpherson was to do. His negligence is not at all accidental, it results from the statute of writing in his text. It is careless in its very essence—it lacks exactly that "self-imposed noble discipline," Goethe was speaking about. Such strategy of writing runs counter to the classical precision of elaboration—a self-conscious procedure of getting rid of all the random and chaotic elements, of attaining such kind of complexity and harmony, necessity and completeness which could transform the text into a Work. The essence of this classical procedure is, of course, the ***repetition*** again; the self-mirroring into a universal, perfect form. And here we are able to transform a little the remarkable words Goethe said to Eckermann and add "***Only*** things that repeat themselves are perfect"—only texts which have interiorized the "noble discipline" of the indigo could become ***good*** texts. And the bad text of Macpherson is just another proof for that. Maybe he didn't forget to put an indigo sheet in his typewriter—but, metaphorically speaking, he was negligent enough to reverse it.

Because—and this is valid for the poor, unfortunate Eckermann as well—the reversal of the indigo is the figure of the Negligence itself, which imprints itself as a quality of a text.

As for Macpherson's attitude to Goethe, it borders on hooliganism. The reference made here is not only to direct disrespectful qualifications which he is not sparing, but also to the unsubstantiated, drastic substitution of the metaphoric paradigm of classical thinking for its ironic duplicate. The epoch of Goethe and Eckermann is not studied in terms of its specifics and differences from the present day (of its "otherness"), while its values transfigure in a kind of monstrous ghost of theirs. Manipulated like this, noblesse turns, naturally, into a pose; mankind—into a printed and multiplied crowd of anonymous, manipulated beings; excitement—into a false pathos; self-restraint—into a control of a somewhat fascizoid super-ego. It is as though Macpherson does not at all assume that "sincerity," "simplicity," "serenity," and "calm" are possible to have! He aggressively claims that there are quite different cultural preconditions in the present epoch, that the contemporary man lives with another "existential aesthetics," and for this reason he regards everything classical as ideology. However, the way the word "contemporary" is used herein, is rather frivolous. Every "contemporary" man has the fragment of his everyday routine in which he lives according to absolutely classical milestones; even the most ever multiplied being has something individual about it, and every one of us has experienced moments of serenity and calm, simplicity and sincerity even amid the social neurosis of the postindustrial society. And, as a whole, it is hardly justifiable to speak of a single and universal "existential aesthetics" of the present reality, because there are many different perceptions of reality; man nowadays lives in a pluralism of many similar kinds of "aesthetics," and the latter are very frequently dated to various periods of their historical origin and have different values.

And yet the crucial negligence and lack of criticism in Macpherson's comments is neither in the impure stylistics, nor in the missed intellectual opportunities. They are not in the reversal of values and metaphors of the classical thinking either. The way in which he slides over the question of authorship and authenticity of this particular fragment by Eckermann (?), is so inadvertent that we may well suspect him of some forethoughts.

Being the discoverer of the fragment Macpherson **must** ask himself, for a very good reason, certain questions which, he, for some inexplicable reasons, doesn't do. Given, that this is indeed a conversation written down by Eckermann, why doesn't Goethe meditate on the indigo in other places of his voluminous creative work? Goethe's huge literary heritage provides no support for his assertion that he deals with the indigo problem in a multitude of scientific and literary works. And though the fragment was invented by Eckermann—has Eckermann any motives to write against himself? If he, through himself, symbolized in general, the figure of the initiated, why then didn't he include it in **Conversations with Goethe** to lend more prestige to it, to "canonize" it as a Goethean idea which supports the contrast between the man of genius and a dilettante?

We may, as well, ask ourselves several questions which Macpherson already could hardly have any reason to do. If the fragment was invented by Macpherson, what then is the function of the mystification? Why is it, indeed—and what does a mystification in a system of semiotic ideas described by Macpherson himself mean? Given that the fragment is a mystification, how should the question of the virtuosity of mystifying (which even experts haven't managed to cope with) on a semiotic plane—how should we interpret the hint dropped by Macpherson that as a whole, Goethe himself was perhaps invented by Eckermann, by his living indigo? The copy, the secondary text, the mystification, etc. (i.e., the indigo), quite paradoxically turn out to be the "primary" text, copies engender their originals, the self-propelled indigo are the reasons for written text to emerge, the artificiality and the secondary element always transcend into a kind of "authenticity." However, isn't the reverse possible too?—if Macpherson invented this text about Eckermann, and "Goethe" stylized a way of writing different from his own, both Goethe and Eckermann are "alive" in him—they are authentic alternatives of the pluralistic discourse Macpherson himself is capable of producing; and from this point of view, Macpherson turns out to be no more than the indigo imprints of a multitude of similar authentic voices, while his own authenticity assumes problematic metadimensions. The truth about authorship in similar questions resembles, ever more, a strange play between interwoven texts and discourses, in which the sheet turns indiscernible from the indigo and the indigo—from the "antique white," untouched paper.

We could go on with the questions.

What, exactly, should the strange pseudonym "Roland Macpherson" mean? The meaning, which is clear enough at first sight—that "Macpherson" is a hint of the famous mystification with **Ossian's Songs** (an in this sense it is an apparent signal that the fragment is not authentic), while "Roland" is the real first name of a famous contemporary semiotician—this obvious meaning does not suffice. Because the name "Roland" corresponds with, the not mentioned by Macpherson but otherwise well known, Madame Roland (of whom Goethe, as already mentioned, also speaks), who wishes to double, by means of the indigo scaffold *Sein zum Tode* itself. However, the names "Macpherson," "Ossian," and "Goethe" are, apart from this, in another peculiar relation. As is known **Die Leiden des jungen Werters** includes entire passages from the **Songs of Ossian**, which Goethe extols for their great natural sincerity and purity (at that time he considered them to be authentic songs by the folklore bard). The texts of these songs are an authentic part of Goethe's novel—but the very texts are Macpherson's mystification. It turns out that Macpherson came, so to say, before Goethe; the mystification is "condition of possibility" of an "authentic" work—the mystified text has engendered a whole range of text reactions, cues, and allusions which, built it in Goethe's novel in an irreversible way, turning **Werter** into a great work (which, as is well known, at the time provoked a wave of most authentic suicides) built on fraud. But this Macpherson is not the Macpherson of the eighteenth century: the contemporary Macpherson relies on Goethe's authentic works, which are not authentic, because they are built on the mystification of that Macpherson, and they are not merely mystifications, because... An interpretation of the pseudonym would lead to a paradoxical and superintricate set of contradictory assertions concerning the authenticity or nonauthenticity of Goethe's authorship (and along with it, of any possible authorship, of the authenticity of the "monuments," the "certificates," the "preservations," the "indigo copies" and... eternity.

Of course, all this is possible, given that the reader is as kind and as good intentioned to Macpherson's "nonclassical" comments as not to stop interpreting them halfway. The very interpretation, however, as we very well know, is a classical philological institution (a precise, repeating, disciplined reading, which avoids every negligence), and it would be impudence "nonclassical" authors who deny its terror to demand that it be applied to them. So that, the

best way to approach texts of the kind of Macpherson's comments, is probably to leave them to themselves. Their impudence will, anyway, fade away with time. The best attitude to them is a classical indifference.

Alexander Kiossev

Notes

1. Initially carbon paper was produced from the indigo plant and for this reason the word "indigo" in the Bulgarian language is still a metonymy of "carbon paper." In the present translation, the word indigo shall be referred as a synonym of "carbon paper."

2. With my comment already published together with Eckermann's fragment, I am left nothing else but express my gratitude for the tolerance displayed by the editors of the *Philemon and Baucis* magazine.

3. In this connection, it would be in the nature of things to recall Goethe's telling maxim "Everyone has something of his character, which, if express publicly, would provoke disapproval."

4. I am not going to introduce the reader in all the paradoxes following from the expression "a universal rule which bears no repetitions." Here just a quotation from Wittgenstein's **Pilosophical Investigations**: "199. Ist was wir" ein Regel folgen" nennen, etwas, was ein Mensch, nur einmal im Leben, tun Könnte?—Und das ist natürlich eine Anmerkung zur Grammatik des Ausdrucks "ein Regel folgen." . . . . Es kann nicht ein einziges Mal nur ein Mensch einer Regel gefolgt sein es kann nicht ein einziges mal nur eine Mitteilung gemacht, eine Befehl gegeben, oder verstanden worden sein, etc.—Einer Regel folgen, eine Mitteilung machen, einen Befehl geben, eine Schachpartie spielen sind Gepflogenheiten (Gebräuche, Institutionen)." Should we interpret Wittgenstein in a following manner—"Death is the single rule which is no institution?"

Part II

Political Aesthetics of Communism

Introduction to the Political Aesthetics of Communism
Vladislav Todorov

Everything has happened in a figurative sense
　　　　　　　　　　　　　　　Pascal

▦ Beginning

Communism created ultimately effective aesthetic structures and ultimately defective economic ones. That is what empowers its strong presence and durability in the world. That is what fortifies it.

Factories are not built to produce commodities. They produce the united-working-class-body. They are allegorical figures of industrialization. Industry represents the leading metaphor of party ideology and factories are the works of this ideology. They result in a deficit of goods, but an overproduction of symbolic meanings. Their essence is aesthetic, not economic. They are the poems of communist ideology. The work process creates just these factory poems, not commodities. Labor is a ceremony begetting the communal body of the working class. The worker labors for the sake of the factory poem, not for the sake of the market. The aim of labor in the factory is the poetic completeness of the factory itself.

Originally published in *Textual Practice* 3(1991): 363–382. Revised for this collection.

A campaign of mass social engineering took place. A definition of the social engineering could be—Power forms the people whom to represent. Party power, according to a certain ideologically justified vision, designs and materializes its own social basis. The Party imagines its constituency and proceeds with its creation. It consolidates and disciplines the historical object summoned to fulfill the party project. The Party has to provide itself with constituency holding the majority of the society which is automatically recruited to build up the Future.

The large-scale industrialization was a political action with the only goal—to produce the Party constituency. Labor was designed to (re)produce the working-class body as the social basis of the Party. Thus, Party power provided itself with historical legitimacy.

The reality of communism is poetically worked out. Society is a poetic work, which reproduces metaphors, not capital. The speech figures of party ideology are the building blocks of the mind. The key metaphors and symbols, the productive means of language, are worked out by the supreme organ of the party-politburo. It is crucial to own not the machines, but the metaphors, the means of production of symbolic meanings, but commodities. Labor forges symbols. The labor force cannot be a commodity, because it is the creator itself.

The fundamental academic field of communism lies in its political aesthetics. The political economy is a simulative one. It generates an initial appearance of an economically motivated society. Actually, it produces the symptoms of such a society, not the causes for it. The working out of metaphors and figures of speech is what generates life forms. The identity of communism reveals itself in the overproduction of words and symbols. The political economy falsifies the genuine character of communism.

The idea has become quite popular that we have lived in an actually fulfilled utopia. The common idea that communism was impending prevented us from seeing that we were actually in it. All the key metaphors of communist

utopia have turned into reality, something which will be discussed further on. We made it through fraternity, equality, the liquidation of money, the disappearance of the state, of property, of economic structures. We experienced the conjuration of communism. We attempted to build it and to live in it. We survived in it.

Utopia is a certain poetic, a certain political genre. It is just that, a genre which has its own structure and generates its own metaphors. Utopia compensates for the displeasure of the overimposed power structure by inventing a fictional perspective of life: an impossible perspective, which helps us to bear the actual order of life and to criticize it from the standpoint of another, nonactual but cherished order of life. The transformation of utopian structures into genuinely political structures creates a society based on political aesthetic and political rhetorical principles and not on economic ones. In such a society, power immediately reigns over bodies with words. It reigns over the social processes through the conjuring of language. It spellbinds.

The final objective that justifies this reality is not the legal order, but the mummy of the leader. The mummy objectivizes political power. It is the superior body. The party power finds its radical representation in the mummy. The political aesthetics of society reaches its sublime terms in the spectacle of the mummified Leader.

Political economy deals with idealized economic models; Political aesthetics with corporeality made eternal. Political aesthetics deals with mummified bodies, objects, and spaces which eternalize the strong presence of communism on earth.

At home, everyone has a measure, which he or she uses to ascertain the real dimensions in space. But somewhere out there, kept in special conditions, is the ideal measure. Its length is a convention. It is the original only by virtue of a social agreement.

Everyone has, at home, images and words of Lenin. They are signs, they are allegorical instruments, which testify to the existence of the original. The original Lenin is kept in a mausoleum and is a unique, not a conventional, body. A mummified uniqueness spellbinds the space embracing it. His images and his words, spread everywhere, is the radiation which imbues minds with communism.

The reality of the communist experiment is guaranteed by the magic reality of the body, stuck to the magic words of the primordial experimenter. Lenin is the author of communism. His immortalized body perpetually authorizes and legitimizes the Party. That is why the mummy must immediately be appropriated and registered in the party inventory.

The problem of the political aesthetics of society is far more general than the problem of communism. In a historical perspective, the merging of the political and aesthetic projects for creation of a purely novel society-poem has existed as a process even before its actual accomplishment in 1917 in Russia. One of the characteristics of modernist culture at the beginning of this century was the idea of radical liquidation of the inherited structures and the generation of a bold phantasm for the organizing of an unprecedented society.

This radical phantasm creates its own genre: the manifesto. The manifesto is the verbal radicalization of the modernist vision and immediately builds the political aesthetics of the modernist endeavor. With a closer look into the different political and aesthetic manifestos, we could reconstruct a global Modernist project for unprecedented corporal integrity of society and for the daring act of building it.

In respect to this global project, political Dadaism in Berlin and the Proletcult in Russia during the 20s have quite decisive roles. The programs and projects of these two movements present to us a decisive merger of political and aesthetic ideas, of the concepts of artistic and civil action.

The 1920s saw the birth of a powerful political art both in Russia and Germany, an art which deliberately scrapped the border between artistic and political action. This political art was subsequently repressed by "Party" art. Nazi and Bolshevik partisanship in the arts, imposed through administrative channels by Hitler in Germany and by Stalin in Russia, liquidated political art. It is symptomatic that Nazis in Germany repressed political Dadaism, whilst the same happened to the Proletcult in Russia, liquidated by Lenin. Party policy abolished political art, especially Proletarian art. This will be discussed in more detail later. For the moment I will say only that identifying the principles of political art with the principles of party art is a gross error. Of course Nazis, as well as Bolsheviks, turned into reality many of the radical metaphors and visions of Modernism, of Futurism, of Constructivism, of Political Dadaism. The political aesthetics of communism manifests the most terrorist recurrence of the modernist phantasms.

My point is that the principles of party art arrested the principles of modernist art, that is, that art in which visions and metaphors of future radical change arise. In short, totalitarianism as a kind of realization of the political aesthetics of Modernism arrested Modernist Art.

In this respect, Lenin is an interesting case. He is the man whom the Dadaists in Zurich pointed out as the greatest Dada on Earth. Political Dadaism in Berlin embraces the ideas of Lenin and gradually melts into the radical communist movement. Lenin is directly involved in the Proletarian modernization of the political ideas of that time. That same Lenin carries out the Bolshevization (read as Modernization) of life through a radical act: the Revolution. After performing it that same Lenin devised party policy as the rule of the starving Bolshevik lands. Party policy liquidated the processes of Modernization.

Lenin's mummy blocks any further modernization. In it, the political and the aesthetic merge as the ultimate party body. The mummy of Lenin is the point at which modernization is terminated and the omnipresence of the Party is imposed. This is the very point at which the idea of a political modernization of society terminates in a totalitarian mummified communism. Communism realized a radical aesthetic, noneconomic modernization of society.

Merger of the Political and the Aesthetic

Dada emerges as an international movement in Zurich in 1916, in reaction to World War I and as a reactive concerted action of radical leftist and anarchist intellectuals of different nationalities and styles who were in Zurich at that time.

Dada is a reaction against bourgeois culture. Dada modernizes the world in an insolent anti-bourgeois style. The motives of artistic action are far wider than the territory of art. Dada presents itself as a daring intervention, which will cure humanity of bourgeois dementia, such as politics, art, and morality. Dada will chase away the monsters which have crawled out on the earth's surface, such as Imperialism, Victorian morals, and prejudices, together with the chef d'oeuvres of classical art. Dada acts, it doesn't produce works of art. Dada shakes up the stiff corpse of European culture. It tramples sanctimonious bourgeois morality. It seethes in the cells of the healthy bourgeois brain. Dada blocks the logical train of thought and thus frees the human being from its importunate training in common sense.

Dada stripped tabooed organs, objects, and actions naked, introducing a new material in art which was base and depressing by bourgeois moral standards. Through blatant musculature of expression, Dada brought to the limit the unrestrained collective will to mock the bourgeois individual cocooned in his morality.

The demand for political efficiency in artistic action leads Dadaist techniques to decisive public operations and offensives which undermine the bourgeois political system, the bourgeois moral imperative, and the phantoms of bourgeois art. All of this helps adapt the project to the radical modernization of society. The will that modernizes society is syncretic in its nature. In it, the aesthetic and the political are inseparable. The chief materialization of this will are photo montage, propaganda posters, allegorical constructions, and assemblages of machinery which disturb the bourgeois order of things. Industry, art, and politics are three heads of a single body, in the throes of one and the same will to modernization.

An exhibition of Soviet avant-garde art was held in Berlin in 1922. Arriving with the exhibition, constructivist Lisitskii started publishing, along with Yerenburg, the magazine *Veshch* (Object), which introduced the West to modern art in Soviet Russia. The spirit of Constructivism, new objectivity, and new materiality promoted by *Veshch* was already popular among Berlin Dadaists. Russian constructivist Tatlin was a dominant influence on the first Dada Fair in Berlin in 1920.

Political Dadaism is infected by the ideas of Machinism and the organizational theories of the Russian Constructivists, obviously mixed with the organizational theories of the Proletcult and its ideologist Bogdanov. Constructivist are neither embellishes life nor creates works beyond it. It organizes life completely. In its aesthetics, the geometrical and the political mind coincide. Constructivism is a syncretic state of science and politics. The modernization of society is guaranteed by such mergers of science, art, and politics.

If Constructivism is called the Socialism of vision, then Dadaism could be called the Bolshevism of action. In Germany Dada is taken over by Bolshevik visions of a "laboroid" space assembled of flesh and metal, of bodies and aggregates, of scaffolds and machines, of clenched fists and chanting mouths. In Berlin, Dada organizes political attractions, mounts centaurs of bodies and machines, in order to make a show of the magic of the endless Proletarian feats of labor.

Contrary to Left Political Expressionism, Dada is remarkably sinuous. After the trampling of the revolutionary movement in Germany, some of the Expressionists retire, others commit suicide, still others sink into a deep mysticism. Dada, on the contrary, experiences exasperation. It accuses Expressionism of consecration of the sick inside of man, of whimpering over its Gothic structures. Dada has no illusions. Dada does not suffer from any prophetic spirit. Dada is a saboteur and is oriented externally, towards expansion. During these years of social shock, the ontology of the world changes for the Expressionists—which destroys them. For Dada, the only thing that changes is the direction of the Proletarian strike, and that doesn't in the least make them turn off the engines. Because the noise of the engines manifests the (idio)syncrasies of the political, industrial, and aesthetic modernization of the world.

The athletic Proletarian body molds details from metal and with a geometrical precision puts together machines with which to attack the complacency of the senile world. Dada amplifies to the limit ideology and practice of the Creator-Machinist.

The Political Aesthetics of the Modernization

The Magic of the Apparatuses

Dada appears in an age already proclaimed modernistic. It extols the beauty of war; Mass-Man's athleticism; synthetic materials; mechanized voice—radio and megaphones; the machine-eye—photo and movie cameras. The legacy of Modernism, has been also absorbed by parties' and organizations' political programs on setting the world straight and replacing it by a radically new, a Brave New World. Marinetti extols war as a natural excess of the senses, of the machinism and communal athleticism of bodies. War is the remarkable transgression through which politics is wholly transformed into aesthetics, and political passion into immediately aesthetic passion. Political interest contorts in a sublime military convulsion and spews forth the charred images of the new world.

The Machine

In it the human is overcome. The organic is surpassed by the mechanical. In the machine, life reaches its ultimate organization. The human body is merely an organ of the machine. The organic element is one of the nodes of a mechanic totality. Only now, and now at last, is the Mind freed from the pathetic body and moves into a dwelling organized and invented by itself—the machine.

The Machinist is Superman. The Machinist is not subjected to subconscious repression, or sense guilt, he is not infected by individuality or sensitivity. The Machinist is the creator of the modernized age, who has decisively overthrown the yoke of the sniffling sentimentality of his perverse body, its ugly organs bandaged with the outfits of culture—clothing. The Creator Machinist represents the mass super-organization of bodies. In this sense, he himself is not a separate body. He is the radically organized state of the laboring bodies with a machine-like principle of common action.

The creative body attains a communal machine-like physiognomy never seen before. In it, the political and the aesthetic are one.

Oculus ex Machina

Eyeglasses are a prosthesis to the eye. They help it see. The snapshot and movie cameras are the superprostheses of the eye. Through them, the eye overcomes its human principle of seeing and becomes a machine. The eye itself becomes Machinist. In this sense, it becomes collective, because it overcomes its individual being, its pathetic partiality and lachrymal. The eye begins to see objectively.

The camera's objective lens overcomes the eye's organic optics. The objective lens is a crystal absolute. It is a superindividual organization of sight. It is the unified being of all possible eyes. The object-glass is the new communal constructivism of sight. It is the ultimately modernized liturgical eye. The Cyclops.

The camera is a prosthesis which has reached its perfection. Its superhuman inventiveness has radically supplanted the function of the organ. The principle of this self-activating prosthesis manifests the essence of the new agent of modernization. The new communal medium. The mass-medium.

On the contrary, according to the classical bourgeois intuition "the subjective genius of art" cannot be political, in that it opens and guards the eternal, age-old order of things. In principle, it transcends the political and the eye opens itself to eternity. "Subjective genius" does not rest on montages and collages, on cutting out and patching up shocking sights, on attractions. It rests on the internal integrity of the chef d'oeuvres. It could not stand prostheses.

Inversely, the political art represents an ultimately focused objective genius, driven by the performance of wonderful aggregates, contraptions and joints, by the vision of unseen laboring automata, which modernize the procession of life. In general, the idea of world modernization is of inordinate political relevance.

The eye becomes agent of the objective lens. The organ appropriates the principle of action of the prosthesis. The natural is overcome. Objective vision marks a decisive victory of the unified automatic mass principle, which stems not from the integrity of bourgeois genius, but from the rhythmic action of the apparatuses.

Objectivity originates in the Machine, which has radically overthrown the Human. Thus, the objective world is always produced and never found. The modernization of the world is represented as mass production of objectivity.

Political Dada does not merely make collages of things and baubles. The world in which Dada raves is not the mercantile world of things, it is not the space of the bourgeois and of things soaked into a small private world. The world is industrial, labor communal, objective; things are uniform, not unique. They refract mass industrial relations. This is a world in which the uniformity reigns. Dada attacks the production of linear uniformity. It attacks common standards of vision. It takes over objective eye, takes over the forms of mass consciousness. It accomplishes wild patching of details and documents, of pieces and industrial wastes. This is a circus of industrially produced uniformity, a sudden breakdown of the prostheses which stimulates an erotic shivering in the organs supported by them.

The camera's objective lens forms a joint between the eye and the view. The change in the optics of the objective lens makes the joint move. The objective lens is an Eye-Centaur who gallops.

The view, as well as the eye, is an agent of the optic structure of the objective lens. Political Dadaism does not merely pick in your eyes and break objects. It attacks the objective structure of vision—the conjuncture formed by the eye and the object in the photograph. It attacks the photograph, that is, the joining of eye with view. Dada is a decisive intervention in the joint. It dismantles it by a kick.

Photo montages, splicing and gluing, the retailoring of ready-made reality—this is the new artistic technique. Objectively snapped reality can only be recut, it cannot be recreated. The reality that appears through the action of the machine reactivates the action of the scissors and the saw, not of the brush and carver. Cutting and fracturing, bandaging and plastering, affixing prostheses—this is the political orthopedics of modernism.

The Cuts of the Collage

The eye armed with scissors and saw insolently crosses the spaces of objective reality by endowing objects with impressive fractures, and then proceeds with plasters, bandages, and prostheses. The scissors, this tireless guillotine, is the magical instrument of modernization. For example, the diaphragm of the photo camera is an eye turned into scissors. It cuts off like a guillotine pieces of vision—frames, snapshots. The diaphragm performs spasm and contracts the vision. This contracted and cut-off view must be bandaged and fortified with prostheses. Then comes the magic of pasting, which reassembles the view chopped up in the camera.

The vision of the artist cannot be embodied in a picture. It can be rejoined after it has been fractured and dismembered by the diaphragm. In this political surgery of sight, the look acquires a distorted body. From this comes the feeling of a disparate and then indecently rejoined defective vision of the artist in political art. It is this principle of vision that Nazism attacks later from its party position, in order to liquidate political art of modernism.

Political Merger of Science and Art

Radical left Modernism feels a strong trust in constructive rationality, which has overcome bourgeois prejudices and developed its own bold visions in the industrial spaces. The political geometric mind is the genius of Modernization and finds its final justification in science. Each action of the new agent of history, the Proletariat, is constructively and scientifically guaranteed in advance in the clear spaces of political Geometrism. It is here that the Utopia of Modernism arises. When the concepts of each scientific field are deliberately generalized and made to solve global problems they turn into metaphors. They turn into crevices, through which gapes the wonderful view of a brand new world. Such an amplification of the scientific concept into a world-building metaphor, into a mythical poetic figure is a political manipulation. To be precise, it is a propaganda manipulation of a political plot for a total and radical world modernization.

The concept as an instrument of a scientific theory is usurped by the actual political design and comes to be used as a metaphor. It becomes pregnant with revolution. That is exactly what was done to the critical spirit of Marxism, to the racial theories, to the organizational theories. That is what was done to the scientific laboratories, whose poetic glorification made possible the mass experiments over immense areas of the Earth.

Science justifies all. The politically perfect world is the one which can be scientifically justified. Modern art builds just such a world. In this sense, Modern art is science turned into a work-world. That is the pinnacle of Modernization.

▦ The Red Geometrist

Man invents and produce ever finer and more perfect implements. Man constantly lowers their weight and thus achieves great technological and social results. These implements make man move ever faster and more precisely. They enable man to master the world and push man to the congenital limits of his corporal being. Propped up by these miraculous prostheses, man surpasses his earthly limitations and enters the spheres of the omnipotent inventive rationality. Art is a sublime organizational condition of those prostheses.

Russian Proletarian art, that is, political art, is in a decisive struggle with the irrational Russian soul, with the forces of its sobbing sentimentality. Proletarian political Constructivism introduces the Nordic spirit of the geometrical mind.

The red Specter of Communism becomes the Geometrist of the new age, the greatest Constructivist and political Dadaist. This Geometrist invented and produced unprecedented prostheses, which would release the laboring body and would throw it into the community of radiant comradeship.

▦ The Body-Aggregate

The modernized commune does not come together on a congregational basis, that is, on the principle of religious faith and initiation. It is built up on "aggregational" basis. The future collective body is represented as an electrified machine-like aggregate. This body, as any aggregate, cannot be described. The descriptive line (discourse) is helpless in this case. That is why the Constructivists and the Dadaists repudiate descriptive lines (discourses), because they have no political constructivist potentialities and power. Such a power has only planning, designing lines. Because of that, the body of the new political agent, the Proletariat, can be neither drawn, nor described. It can only be designed, tailored, and assembled. The red Geometrist designs and cuts out the body-aggregate of the Proletariat using special kind of tailoring machine like film camera and scissors.

Disciplining of the Mass Man

If we attempt to reconstruct the modernist project from the start of this century, we will see that it owes its political aesthetic radicalism to the imperative—"Here and now replace this world with a new one!"—to exchange the old exhausted bourgeois world for a new, differently ordered world. That presupposes two things—invention, design of the new unity of the world, and the disciplining of an agent, or rather an actor, who would erect it. The new Unity of the world and the athletic capability of the Erector—these are prerequisites for the project. What remains to be done is for the action itself to happen to us here, now, immediately. This action is the Modernist act of genius, which will be achieved not by that degraded bourgeois personage the Artist, or by a senile, exhausted God. The decisive act of genius is achieved by the Mass Man. His communal body accomplishes a radical feat of labor by erecting the final work—the New World.

Apparently, the political order of this New World is designed as a work ultimately open, encompassing in its space the body of its creator. The creator moves into his creation. This waste-free act of creation leaves nothing behind itself or outside itself with which its sick body could inflame the new flesh of the world.

The suitability of the Modernist project to life is guaranteed by an already completed rational act, which aspires to the high status of being scientific. The project is scientifically thought out and proven. The designing of the new world is based on the cool minded Geometrist—the predecessor of Scientific Communism. The heat arises only later in the communal body of the Mass Man, who will make the effort of the construction itself. The Modernist Manifesto calls for an immediate mass action. In this sense, behind the manifesto lies the cool mind of the Modernist designer, and after it must be brought out the creative Mass Body. The Manifesto is framed by a scientific Mind and an artistic Creation. Before is the political design, after is the new political order of the world. It might be said that the manifesto is the third position, which stands between the scientifically worked out normative poetics and the concrete work created in accordance with it. In the manifesto, the scientific and the artistic, the political and the aesthetic discourses fuse. The scientific concept and the poetical metaphor merge in the imperative form of Manifesto. And began the Grand construction of scientifically proven metaphors, that is, the imperatives were realized.

The only thing that has been accomplished after the calls of Dada and of Scientific Communism is the party procedure of disciplining Mass Man. The creation of a new world did not take place, because the body refused to accept the communal state as its own creative state. The totalitarian State came to discipline a Mass Body, but it failed and it could not "wither away" as predicted by Scientific Communism.

When speaking of the "old world" one may say that bourgeois society has transformed the social bodies into organs of the personal, the one-sided, and the peculiar. Bourgeois space rests on the principle of heterogenia, because by virtue of its definitions every body is alien to all others. Bourgeois democracy creates a political order capable of governing the segmented social space and enabling the communication of the alien bodies. Bourgeois law regulates the possible concord, accordance, and togetherness of the heterogeneous bodies. It organizes into a community the individuals that occupy a different place in society. According to this juridical principle, no physical body may exist outside the law or above it. The law acts equally both on the body of the President and the Dadaist. In contrast to this, the bodies are entitled to differ with respect to their property, interests, physiognomy, and choice. Equivalent social relations are introduced and ruled by mediators, such as money, alienated from the bodies. Precisely, money enables the expression and realization of the actual differences between the separate bodies and their peculiar intercourse in the common space of the market.

And conversely, in order to create a Mass Man, it is necessary to liquidate all attributes, procedures, and principles which identify the bodies as particular and one-sided, as personal entities in a common space. In this case, equivalence will not be ensured by alienated mediators such as money, but by the physical bodies of the subjects of the new communal world. Thus they become equal and Homo-genius, which makes possible the act of a great Construction that involves a maximum of mass participation and ultimately welds the bodies together. The communal body consists of fragments that have an equal stake in the common entity and an equal interest in everything beyond their physical limits. Thus money is rendered superfluous, and so is the right to be different, and so is the state as an institution which protects the differences. What remains is the body of the Mass Man, left alone with his own will which draws strength from his primal natural drives: to eat, to copulate, to be in a well-lit and warm place.

An interesting example of Mass Man Utopia are the ideas of Bogdanov, that vigorous ideologist of the most outspoken political art in Russia—the Proletcult. This art was suffocated by Lenin because it did not give in to Bolshevization and did not conform to party interests. The political Modernism of Bogdanov became harmful because Lenin had already turned the political idea into a party idea and the Proletariat had to build not a world, but a party.

Bogdanov charged the Proletariat with ontological interests. Lenin charged it with ideological ones. Modernization as the meaning of political art manifests intuitions of a World. Ideology as the meaning of party art manifests intuitions of a Power.

The Center that Unites the Class

It was Bogdanov, the author of the "organizational theory" of society, who worked out various visions and metaphors for the role and place of the new Proletarian art, which captivate the mass conscience even now. Art, he said, is the higher organization of the social experience, the most powerful means for the concentration of the collective forces of the new class. Art is a perfect organization of the class struggle. It is a radically collectivized labor. In it the notion of private property and personality cannot exist. It is a supreme stage of mass Proletarian labor.

Modern grand scale industry is turned into a gymnastic platform with futuristic apparatus assembled on it where Proletarian art demonstrates its stunning "attractions" (Eisenstein), its grotesque "bio-mechanics" (Meyerhold). All of this rests on the scientific justification of modern technology and automation. Here originates the principle of the creative mass force engaged in this process: *Comradeship*. The collectivism of the Proletarians homogenizes their social interest. It unifies them and sensitizes them to all things alien, to all things bourgeois. Comradeship does not arise from religious love, but from the technological togetherness of bodies in the process of labor. Comradeship springs from the new geometrical mode of life. The human corporality must become the immediate substance of comradeship. That is why the Proletarian body of the new class must be united through a common substance.

For Bogdanov, blood is the very substance that should be exchanged between comrades and thus comradeship will flow directly into the bodies of the Proletarians. He founded the first blood transfusion clinic, only not with a medical but with an immediately political purpose. Science thus directly begins serving politics, or to be more exact, directly grows into politics. Blood transfusion as the subject of science becomes a means for homogenizing a united collective political agent: the Proletariat.

Brotherhood solidified through blood fusion is an ancient ritual that is charged with enormous symbolic power. This sacred act, which has its cause in the poetic-mythical constitution of the world, becomes an instrument of science and is conducted through sheer medical procedures ideologically justified and practiced on a mass scale.

This took the life of Bogdanov, himself. He exchanged blood with a man with whom he was totally incompatible. He failed to survive through the antagonism of the alien blood and died. The attempt to produce a purely communal body ended with death.

The Party Modernizes Society by Condensation and Concentration of the Population

The Modernist visions for a Mass Man, inhabiting Sun Cities and Garden Cities find quite a decisive incarnation in the wide Communist land of the Soviets. First of all, because Modernism was directly tied there to Russian universal messianism and thus became a mystery; second, because the party uses of such visions were rather ingenious. Projects for Linear Cities were practically accomplished through the building of gigantic highways and canals. Cities were designed in the form of a grand scale assembly line, or of a linear transmission for the transfer of large masses of live flesh and soil.

The working out of such dynamic communal spaces turned out to be much harder than the building of stationary communal spaces, so-called communal flats. Professional architects take it upon themselves to design and build such stationary spaces called, at that time, the "new social condensers." Such a space condenses the social body in order to make it communal. At the same time, inspired by modern political technology of communism, there arises the idea of concentrating the communal body—the concentration camps.

Now there is a tendency to see the communal flat as a civic place, and the concentration camp as devoid of civil rights. In both cases the communal space is repressive, but it differs in its technology. Besides, in the total absence of civil rights and in the hitherto unseen mass inhabitation of such spaces, the practices of condensation and the practices of concentration become analogous. The condensation and the concentration of the population are two completely equivalent technologies for modernizing society.

One of the spaces, through a simple procedure, fed the other. The subjects concentrated in the camps had already been condensed in the communal flats. The communal flat is something like the entrance to a concentration camp, something like a preparatory chamber. Thus, the process of communization (read as modernization) of society is two-chambered: first condensation, then concentration. Behind this whole process there is no hidden right, no law and order, no legally empowered and constitutionally legitimized procedure. This is a pure case of modernized social technology for the production of a supreme ideological party article—the communal body, or the Mass Man.

Now, let us examine what the space of the condenser is and how exactly are the bodies transferred into the concentration camera. The condenser represents a long row of cell-rooms, connected by a common corridor. At the end of the corridor are the common toilet-bathroom and the common kitchen-dining room. In the projects of official architects, such as Moses Ginsburg, for example, there is also a common library. The library, however, was rarely bothered with.

The cell-room is the place for sleep. There, an individual can be alone with his or her body. The room is the only possible erotically intimate space. But that was not quite so, because the erotically intimate body presupposes a different order of society and its common public spaces. The erotically intimate body can be solely the civic one / but not the communal one / because it has a particular private presence in the social space which excites the "other" bodies. In this sense, the communal homogeneity of the bodies cannot presuppose eroticism. The communal body of the subject is forced to be intimate, for to reproduce itself it must copulate.

In the communal flat, all initiatives of the body are centralized in common public cameras and timetables. There they are trapped and sanctioned as impersonal: eating, cooking, hygiene, etc. The common space presupposes a centralized order in which everything becomes visible except for the sexual act, which is accomplished in the dark of the room.

Fear and Famine

Now let us examine the transfer of bodies from one camera into the other. As the beginning of concentration we can see deadly fear and famine, which is suffered by the bodies in the condensers. Famine stems from the fact that the political economy of communism and all economic laws lead to famine and sustain famine on purpose. Famine is an initial organizational condition of communism. Famine, compared to the plague, is not a calamity, but a social technology for the collectivization and concentration of the population. Famine welds bodies together.

Fear stems from the inexorable course of the transmissions of modern society which rhythmically feeds the concentration camps with bodies. Fear is produced by an already experienced concentration. It welds yet again by causing trembling.

The transferring of bodies from one chamber into another happened at night, when people were withdrawn into acts of forced intimacy. There was a knock on the door and They took them away. The bodies in the adjacent cells used to hear noises of the apprehension and expect every night to be visited by the same knock. At that time demographers registered a sudden lowering of the birth rate. Fear decisively prevented intimacy. The knocking on the door caused an acute castration complex, just as the statue of Commander knocked on the door of Don Juan, in order to punish him with a granite fist.

The concentration of bodies begins already in the condensation camera through a repressive centralization by means of *fear and famine* of the two strongest urges of zoomorphous man: eating and copulating. Thus, the communal body is deprived of all of its natural initiative. It possesses only the party designed initiative.

Thus happened Communism.

Party vs. Political Art

A. The Racial-party Approach. The Racial Eye.

Among the pictures submitted I have observed a number of works which actually lead one to assume that certain people's eyes show them things differently from the way they really are. In other words, there really are men who see today's Germans simply as degenerate cretins and who perceive—or as they would doubtless say "experience"—the meadows as blue, the sky as green, the clouds as sulfurous yellow, and so on. I do not want to enter into an argument as to whether or not these people actually do see and perceive things this way, but in the name of the German people I wish to prohibit such unfortunates, who clearly suffer from defective vision, from trying to foist the products of their faulty observation on to their fellow men as though they were realities, or indeed from dishing them up as "art." No, there are only two possibilities. Either these so-called artists really do see things in this way and so believe in what they are representing—if so one would have to investigate whether their eye defects have arisen by mechanical means or through heredity: in the former case these unfortunate people are profoundly to be pitied; in the latter it would be a matter of great concern for the Reich Ministry of the Interior, which would then have to consider ways of putting a stop to further transmission of such appalling defects of vision—or perhaps, on the other hand,

they themselves believe in the reality of such impressions, but have other reasons for inflicting this humbug on the nation, in which case it would constitute an offense falling within the area of criminal law . . .
Hitler, Adolf. quoted in *German Art in the 20th Century. Painting and Sculpture 1905–1985*. Eds. Ch. Joachimides, and N. Rosenthal, and W. Schmied, Munich: Prastel-Verlag, 1985.

The artists discussed here are the Modernists. In 1937 in Munich, the Nazis organized two parallel exhibitions. One of "degenerative art," in which the Modernist artists are deliberately shown to be total idiots, especially in their particularly imbecile category, Dada. The second offered "healthy" German art, a manifestation of athleticism, of muscular eroticism, of the blue-eyed perspicacity of the German national spirit.

Undoubtedly, the problem of sight and vision is of great importance. How is it solved in this case? Since the artist paints not what is seen by the "healthy" eye, there are three possibilities: first, the damage is mechanical and this induces pity and is a medical case. Second, the damage is genetic or hereditary, and this case is delegated by Hitler not to medicine, but to the Ministry of internal affairs. Third, the damage is mostly simulated and can be directly prosecuted under criminal law. The first two cases suggest pathology, the third suggests sabotage. Or, from another point of view, the first is physical, the latter two are ideological.

The Nazi party ideology penalizes the case of the genetic malformation as an assault against the race. The race-party criterion is the criterion of the "healthy" and the sensible, the one of common sense. Common sense is something typical of party art, because the party is the ideologically organized interest of a homogeneous mass of people, with their own common sense for the order of things, with their own organ for uniform vision, *sensus communis*. In contrast, eccentricity is typical of political, not of party art, because the political act demonstrates and identifies a particular agent with his own acute partial social interest. The fighting political agent publishes his own interest differently from the party agent. From the standpoint of common sense of the party agent, the publications of the political agent are always subversive. In this case even genetic malformation is treated as subversive, that is, as a political phenomenon, because genetics is loaded by National Socialism with a party sense.

Let us get back to defective vision. We have spoken already of the machine eye, of machinism in general, and of the collage principle of modernizing normal sight. The Modernist principle of representation is just such a machine for reorganizing vision. In this sense, Modernism does not represent, but reorganizes the organic principle of sight into a mechanic, technological, geometric one. The Modernist eye invents the view. Of course, from the point of view of normal vision, and the more so when it is loaded with ultimate party sense, this eye is faulty. The spectator looking at the canvas does not find a recreated reality there but a set of prostheses belonging to the handicapped eye of the painter.

The racial-party approach elevates the organic into an ultimate value and considers as an assault against it any attempt at attaching prostheses. This same Nazism deifies the machine, but only as a means of exhibiting the will of the organic. The mechanic as a willful extrapolation of the organic.

The Modernist idea of radical replacement of the naturally organic with the machine is a sabotage. In this sense, the party ideology of National Socialism is the opposite of the Modernist one. Hitler attacks Modernism as a phenomenon that is political in its nature.

Nazi art is open to the *sensus comunis*. And common sense dictates the following: art organizes the vision and virtually represents the organics of the visualized. A painting does not represent merely some object or body, but the principle of its natural organics. If the object-prototype is slightly marred, then its image brings back its organics. In this sense, defective images are not possible in art, because art itself is a regenerative, not a degenerative activity.

The problem of party censorship lies in the depiction of the "representable," because party truth is connected to it. The image is neither an actual empirical prototype, nor the thing immediately represented on the canvas. The representable offers the ideal integrity of the image. The representable cannot pose technical problems, but only ideological ones. In it resides a Truth lying beyond any empirical manifestation. Artistic mastery lies in the act of making the image ultimately transparent, so that the representable can stand before the eye clearly and fully.

Such censorship is a party institution, not a political one. It does not come from any concrete political agent who is in power and who says what can and what cannot be published. This censorship is not a political institution, defined as a state structure. The censorship which guards party truth works by giving form to thought and imagination.

Party censorship is not a separate institution, which permits one type of thought and prohibits others. It acts as the structure of thought or sight. It poses the organically fundamental state of things, and not their politically defined state. Such a censorship does not censure the phenomenon, but the person who gives birth to it. It does not outlaw the painting, but the person who has seen the real that way. On the contrary, political censorship prosecutes the phenomenon, the thing born. Ideological party censorship prosecutes the nature of the birth. Because it prosecutes persons, and not phenomena, it is not defined as a state institution, but acts through the organs of security.

Party truth liquidates political art, because it liquidates the political personality in general: either everybody in the party or everybody in the camps!

B. The Class Party Approach. Party Replaces Class.

Now let us discuss the class party approach as similar to and different from the racial party approach. The one liquidated political art in Germany, the other in Russia. And everything began with Dada and the Proletcult.

The racial party approach stems from the organic unity of "blood and soil" as a genetic source of national purity and the historical mission of the race. Things are not so simple with the class party approach, because the communist party claims to be one thing, but is, in fact, quite another. But let us begin elsewhere.

> Literature must become party literature. Down with non-party writers. Down with the writer-supermen.
>
> The literary work must become a building block of the organized, planned, united. . . . party work.
>
> Writers must necessarily enter the party organizations. Publishing houses, reading rooms, libraries—all of these must come under party control.
>
> In defining the borders between party and anti-party writing, the criterion must be the party program. . . . its statute. . . .
>
> Lenin, Vladimir. "Partiinaia organizatsiia i partiinaia literature." *Iz istorii Sovetskoi esteticheskoi mysli; 1917–1932.* Eds. G. A. Belaia, and A. E. Gorpenko. Moscow: Iskusstvo, 1980.

It is evident from Lenin's thought, cited above, that the Communist party idea, even as far back as its prerevolutionary state, has been developing as an imperial idea. The new emperor is the party.

What Lenin wanted in 1905 was actually accomplished in 1932 at the writers' conference, where Formalism (read as Modernism) was totally liquidated and the omnipotence of the new party truth in art was proclaimed. Thus the writers enter the party. Those who do not go to the camps. Thus the political person in art is liquidated. Party truth flourishes and recruits its shamans and priests. Party truth or Party justice *(Pravda),* becomes the basis of the new Inquisition. True art is justified by Party art.

In 1920, Lenin devises an attack against the Proletcult. The motives are that in its ideas and practices the Proletcult is decisively independent of the party line and party interests. And that is true, because the Proletcult is the actual political Proletarian art of that time with its ideology and action program, with its own organizational structure independent from the party. Not party literature, but Proletcult is the politically representative art of the Proletariat. The ideologists of Proletcult are people, all of whom have been trampled by Lenin and thrown out of the party. We are not discussing here the extremism of this art and this idea in general. We have already discussed that in relation to Dada. Here, the important thing is that a structure is being built independent of the party, which represents the Proletariat itself. But the party liquidates all this, because it subverts and competes with its political representativeness. Everything which might undermine the political representativeness of the party comes under the knife. The peasant for example, a political person, whom the party does not represent, is totally stripped of rights, if not physically exterminated with administrative executions and deliberately caused mass famine. The deprivation of rights goes as far as the peasant's lack of a passport, because of which he cannot leave his village. He is actually not a citizen and cannot represent even himself, because he is totally illegitimate from the party point of view.

Thus a new class is formed—the party oligarchy which holds the entire power. It is not the means of production, but the means of power, which organize the new communist social relations. Who holds and who reproduces political power through its own means? Not the Proletariat! The party interest has nothing in common with the Proletarian interest. The party represents the interests of those who are the immediate body of power—the so-called "nomenclature." The party membership mass organized on horizontal principle is a totally fabricated phenomenon. But party interest continues to fake a Proletarian class interest and constituency. Party art vigorously continues to express the workers' presence in the world. Why? The laboroid imagery in no way represents the virtual social interest of the party oligarchy.

Why doesn't it glorify itself? It remains hidden, invisible, and untouchable. It acts as a lizard, which tears off its tail as soon as it is stepped on. Because, from the point of view of civil law and order, from the point of view of the politically public agent this oligarchy is illegal. So Party art represents a fabricated political agent: the Proletariat.

The question of the legality of the party and party policy in art is central. In his article about party literature Lenin elaborates this question. At that time, before 1917, the party and all its publications are illegal. Legal publications are nonparty. But there comes a time when the party begins functioning legally and then all possible publications have to become party ones. Coming out of illegality, the party usurps the whole press and there is no need of any law for the press (because law is necessary where there are different political interests, i.e., different political agents). In a state of all-encompassing party policy, a law is unnecessary because the only differentiation is party/anti-party, and that differentiation is ruled upon by the program and statute of the party. The statute of the party is the very law which constitutes the possible relations. In this case, the state actually does begin dying off, because the party takes up its functions and gradually replaces it.

Not until now have there been preparations for legislating a law of the press and not only of the press. Only now has the possibility of the existence of political agents outside the party been admitted.

Inter-party life is conspiratorially closed from the point of view of the state and the few laws there are in it. But it is legal, nevertheless. Lenin begins, but does not develop his thoughts on the legality of the party. That the party is legal does not prevent it from developing an internally conspiratorial life, with its own structure, discipline, and secrets. Any change in the power structure happens in the form of a conspiratorial plot.

Through Revolution, Party conspiracy seized the whole power and became legal. We make the difference between the concepts of **legal** and **legitimate**. Something is legal if it does not contradict the law and justifies its existence through the law. The law may not contain explicit provisions for the existence of any such particular phenomenon. For example, the law does not say whether a workers' party should or should not exist. It comes under the competence of the law only after such party has appeared by itself. On the other hand, a phenomenon is **legitimate** if: (1) It has been categorically enacted and regulated by the law. In this sense, Parliament is a legitimate division of power. A legitimate entity cannot be regarded as legal or illegal insofar as it is made by the law and do not depend on someone's will expressed in accordance with the law or in spite of the law. (2) Besides, legitimacy insists on the representative character of the political phenomena, delegated through a due legislative process. From this point of view the Communist Party by its conspiratorial principle may be "legal" if it does not break any existing law, but it is not legitimate as the only party on power, at least for two reasons: its party leadership that has merged with the State power has been elected through party vote and discipline rather than by general elections. Thus Party imposes the interests of the conspiracy onto the structures of the State. Moreover, its exclusively leading role is decreed by the Constitution. Its first article reads that the only party—the communist one—has the leading role in the Socialist State and that the communist party turned into an all-national representative. That automatically undermines the very essence of a constitution as fundamental law of the State, which ought to decree the possible forms of political life, not the specific entities involved in it. Legitimacy concerns the procedure of authorization. There is a difference between the legal existence and the legitimate power of a party.

The existence of the party is legal, but it is illegitimate in holding and executing the whole power, which it has actually usurped through conspiracy. It actually represents the interests of the party oligarchy and no one else; it is not sheathed in a law, voted for by free citizens. It does not possess delegated rights from a multitude of citizens; it endows itself with power through its program, the State constitution is only a repetition of this program. The territories, where party interests act most strongly, are not regulated by law, because there no other political agent can exist, or have a legal status. The law is possible only where there are relations between independent political agents.

The party suffers from a chronic insufficiency of representativeness, that is, of legitimacy. From here on it begins to liquidate and take away the rights of anything which might compete with it, or subvert it, or sabotage its representativeness. It liquidates Modern political art, precisely because it competes with its right to represent the Proletariat. The Party collects a great mass of members, and creates its own simulated social-political interests, which only it can represent. It invents a class party approach, which should define good and evil and other tricks, so that the real class, the real interest should sink into conspiratorial darkness, since it cannot have public forms, because it is illegitimate, and rules over the public, visible world through ghosts. The Proletariat as a class, as an actual political agent has long ago disappeared, because the structure of social relations is ruled not through ownership of the means of production but through possession of power and by the degree of initiation into the party conspiracy.

The phantom of Proletarian class interest continues to exist as a means, not as an end. The class party approach is the means of production of power.

The trick with the party policy of art is in the following—that which is given to us as party criterion, that which we have caught and hold on to as a party truth is only the tail of the lizard. The lizard has long ago escaped unharmed. We hold on to words, phrases, slogans, hammers, tanks, images of laboring hands and brave blood donors, of bridges and golden wheat, with the ontological certainty that we are holding on to the whole new and daring

Communist reality. But this is only the lizard's tail. Whoever does not wish to hold on to the lizard's tail and pretend to be holding the Proletarian hammer in hand, is liquidated. The lizard comes back to feed itself.

The racial party approach of Nazism is clear. National Socialism comes to Germany through a legal procedure and for a short while it really begins to express and represent the German national mind which is inspired by it. The party is legal and its structures are not conspiratorial. The power which it holds becomes legitimate organ of highly organized national interest.

The class party approach of Bolshevism, the internally conspiratorial structures of party life, the publicly simulated structures of party truth—this drenches the whole physical space of society with permanent revolution.

The mummy of the Leader! Why does a civic legal political power need mummies?

The class struggle and the dictatorship of the Proletariat become the main ideological alibi for the liquidation, which the party carries on against all evidence and witnesses of its own illegitimacy.

The class motive and the racial motive of the totalitarian parties liquidated Modern political art. The two motives are completely different, as I have attempted to explain. The link between them is that both have worked out their own technologies and ideologies for the liquidation of possible political agents, who by definition represent nonparty interests.

Presently, when the serious work on the analysis and criticism of the Class Party Empire—in art and public forms of life in general—is forthcoming, we have to take into account what Dada virtually is, what a scandal this crocodile is, what a saboteur it is, that Party truth did crush it in panic with a ferro-concrete fist.

From Anatomy of the Political Body
Ivan Kristev

Even when Ilyich is no more, we still have Lenin.

▦ I. A Political Anatomy of Communism

The autopsy took four hours and forty minutes. The press release was a triumph of materialism. It described Lenin's body in minute detail, with a special emphasis on his brains—1,340 g of them. One is left with the impression that the main purpose of the press release was to show that LENIN HAD A BODY, which had functioned through all physiological processes typical of the human body. LENIN'S BODY WAS A HUMAN BODY.

Such a statement is plain as plain—to the point of absurdity. However, this absurdity is logical. The monstrous minuteness of the press release was actually directly linked with "the principal question," "the question of power"—a total political power which was ubiquitous and "expropriated" medical authority. Health turned into a political, rather than a medical problem.

In 1922, Lenin wrote to Molotov: "I have two letters from Chicherin. He wonders whether, at the Genoa Conference, we shouldn't concede—if we get reasonable compensation (supplies, etc.)—to minor amendments in our Constitution, namely the participation of other parties in the Soviets.

"This suggestion shows, I believe, that Chicherin needs treatment, send him to a sanatorium at once."

Had Lenin written "send him to prison at once," the idea would have sounded perfectly alright. A similar resolution was fully justified when one was accused of pluralism. But why send one to a sanatorium? Nor was Chicherin's case an exception. Krassin, for instance, was one of dozens of people who were ordered to undergo psychiatric treatment. Lenin behaved like a GP, rather than a government leader.

The dividing line between medicine and politics was obliterated. A closer analysis of Lenin's political medicalism shows that "sending Chicherin to a sanatorium" exemplifies certain theoretical attitudes.

Bolshevik metaphor makes abundant use of medical imagery to express the idea of social reform. The old bourgeois world is malignant and decaying, and it is in agony. Headed by its vanguard—the communist party, the working class has no choice but to "excise" the bourgeois tumour from society like an expert surgeon. Strangely enough, this places the very political act in an entirely new light. Executing "the enemies of the revolution" becomes a medication, rather than the killing of people.

Total political power proved possible insofar as it constantly posed as medical, intellectual, or any other power.

The blurred line between politics and medicine also blurred the line between sanatoriums and prison. Sanatoriums and prison were just two different asylums for the political body. Physiology was thoroughly politicized. Lenin himself fell victim to political medicine. Lenin was not treated by doctors—he was treated by the Politburo. Politburo sessions approved Lenin's regimen by vote and prescribed his daily walks, diet, etc.

The problem of the political body and the problem of mortality clashed.

The doctors who autopsied Lenin tried to show that Lenin's body was human—but failed.

The commission in charge of Lenin's funeral was renamed a Commission for the Immortalization of Lenin's Memory. A government resolution recognized Lenin's body as a political body. A mausoleum was built. Earlier, at the Soviets' Second Congress, Stalin "spilt the beans," making the crucial admission: we, Bolsheviks, are made from special stuff.[1]

Exactly what sort of stuff Bolsheviks are made of has remained unclear.

The mausoleum is the true home of totalitarian power.

II. The Guillotine and Acid

This wasn't waxwork.

Is there a wax figure of Lenin at Madame Tussaud's? Is the fire which destroyed Madame Tussaud's in 1925 in any way connected with Western press allegations of the period that what was displayed at the Mausoleum was a wax figure, not Lenin's embalmed body?

Lewis Fischer's book *The Life of Lenin* does not answer these questions, but it does cite facts relevant to one possible answer.

To dispel doubts about the mummy's authenticity, a group of journalists, Fischer included, were invited to inspect the relics. Professor Zbarsky, the world famous biochemist (who took part in Lenin's embalming) delivered a short lecture. Claiming that the body would keep for about a century, the professor opened the hermetically sealed glass case, caught Lenin's nose and turned his head to the left and to the right. "This wasn't waxwork," wrote Fischer. "This was Lenin."

This statement of paramount importance in 20th century history dispelled a dangerous illusion. Faced with the ultimate Bolshevik objectification—the mummy, the West suddenly realized that the Bolshevik revolution was not a 1917 version of the storming of the Bastille. Having "interpreted" events in Russia behind Western intellectuals' backs for years, Jacobean metaphor started having fits of claustrophobia. Lenin could have no wax figure—his body symbolically ruled out the creation of one.

The parallel between the wax figure and the mummy, between Madame Tussaud's and the Mausoleum, completely objectifies the polar notions of power, and hence, the different anatomy of the political bodies at the heart of the two revolutions: in France in 1789 and in Russia in October 1917.

This excerpt deals with the execution of Louis XVI and the liquidation of Nicholas II. The murders of the king and the emperor, the symbolic aspect of the murder techniques, are treated as a code which can be applied to decode the programmes of the French and Russian revolutions.

The idea of the new revolutionary corporeality, the "new political Adam," is not inferred from the ideologues' utopian works, but from the method used to execute the symbols of the old world.

The Guillotine

"The execution of Louis XVI was a political act." The trial against the king was a trial against justice. Today, similar statements are generally accepted. To a large extent, the decline of French Marxism has proven to be the end of "the notion of the French Revolution as fateful." It is now clear that the French Revolution solved one basic problem: the king's physical elimination. The king's body proved to be the insoluble contradiction in a changing French society. For 18th century French society saw the king's body as a political reality rather than a metaphor. To function, the monarchy needed the corporeal presence of the king. The revolution had to metaphorize the king's body. In a certain sense, the guillotine was a workshop for metaphors.

The revolution had to execute the body of the existing power, the divine right, and constitutional inviolability of the monarchy. To strip someone or something of their inviolability is one way of producing political metaphors. But the monarch's constitutional inviolability was guaranteed by the revolution itself. The 1791 Constitution ruled out the possibility of executing the king. Since royal authority was divine, the king was inviolable as long as he was king; deprived of his sanctity, he could be tried only for crimes which he had committed as an ordinary citizen, as non-king.

To execute the king, the revolution had to execute its own legitimacy. The guillotine thus became a workshop for the illegal production of metaphors.

On November 13, 1792, Saint-Just addressed the National Convention in a speech which should have cut the Gordian knot: "I have taken the floor, citizens," said he, "to prove that the king may be tried because both the opinion upholding royal inviolability and that of the Committee, which wants to try the king as an ordinary citizen, are equally wrong." The important point for Saint-Just was to try the king in his capacity as king, so he accused him of a metaphysical crime—"the crime of being a king."

The symbolic separation of powers proved possible only as a physical severance of the king's two bodies: the political body of Louis XVI and the body of Louis Capet, father and husband. Figuratively speaking, in this case the guillotine did not kill—it separated the one from the other. Having failed to survive this separation, the innocent Louis Capet was buried, while Louis XVI's body was displayed in its metaphoric integrity at Madame Tussaud's. On the orders of the revolutionary authorities, Madame Tussaud moulded Louis XVI's portrait before his execution.

The body of power was amputated from the body of the king. The king's head was moulded in wax, yet wax was the body of seals. Having embodied absolute power, Louis XVI also embodied the absolute seal. The revolution separated the bodies of Louis and the seal. Madame Tussaud put them together again in a parody.

Acid

The meaning of the Bolshevik revolution is to be found in the symbolic interpretation of two biochemical processes. The first process took place in July 1918 and may be described as decomposition of a base through acid; the second was in January 1924 and may be defined as the transformation of death into eternal life—in a certain sense, this biochemical process was a miracle.

This paper will discuss the decomposition of a base through acid only. Or it will examine the murder of the Russian Emperor Nicholas Romanoff as one stage in the process of turning society into a conspiracy. The emperor's murder was itself part of this conspiracy. It was no different from the murder of any petty bourgeois. There were no trial, dramatic speeches, charges, or crimes. One night the Romanoffs were shot dead; their bodies were then loaded on a truck, driven out of town (Yekaterinburg), and buried. We do not even know who ordered the execution. Paradoxically, the murder of the Russian emperor lacked a symbolic dimension. Louis XVI's head rolled in the heart of Paris, at the heart of the French Revolution. Nicholas Romanoff was killed as a dog "at the back of the beyond." The emperor's crime was covered up. If in killing Louis the French Revolution executed its own legitimacy, the murder of Nicholas was tantamount to rejecting legality. The problem facing the Bolshevik revolution had nothing to do with the legalization of a purely political act like the execution of Louis XVI. The problem of the Bolshevik revolution was that of any criminal: how to hide the corpse so as to avoid discovery. The emperor's corpse—not his body—actually foiled Bolshevik plans. After burial, the royal corpses were exhumed and drenched with acid. Later, the building where the Romanoffs had been imprisoned was destroyed as well. If the execution of Louis XVI was a political crime, the murder of Nicholas II was a criminal offence, depriving a person of his life with the purpose of robbery.

The idea of destroying the old power and abolishing classes automatically placed Bolshevism beyond politics and the political. Liquidating power proved possible only as an infinite exhaustion of a total and unlimited power. The idea itself lent an absolute value to this very power. In this sense the body of Nicholas II was no longer different from the millions of other bodies that populated the underground.

The very act of going underground practically stripped the emperor of his power, for the strength of his power lay in its legitimacy—yet this legitimacy was outlawed. Nicholas II posed a threat in time only, therefore his corpse alone constituted a threat.

The public and the underground reversed roles once and for all. The guillotine was absolutely useless. The only power which the emperor's body had was the power of history, of time. The emperor's body lost its organic essence, becoming dangerous only as a geological formation.

The acid poured over Romanoff was the real weapon of the revolution. The new government did not execute—it wiped people out. Socialism proved to be the end of sociality.

Certain hypotheses claim that the acid used on the emperor's corpse was the main component of the stuff with which Lenin was mummified.

Note

1. "We are such stuff / As dreams are made on" (William Shakespeare, *The Tempest,* IV. i. 148).

Part III

The Post-Paranoid Condition

The Post-Paranoid Condition
Ivaylo Ditchev

In the times of allegory I had imagined a fantastic country that had decided to base its politics on science, rather than irrational values. Unlike communism, it was not political economy, but genetic engineering which was supposed to make it possible to improve human nature at any moment. The result was not exactly predictable. To begin with, the geneticians themselves seized the opportunity to make their own genitals several times bigger, which resulted in massive shortage of blood supply to the brain, fainting-fits, and bad government. Metabolism had to be speeded up, and consequently more food was needed, so geneticians devised supplementary elephant trunks for the fruit-pickers in order to raise the productivity of labor (realizing thus Fourier's dream of what he called the "archy-hand"). This necessitated the reduction of feet and the introduction of new means of transportation like wings, the latter implying a diminuation of the fruit-picker's body and, respectively, a decrease of productivity.

The revolutionary process went on and on even after gradual discontent began to spread among the creatures, who had lost all resemblance to the human race. But who else, if not the geneticians again, could find the way back to the natural state? Genetics was now largely taught at school and the best engineers, chosen in the most democratic way, were asked to increase their brains to such an extent that they could no longer do anything but lie in bed, like the famous philosopher, and invent clever traps for nature to show up on its own; but any time someone pretended to have got hold of it, there burst out a terrible quarrel, for you couldn't be sure whether this was Nature at last, or whether the engineer in question was not furthering a self-interested project, and he was remodelled, and someone else took his place, and the political struggle had no end.

There is no transcendence about capitalism, no eternal truth, no image or example (from Mirandola to Marx and Sartre). What does it mean, then, to return to capitalism? Return to shapelessness, to the void of freedom? But was communism really a shape for man, transcending him? All constraints imposed upon him were but "political decisions," that is, based on the struggle for power between forces in a historical situation; they were not real in the way a taboo or the obligations of honor are. (The Berlin wall was never anything but an act of political force, for both sides—unlike the Chinese wall, for instance.)

That's why the villain disappeared miraculously, like a computer-game-enemy, who leaves no trace behind. The irrational thing about the fall of communism is due to the fact that in itself it was but an act of force, but off from eternity: the moment it is defeated, it seems to have never been there at all. Like the ghost in a bad dream it has no other reality outside the fact of struggling with you; it was you, in opposing it, who made it exist (you = the democratic world, common reason, the dissidents, etc.).

In a way, politicizing the world leads naturally to paranoia: everything and everybody is turned into a pawn of the great mortal struggle; things have no value in themselves outside the interpretation with respect to the big stratagem. Unlike its medical counterpart, political paranoia presupposes a certain control of the process, that is, you may interpret everything in the political perspective, but then you go home and read a book or kiss your wife without planning these as moves in the final destruction of imperialism. In his *Meditationes* Descartes seems to suggest something like controlled paranoia to be the ultimate foundation of reason (the extreme example of doubt). What if

a *malin génie* were tricking me and all my sensations were false? There is no way to prove that everything around me is not the product of someone's wicked will; one thing is nevertheless certain: my doubt, my ability to evoke this possibility, to imagine my total defeat and the irreality of the world I am familiar with. Is it **me** who controls the situation—even to the point of self-negation?—I have the upper hand over the demon, I create him, not he me.

Descartes, however, did not envisage the case when doubt could be imposed upon the subject by the alleged demon himself by the means of terror, propaganda, ideology, etc. "I doubt, therefore I am" turns into "he forces me into doubt, therefore **he** is." Now there is no way out: both certitude and doubt are at the side of the demon, he asserts at the same time that he does and that he doesn't exist; that everything is and is not manipulated. Getting rid of the demon then actually means having him back on your shoulders, as it was he who constantly wanted you to do away with him... In other words, the question of post-communism is: how do you get rid of a **revolutionary** power, aiming to abolish all power in the world?

The Department of Rumors

There is a rumor that the department for spreading rumors among the population at the State security still exists. You can't even say that it has gone underground, for departments like that are underground in principle. It may have spread the rumor of its own dissolution, but also, and this is even worse, of its existence (which is perhaps its only form of being!). After some reflection, you come to the conclusion that there is no way to get rid of the rumor-department: it will be there the moment you think of it.

Rumors were indispensable in the great communist deconstruction of the subject. "Department for disinformation," as we used to call such institutions, is incorrect, as it implies that rumors are definitely false. Rumors may be true, but not necessarily. Usually there is the eroticism of eavesdropping, of getting more than you should, but it

might be just a piece of useful information that is nowhere to find. For instance, during the Chernobyl catastrophe while the media went on and on repeating there was no danger whatsoever, an elderly lady from the local party headquarters in Sofia rang at people's doors, saying confidentially to everyone that she had some friend at the Ministry who told her it might be better for the children not to drink milk.

The essential about a rumor is the subjective way it represents reality—it is a *doxa* needing to be proved by public procedures (i.e., to be universalized in some way). The central paradox of communist culture lies in the fact that public representations were no less subjective than rumors themselves: they were not intended to be true, but to help the victory of communism (the preservation of power), that is, open and frank ideology. Note the obscene character of the very notion of ideology in a Marxist-oriented type of discourse: what does it mean if I call my ideas "false consciousness," if I consider them to be but a means for something else? It means I'm not ready to **die** for them; I will die even more readily for bread, for a better life, for power, but never for truth, as stupid people did for ages. Thus, when you neighbor tells you she heard a rumor and when a party chief says he adopted an ideology, there is not much of a difference: neither **is** what she or he says.

Deficiency of the official ideological information presupposes rumor and the subjectivity of rumors presupposes official confirmation—this is a vicious circle. In such a system of total relativity, man can no longer be an identical, responsible social subject: he acts according the fluxes and refluxes of desire, of hope, and despair (accordingly, you believe or disbelieve radiation).

The class struggle of representations—socialist versus capitalist, official versus unofficial, tactic versus strategic—is aimed not at imposing the true one, but at maintaining the struggle, at undermining the principle of truth in itself and reducing man to a series of situations of desire. The most amazing thing is that class struggle begins the mo-

ment you want it to begin. Between the point of view of the theoretician, stating that there is such a thing as class struggle and the ideologue, who produces purposeful theories that would serve one side of the struggle there lies nothing more and nothing less but readiness to die—asceticism, sacrifice, self-negation, whatever we will call it. Eternity, as a transcending point of reference, attained through the irreversible, is the most forbidden thing under communism, as it undermines the principle of the mass, which should be in constant movement (H. Arendt); the masses are life, whereas the individual begins with the awareness that he or she is mortal. Communism abolished death just like the Russian utopia dreamt of (the result was the *evaporization* (Orwell) of millions and millions, deprived of their own death). We can't deny a certain gratification in this new erotic structure: total uncertainty implies the immortality of timelessness.

Now let us make one more step. In a world of all-embracing (class) struggle man could at least *engage* himself, take sides, that is, the side of he, who is going to win in the course of history. This was obviously the case with many western leftists, having nothing to do with the *real socialism*. But what happens if you begin to think that both conflicting representations are produced by the same author, that is, that power produces its own enemies (as in "1984")? The heroic choice itself becomes dubious. Who would sacrifice his life fighting a fictitious enemy?

In telling the story of Andropov, Vosslensky relates the fact that in the beginning of the eighties there were quite a number of accidents with high-ranking officials. This, he says, might have been:

1. just a coincidence;
2. the elimination of rivals by the KGB;
3. an elimination of some rivals, done to intimidate other rivals;
4. just a rumor, spread by the KGB on the occasion of an accidental fact in order to intimidate rivals; or

5. a rumor, spread to intimidate rivals, having no relation to reality.

We have arranged these gradual steps of collapse into class struggle paranoia in an order, quite similar to Baudrillard's *precession of simulacra*. You have:

1. event; no power
2. power over event
3. power over event and power over man
4. power over man; no power over event
5. power; no event.

The beginning resembles dogmatic metaphysics; at the end Nietzsche's thesis is realized: there are no facts but only interpretations, which are acts of will to power. The problem is you have no fixed place on the scale; your own position in the process of collapse is not a fact but an interpretation again. The very moment you start suspecting the world, it yields political phantoms and disintegrates; the stronger your interpretation, the greater the collapse. It seems that the subject was all of a sudden forced into a state of unexpected and ill-timed freedom (as he or she was detached from death and eternity), and this deconstructed him or her into a series of paranoid situations.

There was no total control under communism,[1] there was the rumor of total control; but how do you get rid of a rumor?

The Nomenclatura of Dissidents

It has often been said that anti-Communists form a sort of new nomenclatura: the origin of their movement is conspiracy; the principle of nomination, at least in the first days after the victory, is personal loyalty. Anyway, you can always suspect people in a classless society of representing no one but themselves, as there are no articulated interests of the different social groups. Except for a few outspoken dissidents, the new political elite is totally unknown to the population; they are accepted as a team in thanks to the general (eschatological) wish for change.

Nomenclatura comes from *nomen* + *clamo*, "to call names," that is, an enumeration of names, a **list**. In the linguistic intuition of a Bulgarian or Russian, they form an arbitrary group (like the items present in a storehouse). Now let us imagine what it would mean to replace a traditional class by a nomenclatura. There would no longer be any content, economic, cultural, symbolic or whatsoever behind the constellation of people designed; nothing transcendent to the (political) situation would motivate the adherence to it—a name is either present on the list or it is not, and that is all. To be present on the list does not necessarily imply that you occupy a certain post or share some privilege: it only makes these probable, as the list is not a description, but an act of power. And when we ask "whose power?," we get a circular definition: the power, acquired thanks to the list.

Once social differences are abolished society is about to collapse into chaos, and this was precisely the case of the Soviet union under the modernist rule of Lenin. In an act of postmodern genius Stalin succeeded in both preserving the modernist deconstruction of hierarchies and the social functioning: by introducing the system of lists, he made social differences **arbitrary**. He knew that the other name of equality is arbitrary inequality. The masses don't just need to have no superiors, they need superiors who have their own superiors, and feel guilty; superiors who are constantly sacrificed. The masses need to feel that the rule over them is not eternal, that there is a basic **reversibility** of roles (like in the carnival). In tradition there was always the transcending principle of death (eternity, God, the ancestors), which legitimated power by undermining it at the same time; because the beyond not only gives the ruler his power, but also puts limits to it. The Bolsheviks carried this to the extreme: for the first time in history power undermined itself, affirming that it was no longer based on eternity, but just on the political situation—power stated "I am but a situation of power, my main goal is to abolish all power in the world including myself." It was constantly moving, reforming, purging itself, being thus even harder with its own people than with the population.²

The western use of "nomenclatura" to design what Jillas called the *new class* ignores the amplitude of the phenomenon. Here are some other examples. The list of all who live in Moscow (or: of those, who have to live in Magadan). The list of *kulaks*, that is not of the rich peasants, but of those who have been interpreted as such (sometimes in order to cover a percentage, required "from above"—the abstract figure makes the process even more arbitrary). The list of party members, percentage again according to sex, occupation, nationality, etc. The list of those who should no be seen on TV, but are allowed to publish in the press. The list of those who are not allowed to publish anywhere, but are not to be fired. The list of potential collaborators (of the police, of local authorities). The list of people who might (or might not) be shown to foreigners. The list of writers, composers (the "unions"). The list of Hungarians, Tatars, Turks. The list of the persons allowed to buy a flat of more than 120 square meters . . . We could go on like this until we have described the whole of the communist society. The ideal, thus, would be a state where **all** the relations are alienated in such (public) lists and **all** the efforts of the individual are directed towards moving from list to list³—that is, of being interpreted in such a way as to become a member of the desired nomenclatura group or to escape from the undesired one. At that point, man has no "inside" and is entirely public, as everything in him is language. Thus factories produce signs instead of goods (to use V. Todorov's expression). Boss X does not manufacture shoes for shoes' sake, he manufactures shoes in order to be interpreted by boss Y as "manufacturing shoes"; it is no longer consumption by the buyer that motivates him (or rather its representation in the field of exchange), but interpretation by the superior (or rather the interpretation pattern, that is "ideology"). The mode of production (public property, application of the Marxist-Leninist formula, etc.), becomes more important than the product itself and this has become possible thanks to the new social mediator, power without content, alienated in the bureaucratic list. By it, an age-long ambiguity of culture seems to be resolved: the project for the control of man over nature (the utopian limit of which is consumption) has been entirely engulfed by the one for the control of man over man (implying a potentially endless struggle for power). The various "triumphs" over nature, from agriculture to space travel, are nothing but *simulacra:* they have no value outside the great struggle (of classes, of systems, of gangs).

And yet, real communist societies differ from the ideal one in an important aspect: not all lists are public, they form a sort of conspirative hierarchy. For instance, a common man knows the list of party members, but the list of district-committee nomenclatura remains in principle a secret (a party member has more chances to know who participates at level No. 2). Ordinary police collaborators know nothing of the collaborators of the KGB. And maybe still less people know the list of those allowed to buy U.S. dollars or to grow mushrooms in their cellar. All this bears the traces of the underground period, when communists had to rely on pure secrecy with no properties. To found structures on the existing values (such as personal honor, truth, morals, etc.) would mean to accept the old world, which was supposed to be *demolished to the foundations.* The proletariat was supposed to be the radical negation of capitalist society and its avant-garde, communist party, could not base his activity on immediate positive values (the positive side of it should come afterwards, that is, it was **mediated** through the bright-future image). This is how Brecht puts it in **The Measure:**

> He who fights for Communism should be ready to fight and not to fight; to say the truth and not to say the truth; to do favours and not to do favours; to hold promises and not to hold promises; to seek danger and not to seek danger; to be seen and not to be seen. He who fights for Communism has only one of all the possible virtues: that he is fighting for Communism.

Today we perceive a macabre note in what Brecht thought to be an eulogy, although the description is quite right. The radical revolutionary, the communist, has only one trait, which amounts to tautology: that he is a revolutionary. Thus, the only way for him to be identified by his collaborators is the interplay of presence and absence—the secret list (absence from the public field, presence to conspiracy). When the underground revolutionary turns into an anonymous *aparatchick* the conspirative link becomes bureaucratic, but does not change in principle. All "depth" of the individual is but an artefact, the result of political decisions with no transcendence; all his or her traditional "contents" like competence, responsibility, morality, are reduced to the surface of pure presence or absence from the list. Even the will of those who interpret his behavior, as to range him or her into a given list, is not transcendental to the situation, as power is assumed in a collective way; for the first time in history the ruler has renounced to the essence of power—to have a face, an identity, a name, an opinion, a sense of pride or honor. Power is **anonymous** and consequently completely irresponsible, as there is no individual to assume personal responsibility. The mythical figure of the Leader carries this to the extreme—standing for the masses and for History itself, he is always right and never guilty, he won't die for anything, he personifies the masses' immortality (as a mummy, if necessary).

As a new type of social mediator, replacing money, laws, knowledge, etc., the nomenclatura list brings about a real revolution in human relations. It is the rationalization of the situation itself, making it possible to think and calculate the bare power-constellations without reference to anything else; thanks to it power can be from now on thought of in terms of being or not being there. (A similar revolution was, in its time, the invention of money, representing the bare value of a thing with no relation to its essence.[4]) In traditional representations of power, we are always "distracted" by something transcending it: a king makes us think of ancestors, blood, tradition, ritual; a president evokes the principle of representation; even a conqueror is associated with something other than pure presence like force or cruelty. The nomenclatura-member is the man without qualities, the relation between him and his place in society is mediated through the anonymous interpretative process.

All people living in such a society become members of **some** nomenclatura list, whether they wish it or not. In the course of the decencies this has a strange effect: little by little the seriousness of life disappears; instead of being interested by the depth of things, you turn more and more to the surface of language; instead of living, you represent yourself as somebody living. On the surface of simulation there is no place for the tragic essence of life, this is the kingdom of fiction, that is, of immortality. It is maybe the feeling of this tragic seriousness that makes the changes so difficult, almost impossible: how could a fiction become reality?

Storming the TV

The building of television was in the center of the Romanian revolution. In Sofia it was under siege for months, first by the one, then by the other, finally by both groups shouting at each other across the police cordon.[5] Unlike the riots in '68, no students demanded broadcasting time; it was *das Man* itself that attacked the media.

In the days of the French revolution, clocks are said to be shot at by the armed crowds; new religions burn the sacred books and destroy the temples of the old ones—in short, man fights not only with a body, but with a symbolic reality as well. But what does TV stand for? Its aim is no longer to represent some event or value: in its principle television is a substitute for reality, it is reality-as-artifact.

This makes storming the TV paradoxical: there is no longer any wax-enemy to be stabbed, nothing to be burnt, no symbols to be replaced; there simply is nothing but television as all aother representation can be televised. Thus the revolutionary masses don't seem to have much to communicate. It is as if Vladimir and Estragon had taken the stage by storm in order to find out there is nothing to do but be present there. And we saw them in Bucharest, crowding by dozens in front of the camera, pressing into the frame without a word. These were the revolutions of pure presence: no stratagem, no project for a better world was motivating them, as all that smells of transcendence had been discredited long ago.

Totalitarian culture once had largely been a culture of cinema. A film, being a closed system, produces both its text and its context (you watch it silently in the dark, as any other point of reference may disturb your perception). This creates a world of total relativity—Laurel & Hardy are small when the furniture around them is big; the voice of the commentator denotes the item shown on the screen as one does in real life, but in the film both voice and thing are man made. The Russian montage-school founded its whole theory on this; the experiments of Kuleshov showed that the whole meaning of a sequence may be changed; prisoner's face followed by window suggests longing for freedom, but that very same face, followed by a plate of soup, all of a sudden begins to express simple hunger. And yet we are persuaded that this is reality itself, as we identify the events and objects of life, being transcribed faithfully by the machine. Reality itself seems to be totally manipulated by a new, completely different type of author: not the one that speaks, writes, plays, but someone who mounts all these, a meta-author, placed above reality as a whole, he is born by our paranoid suspicion. The meta-author is often personalized in the person of the director of the film, but in fact "he" is a semiotic function, not less than the Leader in the fictionalized communist reality. You need a stratagem, a focus of some invisible interest behind in order to understand the mutilated—by scissors or by decrees—reality.

Totalitarianism went on and on with this film-editing *montage* principle: left in the dark with no outside points of reference, man was caught in a system of absolute relativity where life was lived to be represented and representations had to be acted out—take a 5-year plan, a party congress,[6] a brigade, a space rocket: was this fiction or reality? The edited reality produced, as in cinema, the figure of the "He who manipulates all this"—the Party and its Leader. You could prove or refute the existence of the meta-author no more than the existence of God; though He was badly needed to understand what had been deprived of sense.

The boredom of TV suddenly interrupts this paranoid process. There couldn't be an author behind televised reality as there couldn't be one behind the clock. As a form of synchronization of social life, as a measure of the public, TV seems to go back to what Weber called *formal rationality*. It is the becoming of the world itself—day after day things happen, information piles up, images seduce us, and there is no sense, no end, no transcendent meaning. No final touch, no summing up, no sacrifice is thinkable in this new medium: TV is life itself, it never stops, never leaves a trace upon eternity—as it is eternity itself. This makes it the ideal medium of post-communism (and maybe a determining factor of the changes, as well). By storming into the frame of TV, the masses destroyed not only the function of the meta-author, but with him the very possibility of history, which, as they have learnt from Hegel, begins with negativity, with death. And this seems to be the ultimate sense of this new, postmodern, postparanoid democracy: no power, no walls and borders, no progress, nothing—just being there, forever.

Dubrovnik, November 1990

Notes

1. It is ridiculous to talk about total control in underdeveloped countries, where a train can never leave on time. H. Arendt and others have explained the phenomenon by the principle of terror.

2. The priviledges of the elite (before the Briejnev era, which was of course the time of decay) cannot be compared to the

insecurity they lived. No one would risk his or her life just for a *datcha*; some quite different type of mivation was obviously moving people.

3. This can be clearly seen in the classic utopias: social regulations take the form of bureaucracy as it is the case with More's permissions to travel, Plato's—to have children, etc.

4. Could we go on with the parallel and speak of use-power and exchange-power?

5. Moscow putsch and counter-putsch were no less centered round the TV screen.

6. It's interesting how S. Krakauer relates the shooting of "The Triumph of Will": the Nazi congress in Nuremberg was apparently the event to be filmed, but actually the congress itself was prepared in such a way as to be filmed.

Epitaph for Sacrifice, Epitaph for the Left
Ivaylo Ditchev

▨ No Misery

The most significant trait of the times we live through: no one is willing to die for whatsoever. Their emblem: the delirious Gulf war, having as main objective to avoid casualties in the first place, a war, carried out to demonstrate that "all is under control" and thus negate death and loss.

"All that is not given is lost," says an Indian proverb; but in our contemporary world nothing is ever given and all seems lost. Unhappiness itself has been deprived of its Christian attraction: being poor and ill today provokes but repulsion, mixed with a 19th-century-styled philanthropic attempt to buy oneself out, to have no longer misery before one's eyes. Unhappiness frightens to death modern man, who, in plunging into a world of boundless positivity, has been left without defense against evil. Suffering no longer makes sense, therefore suffering is unbearable.

The name for it is decadence. Samuel Butler's witty anti-utopia "Erewhon" (= nowhere) was an introduction to the decadence of the last century. In his imaginary land, people are despised, sentenced, or even punished as criminals for the bare fact of being unhappy. Society has placed itself entirely on the side of fortune and order, and all of a sudden misery has become a much greater menace than crime: it has to be banned. The Malta talks can be seen as an introduction to the 20th *fin-de-siècle:* evil was suddenly ordered out of the world. In this way, an essentially tragic vision of duel between two superpowers, the outcome of which tended to apocalypse, was replaced by the comic one of a world where minor villains menace peace and happiness, but the centralized forces of good quickly teach them a lesson without really risking anything. Thus suffering, hardships, endurance, victims are from now on, denied legitimate right to exist; it is but a complication, a peripeteia before the burst of laughter. The miracle of fraternization is everywhere—East and West, then Jews and Arabs, who'll be the next? What's the use to fight, to defend interests, to try and return universal tendencies; the world is what it is, there are the rich countries and the poor ones, experience has shown that it is better for the poor to let themselves be guided by the rich. Every problem can be resolved by peaceful means under the new pax americana. Opposing, confronting, politicizing—these are remnants of a delirious sado-masochist past, when man thought he was concerned with power. Today power seems to disappear behind technicians, journalists, opinion polls, and currency rates and man seek his identity at home.

In such a tender decadent world, the Iraqi occupation of Kuwait or the Serbian aggression are but dead ends of history wherefrom nothing could follow: they are to be simply skipped (Kant defined the comic as an intensive expectation that dissolves suddenly into nothing). All local suffering, denied access to history, becomes an act of terrorism; instead of being defeated, it is to be punished. In the good old times of duel between good and evil, you sympathized with one party taking, if he had the courage to do so, the risk to engage oneself on his side. In the times when good is a sort of police for evil, one no longer fights evil or wishes to do so, he or she simply wants to do away with the center of infection, as wars and conflicts terrorize with the very fact that they exist. No one wishes to knows who is to blame for the horrors in Somalia or Bosnia, first comes "stop the war," and only after that "may the just cause win, if possible." The West has, so to say, assumed the role of a parent for the rest of the world. In between small local terrorists, children have quickly learnt to cheat on the police of good: they know perfectly well that they will never be defeated, as they are but the shadow of the New World Order, that is, they are not fighting, but producing signs of evil that block the system of centralized good (as any signs these can be bargained at a profit).

In Erewhon, as in the New World (Dis)Order, the negative is no full-right enemy, defying the positive in dubious battle. If negative exists at all, it is but a lack of self-confidence, a neurotic tic of the positive. Suffering, violence, and death are no longer a necessary element in the development of society, as the forces of good and reason have things under control; Mephisto is discharged. But if we are already there, then progress itself is no longer real; if it can be effectuated in a reasonable way, the forces of reason themselves should have attained the ideal and wouldn't be supposed to develop any longer. No need for the future to extract itself from the present in tragic labor; it is the sweet memories of past happiness that have replaced the vision of a better future. What comes can only frighten in its irrationality and absurdity. The future terrorizes exactly like the Somalian skeletons, the Yugoslav concentration camps, or the German burnt Turks. What will happen? Why should anything happen at all? What, if not final catastrophe and death, could bring us the future? The police of good and reason tries to keep, here as well, things under hand, to make believe that nothing will happen, or, as this is somewhat difficult a task, at least to play the Malta trick and turn tragedy into comedy, affirming that whatever happens will be of no importance. All great notions are back out of the cupboard, all eternal values, all fashions, all nostalgias to assure us magically that the world has always been the same, nothing ever changes, nothing really important is at stake.

This seems to be the real end to two millennia of Christian civilization. Because, paradoxically, the *laic* (people) fight for a better future, from the French revolution to the fight against fascism or against the Vietnam war, was the final crescendo of this civilization. In fact, the deepest motive force of the European left movements has neither been the striving for the public (at the expense of the private), nor for equality (at the expense of liberty), but the readiness to assume the tragic break between present and future, that is the willingness to sacrifice. It may be objected that many other political currents call on selflessness as well (in *Mein Kampf*, for instance, the Aryan is presented as superior to the Jew, in that he is able to sacrifice himself, the latter being condemned to die like a beast). However, there is a world of difference between the self-affirming sacrifice on the right, through which the "master" (in Hegel's terms) imposes his name, his will, his passions, his race, his masculinity, and the radical sacrifice on the left, experienced in the name of the oppressed as self-effacement of an anonymous, if not androgynous comrade in the "class," the "cause," the "historical necessity." (Or, if you wish, between phallus and castration.)

This explains why communism never won in the West: the East offers a better milieu for self-effacement. To take away private property or to erase the differences of class, knowledge, or sex is in its essence a sacrificial act, for he who does fight for such erasement, in expropriating the "phallus" of the ruling class, cancels the very possibility to acquire it himself, that is to be male, master, proprietor, etc. Envy destroys not only the other but oneself, as it undermines the very ideal of the ego (the "good object" of M. Klein). Nazism, if it had survived, would have ended up in liquidating all others; communism, after destroying all the ideal projects of the I (ancestors, tradition, identity, truth, dignity, law, wealth, science, and party members themselves) went as far as destroying itself in the supreme gesture of the Perestroika. The ultimate sacrifice of communism was the sacrificing of communism itself. (Is then communism dead or does it still live: here you are a logical paradox similar to the one of the liar saying "I am a liar.")

▨ Communism's Guilt Machine

It is not by chance that the fall of the Berlin wall brought about such unaccountable despair, and that, on both sides. It seems that the communist bloc played a greater role than people inside and outside it would be willing to admit. Today we could argue that the whole thing was a tasteless combination of Schlaraffenland and Gulag. And yet, in another perspective, the essential was not what communists were ready to die and kill for, but that they were ready to do so in a world of positivity, that had no defense against death: it was they who assumed to be the agent of the destruction of the old and the birth of the new, to be the ecstasy of rupture itself as scapegoats and hangmen at the same time.

The notion of sacrifice has been banalized by Stalinist propaganda, as well as by the anti-Communist folklore, but this should not mislead us. We simply have to get rid of its positive connotation: sacrificial exchange was but a type of social relation. In fact, being transformed into a state policy, manipulated, perverted, it became a terrible burden for the "liberated" populations. This side of communism is rarely analyzed; normally one is tempted to see the utilitarian side of the thing—the regime confiscates, the envious populations rob the individual of rights and property. But in fact the interaction had a deeper symbolic dimension. To make of the "proletarian"—by definition being deprived of property, power, knowledge, sex[1]—the basis of society means to incriminate all "phallic" attributes of man (power, property), and to impose symbolic castration as a moral (and even a juridical) norm: any form of existence above the imaginary zero-point called "proletarian" was branded with guilt. This has certainly been the utmost radicalization of Christian culture.

According to the official doctrine of the Stalin-era, the present generation had to be sacrificed for the one to come (this seems to be a "cosmization" of the convictions in the Slav-orthodox family that parents should "sacrifice" themselves for their children). Agriculture had to be sacrificed to industry, consumer-good production to the production of means of production. We could analyze the whole (pseudo-) Marxist economic theology in terms of what is due to what. Besides, children had to sacrifice their parents (Pavlik Morosov), party officials, accused by mistake, had to sacrifice their honor for the honor of the Party, etc.

Or take the example of the communist party, this strange structure that was supposed to govern the Soviet-style countries and that, according to Stalinist norms, covered up to 14 percent of the population. The Party was based neither on property, nor on birth, nor even on some special function or knowledge (the 14 percent pierced through all levels of society). What united its members, motivated by the normal human wish for social success, was the readiness to sacrifice themselves and feel guilty for what they would not sacrifice. A party member was supposed to work more than the rest; I do not say that he or she in fact did work, what matters is that they were expected to, both by official discourse of propaganda and by private grumble. He or she had to be at the disposal of the Party, because the Party had given them everything (work, house, life) and had thus infinitely indebted them: the member had to be ready, in return, at any moment to organize, to put into practice, to rouse enthusiasm, to be the avant-garde model for the rest. What observers rarely notice is that other stranger "moral" expectations were attached to those: for instance, the party member was supposed not only to be modest in his or her private life (initially: poor, of "proletarian background"), but also sociable, that is a "collectivist," transparent. There was a typical story of the party secretary who lived with no curtains. Privacy and selfishness was supposed to be sacrificed: the first step upwards in the social hierarchy (Komsomol, Party) implied an amount of self-denial or at least its simulacrum (the latter was obviously more often the case). But even then, imagine the identity of a person who is constantly torn between pretention and intention, imagine the lack of freedom that person would have to live with. What is more, the sacrifice/guilt pattern was linked to a monstrous apparatus of secrecy. Vague rumors of crimes, tortures and murders, racist and imperialist phantasms behind closed doors, secret, semicriminal advantages and benefits: this is what made the strange conspiratory organization in power stick together. It makes no sense to compare the privileges of the elites of "real socialism" with those in the developed countries or in Africa; the essential problem is that everything these elites possessed was outlawed and nevertheless tolerated, if not secretly encouraged; that the overall incrimination of social differences, opposed to the practice of such differences, created a situation of general indebtedness. One should not be astonished that ex-communist parties do not dissolve after the fall of the regimes: they are more than a political structure.

Power reposes on symbolic exchange; in order to rule you have to give. And yet, there seems to be no other example in history of such a systematic culpabilization of a ruling group.[2] One may think of early Islam, a culture imposing severe self-restrictions of those in power and equally tending towards military and ideological expansion; although Islamic culture guaranteed—at least to men—the superiority over women, providing thus the "natural" basis on which a minimum of power could be built up. Under communism all power had to be reconquered again and again by acts of sacrifice, as it had been deprived of "substance" (property, blood, sex). On the top of the pyramid there was the image of the sacrifice as such: Stalin, in his plain "stalinka," who didn't sleep at night, thinking so much of the well-being of the people and who even sacrificed his only son ("I don't exchange a soldier for a general"). He represented the perfekt I, the sublime effacement of individuality, melting into the anonymous masses. If we know today that despite his outward modesty and impersonality there was the perverse eroticism (or paranoia) of unlimited power, symbolic exchange remains the same: Stalin sacrifices his personal life to the people, the people ought to return the gift, in offering their freedom.

Thus communism, as designed by the Stalin era, transformed the purest essence of human nature: that is the faculty of giving, sacrificing, and owing into a monstrous technology of domination. The guilt machine it engendered seems perfect today, none the less it was—the result of a chaotic mixture of traditional Russian cultural structures, revolutionary ideas imported from the West, and a concurrence of circumstances. In fact, it was not giving, but taking away that came first historically: the Party had confiscated the whole of social reality, and thus everything, even life itself, became a gift and the object of symbolic exchange. Such relations with power were obviously an anachronism in the 20th century, for gifts are the exact opposite of rights. For instance, if travelling abroad were a right, you wouldn't have to feel grateful for being "let" abroad or guilty for having "fled." If there were public procedures of applying for a post and legal guarantees against being thrown out at any moment, the employee would not be indebted to the Party and could act as a free person according to his moral conscience. If you could buy all you need on the market using your own money, you would not be indebted to the seller, etc. Rights break the links and liberate the individual, symbolic exchange binds them to produce a community.

The greatest discovery of the system was the combining of the gift-and-sacrifice mode with bureaucratic anonymity. The unprecedented centralization of all that touched to representation aimed, primarily, at dissociating humans from their bodies. The physical, sexual, passionate subject, who in the traditional societies exchanged gifts and acts of generosity, were now replaced by an abstract bureaucratic file; humans were reduced to a point in the topography of nomenclatura. It was not the glorious chief X who was indebted to the notorious warrior Y, but an abstract bureaucratic position, defined in abstract terms (did he or she own a cow before the revolution? join the Komsomol? celebrate Lenin's anniversary?). Imagine that the glorious chief is not a desiring body, but a construction, a collage: some clerk registers a great victory he won, another sticks to him the glorious phallus, yet another makes the inventory of his ancestors. The file completed, he can be situated on nomenclatura level "chief" and effectuate a great, generous potlatch. Then some clerk (for some quite personal reason) inserts into the file the observation that the chief was telling political jokes, offending another chief: he is immediately placed into another level, and becomes, say, "foreigner" or "woman."

For the West, modernization implied the destruction of the symbolic exchange between social positions and persons, in introducing rights, mediators, neutral (Wertfreie-Weber) spheres of transaction and thought where the subject doesn't oblige and isn't obliged to anyone. Marx, one of the most radical thinkers of western modernity, as well as Nietzsche and Freud, concentrated their fire in the first place on the symbolic debt that mystified the relations between man and power. They were obviously working in the right direction; by the end of modernization, not only the notion of morals and guilt, but the overall system of giving and sacrificing was eliminated from culture. Thus loss, misery, and death loosed all their sense and became an object of dumb horror for the individual.

The East, and Slav orthodoxy in particular, lived the shock of modernization in quite another way: it radicalized and globalized the sacrifice/guilt pattern, extending it to cosmic, eschatological dimensions. No single spot of reality was left untouched by owing-and-being-owed, no indifferent nature or rational, pragmatic interaction sphere outside the splitting into friends and enemies, progressive and reactionary, good and evil. The heroic movement forward to industrialization seemed to be but the ideological facade for its opposite—the radicalization of the symbolic exchange pattern; and it is Dostoievsky rather than Marx who can explain to us this universe, attempting to jump over modernity: "Everyone is guilty before everyone for everything and this is paradise."[3]

▨ Seduction International

The symbolic exchange had its international dimension. On one side you had countries that kept their habits, brands of whiskey, names of the streets; on the other, the five-year-period is the maximum that reality can hold out. Apart from the heroic side of suffering, representing the great socialist experiment as the guiding star of humanity, in everyday life the East developed a strange discursive masochism, a morbid delight to dwell in misery under the gaze of the prosperous West, horrified by unhappiness. It was as if division of labor was effectuated throughout Christian civilization: one half had undertaken to be happy and enjoy itself, the other to sacrifice and suffer. (As far as the facts it was the contrary, for it was the West that worked harder, but I am considering images, not economy). There exists an ancient archetype: some renounce to life, that is, to pleasures, sex, freedom, power, success, and wealth and submit of their own free will to discipline and privations by going to a monastery/convent. Monasteries are miniworlds, situated by the side of the real one, they have social structures, culture, laws, power relations, and even economic production of their own—only life is supposed to be harder than outside. They are worlds of permanent sacrifice, especially concerning the sexual side of the human being,[4] worlds that take onto themselves suffering in order to liberate the "real" one from it.

We can see the communist bloc as a planet-scale monastery, where suffering and misery is assumed to liberate the rest of the world from the anxiety before it. Symbolic exchange was globalized through the massmedial unification of the world. Note the strange fight carried out of communist and Stalinist ideology against all that might be pleasant: fashion, dancing, chewing gum, entertainment, "art for art's sake," infidelity, and all hints of eroticism. How does this fit into a "materialist" ideology? In a strange way the phantasms as Slav (Russian) soul, communist martyrdom, and postcommunist "miserabilism" merge. One somehow expects suffering to take place in this part of the world, that is, voluntary suffering (and this is why the third world can hardly play the role of monastery). It seems—or seemed for some time—quite natural that whole postcommunist populations bombard the West with victimary discourses, saying that everything of the life "before" was awful, absurd, ugly, terrible, every single minute of it.

Leave aside the question whether it was really that awful and if it could have been much better without communism. Just imagine, say, a well-bred healthy engineer, head of a family, coming up to you and saying: "I was a slave, all my life they humiliated me, you cannot understand." What noble ideals of personal freedom he must have, if he feels like this. Even if the man had really been a slave during the whole of his life, why should he tell it with so much excitement? Why should he draw an almost masochistic pleasure in the idea of his real or imaginary sufferings? Moreover, the real martyrs of the regime, for example, survivors from the camps, are much more reluctant to complain, trying to save their dignity in some way or another. Miserabilism is the cultural norm, a sort of perverted identity and you should not be surprised to hear the victimary discourse even from high-ranking communist officials. Living under the conditions of chronic indebtedness has evoked chronic self-hatred.

The self-hatred discourse became a genre of communication long before the fall of communism, and in some of the countries long before its establishment: standing in queues or having a dull time in an office, people amused each other with facts or jokes showing "how normal everything is abroad and how absurd it is at home." Here is a real one: a Japanese literary scholar was said to have expressed astonishment at the bold imagination of a bulgarian poet having written: "if suddenly there were a power cut." Whereas to the Japanese the image of electricity being cut off all of a sudden is a metaphor, similar to the one of the sun being extinguished, no Bulgarian will ever suspect it to be a figure of speech. In fact metaphor was the chief strategy of the genre, that is, the comic jump from "here" onto "there": everything "here" is a metaphor of the original "there." And if propaganda projected this original onto the communist future, whereas everyday life discourse projected onto the consumer paradise, it boils down to the same (in fact by the end of the '70s this difference began to disappear, as the regimes looked more and more westwards). What persists is self-hatred.

Here is one more sample of the genre, this time a fiction. A Russian specialist falls among man-eaters, who capture him and prepare the cauldron. "Comrades"—he addresses them—"Have you ever heard of the Great Socialist October Revolution?" "No."—the tribe answers. "Do you know what in means to built socialism?" "No." "Have you ever celebrated the centenary of the great Lenin?" "No." "Then why have you become man-eaters?" The joke obviously attacks the communist thing; note however the masochist axis on which it has been built: the "we" is degraded to savagery. This is not the irony that every "normal" (non-monastic) nation has for its shortcomings. Pretending to boast that the USSR is the best (the sacrificial avant-garde of humanity), it effectuates an about-turn in order to present them as being the worst (cannibals). Curiously, however, the two extremes merge, because to confess you are bad, sacrificing your pride and identity, means that you become even better then those who have lead a normal virtuous life. (This paradox used to be the kernel of Christianity: you cannot be virtuous, affirm it, remain it without committing the "sin of pride"; you have to sin and repent.) The "we-are-the-worst" genre is running higher and higher these days; the whole of life "before," that is economy, politics, art, is not only rejected, but bluntly destroyed, sacrificed before the fascinated eye of the West. (What noble ideals of economy and social life they must have to act like this.)

Certainly there has much to be changed, and certainly it has to be done quickly. There is, however, something suspect in the readiness and euphoria with which whole populations engage, for the second time in less than a century, in the making *tabula rasa* of the past, sacrificing the totality of social reality before the altar of modernity. It is this belief in miracles, more typical of the countries of orthodox culture, and particularly of Russia, that combine in a strange way with the armchair theories now of Marx, now of the Monetary Fund. The economic miracle, as any other one, is to be paid for by suffering; although, unlike the individual everyday sacrifice, required by the "protestant ethic" (M. Weber), the orthodox ethic exalts unrealistic hope, cataclysm, fusion in the community, Easter.

No one has the right to judge a whole culture; the problem consists in the fact that today this (as any other) culture is no longer isolated, being involved in the worldwide seduction game with the West. In destroying itself, the East tries to capture, once more, the love of the West, to impose an obligation on it. In fact, the two central figures in the transition period discourse are the debt of the respective country towards the West (no one ever bothers to specify who the creditors are and whether the western countries themselves are not even more indebted) and the duty of the West towards the East (you have let us suffer in signing the Yalta agreement, in not declaring us war). The West has, so to say, given credit to the communist fathers, then indebted them, now it ought to give new credit to the sons. The fathers won over the West by sacrificing themselves in the fight against fascism; the sons have to win their heart by equal selflessness in fighting communism. All around the ex-soviet bloc there is the rumor of a new Marshall plan, which the West is somehow obliged to launch, and this makes one think of the Bolsheviks, who awaited the general proletarian revolution as help, reward, and recognition. What will happen when the "masochistic" peoples realize that misery is banned and that the wealthy democracies are not involved in symbolic exchange with them, but only in selling images?

Towards Ecophilanthropy

Today it seems that Soviet communism, in making perverse usage of sacrifice and generosity, compromised the very possibility of left-wing ethics. But then why did the Brezhnev universe itself decay in introducing hereditary principles of power, open privileges, security, cynicism?

Demographers would tell us that along about the '70s the massive processes of migration were stabilized, the flux of rural populations to the industrial zones diminished parallel with the slowing down of extensive growth of production. All desired liberations were, if not fulfilled, at least accepted by public discourse. In fact the Fourierist revolution of '68, based not on sacrifice and misery, but on sex and happiness, was a sort of suicide for the European left and it was not by chance that the aging communist parties were instinctively against it. Pleasure was enthroned, nothing in principle was any longer opposed to desire: it remained just to devise technologies to fulfill it. Somehow the world need no longer change. Even the scientific euphoria seemed over, after man had marched on the moon: a dream had come true and what of it? If television had not existed, this epoch would have invented it. Wasn't it in fact TV that killed the left, as well as real socialism? Its pan-aesthetic mode of life was a perfect shield against sacrifice and generosity. Even the fall of communism turned out to be but a media scoop, implying neither risk nor engagement. There is nothing to take or give to the picture-world; being situated outside it, you cannot even answer by a picture of your own, as this, unlike using normal language, is technically impossible. The only thing you are supposed to do is contemplate it motionless in the dark.

Trying to do without the ordeal of change, a happiness-bound world replaces the tragic figure of the revolutionary by the comic one of the philanthropist. Neither left-wing nor right-wing, he is a protagonist of decadence. In the imaginary world of the 19th century, he never risks his life, nor even seriously damages his wealth; he gives without really losing, resolving thus miraculously the fundamental problem of human existence. If today the good-natured uncle with the top hat has been replaced by televised humanitarian missions, the desire they express is still the same. So to say, the "master," the former colonialist, the postindustrial capitalist has suspended the give-and-take exchange with the "slave," he will give, although, seemingly not in order to bind and subject the latter to his will, but to get rid of him! The gift draws lines of demarcation: we rich are here, you poor stay there. The ideology of this new status quo is a sort of racist, cultural or other ecology, aiming at preserving everything as it is. The industrialized West accepts to pay ransom in order to get rid of the suffering, straining in all over the world.

According to psychoanalysis, the repressed never does disappear, at one time or another it re-emerges in an irrational form; similarly, repressed misery and suffering shall certainly be back one day, the whole problem is under what a monstrous shape they will manifest themselves. I wonder whether the western TV-watcher realizes what humiliating, degrading effect this sort of "ecological" aid has on the population, denied forever access to the community of their benefactors? And that what the wretches on the far side of TV really need is someone to fight shoulder to shoulder with them, moved by the project of unification for mankind.

The world seems never to get wiser. If you want to know about today, look back at post-Fourierist 19th century decadence with its horror of death and the future, with its obsession with beauty and well-being. If you want to know about tomorrow, think of what followed.

Notes

1. In the *Manifesto* capitalist machine production is accused of effacing the differences between men and women, which was, in fact, another culpabilizing phantasm (if so, why should spinning factories be reserved for women?)
2. The communist party was obviously not a ruling class: not all members had power, though all in power had to be members. It was a virtual identity, a promise of power, provoking shared crime and shared guilt.
3. This is the sublime revelation of the future saga Zossima after having renounced the idea of duel, that is, of personal masculine honour ("The Karamazov Brothers").
4. Note the equation that Freud establishes between the fear of death and the fear of castration. Assuming castration would equal assuming death. Note the Puritan obsession of Soviet-style communism after the 20s.

An Essay on Terror
Alexander Kiossev

To Vladislav Todorov (by whom this text has doubtless been influenced)

1. The Ultimate Revolution

In a sense, all revolutions have been a failure. Not that they failed to achieve their ends (although this is also true): they were not truly revolutionary—they were no radical utopias.

All utopias dream of a future fairer order, which presupposes that the current order will be destroyed. However, all interpretations of social systems or orders to date have been rather narrow minded: changes have affected the political, economic, or class order alone, overlooking the global symbolic order of which the affected order is a part. Total power, which revolution craves to seize and change, belongs to neither politicians nor the rich, nor to any classes—for they all must conform to realities. "Realities" are nothing but symbolic products, effects of the symbolic order, of its infinite mesh of symbolic games generating its own referents within itself.

What could the idea of an ultimate revolution possibly be? To replace the symbolic order by another, juster one. This is tantamount to replacing realities by other, juster ones.

Of course, empirical revolutions destroy and replace certain old symbolic subsystems—they rename streets and months, change the spelling, rewrite history, or introduce a new chronology. As all things empirical, however, this is far from the eidos of total revolution which will replace everything—from the structure of social groups to the structure of dreams, from comprehensible everyday vocabulary to the cultural and physiological mechanisms of erection—by something else which is juster. Something juster will also replace the very notion of justice, for this notion also belongs to the old symbolic order, along with that of change. And with the notion of a notion.

The ultimate revolution will not materialize when everything written by poets and philosophers comes true, but when something more—all they have not written—comes true, too (for writings and inventions are also captives of the old, unjust social order). The ultimate revolution dissolves into its own infinity (which is paradoxical?, vicious?—we cannot know since the laws of logic have been replaced by other, juster ones).

The only thing that cannot be conceived of as changed is the instrument which will effect "the change." Terror.

In this sense the "velvet revolutions" that swept across Eastern Europe are revolutions without a specific quality. Their lack of a reign of terror is a problem. It can be formulated in two ways: 1. Why was there no reign of terror? Now this is a theoretical problem. 2. When will there be a reign of terror? This is a practical problem.

Because of his innate, irrational optimism, this writer opts for the theoretical problem.

2. Symbol and Blood

It is an ancient truth written in blood that major values, standards, and norms are imposed by force. Violence, however, should not be regarded as limited and localized in those high levels of symbolic order only. It is not to be found within "the values" only—violence is all-pervasive.

From Plato's *Cratylus* to Ferdinand de Saussure's and Benvenist's courses in general linguistics, all projects on semiotics have focused on one problem: is the relation between signifier and signified arbitrary? The answer depends on the type of mediating "third term," which is in-between the signifier and the signified. It could be a "natural rightness" of the relationship—or again, it could be a "pure convention." The signifier could be related to the signified by the very nature of the latter, by the reality of the signified. The polar view holds that they are bound by the conventional reality of social habits.

A view which invalidates the "natural"-vs.-"conventional" opposition eliminates this pointless alternative. Realities are symbolic conventions which are forgotten to have been conventions. Far more force has been used and far more blood shed to strike THEM out from memory, than for "the values" and "models." Conventions are the result of ultimate violence—a violence which does not concentrate on a visible bursting point, but drains through an infinite network of invisible channels: violence so stark that it suppresses its own terror by turning it into a habit, into naturalness, naturality, reality.

Realities are conventions which are forgotten to have been conventions; conventions are violence forgotten to have been violent.

Suppressed (from "suppression" or *Verdrängung*) violence is what welds the signifier and the signified together. To be born, "the world" was terrorized.

3. Tattooing and Articulation

The human body seems to be a reality. It seems to be the ultimate reality which will survive even when all others have crumbled. Everyone from Protagoras to modern philosophical anthropologists have seen this reality as a measure, a scale of all other realities. The reality of the human body seems to be the foundation that makes possible all other symbolic-system-realities (even the Lord bows before it during the Last Judgement—and obeys the need to raise the dead in flesh and bone in order to administer divine justice).

Yet as a transcendent signified, the human body cannot survive the infinite symbolic dynamics, the game of signifiers. The symbolic order(s) scars the body with social labels of sex, status, age, ethnicity. These, however—clothes, colors, accessories—are just the body's outermost semiotic crust.

On a more inward plane, the symbolic order of a certain culture is tattooed on the body irreversibly: it pricks a pattern into the skin, cuts the breasts into shape, moulds Chinese feet, stretches the native's lip to the ground, or circumcises the Muslim.

On an even deeper level, the symbolic order may interfere with the so-called physiology of the body itself—it could make the body vomit in disgust, infect or heal it, change its sex, delimit it from (or merge it with) other bodies. This is a kind of deeper tattoo: a deep engraving which determines the form of the body's very "reality." The ultimate in this tattoo is articulation: the body is articulated in parts, zones, members.

Lacan claims that the subconscious is structured like language, or more precisely, like a multitude of superseding vertical levels of signifiers: the prototypal text of the subconscious is the unattainable point at which the symbolic order has clashed with nonarticulated biologism over what ought to be called the proto-body. This is where it was tattooed, engraved in this proto-body, sinking ever deeper, shaping its amorphousness, articulating within it differentiated parts, coherent forms, erogenous zones for the first time ... Only thanks to articulation did amorphousness evolve into a body, into a reality identical to itself.

The constitution of the body's reality is an act of violence doomed to oblivion. At the same time, it is a mystery (since all violence is, among other things, a mystery phenomenon). In ancient rituals, the human sacrifice objectified this mystery violence: one could see the axe of symbolic order drop and dismember the body. Mysteries are not just violence. They are also a revelation: one can see the dismembered becoming articulate, categorical, definite.

In his short story "The Penal Colony," Franz Kafka invented a machine for ultimate revolutions. This machine radically engraves the new symbolic order straight onto the body of the condemned, which for an instant flutters on the verge between life and death, in the domain of revelation. At first the uninitiated take the engraved body for a terrorized body—but terror in the colony follows rigid rules and conventions. From the colony's perspective, the body is conventionalized so as to be transformed into a new, changed body—into a new reality. The new body's passage unto death is more than a matter of pure biology. A reversal is still possible until this moment: the body can revert to its old reality, the new reality proving to be pure convention, pure arbitrariness, pure violence. Death rules out the possibility of a reversal as the new reality evolves into something which seems to escape the symbolic order and pass into a beyond of sorts: it becomes super-reality. The referent becomes a Transcendent Referent. Nothing can provide a more efficient foundation for the new symbolic order than the guarantee of death—death provides the fixed point which transcends all structures and avoids the endless game of signifiers. At the same time this game, which *per se* would build a network of equally arbitrary terrorist conventions, gets a chance to produce reliable, resistant realities guaranteed by superreality: death.

A revolution which does not terrorize, tattoo, engrave and/or articulate the body, which does not bring it to the verge of death, is an unstable revolution. The enforcement of its symbolic order is reversible. It lacks a foundation. That is why this revolution could always crumble back into laughter: uncemented by terror, its symbolic constructs could always rebound; they could always be denounced as being entirely arbitrary, brazen. It is constantly threatened by its own (latent) comic metamorphosis: to become an unfounded claim.

Lyotard recounts how the King of Ou ordered his general, Sun Tze, to make fine soldiers out of 180 of the his favorite wives. The general started drilling them to turn "right!," "left!," and "about face!" to the drumbeat. The women giggled, chatted, and refused to obey. The general drew his sword and chopped off the heads of two of the king's best-loved wives. He got perfect discipline. The new symbolic order promptly triumphed: the women started behaving as soldiers. The lapse into laughter was no longer possible. Death stabilized the new realities.

4. Nonspecific Revolutions

The velvet revolutions have been velvet until now. They have not exploded into a mass reign of terror so far (at the time of this writing, 20 August 1991). Perhaps there will be no reign of terror, and this will set a precedent in history.

The velvet revolutions did not make a terrorist attempt to engrave a new symbolic order onto the biological body of the individual or group social bodies. They presupposed that, in fact, nothing new needed to be imposed—it was enough to simply clear the way for the old order, a "natural" order, which had always existed and had merely been subjected to terrorist repression under totalitarianism. Therefore, many people declared the velvet revolutions to be restorations or counter-revolutions rather than revolutions. However, something was wrong, and this was obvious in the paradoxical names tagged on to them: "velvet revolution," "counter-revolution of normality." Something "natural" and "normal" needed to be restored—but the restoration itself had to be effected through a paradoxical gesture which went beyond a simple establishment of normalcy. It was not necessary to resort to terror since the "normal" and "natural" symbolic order was conceived of as the hitherto suppressed reality itself, which now had a right to free expression. However, this reality had been suppressed too hard too long—it could no longer merely set in, it had to triumph. This was possible in only one way—which was radically different from terror—as a festival.

In festivals, reality is manifested as joy. The problem velvet revolutions seemed to face was not the forcible installation of a new symbolic order, but an ecstatic expression of the old one. Imbued with humanistic and liberal values, the "natural" bodies emerged in the menacing public space of totalitarianism and started eliminating its external limitations. They broke all public rules, reshuffled present perspectives of totalitarian architectural space, pronounced tabooed words and sang tabooed songs, used an inconceivable language, proceeded from "eternal" symbols. The conflict seemed to be between "inward" naturalness and "outward" violence; reality vs. fear. The festival got in full swing when, identified in its arbitrariness, terror (seen as a purely external limitation, a threat external to the free "natural" will) seemed to have vanished—the totalitarian world collapsed as a house of cards: a world without a foundation.

In fact, this was just underrating totalitarianism and totalitarian terror.

In the wake of the radical festival, the bodies, which had gotten an opportunity for expression, were expected to remain in the everyday world and face their "normalcy" and "naturalness." This did not happen. After the symbolic order of totalitarianism was denounced, the signifiers—declared "old" and "normal"—of democracy, freedom, and perennial values refused to meld with the available signified: mutants, mute chthonic creatures for which there were no symbols, crawled out of the crack between the symbolic orders. The "normal" became a post-totalitarian utopia—the average "das Man" was crowned with a transcendent nimbus in the West.

5. The Post-totalitarian Mutant

The mutant metaphor is important here. A mutant is any articulation with an error, an aberration in the programming code. Of course, "error" and "aberration" are other, already obsolete metaphors. They are figures of the suppression of a "rightness" whose model has been imposed by violence. That is why we will take a different approach to mutation: a mutant is an articulation which results from the interbreeding of two (or more) codes; a mutant is any articulation in which the symbolic order is engraved incompletely, any misprint: its "incompletion" and "misprinting" are the result of another code in action.

In a mutant, the violence of symbolism could never settle completely—in oblivion. The two intersecting symbolic orders mutually demonstrate their arbitrariness. Mutant articulations cannot petrify in "naturalness"; they are the eternal burning memory of the fact that every reality is semiotically (i.e., violently) articulated.

Totalitarianism did its best to articulate correct, nondeformed totalitarian bodies. Both the theory and practice of terror were radicalized precisely under totalitarianism: dozens of millions were liquidated and as many were concentrated: the collective bodies were subjected to new discipline in camps, the construction of motorways, sun cities, inter-sea canals, and tenements (Vladislav Todorov). All former spaces, institutions whose mazes and channels used to traditionally discipline the bodies, were transformed.

Still, communist totalitarianism suffered from a rashness and incompleteness. It was rash because it wanted to achieve in dozens of years what other civilizations had done in centuries; it wanted to carry out too quickly the terror-convention-reality transition. In earlier civilizations, the violent engraving of symbolic order spanned dozens of generations, it ramified and scattered into myriad small centers of violence (family, informal communities, professional groups, school, hospital, army...). Communist totalitarianism set out to radically centralize all violence—and to do it fast on an industrial scale. This, however, triggered local resistance—micro-institutions of the former symbolic reality conspired against the new symbolic order and cocooned a series of old symbolic chains: the radical centralization project proved to be a utopia.

The other flaw of communist totalitarianism was that it failed to achieve the radical expansion which would have left it without competition as regards the criteria of "reality." It coexisted with another reality-producing system of a relatively traditional type (Western society, "realized" through the symbolic order of the Modern Age). Thus conspiratorial foci, which produced alternative reality within the totalitarian society, acquired an external verification of their symbolic production: alternative reality existed out there somewhere as "normal" reality.

This prevented totalitarian terror from becoming total terror: it remained a "reality" in *statu nascendi*, heterogeneous and at war with former traditional forms of "reality."

The body of totalitarian man was in a constant process of double, militant engraving: it was articulated as a mutant of the incomplete and ongoing war between two incompatible symbolic orders. Totalitarian man proper thus remained incomplete. His body wavered between two conflicting engravings—it was a traumatic body as an experience of an unachieved terrorist-conventional identity. However, it was also a mutant body due to the impossibility of such an achievement—because of the interference of incompatible symbolic models.

6. Velvet Revolutions as a Festival; Festivals as Tics of the Schizoid Body

Minimal revolutions could not have resorted to terror because of the utopia of normalcy—this would have run counter to the immanent meaning of the utopia. As mentioned above, they acquired their purely symbolic expression in the festival—the wild revelry and abandonment of liberated "natural" bodies expressing the "perennial" articulations of democracy, freedom, humane justice, etc.

Festivals radically changed these bodies' habitat—but could not interfere in their tattoos and engravings as radically. Bodies remained mutants with a traumatic self-awareness of being "abnormal" (which, in fact, was only a memory of the terror).

Presumably, festivals could not solve this problem. They are conservative in their very function—their task is to disperse maturing destructive energies in an established symbolic reality so as to reproduce this same reality, stabilizing its referents. The festival is a ritual act for the purge-innovation-reproduction of the everyday world—the ruling symbolic order. Revolutions are catastrophically providential, whereas festivals are cyclic; revolutions change the ruling order, while festivals reproduce and consolidate it. Revolutions are followed by a totally new everyday life, and festivals—by an old, traditional everyday life.

The revolution-presented-as-restoration called to life street festivals—they were only to purge and establish "the order of normalcy." These festivals were to have expressed "living in truth" and restored the cycle of a normal everyday life. This meant that the body had to carry out procedures and acts intended to purge and peel former symbolic cumuli—cumuli of the totalitarian "unnatural" symbolic order. Unlike terror, however, festivals did not rearticulate the body once and for all (bringing it near death), but merely masked, disguised it. Terror engraves the body; festivals paint on the body—they paint on it, hyperbolically doubling this body's own members. Terror engraves and articulates a new body. Festivals only explicate and celebrate the old body's traditional symbolic elements.

Totalitarian engravings had to be cast aside, shed through festive cries, grimaces, and dances. This, of course, was impossible. The festivals of velvet revolutions painted on bodies their own normalcy—but under the surface, their distorted, nonfocused, mutant members struggled to break out. In the upended public and architectural space, the bodies danced, grimaced, and twisted in an effort to shed their tattoos and tear their own monstrous members engraved by totalitarian terror.

This was impossible. More and more festivals were held. The street gestures and grimaces of mutant bodies struggling to break free and purge themselves, froze in tics.

Tics are the festivals of mutants turned into a fixation. Tic-festivals were to have made up for the lack of a reign of terror—that is why conventionally enacted mystery forms of terror could be made out in the motions of the feting bodies. There was a universal yearning for some kind of grand Orgasm-Catharsis-Repentance, some beyond-Terror, which would have made a new life possible.

7. The Unbearable Everyday World

Traditional festivals impose and establish a cosmic order—an everyday world. Festivals present forgotten (conventionalized and suppressed) terror as harmony and meaning which permeate the everyday world.

The post-totalitarian everyday world could not produce the order and meaning yearned for by the festivals of velvet revolutions. It was a somber space of hunger and futurelessness. In the everyday world, mutation affected not only bodies, but also all foci of the socium: there was no bread in the bakeries which sold shirts, tons of meat were dumped during the worst famine, writers and cops turned businessmen, decaying animals floated in the Black Sea and fish died, streets were littered all over, leaders of the opposition proved to be liars, mutant communists increased their mutant electorate.

In this sense, the post-totalitarian everyday world was a reign of terror—but a peculiar kind of terror. It was in the bodies themselves: social space terrorized itself through an immanent terror. A traditional reign of terror imposes an order-and-meaning. Post-totalitarian terror ensued from the painful experience of the absence of order and meaning: a chaotic machine which inscribes a set of meaningless letters and pseudo-signs on bodies—it tattoos them with scribbles, with disgusting drawings, and articulates them in line with the forms of chaos. Unlike all other kinds of violence, which transcended into a conventional order and meaning (and were therefore bearable), this terror was unbearable. It did not lead to the realm of revelation.

There is only one salvation from unbearable terror: flight. Some people took flight to the space west, which blinded them with its radiant "Normalcy" (a geographical utopia).

Others sought refuge in religion—the meaninglessness of the post-totalitarian everyday world was declared to be an excruciating Trial on the way to the future Revelation.

Still others took to flight in a recurrent Tic-festival which enabled them to scream "Down with communism" until breathless, and went on and on as a permanent street promise of the Great Catharsis.

All fugitives bore along their mutant bodies—which in fact generated the meaningless terror.

8. Instead of an End

This text stops at this point—at the point where history has stopped. It will not mutate into forecasts and optimistic versions. This makes it meaningless; an essay with neither a future nor a hope—a text which emanates the violence it describes.

August, 1991

An Essay on Theoretical Terror
Ivan Kristev

The 1694 *Dictionnaire of the Academie Francaise* already distinguishes the political meaning of the word "revolution": "a vicissitude, a major change in the destiny and in the things of the world." Furthermore, the *Dictionnaire* recommends six appropriate adjectives qualifying the revolution: "great, timely, surprising, strange, wonderful, amazing."

In "An Essay on Terror," Alexander Kiossev is also faced with the need to define the revolution and to specify it through adjectives. In a mystic way, he likewise ends up with six adjectives: "ultimate, empirical, total, velvet, unstable, minimal."

The discrepancy is full and symptomatic. The fate of the word "revolution" has undergone a great change. What characterizes the concept vested in the Academie Francaise *Dictionnaire* is that "it (the revolution) is a category of historical awareness, an event which could be identified only *ex post facto.*" The intuition of the *Dictionnaire's* authors is that revolutions are not made—they happen. This intuition stems from a definite historical reality: The Glorious English Revolution. Until the mid-18th century, the word "Revolution" was capitalized only when referring to the events in England in 1688.

On hindsight, however, this first European revolution strikes one with its unspecificness. It was not brought to life by a radical utopia nor based on a project which was to be fulfilled. It seems as though the sole purpose of this revolution was for it to be forgotten. Nor is this accidental. The Glorious English Revolution problemizes the "apparent" connection between utopia and revolution. For unlike Alexander Kiossev, this writer could hardly assume that utopia can boil down to the "dream of a future fairer order, which presupposes that the current order will be destroyed." Utopia or, to be precise, the utopia of the Modern Age is an alternative world not in the sense of an idyllic picture but as a rational construct, a project which is fulfillable under certain circumstances. That is why utopia is first and foremost a text or a family of texts: a text which precedes revolution and should be substantiated.

"The Glorious Revolution" of 1688 lacked such a text. It was, rather, mottoed by the restoration of an erstwhile political order as a new interpretation of an already substantiated text: the Holy Bible. The English Revolution was conceived at that time as a rejection of political anarchy and rampant instability—events which were known at that time as "revolutions." It was a Revolution-Restoration, a restoration of fundamental political laws; a Revolution bracketed off by modernity. Much later, in 1790, Edmund Burke was to admit that what attracted him in the "Glorious Revolution" was its nonrevolutionariness. This admission was made possible by the storming of the Bastille on 14 July 1789.

The Invisible Geography

In Kiossev's concept—a concept wholly in the spirit of the modern age—the revolution presupposes a radical utopia, the making of a world, the creation of a new political Adam. Kiossev's intuition with regard to revolutions is based entirely on the experience of the French Revolution, which became a model in the mid-19th century and was "repeated" as such in 1917. Imposing the French Revolution as a model was closely related to the intellectual dominance of radical ideologies (and Marxism in particular), which elaborated the doctrine of typical (the French) and untypical (the English) revolutions. The utopia-revolution-Terror relation also emerges within the thus imposed "typicality"; in Kiossev's view, this relation acquires the dimension of universality. This makes it possible to construe "the ultimate revolution"—a revolution which is not confined to political change but "replaces realities by other, juster ones." The ultimate revolution may be triggered only by an ultimate utopia. It cannot have conscious agents; it is a text which cannot be interpreted because all interpretations are locked within existing realities. The ultimate revolution changes EVERYTHING: "the only thing that cannot be conceived of as changed," writes Kiossev, "is the instrument which will effect 'the change.' Terror." Terror is the *differencia specifica* of all revolutions. In talking of revolutions, we talk of Terror. That is why the study is entitled "An Essay on Terror." An essay provoked by the complex reality of "gentle revolutions," of their "abnormality," "misconstrued modernity." An essay provoked by the fact that the theoretical reflections on these revolutions resign themselves to the absence of a Reign of Terror, to the disruption of the link between Terror and revolution. Kiossev regards his own text as radical (a text "beyond good and evil") precisely because he refuses to accept the apparent naturalness of this absence.

The ultimate revolution, the universal Terror-convention-reality transition, the Terror-festival opposition: radicalized, Kiossev needs all those fundamental "prostheses" (to quote Vladislav Todorov) so as to regard the Eastern European change as a revolution, as the making of a world.

Yet isn't "An Essay on Terror" an attempt at Terror? How should one interpret the stance of Kiossev, perched on the Danton-Derrida line and engulfed by the hysterical chaos or chaotic hysteria of a political situation which counters any attempt at being rationalized? A public inquiry into Alexander Kiossev's eroticized metaphors presupposes applying historicism (this is the only way they can be made comprehensible and responsible). In this case, historicism is an instrument for deradicalization, for decoding the aforementioned text in its preconception, in its ultimate gesticulation.

The primary metaphor is the Reign of Terror. It is branded with a metaphysical metaphoricalness. The Reign of Terror is taken out of all context whatsoever and stripped of its traditional content. It stands for terror, fear, a premonition of terror, and something else, plus other things. It creates the world (visions the world); forgetting Terror makes it possible for the world to exist. Terror is forgotten in its excess. Applying historicism presupposes treating the Reign of Terror not as spontaneous violence but as an instrument for the creation of a "juster world" which is, at the same time, like this selfsame world. If in Kiossev's radical concept Terror and violence are synonymous, this writer's stance is radically different. The very idea of regarding them as two words with the same meaning seems to me ultimately suspicious, terrorist.

The French Connection

The Reign of Terror is no spontaneous violence. It must be organized and motivated. In his brilliant study "Revolutionary Terror," French philosopher Claude Leforte upholds the thesis that the debates on Terror which flared up in the Convent in Year II were part of the Terror itself. The Reign of Terror is unthinkable without a constant self-quotation of motives or an incessant emphasis on its mystic association with Liberty and Equality. Terror talks—it talks about itself—and this makes it different from the mute violence against tyrants. Terror is theatricalized and performed before an audience in the squares of the Republic. It is not accidental that the main points motivating every Reign of Terror are: first, the idea of the latter's inevitability and second, the creation of a polar space where revolutionary Terror is opposed to counter-revolutionary Terror, red to white Terror. "What constitutes the Republic," says Saint-Just, "is the total annihilation of everything that opposes it." Terror visualizes the relation of death to Liberty and Equality. The world of the dead is symmetrical to the utopian world which is to be imposed. Rousseau's prerevolutionary view that man is born free was enhanced by the idea, born in the years of revolutionary practice, that people are equal in death.

Precisely this disposition was the mechanism which set in motion the first utopian machine of the Modern Age: the guillotine. As Dr. Guillotin himself noted in the project he submitted to the Constitutional Assembly, "the means of punishment ought to be identical for all sentenced by the law to death regardless of the crime they are charged with. Criminals should be beheaded. The beheading should be achieved by a simple mechanism." Unlike the executioner's axe, the guillotine does not deprive of life but restores Liberty and Equality in the form of death. The guillotine symbolizes a type of violence which is radically different from that known in the premodern age; it symbolizes Terror—the Terror which replaces the life-death opposition by the ideological oppositions of freedom-nonfreedom, equality-inequality. Death is instrumentalized. It is not a border we are faced with nor is it truly important. From an instrument, Terror itself has turned into a world. Terror is not synonymous with violence—it is synonymous with a new world.

▦ The Body

Kiossev's essay asks how is Terror possible. It associates the possibility of tattooing new symbolic orders with the ideology that "the reality of the human body seems to be the foundation which makes possible all other realities." The revolution does not destroy this "appearance." In the domain of Terror, "we have no bodies, we are bodies" (Reich). The annihilation of corporeality, pain, death are so irrefutably real that they transfer the quality of "irrefutable reality" onto the power that breeds them. The deprivation of Terror is a deprivation of reality. This is one of the existential insights of the case in point. What upsets the writer is that the "velvet revolutions" produce societies suffering from a chronic shortage of reality. The "gentle revolutions" themselves are unreal, unspecifically gentle.

Alexander Kiossev's basic intuition is that Terror alone makes us real, enabling us to experience the reality of the world. This intuition is reproduced in our political situation in a spontaneous and very strange manner. The body is present in the "velvet revolutions" in a peculiar way. It builds "live chains" and merges in marches to push itself to the limit in the act of a hunger strike. The hunger strike expresses the impossibility of forgetting a Terror that was. Revolutionaries do not terrorize but relive the terrorization of their own bodies over and over again. The body of the Other, of the enemy, proves incorporated into our own body. The hunger strike expresses the impossibility of forgetting the old Terror, as well as the impossibility of having a new one.

The Impossible Terror

Alexander Kiossev's "An Essay on Terror" raises two fateful questions, a theoretical: "why was there no reign of terror?" and a practical one: "when will there be a reign of terror?"

In regard to the latter, the practical question, the writer confines himself to a humanistic ἐποχή (refraining from judgment). The entire essay is meant to motivate the legitimacy of these two questions. Questions which legitimize the study of "velvet revolutions" in their "defectiveness," their deviation from the model. Strange as it might be, Kiossev falls prey to the idea of a "normal revolution," of the universalization of specific features of modernity. The question which Kiossev will not ask is: "is Terror possible in a post-utopian situation?" As he himself notes, the Eastern European revolutions are deprived of a radical utopia.

They lack a text which is to be substantiated. The end of communism marks the exhaustion of modernity, of its projectionism. The ideological basis of the Eastern European revolutions were not utopias but anti-utopias. Modernity has thus proved to be in a hall of mirrors—it cannot simultaneously escape from the hall and from its own image. It is the lack of radical utopias, the rejection of utopias that makes the Reign of Terror impossible. Violence, monstrous violence is possible, but it will not be legitimized as ensuing from Liberty and Truth. The prerequisite for this legitimacy is destroyed—the conviction that a "juster world" can be imposed; furthermore, that a "juster world" can be invented. The "utopia of normalcy," and Kiossev perceives this, is de facto a rejection of utopia—it does not vision the world but displays it. It displays the world not in its naturalness but in its conventionality. The future lies several hundred miles away, the aspiration for liberty is replaced by the demand for democracy, no one cares about the materialization of the human essence. Churchill loved saying that democracy is not the perfect but the best of familiar forms of government. Something in the world has changed radically.

▓ A Short Anti-Kiossev Manifesto

The Reign of Terror did not nor will it take place. It is over. The violence which might erupt is stripped of its ideological motives and doomed to muteness. The "brave new world" in which we have ended up is also doomed to muteness or nonarticulation. This muteness spawns a desire for radical gestures, radical theoretical gestures. The theoretical intuition of modernity tries to terrorize the world which does not fit into its patterns. In this sense, one can say that Kiossev's essay "stinks of guts": the guts of the gutted classical viewpoint.

Kiossev's text resembles Spielberg's world: a world enamoured of its own mutation. Kiossev's stance also laments the radically new stance of the intellectual, the fact that it is no longer possible for men of letters to build worlds and create pedagogical dictatorships. A lament which cannot hear itself.

The End[1]

Note

1. The present text has doubtless been influenced by Vladislav Todorov—not by his radical mode of thinking and metaphor but by his Departure.

Epilogue:
Health Takes the Power
Alexander Kiossev

This book happens to end with Ivan Kristev's essay—a fact which, of course, is accidental and yet could hardly be more symptomatic. For it quite unequivocally demonstrates that the texts included in the book do not end on their own but have been **forced** to end.

They were, one could say, suppressed: placed beyond the Symbolic Law of the post-totalitarian world. The suppression did not, of course, take the form of a direct administrative sanction—it did not deprive individual persons of their public voice, did not overtly taboo one or another topic which these texts dealt with (and, therefore, had nothing to do with totalitarian censorship). In fact, after the change of 1989 in Bulgaria, as in the other Eastern European countries, such overt suppressions, sanctions, and acts of censorship did not seem to be possible at all: for a short period of time the Bulgarian public domain seemed to enjoy the greatest degree of freedom, if not of frivolity, in the world.

Still, a kind of suppression existed: in the Bulgarian public domain a consensus was being established that such mode of writing was "out of date." The rationalized hostility against it took various forms (the accusations ranged from the claim that it was unforgivably irresponsible to the charge that it was terrorist, from the reproach that it was incoherent and intellectually undisciplined, to the attack that it was perverse and sacrilegious); its effect, however, was all of a pattern: it manifested itself in a kind of idiosyncratic hostility to that type of discourse—to its mechanisms of meaning-generation and its significant practices.

At least one of the reasons for this "suppression" seemed comparatively clear. It consisted in the effort to quickly and efficiently forget one's own past. This mode of writing, by virtue of being bound up with a particular human group (with the hermetic nature of the intertextual games of the "intellectual oasis" referred to in the introduction), was pregnant with far too many shameful memories. The most important of those was not at all the fact that, in the long run, the group never got beyond the state of half-resistance and never overtly challenged the totalitarian institutions, thus making it impossible for any one of its members to morally capitalize on it in the post-totalitarian situation. It seems to me that for each one of the members the shame actually bore a purely personal aspect—the identities that the group allowed room for were amorphous, uncompleted, compensatory identities. Given the lack of creditable models of social behaviour to be followed, every one was doomed to an ex-centric existence: the young intellectuals in this group existed in too great a measure **through one another**—they existed through mutually inspired ambitions, rivalries, friendships, dialogues, quarrels; they projected their personalities into and developed them by means of the intellectual-erotic togetherness which was supposed to make up not only for the lack of authoritative figures but also for the lack of a broad public, intellectual, and political horizon. In the post-totalitarian period the craving for such well-defined, solid models of authority became particularly acute: after so many years of a dependent, inarticulate life, a huge number of people came to need the belief that such well-defined, "mature" identities really existed. Thus, the members of the group became even more acutely aware of the compensatory and amorphous character of their former undefined positions. Their awareness seemed to reach a kind of breaking point when, in the eyes of many, those positions began to appear as solely defined by their amorphousness and unautonomousness, when they began to be seen as anchored in the safe haven of a well-protected, promiscuous, and game-playing minority, that is, to be seen as some intellectual and political puberty from the past when the human identity and the human choice are still shamefully incompleted. A puberty which was once and for all outgrown. The narrative about how everybody had moved from an unautonomous "then" to a self-autonomous "now" came to wield tremendous power—all of a sudden in post-totalitarian Bulgaria everybody felt grown-up. The ironically transgressive discourse of the former intellectual group, playing not only with the context of the group but also with the global symbolic mechanisms of totalitarianism, suddenly lost its chances of survival: for the Bulgarian public domain as well as for many of the exponents of this discourse it came to represent only the shameful and infantile aspects of their own past. It was, therefore, to be forgotten as soon as possible.

In a sense, despite all its attempts at *Vergangenheitsbewältigung* (public debates about the guilt, mutual accusations of dishonour, revelations about the victims of totalitarianism, and the coercive pressures upon intellectual life in communist times, acts of repentance and pseudo-repentance), the post-totalitarian world represented—and still represents—a typical example of *Vergangenheitsverdrängung*. The case in point proved to be no exception. Stripping down the simulative and play-acting intellectual discourse to bare shameful puberty was a typical attempt to repress the past. The hostile idiosyncrasy towards this puberty aspect blocked the hermeneutic access to other dimensions of the discourse: its intellectual and political potential was declared nonexistent, its complex rhetoric began to irritate, its dialogue with certain Western postmodern and poststructuralist thought-strategies was seen as an empty fashion. Public consensus prevented its being carried across into the "new" post-totalitarian age as specific intellectual experience. Its reduction to figures of shame and amorphous identity constituted, in fact, an attempt to lose the key to its understanding—the reduction was part of the wholesale process of the oversimplified rewriting of the totalitarian past.

It was also part of something else, however—what engendered it was yet another important context without which the above mentioned "suppression" would have been hard to imagine or comprehend: the context of the general discursive situation of post-totalitarianism. In other words, the attempt to confine the respective discourse to only one of its aspects was part and parcel of the struggle of dominant rival discourses; it was indicative of the disposition of the rhetorical forces and interpretative strategies defining the post-totalitarian *Öffentlichkeit*.

This discursive situation characteristic of Eastern Europe after the fall of its totalitarian rules can, of course, be described in much greater detail, yet it is beyond the scope of this brief epilogue to do so. I will, therefore, allow myself to define it from a rather general and one-sided perspective—it was simply a **blockage of all critical discourses.** The situation which actually arose in the East has been termed by me in my *Essay on Terror* "the utopia of normalcy." In this process, the repression of the totalitarian past was, in fact, mirrored upside down by an opposite process—the repressed was now being replaced by new, "grown-up," one-dimensional identification models invading with imperialist aggressiveness the vacant space—now cleansed of shame—in their self-appointed guises of final Freedom, Democracy, Free Market, Truth, Faith, Maturity, and National Sentiment. This urge to restore traditional social models of Modernity (which in post-totalitarian Eastern Europe were perceived as the only "natural," "organic" patterns of social behavior) made virtually impossible any criticism of the fundamental conditions of post-totalitarian society despite the unceasing discussions and debates, the public scandals, and the mutual attacks on political and cultural party-programmes. The traditional social models (predominantly of a right-conservative type) came to life again carrying a transcendental aura round their empirical substance: in the East one could, for instance, quite seriously claim that private ownership was **sacred**, that communism was **demonic**, that in the moral human being, public and private behaviour fully coincided, that it was bad if "homosexuals," "Turks," "gypsies," and other "deviants" ruled the country. In the post-totalitarian world new taboos revived—in Poland it became difficult to utter public critiques of Catholicism, in Bulgaria the same applied to free-market economy, Eastern Orthodox religion or patriotic sentiments. This was determined by the specific normative horizon of the post-totalitarian public domain: on the one hand, it was characterized by the taken-for-granted Western models in which the West functioned as utopia for the East (the so called *zapadniki,* the programmes seeking "a way to Europe," "a place among the civilized nations of the world," etc.); on the other hand, it was marked by an equally strong reaction against such models, the *ressentiment of potchveniki,* seeking the West as anti-utopia and identity-loss, the homegrown doctrines of "native originality," of metaphysical superiority of the East over the West, etc. The overall effect, however, was that the critical potential of Eastern Europe diminished in a socially dangerous measure. All this found concentrated expression in the specific post-totalitarian "economy of truth" (in the Foucauldian meaning of the term—an ensemble of institutionalized mechanisms for the production, legitimation, distribution, circulation, and impact of "truth-telling" discourses.)

Here I will confine these institutionalized mechanisms—despite their multiple variants—to two basic rival discourses. The two dominant truth-telling Modes of Rhetoric—two matrices for the production and distribution of "truths" which blocked the access to intellectually informed critique—were exemplified by and embodied in two public figures representing the two Authors of Truth which post-totalitarian society recognized as the only legitimate ones. These were the Intellectual-Parrhesiast and the Expert.

The antique term *parrhesia* (studied by Michel Foucault), denoting "free utterance," "freedom of speech," "the risk of openly speaking the truth in the tyrant's face," can give us an idea of the first type of the "political economy of truth." This type can be regarded as hypertrophied dissident discourse, which in totalitarian times—heroically, putting at stake its own body and social position—categorically denounced "the world of the lie": that is, the self-reproducing totalitarian ideology. In post-totalitarian time this discourse paradoxically came to occupy a position of power, undergoing quite unexpected transformations. Irrespective of its actual substance, the parrhesiastic utterance (the scandalizingly transgressive, outright, and uncompromising pronouncement of the "truth" in everybody's face) began to be seen as produced by a taken-for-granted moral position: it carried a preconceptional form of truth and could not be refuted by facts. Its traditional form—the form of a simple and direct negation of a *whole* order of symbolic representation—prevented this utterance from entering into dialogue with **any** localized, **detailed**, specialized truths; it inevitably proved hostile to all other "expert truths" (which were morally neutral as such and did not preclude being integrated into a potential "world of the lie"). Thus, in Bulgaria the parrhesiastic mode of rhetoric at a certain moment generated a series of militant arguments crusading against sociology, demoscopy, and the political studies. The image of the individual sacrificing himself in the name of Truth (there were "cities of truth" in which those sacrificing themselves tried to start a new life; there were also hunger strikes against the lie) was radically opposed to that of the individual who did not live "globally" but was content to perform a certain professional role. The expert, the administrator, the politician, the man of science or business were paranoidly suspected of belonging to the communist Mafia and conniving at the grandiose secret Conspiracy of the Lie meant to prevent the regeneration of Eastern Europe. This was another of the unexpected transformations of the dissident parrhesiastic mode—in order to be able to reproduce its globally negative form it, at the same time, had to proclaim again and again that the world of the lie had not yet come to an end; it had to evoke transcendental-paranoid representations of the communist Enemy and to produce unending images of its metaphysical battle with this enemy (a Bulgarian writer was quite in earnest when he declared that the failed coup in Moscow of August 1991 had been "an astral battle between the Armies of Good and Evil"). Post-totalitarian parrhesia turned into a cult of the literal, plain word which shook society to its very foundations. It consequently demanded from the parrhesiasts a constant perpetuation of the tumultuously scandalizing attack upon those foundations and endowed the word with a specifically nonempirical and sacred aura.

Thus, most paradoxically, the parrhesiastic mode of rhetoric produced two diametrically opposed results: on the one hand, it subjected the post-totalitarian public sphere to tumultuous scandal, making brutality and the dismissal of every convention the be-all and end-all of the discursive space; on the other hand, it revealed its unsuspected kinship with resurgent fundamentalist and religious movements which also felt the need to publicly proclaim unquestionable, sacred, shattering, and global metaphysical truths.

The figure of the Expert—agent of specialized languages, disciplined techniques, and professionally acquired stratagems for solving problems—was the other important figure in the post-totalitarian space. This figure, typical of every modern society in which there exist autonomous institutionalized fields with a "rationality" of their own (sciences, law, religion, art, media, sport, etc.) took on quite a different aspect in post-totalitarian Eastern Europe. For, after the end of the "Great Historical Experiment" the Eastern European societies turned out to be in a unique nonexpert state for which no precedent was available and no "specialists" existed. As the professionally acquired stratagems for solving the various distressing problems were simply not available and as these problems arose not in the well-articulated disciplinary fields but in the chaotic society as a whole (i.e., they were not of a local and professional but of a constitutive and global nature), the above-mentioned societies were, in actual fact, characterized by "a crisis of the Expert Reason": the numerous groups of both Eastern and Western "specialists" unceasingly and noisily turned out projects for improving the situation which were then as noiselessly abandoned for having been proven totally inadequate. As, however, the expert discourses constituted one of the main attributes of the utopia of "a normal society" (in it, of course, there **had** to be specialists and specialized practices capable of dealing with every problem; there **had** to be experts producing the illusion that all was under control) this actual crisis had hardly any effect upon the public position of authority occupied by the expert discourse—it represented one of those solid identificational models of the New World Order which couldn't be subjected to questioning and critical reappraisal (only the parrhesiast's paranoid attack was to have validity against this discourse). In fact, the basic social function of this type of discourse was to offer models of social behaviour alternative to the parrhesiastic ones. In contrast to the "global" historical identity of the parrhesiast, craving to resolve the problems with one single gesture of soul and body, desiring to "begin to live in the truth," both individually and collectively, privately, and publicly, those models were to offer the alternative of a normalized averaged "identity," preserving such "normal" distinctions as professional function-existential position, ethics-politics, individual identity-social role, private-public, etc., and creating the illusion that these distinctions really existed in the mutated Bulgarian society. In other words, the "expert" represented merely one discursive possibility for producing utterances which **did not insist** that the public role of an individual should become identical with his self-sacrificing body; unlike parrhesia, they **did not insist** that the biographical dilemma of totalitarian man should sublimate into a scandalizing verbal act—they would rather repress it into a value-indifferent, detached social role. This was to be the **alienated** and **neutral** mirror-discourse opposing the parrhesiastic one: it consisted in stratagems of action, which were at least seemingly effective, in detailed and specialized rational practices which were at least seemingly verifiable. Prevented, however, from functioning effectively in the warped social space of post-totalitarianism, the expert discourse turned out in many cases to be mere Rhetoric, that is, a mirror-discourse, the marked member in the opposition of expert vs. parrhesiastic rhetoric. Consequently, the Expert—despite the potential of this social role (a real specialist solving particular problems in a localized professional field) turned out to be in much greater measure a political and public figure—a "politologist," a political "expert," an antagonist of the Intellectual-Parrhesiast. The paranoid, scandalizing version of Truth was contrasted with a self-confident and alienated technological version of it whose main function was to induce the sense of peace and social stability at all costs.

Bearing in mind the discursive situation described above, the ironic, game-playing, transgressive language of the former "intellectual oasis" was, in fact, left with no choice but to be suppressed. In its essence, the suppression was not direct (although there were instances of direct and vicious open attacks against this language)—rather, the suppression consisted in such retrospective interpretation of the merits and demerits of the language that it was bound— much in keeping with the supply and demand of new voices on the discursive market—to turn mute.

One of the objectives of the present book was to prevent the occurrence of this muteness. Refusing to conform to the newly established discursive *conjunctura*, it sought to preserve and protect from repression and oblivion the intellectual and political experience of this language. So, let us at this point—at the very end of the book—try to make explicit some of its dimensions which, in totalitarian times, were obliquely referred to, even its exponents not being entirely aware of them, let alone developing an ideology about them.

If the shameful memories were the first reason for "suppressing" the ironical, game-playing discourse of the "intellectual oasis," it was its rather specific "critical" potential which constituted the second reason for doing so. Clenched between the pressures of the "truth-telling discourses" of post-totalitarian time, silenced by shattering, global, paranoid-metaphysical truths on the one hand, and by mutated theoretic-expert languages on the other, it was given no chance to carry across its ability (an ability which failed to realize its own full potential anyway, which failed to fully shake off its infantilism and aesthetic narcissism) with active political irony to **transgress, promiscualize,** and **madden** orders of discourse which appeared grown-up and preconceptional, eternal and natural. We mean, in short—to use Vladislav Todorov's key metaphor—its ability to **inflame.**

In some of its aspects the mode of discourse called "inflammation" was an attempt at "writing as experience of limit" (in the sense that so many different scholars as George Battaille, Michel Foucault, Julia Kristeva attach to it). In this sense the phrase "critical potential" is not adequately chosen: the "inflammation" was not criticizing totalitarianism—it was trying to aggressively interfere with it, disruptively testing the limits of its Symbolic Order.

The inflammation-mode aimed at scandalizing the totalitarian public domain. But the scandal engendered by it was to also have political and philosophic dimensions. Along with its social and political task it was to be a philosophic act as well (or rather "action" as the intellectual group used to call it). In a not too complicated a manner the mode was to attempt practical solutions to some well-known philosophic and social problems: the first of those being contained in Wittgenstein's dictum that the function cannot be its own argument—that is, that a social system cannot evolve a final and objective self-reflexivity focused upon its structural framework, as such self-reflexivity will inevitably be **a part which seeks to encompass the whole.** In political terms, this was an attempt to overcome the above antinomy inherent in any social criticism of totalitarianism: such criticism not only invariably proved intrinsic to the totalitarian whole (i.e., it posited as a premise for its existence what it actually criticized) but also—in terms of its conceptual apparatus—already actualized the opposition of "ideological appearance vs. truth" and thus fell back into the "power of truth" and the "will to knowledge" of modern instrumental reason.

The "inflammation" attempted to solve these problems simply and by force: its aim was to demonstrate that in the totalitarian symbolic order there were central joints of symbolic representation that could be attacked (i.e., acts of intervention could be carried out against what has been termed by some the "Master signifier" of a symbolic order), and that it was possible for these joints to become "inflamed" so that their "non-naturalness," their morbidity could be revealed. The inflammation did not criticize—it simulatively replaced: it subverted the very constitutive metaphors of the Great Discourse of the Left, transformed by totalitarianism into a bureaucracy-police machine. It spawned their doubles in such a way that, instead of seeming the glorious projects conceived by reason, they turned out to be those awful monsters born from its sleep. Thus, in contrast to the situation in the West, the inflammation was a discourse of the anti-Left (without being, however, a discourse of the Right). After they had been inflamed, the key utopian metaphors and visions of the totalitarian world were not to be seen any longer as this world's natural foundations but rather as constitutive distortions in its very generative grammar.

To put it metaphorically: what had seemed the root of this world was now to be perceived—through an abrupt change of the *Gestalt*—as an inflamed wound, as a root-wound, which made the texture of this world (its Symbolic

Order) "radiate" with a nauseatingly non-natural, morbid light. In other words, this was to be the reverse of mystical revelation where one contemplates in a state of sublime ecstasy the very foundations of the world—as in Canto XXIX and XXX of his *Paradise,* Dante contemplates the Divine Center of the circle in which all time and space, all energy and force, all wisdom and love converge. A paraphrase of a famous Shakespearean line would more suitably describe this kind of operation: the inflammation made one feel that "the world is out of joint." It was thus to be perceived neither as "theoretical activity" nor as "theoretical criticism" in the exact sense of these words. Its gesture was far more excessive: it constituted a political transgression which—unlike the direct dissident challenge—was to be an "ontological" transgression too. What was being transgressed were not some specific coercive regulations and laws of totalitarian rule but the very constitutive principle of the totalitarian world—the inflammation sought to transform "the center," the sacrosanct "joint" of this world into a sacrilegious mutant. Rendered into the inflammation-mode the communist and avantgardist utopian visions revealed themselves as prostheses of the world's organics: Lenin's sacrosanct mummy which—according to Todorov—should be the focal point of the totalitarian symbolic order, is transformed by the inflammation into a monstrous stub; "terror" is perceived as the constitutive code of a profoundly "inauthentic" reality. The inflammation was to be an inverted act of the mystical *contemplatio* invoking not exultation but horror—causing a revulsion which, in its negative energy, was to be compared only to ecstasy.

To put it in more theoretical terms—this aggressive mode of discourse transgressively transformed the constitutive metaphors of a symbolic universe so that they lost their self-evidence and naturalness; it not only actually and violently inverted the "normal" value-oppositions and hierarchies of this world but also—through sacrilegious transfigurative acts—activated the whole "dark" potential of what Freud termed *Das Unheimliche.* The inflammation—

as it was introduced by Vladislav Todorov—was not a descriptive or argumentative mode (consequently, no theoretical counterarguments, no parrhesiastic or expert strategies, can deal with it) but an aggressive mode of discourse: it was an intervention, an attempt at a semantic scandal directed against the Master Signifier in order to set the dislocated joint of the totalitarian world: it was writing as experience of the utopian limit which was to have provocative and therapeutic functions. It strove to render the most glorious—the utopian vision—as disgusting cosmic voluntarism, sought to reveal the most horrible—terror—as the necessary solder of every "natural reality"; it represented an analysis in the mode of apocalyptic hypothesis. Its strategy was anti-Baudrillardian—not seduction but antiseduction; an aggression against the cultural schematisms governing the economy of Desire; it was the strategy of invoking an almost hypnotic revulsion and horror by revealing the existent symbolic-institutional jointure of the world. This mode demanded from the reader that he should feel his own body as a totalitarian prosthesis; it called for a style which pricked the skin under the reader's ideological nails making it smart and sting; it did not exert actual terror upon the reader but forced him to become aware of the **already having happened**, the **already existent** terrorized totalitarian constitution of his social body.

The inflammation-mode, which I have described as anti-utopian, bore in itself, however (as does every anti-utopia), an empty utopian structure inherent in the belief that there existed such a thing as totality, that there **was** a "center" that could be inflamed. This structure embodied a longing which was the Other of the terror and claustrophobia instilled by totalitarianism. The political danger for this mode was that its global "discursive-ontological" ambitions cut it off from any open and "naive" political resistance. They risked to turn it into a self-contained stylistic curiosity unintelligible to the mass agent of political activity—a curiosity to be used in a purely "disinterested," aesthetic manner (in the Kantian sense of this term). The inflammation intertwined in a curious way with the other discursive strategy of the intellectual group referred to in the introduction to this book—the strategy of simulating, of producing subversive doubles, of anonymity and dissemination; the strategy which revealed itself in the impossibility of identification, in the play with quotations, authorships, and identities allowing no location of a "center" to be inflamed, no clear definition of "protagonists" and "antagonists," in short—no Minotaur to be slain by the hero. The implicit heroism of the inflammation mode was systematically parodied and deflatingly doubled by its own imitations—it transformed itself into laughter and play, into frivolity, into hermetic aestheticism, and even snobbery. Being subversively doubled, ironized, quoted out of context, this heroism underwent strange transformations: young people appropriated without asking Vladislav Todorov's authorship and used his inflammations for their own purposes. Todorov wanted to be a "virus" in the totalitarian discourse—yet the virus mutated into new races with different biological parameters: again and again the inflammation encountered Pierre Menard's paradoxes. The quoting simulations and games disrupted the "heroic centralism" of the inflammation-mode yet, at the same time, they made impossible that global politico-ontological action which constituted the structural utopianism of this mode.

In this context, it was perhaps exactly the "reversed indigo"—the image of the "inflamed quotation," of the scandalous and impossible duplication—which was the limit-point of all writing strategies available to the intellectual group: a limit point of incomprehensibility and pain.

The debate between *Essay on Terror* and *Essay on Theoretical Terror*, with which the present book ends, must be seen exactly in terms of this context—as part of the general process of "deradicalizing" and marginalizing these limit-texts (and as part of the specific process of Ivan Kristev's own "deradicalization"). Here operated the already mentioned regularity: the marginalization of the texts which sought to be "writing as experience of limit." Ivan Kristev's text attacked the discourse of the group rather than the actual *Essay on Terror*. The suppression discussed above is implicitly at work throughout the whole text: it represents, in fact, a hermeneutic blockade, a refusal to understand the strategy of the inflammation-mode. In short, *Essay on Terror* has been read in an arrogant manner—as something which it is not: as an avantgardist leftist manifesto which dreams of world engineering. Without much hesitation Ivan Kristev has turned the empty utopian structure of inflammation into its opposite: into a dream of an utopian project and of terror(?). Consequently, the laments caused by the lack of terror are laments uttered by a belated agent of Modernity (destroyer or constructor of worlds) against the new, ironic, and mute Postmodernity. The postmodern reality allows no destructions/constructions: its future has geographical dimensions—"it lies several hundred miles away"—and, therefore, the intellectual has to give up his pedagogical dictatorships.

However, Kristev is not content to be postmodern himself while the others are confined to the past of Modernity. He undertakes to do something different, quite incompatible with his postmodern pose: to correct the "branded metaphors" of the *Essay on Terror* (revolution, utopia, terror, etc.) by making them historically responsible and reducing them to the concepts of political science and history. (Let us here ignore the fact that such an act does not recognize the intention of inflammation to intervene not in the field of the expert, "sane" concepts, theoretically controlled and specified, but in a quite different semantic sphere—the sphere of nontheoretical mass intuitions which are in power in the post-totalitarian society.) *Essay on Theoretical Terror* insists upon a "normal" theoretical use of concepts, imagining it as meticulous historical specifying and terminological disciplining of concepts: demands which are attributes of a traditional figure of Modernity—the Expert. Kristev wants to examine, consult dictionaries and encyclopedias, to quote voices of authority, correct and analyse, to specify and "apply historicism." Read through an alien interpretative grid, the aggressive metaphors of inflammation are tamed into convenient concepts inscribed in a traditional disciplinary field. (This field, i.e., political science, has gained new authority from the radiance of the New World Order: the "politologists" were one of the most sought after scholarly commodities in post-totalitarian Eastern Europe.)

At the same time, however, in *Essay on Theoretical Terror* (and it is at this point that the repressed past rather than the "glorious postmodern future" reveals itself in the form of a stylistic symptom) the pose of the expert proves to be a merely simulated one. It is a quotation from the expert discourse which, however, is still punctuated by other non-expert rhetorics. Ivan Kristev's text is characterized by a succinctness, swiftness, and even frivolousness of its logical enthymemes its proofs and conclusions are often premature, it contains jokes and teasing remarks, produces undisciplined, wild metaphors—"laments," "guts," "Danton-Derrida lines"—which as a stylistic approach and terminological apparatus are quite incompatible with the pedantic, neutral, and positivistically scrupulous expert discourse. They can be regarded as one thing only—as a trace of the free, scandalizing game playing of the "oasis." Ivan Kristev is simply trying to forget that there was a time when he, too, played Pierre-Menard-games. He now longs to assume the stable professional identity of a politologist and historian. And he almost seems to be taking the game seriously (somehow, among other things, he had become the head of a certain foundation as well as adviser of the president). The problem he faces is that, no matter how hard he tries to shake off his former inflammation, it breaks through the surface of his expert style in the form of a discursive subconscious undermining his serious professional pose of an Author of Truth.

In spite of all that, however—and quite independently of the stylistic symptoms of the repressed past visible to only a few observers—"expert texts" such as Kristev's performed a clear function in the discursive struggle of post-totalitarianism. The "serious," "professional" voices of such texts counterbalanced the parrhesiastic Truth and marginalized other discourse possibilities doing, no doubt, their share in establishing the new discursive status quo. This is a function which comes surprisingly close to the one described by Foucault: the "great confinement" of the respective "mad" discourses and symbolic formations; the appropriation of their voices and their alternative position by virtue of which they can be the Other of modern instrumental rationality; the introduction of the norms of "power/knowledge" regarding the deviant voices as mute objects, describing and classifying them in its conceptual grids in order to confine them at last to theoretical and political silence. Deep down, beyond the flirtation with words like "modern" and "postmodern" Ivan Kristev's text reveals the hostility of every neutral expert position towards any attempt to make the **individual biographical body of the expert himself part of the theoretical subject of his discipline** and to "**inflame**" the concepts of his value-neutral specialized language in such a way that they begin to appear as Dionysian metaphors branching out into trees of figurative exuberance.*

To summarize briefly—this was the hostility which a new, solid model of identity manifested towards the possibility of its own problematizing by the totalitarian past. Ivan Kristev's *Essay* exemplifies the position of the post-totalitarian expert—a position of which there have remained only the concern for its own preservation as well as its mass medial self-advertising. Not forgetting, of course, its sanctions against the other existing discourses. What it lacks, however, is something of crucial importance (something which alone justifies the existence of an expert discourse)—it lacks the theoretically detailed and practically operative formulation of what "velvet revolutions" are and how the problems which they left in their post-totalitarian wake are to be solved.

Some time after the publication of *Essay on Theoretical Terror* the transgressive-ironic discourse of "inflammations" and quotation-interplay was also attacked and mercilessly penalized by the other discursive position of authority—the parrhesiastic one. It received a few heavy religious (almost fundamentalist) blows from the newly established group of Orthodox-Christian philosophers. On the surface, the discourse and the group associated with it were accused in this religious attack of being infantile and immature and thus incapable of moral and political choice. However, the outburst of biblical fury and fierce abhorrence on the part of the young prophets spoke of deeper reasons. The discursive experience of the former intellectual group posed a threat to the very core of the new-old religiosity. This experience was still informed with the memory of how a "parasitic" existence could be led inside languages which proclaimed immutable values and postulated a nonverbal eidetic beyondness: "the Genuine Reality." This discourse was still able to inflame and incestuously transgress the indisputable hierarchies of Being which purport to be beyond any discourse (no matter what names they had been given—"historical necessity" or "Providence") perceiving them as invariably integrated in certain symbolic practices, and what is more—regarding them as constituted by such practices. For it was also able to recreate the genealogy of those "immutable values"—a genealogy which was in many respects intertwined with its own. Their profane, controversial, and noneidetic *Herkunft* could be traced back to the small proto-religious groups emerging from the same controversially simulative and not so radically subversive intellectual environment. The new religious variant of parrhesia was genealogically related to the collectively experienced, dark side of totalitarian discourse: it was no stranger to the dark, painfully devoid of language, agonizing and amorphous traumatic experience which now manifested itself in the impulse towards fundamental Truths and absolute forms of Eastern Orthodox philosophy. The transgressive discourse still carried within itself the memory of how such "fundamental" thinking could be hypothetically unfolded into its dark, anti-utopian variants. For years it had been carrying out—albeit not purposefully—an actual process of deconstructing the fundamental Christian opposition of word vs. Word. In terms of its experience, all symbolic practices, all names, in short—every verbal reality—were to be seen as a reality **of** this nonabsolute, empirical world; a reality which was ordinary and pregnant with conflicting potentials; a reality which could simultaneously liberate and enslave, invoke insight and blindness, be natural and unnatural. The possibility of "inflaming" the Word which claimed to possess eidetic values, of making transparent—as Roland Barthes would put it—its fascist dimension—all this was part of what the group had experienced and thought through. The insight it had gained spelt a whole range of possibilities which posed a threat to the new eastern-orthodox fundamentalism. This was a threat to any eidos, any Master signifier and thus also to the mystical contemplation of the Center: the transgressive discourse could inflame the existentials, the hierarchies, the ecstasy . . . Having outgrown the "puberty" of the intellectual group, having become "mature" and "wise"—possessors of an unshakeable identity—the religious-orthodox thinkers in Bulgaria could not allow this to go on with impunity. They could not remain indifferent in the face of the promiscuous, transgressive, travestive approach to the body which proved to be created not by God but by the totalitarian symbolic order, and thus deprived of all its "normal" and "natural" properties, divested of the "normal" periods of its aging or its "natural" sexual identity. This was the body which revealed itself in the unnaturalness of "its prostheses and bandages" (V. Todorov); the body which was terrorized and traumatized, marked by its morbidity, amorphousness, and plurality. Such an unnatural body could not have a "natural identity": a product of totalitarianism and branded in its very heart with totalitarian engravings, this body continued to feel the tragedy and physical distress of unfreedom being, thus unable to fulfill its fundamental

Christian mission, namely—to be the Body which fulfilled its own potential in the act of sacrifice. This act could be the dreamed-of release of dissemination, stabilizing the Word and thus realizing the economy of parrhesiastic Truth. Yet, in terms of the experience gained by the "oasis" every heroically sacrificial, "ontological" gesture deserved to be "inflamed" and thus stretched to the point where it revealed its conflicting disseminative potentials. This could no longer be infantile behavior—it represented a position of moral and political principle. In view of it, the wholesale religious crusade against the discourse of the group was to be expected—this discourse had to be discredited at all costs, it had to be stripped down to its unnatural, nauseating, shameful dimensions and seen as mere clownish posturing. According to the paranoid logic I have already described, it was, in the last analysis, labeled as communist (which to the representatives of the religious-orthodox variant of parrhesia was nothing else but a grimacing hypostasis of the satanic).

Must we now (and is such a procedure at all possible) assign heroic dimensions to both this simulative and inflaming discourse and the no longer existent intellectual group associated with it only because they did not hold out against the fierce discursive pressures and were forced to drop out of the social race? Is it possible to deny that the existence and the mode of this group represented in themselves a much too conspiratorial, esoteric, and "discursive" resistance which was unable to transcend the boundaries of its oasis and did not in any way predict the collapse of totalitarianism? Is it also possible to deny that the behavior of this group had a special erotic tinge? And that intrinsic to it was a certain self-contained and, no doubt, infantile narcissistic aestheticism, a certain self-delusion that scandalous verbal constructions represent the only creditable social action?

All this cannot be denied, of course. Yet, let others (and there is no shortage of them in the post-totalitarian world) fall into fits of rage over the above-mentioned features of this discourse, reducing it solely to them and thus coming to terms—in the easiest possible way—with their own past.

For, what proved fatal to this discourse were not the outside attacks and sanctions against it. Fatal to it was the "losing of the key" by its carriers themselves owing to the newly established political economy of truth. The members of the group yielded to the power of the new identificational models, assuming themselves the roles of parrhesiasts or experts and ceasing to understand **why**, in fact, they had been doing all this, **why** they had been seized by this insanity? They began to internalize the New Symbolic Order, themselves repressing their own past. In view of this we can say that the censorship against them was not of a bureaucratic-totalitarian but of a Freudian kind. Thanks to it, they began to forget quite effectively: to forget the political and philosophic charge of their own language and its mechanisms of resistance; to forget its intellectual and philosophic **potential**, the space of freedom which could be won by means of this language. Nobody wished to "test their own limits" any longer because they felt content within them. The members of the group had meanwhile also "grown-up," becoming members of parliament, ambassadors, advisers of the president, businessmen, and mass media stars in post-totalitarian Bulgaria. Others successfully stepped into similar well-established professional roles in the postmodern West, figuring there as paid experts on Eastern Europe. In their new environment they were, however, to encounter another sanction—this time imposed by the academic Left of the American and European universities which did not allow any excessive, libertarian acts of aggression against the Great Discourse of the Left, trying hard to preserve it from turning into a fossil. They were also to encounter the sanction of long-recognized experts who could not allow just anybody to undermine the authority of their professionally informed and strategic word.

The utopia of normalcy sought to represent the existing world as involved in the process of a global recovery to which any inflammatory process could only be detrimental.

In fact, in his text *Epitaph for Sacrifice, Epitaph for the Left* Ivaylo Ditchev deals with this very same situation, looking at it from a somewhat more general perspective: he sets out to examine that general atmosphere of the postmodern world which, in a way, naturally engenders such outlooks. This is a world where the great metaphysical struggle between Good and Evil, Reason and Madness has finally spent itself—nobody is seriously fighting for the negative cause any more, Mephisto has been fired; the sleep of reason no longer gives birth to monsters—it only produces small disagreeable insects. Even wars have become only local demonstrating that, in the long run, everything really is under control. The centralized forces of Good and Reason are quick to teach every aberrant act of frenzy a lesson. Local misery, suffering, madness—none of these, although encountered here and there, have a legitimate right to universal existence any more. In a sense, they are all improper for they no longer represent only one side of the metaphysical struggle and are thus merely regarded as a disgraceful incident which the police (in the old sense of this word—the institutional body entrusted with the duty of maintaining the harmony and well being of the world polis, including its good health) will quickly get out of the way.

And thus today, amidst the harmony of the New World Order, the inflammations gradually begin to disperse. One by one, the mad traumatic voices are falling into silence.

And if this book is not always behaving in a proper and healthy manner, the only choice left to it is to ask forgiveness.

And perhaps to come to an end?

Or to tell about all this in an act of muted resistance, in a style which can hardly inflame any one.

The style of an epilogue.

Note

* To quote just one example of this, *Revolutio* derives its origin from the field of astronomy where it referred to the cyclic movement of the planets and stars on the firmament. Experts argue that the original meaning of this word underwent a metaphorical change in the works of Seneca and Cicero where it came to denote "fateful" or "historic" processes. The meaning of cyclic movement was preserved as late as Shakespeare—in *Hamlet* "revolution" is said to refer to the turning of fortune's wheel. In Italian the use of the word *rivoluzione* in the sense of political unrest supposedly goes back to the beginning of the 13th century: Alexander Demand, from whose book *Metaphern für Geschichte, München 1978* these facts have been taken, argues that the use of the word "revolution" in this "inglorious" sense was already in existence at that early period. At this point we must ask ourselves by which of these meanings—the astronomical, the fateful, the Italian, the "glorious English" or the "modern French" one—we should be actually guided. And what, in reality, are we supposed to gain from being reminded of them? Which is the typical revolution (if this word does, indeed, mean anything beside will to power and politics of representation)—the French or the English one? Or maybe the astronomical one? Perhaps the "model-generating" ability of the French revolution has been exhausted to the extent that we could gain better insight into the next "revolutions" by turning to the stellar or fateful models. Traced in all its directions, the history of a word resembles not so much a tree with many branches as a tangled, madly chaotic bush which can disrupt the self-evidence of **all** of the word's sematic connotations, of **any one** of its modern uses: from the experimental to the "legitimate" theoretical one. Looking back into the abyss of its historical uses a concept can only become giddy. The vertigo is the only gain.

Contributors

Alexander Kiossev (born in 1953 in Sofia, Bulgaria) teaches cultural history of the Modernity at the university of Sofia. At the present moment he is a lecturer in Bulgarian language and literature at the University of Göttingen, Germany. His publications include a book in history of Bulgarian poetry, many theoretical essays (some of them translated in English, German, French, Hungarian, and Romanian) and a forthcoming book in Bulgarian about the discursive production of truth in totalitarianism and post-totalitarianism.

Ivaylo Ditchev (born in 1955 in Sofia, Bulgaria) teaches aesthetics at the University of Sofia. At the present moment he holds his Ph.D. at Paris 7 in France and participates at the French investigation group *The grey memory of the East*. He is author of several collections of short stories, a novel, and two collections of theoretical essays (some of them translated in English, German, French, and Hungarian).

Vladislav Todorov (born in 1956 in Sofia, Bulgaria) He was member of the Bulgarian Institute of Arts, the department of theater studies. At the present moment he holds his Ph.D. and teaches Russian literature at the University of Pennsylvania, Philadelphia, USA. His publications include a book in Bulgarian about the transformation of the utopian manifestos of avant-garde left art into a Symbolic Order ot totalitarianism and a forthcoming book in English (to be published by SUNY). Some of his theoretical essays are translated in English, German, French, Russian, and Hungarian.

Ivan Kristev (born in 1965 in Sofia, Bulgaria) He studied philosophy at the University of Sofia and specialized in political science at the University of Oxford. At the present moment he is director of the *Friedrich-Naumann foundation* in Sofia. His publications include a book of poetry and several theoretical essays (some of them translated in English, German, and Hungarian).

All four contributors were, in the period between 1987 and 1991, members of the intellectual group *Synthesis* in Sofia. The group published the semi-Samizdat collection of essays *Ars Simulacri (1989)* and the collection *Ars Erotica (1992)*. In 1993 the Hungarian publishing house *2000-Orpheus* published another collection in Hungarian: *A mutants egzotikuma. Bolgar postmodern essek (The Exotics of Mutants. Bulgarian Postmodern Essays)*.

Index

acid, 99–101
action, 66, 68, 70, 78, 164, 174; mass action, 79
aesthetic and economic structures, 65
aesthetics, political, 65–94
allegory, 105; allegorical, 65, 67
anatomy, political, 95–101
angle (Angulus), 10–14
archive, 25, 26, 35, 45, 54
Ars Simulacri, xvii, xviii
articulation, 137–140, 143; mutant as articulation with error, 141; nonarticulation, 153
assemblage, 71
author, 11, 25–32; author of Truth, 159, 170; Lenin as author of communism, 68; meta-author, 116–117. *See also* authorship, 25–32, 58–61, 168
avant-garde art, 71. *See also* Constructivism, Dadaism, Expressionism, Formalism, Futurism, Proletcult

blood, 81–82, 114, 125, 137; blood and soil, 89; blood transfusion as means for homogenizing, 81–82
Body, xi, 67, 68, 71, 75, 78–80, 84, 87, 95, 97, 100, 126, 127, 140, 142–146, 151, 152, 160, 173; biographical body, 171; bodies and aggregates, 71; body of the Other, 152; body's reality as act of violence, 138; collective body as aggregate, 77, 78, 142; communal body, 65, 78, 80–85; communal athleticism of the bodies, 72; conventionalized body, 139, engraved body, 139;erotically intimate body, 83; human body as reality, 137, 151; as transcendental signified, 138; king's body, 98; king's two bodies, 99; laboring body, 77; Lenin's body, 95, 96, 97; mass superorganization of bodies, 73; mutant body, 143, 145, 146; "natural" body, 141, 143 (*See* unnatural body, 173); party body, 69; political body, 96, 97, 98; Proletarian body, 81; proto-body, 138; reader's body as totalitarian prosthesis, 167; self-sacrificing Body, 162, 174; schizoid body, 143; social body, 82; superior body, 67; technological togetherness of the bodies, 81; totalitarian body, 142–143; traumatic body, 143; working class body, 65, 66, 140. *See also* corporeality, 67, 98; annihilation of corporeality, 151; corporeal being, 77
book, 26, 27, 28, 30, 155, 163; book-world, 28; life as a book. *See also* life-work, 51; transparent book, x, 1–2
Bull-God, 18–20

capitalism, 106
carbon paper, 61
castration, 17–18, 85, 122, 123, 134
catalog, 27, 28, 31, 32
censorship as political (party) institution, 88, 175
circle, x, xii, xiii, xiv, xvii, xx. *See also* community, group, milieu
city. *See* city of truth, 160; Garden cities; Linear cities; Sun cities, 82; The Luminous city of Luxembourg, 15–17; The Dissipated City of Luxembourg, 17–18; The Twisted City of Luxembourg, 18–20; The Phantom city, 20–23
classical, 34, 35, 43, 44, 49, 50, 51, 53, 54, 55, 56, 57, 58, 60, 61, 70, 74, 153; classics, 33, 35; nonclassical, 51, 53, 54, 55, 60
collage, 74, 75
collecting, 28, 30, 31, 32, 36
communism, 65–94, 95, 105, 106, 108, 109, 110, 113, 123, 125, 129, 131, 132, 146, 153, 159. *See also* communist bloc as planet scale monastery, 128
community, x, xi, xii, xiv, xv, xvi, xvii, 126, 131, 133. *See also* circle, group, milieu
comradeship, 81
concentration camp, 82, 83, 129, 142; Yugoslav concentration camps, 121
condensation and concentration of the population, 82–85
conspiracy, 92, 100, 110, 114; conspiracy of the Lie. *See* conspiratorial life, 91; meaning, xx; plot, 91; principle, 92; resistance, 174
Constructivism, 69, 71, 77; communal constructivism of sight, 73
convention, 67, 137, 139; convention as result of ultimate violence, 137; symbolic convention, 137; (terror-) convention-reality transition, 142, 149; conventionality, 153
coping, 28, 36, 39; copy, 36, 39, 40, 42, 54, 60; copyist, 27

Dada, 54, 69, 71, 72, 74, 86, 89, 90, 94. *See also,* Dadaism, 68, 69, 74; Dadaist, 22, 77
death, 100, 109, 111, 117, 119, 121, 123, 133, 134, 144, 151; death as supereality guaranteeing the symbolic order, 139–140; relation of Death to Liberty and Equality, 151
Desire, xix, 167
dialogue, x, xv, 157, 160
difference, 53
dilettantism, xv
discourse, xi, xiv, xix, 50, 77, 78, 79, 124, 156, 162, 175; blockage of all critical discourses, 159; discursive *conjunctura*, 163; discursive market, 163; discursive masochism, 128; discursive subconscious, 170; dissident discourse, 160–161. (*See* parrhesiastic discourse, 172); every day life discourse, 130; expert discourse, 162–163, 170; "great confinement" of the "mad" discourses, 171; Great Discourse of the Left, 165; mirror-discourse, 163; struggle of dominant rival discourses (discursive struggle), 158, 171; (suppression of) the ironically transgressive (play-acting) discourse, 156, 157, 163, 164, 172. (*See* discourse of the group, 169, 174); transition period discourse, 131; truth-telling discourse, 159, 163; "virus" in the totalitarian discourse, 168. (*See* parrhesiastic discourse, 163); victimary discourse, 129

disfiguring figures, xiii
Disgust, xix, *See* revulsion (negative ecstasy), 166–167
disintegrity, hermeneutic, xvi
dissemination, 168, 174
dissident, xii, xv, xvii, 106, 110
dissimulation, xv, xvi, xvii, *See also* imitation, xix; repetition; simulacrum, xviii, 110, 113, 124; simulation, xvii, xviii, xix, 115, 168; simulations simulate, xix.
door, 10–14

ecophilantropy, 132
ecstasy, 123, 166; ecstatic energy, expression of, xx, 141
empire, 26, 32; Library-Empire, 27
engineering, genetic, 105; social, 66, world engineering, 169
engraving, 44, 138–144. *See also* imprint, 44, 45, 46, 59
eroticism, xi, 84, 86, 107, 125, 128; erotics, xii, 74. *See also* Eros, claustrophobic, xi; intellectual-erotic togetherness, 156
evil, 119. *See* duel between good and evil
expert, 159, 161–163, 169, 171, 177; crisis of the expert reason, 162; expert discourse, 162–163
Expressionism, 71–72
eye. *See* look, oxulus, sight, vision, 73–76, 81–82, 86, 87, 88. *See also* fascinated eye of the West, 130; gaze of the prosperous West, 128; "healthy eye," 86; machine eye, 87; racial eye, 85
eye-sun. *See* all-pervasive gaze; illumination; organ of light, 15–17; eye-sun as phallus, 17

festival, 141, 143, 145; tic-festival, 143–145, 146
form of life, xi; alternative, xx
Formalism, 89
Futurism, 69

game, xii, xv, xvii, 30, 52, 168; game of signifiers, 138, 139; intertextual game, 155; Pierre-Menard games, 170; scandalizing game, 170; seduction game, 131, symbolic game, 135
generation, xiv
genetics, 105
genre, ix, xiii, xxi, 1, 67, 130; genre of self-hatred discourse, 129; we-are-the-worst genre, 130
good, 120; duel (battle, struggle) between good and evil, 120, 161, 176; good as police for evil, 120–121, 176
group, xiii, xiv, xv, 156, 168, 172. *See also* circle, community, milieu
guillotine, 98–99, 151
guilt, 123, 127, 157; guilt machine, 123, 126

happening, intellectual, x
health as political problem, 95, 155, 176
Herkunft, 172
hero, 19–20, 168
hunger strike, 152

identification, xv, 28, 168; one dimensional identification, 158, identification models of the New World Orders, 162
identity, xvii, 26, 120, 122, 124, 134, 162, 168, 170, 171; identity of communism, 66. *See also* sameness, 10–14; preserving who you are, be always one and the same, 43, 121; self-duplicating sameness, 20; uncompleted, compensatory, amorphous identity, 156, 158, 173; sexual identity, 173; terrorist-conventional identity, 143

ideology, x, xv, xix, 50, 57, 65, 72, 80, 86, 90, 94, 107, 112, 128, 129, 133, 148, 151, 160, 163; ideology of National Socialism, 87
indigo, x, 33–62, 168; indigo-scaffold, 60; living indigo, 59; reversed indigo as inflamed quotation, 168. *See also* symbol of the indigo, 35, 37, 38, 39, 40, 41, 42, 56. *See also* secret of the indigo, 36; super-indigo-super-Ego, 50
inflammation, xiii, xxi, 164–168, 169, 170, 172, 176; inflammation as empty utopian structure, 167. *See also* aggressive mode of discourse, 166–167
inter-disciplinary, xv
interpretation, xvii, 1, 11, 15, 23, 60, 106, 110, 112, 148, 163; as a classical philological institution, 60; living as the only privileged interpretation, 29

key hermeneutic, x, xii; "great key," 35; key metaphor, 66. *See also* key to understanding, 158; losing the key, 175

labor, 65–66, 71, 81, 105; division of labor between East and West, 128; tragic labor, 121
labyrinth, 19–20
language, total, 21; as virtual reality, 21; language-world-textuality, 53
Left, 119, 122, 132, 175, 176. *See also* leftist, 109, 169; Great Discourse of the Left, 165, 175
legality and illegality, 91
legitimacy, 92, 93, 98–101, 152; illegitimacy, 94
library, 26–32, 54; Alexandrine, 27; burned, 27, common, 83; Library-Empire, 27; library under party control, 89; library-utopia, 26. *See* librarian, 26
list, 110–115; list as a new social mediator, 114. *See also* catalogue
literal, 3, 7, 8

machine, 11, 72–75; chaotic machine, 145; guilt machine, 123, 126; machine for ultimate revolution, 139; utopian machine, 151. *See* Machinism, 71, 72. *See also* Creator-Machinist, 72, 73; Machinist as Superman, 73; Oculus ex Machina, 75
manifesto, 68, 78–79, 134, 153, 169
mask, xv, xvii,
Mass Man, 78–80, 82–83
Master signifier, 165, 167, 173
mausoleum, 68, 97, 98
merger of science, art and politics, 70–72, 73, 76–77
metaphor; 67, 69, 81, 97, 98, 99, 130, 142, 150, 154; aggressive metaphors, 170; Bolshevik's metaphors, 96; branded metaphors, 169; concepts turned to metaphors, 69, 76, 79; constitutive metaphors, 166; Dionisian metaphors, 71; eroticized metaphors, 149; Jacobean metaphors, 97; key metaphor, 66, 164, 165; metaphor as means of production, 66; political metaphors, 98; wild metaphors, 170. *See* metaphysical metaphoricalness, 50. *See also* Metaphern für Geschichte, 177
milieu, intellectual, xii, xiv, xv, xvi, xviii, xix; semi-academic-semi-artistic, xiii, structural ambiguity of, xvii. *See also* circle, community, group

modernization of society, 70, 71, 74, 76, 80, 83, 127; agent of modernization, 73. *See also* industrialization, 65, 127; production and overproduction, xviii
Modernism, 69, 72, 76, 82, 87, 89
Modernists, 86
montage, 70, 74, 75, 116
monument, 39, 40
mummy, 67–69, 94, 97, 98, 114, 166
mutant, post-totalitarian, 141–145; mutation, 153
mystification, xiii, 34, 59–60

narrative, ix, x, xi, 49, 157; narration, x
negligence, postmodern, 55–57, 58
nomenclatura, 90, 110–115, 129
normalcy, 140–141, 144, 146

opposition, xv, xvii. *See also* resistance
order, 51, 119, 145, 148, 160; actual, 67; bourgeois order of things, 71, 79; centralized, 84; conventional, 146; eternal, 74; legal, 67; metaphoric, 49; New World (Dis)Order, 121, 162, 170, 176; old order, 140; order-and-meaning, 145; order of discourse, 164; order of normalcy, 144; political order of the new world, 78; sacred, 16; symbolic order, xviii, 135–136, 138–144, 151, 164, 165, 166, 173, 175. *See also* space, bourgeois, 79; common, communal, 80, 82–83; physical and allegorical, 19–20, 94; public, 83; grammar of instructive language, 21
organics, 87; world's organics, 166. *See* organic, organ, 73, 89; organic into mechanic, 87, organic patterns of social behavior, 158
Other, the, 14, 18; Otherness, 53. *See* body of the Other, 152; the Other of the modern instrumental rationality, 171; the Other of terror, 167

Paranoia, 106, 125; class struggle, 110; controlled, 106; political, 106; paranoid attack, 162; logic, 174; space, xvi, xvii; suspicion, 116. *See also* post-paranoid condition, 105–117; democracy, 117
parrhesia, 160; parrhesiast, 159, 162–163, 171, 175
Party, 66, 68, 80, 82, 89, 90, 91, 93, 94, 96, 112, 113, 117, 124, 126, 134; race-party criterion, 86
party art, 68, 86, 89, 90
phallus of the ruling class, 122
phantasm, 134; imperialist, 125; modernist, 68, 69; Slav, 129
philosophy of language, 35
plagiarist, xviii, 27
political, 74; action, 66; art, 68, 69, 76, 77, 86, 88, 89, 93, 94; attraction, 71; changes, xi; collective political agent, 81; force, 106; intuition, xv; puberty, 157; struggle, 106; political transgression as ontological transgression, 166; political unconscious, xviii
post-totalitarian age, 157; Bulgaria, 157, 175; Eastern Europe, 158, 161, 170; expert, 171; mutant, 141; Öffentlichkeit, 158. *See also* discursive situation of post-totalitarianism, 158; post-totalitarian public domain, 155, 159; 161; period, 156; society, 158, 169; world, xi, 145–146, 155, 157, 159, 174;

Post-totalitarian age *(continued)*
  post-communism, 107, 117;
  post-utopian situation, 152
power, 66, 67, 80, 90, 92, 93, 95, 96–101, 107, 108, 111, 114, 117, 118, 120, 123, 126, 127, 128, 132, 134, 151, 155, 177; body of power, 99; essence of power, 114; games with the power, xv; minimum of power, 125; nomenclatura as the immediate body of power, 90; parliament as legitimate division of power, 92; power as reposing on symbolic exchange, 125; power/knowledge, 171; preservation of power, 39, 108; production of power, 93; reality as total power, 135; traditional representations of power, 114
Proletcult, 68, 69, 71, 80; Proletcult as the actual Proletarian art, 89–90

quoting, 28; quotation, 168, 170, 172

race, 86, 89
reading, xviii–xix, 1–2, 28, 31, 32; as act of intercoursing, 26; as conquering, 30; as modus of existence, 26; as proceeding writing, 27; as rereading, 27. *See* reader, 1–2, 26, 29, 55, ideal reader, 26, 29, 30
reality, xviii, xix, 69, 110, 115–117, 126, 128, 131, 143, 149, 151, 152; alternative, 143; a-semiotic, pure, xix; communist, 94; cultural, 28; Don Quixote and the Problem of Reality, 29; figurative reality, 19; Genuine Reality, 172; historical reality, 147; inauthentic reality, 166; political reality, 98; postmodern reality, 169; potential or actual, 30; ready-made, 75; reality as convention, 137; reality as a narrow slit between two books, 29; reality as suppressed violence, 137; reality as symbolic product (as semiotically articulated), 135, 142; reality in *statu nascendi*, 143; reality of communism, 67; reality producing system, 143; suppressed reality, 140; symbolic reality, 115, 144; utopia as reality, 67; verbal reality, 173; virtual reality, xviii–xix, 21. *See also* criterion of reality, 143; production of objectivity, 74
reception, xx
repetition, 3–9, 46, 50, 53, 60, 61, 93; eternal repetition, 53. *See also* copy, double, twin, xviii, xxi, 3–9, 12, 13, 26, 39, 40, 42, 143, 164, 168; indigo doubled life, 50; dissimulation
representation, ix, 12, 109, 112, 115, 117, 126, 160, 165, 177; class struggle of representations, 108; modernist principle of representation, 87; political representativeness, 90, 93; public representations and rumors, 108; representable, 88; transcendental paranoid representation, 161
repression, subconcious, 73
resistance, xiii, xvi, xvii, 175, 176; half resistance, 156; local resistance, 142; "naive" political resistance, 167. *See also* opposition
revolution, 69, 76, 92, 94, 96–101, 115, 116, 122, 127, 130, 131, 132, 135, 144, 145, 147–149, 169, 177; empirical vs. ultimate (total) revolution, 135–136,

147, 149; normal revolution, 139, 147; untypical revolution, 149; velvet (nonspecific, minimal) revolution, 136, 143–144, 147, 148, 149, 152, 171. *See also* counter-revolution, 140; restoration, 140; revolution-presented-as-restoration, 144; revolution-restoration, 148

rumor, 107–110, 125. *See also* doxa, 108

sacrifice, 109, 117, 119, 122, 123, 125, 128, 131, 132, 174, 175; sacrificing as a monstrous technology of domination, 126; sacrificial exchange, 123; sacrifice/guilt pattern, 125, 127; self-sacrificing body, 162; *See also* perestroika (sacrifying of the communism itself), 122; self-effacement, 122, 125

scandal, 27, 33, 34, 54, 94, 164; semantic scandal, 167

seduction, 128, 131, 167; anti-seduction, 167. *See also* tempting and luxurious reality, xviii

semiotics, 34, 35, 55; nonclassical semiotics, 52, 137; semiosphere, xii

sign, 44, 48, 51–53; anti-sign, 53; nonclassical sign, 53; sign function, signifying function, 52, 53. *See also* signifier-signified relation, 51–53, 137

suffering, 119, 121, 128, 129, 131, 133, 176. *See also* loss, 119; miserabilism as cultural norm, 129; misery, 128, 131; unhappiness, 119, 128

suppression, 155–158, 169

symbol, xiii, 4, 42, 48, 54, 98, 115, 136, 141; instant-symbol, 52; symbolic exchange, 123–132. *See also* violence of symbolism, 142, 146

tattooing, tattoo, 137–140, 144–146, 151. *See also* articulation, engraving, 138–144

television, 115–117, 132; television as a substitute for reality, 115

terror, xix, xxi, 107, 135–146, 147–154, 158, 166, 167, 168, 169, 170, 172; post-totalitarian terror as an immanent terror, 145. *See also* violence

text, 2, 28, 31, 33, 53, 54, 55, 56, 59, 60; limit-text, 168; prototypal text of the subconscious, 138; substantiated text, 148, 153; text and context, 116; text beyond good and evil, 149; sing/understanding, ix

theory of communication, 36

totalitarianism, xi, xiv, 116, 141–143, 155–177; as realization of the political aesthetics of Modernism, 69; totalitarianism as linguistic phenomenon, xiii. *See* totalitarian, age (times, past, world, etc.), 155–177; anonymity, 55; censorship, 155; culture, xi, xiii, 116; discourse, xix, 172; hierarchy, xvii; man, 143; institution, 156; mask, xv; mechanism, xvii; past, 158; power, 97; simulacra, xviii; situation, 156; system, xvi, writers, xvii

trace, 37, 42, 53, 170; trace of eternity, 117; trace of the Other, 53. *See also* deferment, 53; *les grammes*, 53; supplement, 53

truth, 28, 39, 59, 88, 106, 108, 113, 122, 136, 153; cities of truth, 160; deconstructivist "truth," ix; expert truths, 160; fundamental truths, 172; ideological appearance vs. truth, 165; living in truth, xiii, xvi, 143, 162; metaphysical

truth *(continued)*
 truths, 161; paranoid version of truth, 163, 164; (economy of) parrhesiastic truth, 171, 174, 175; party truth (pravda), 88, 89, 93, 94; post-totalitarian "economy of truth," 159–160; power of truth, 165; preconceptional form of truths, 160; production and distribution of "truths," 159; saying the truth in a tyrant's face, 160. *See* parrhesia; truth-telling discourse, 159; twin paradox, 8–9

utopia, xviii, 66–67, 74, 80, 118, 143, 148, 153, 169; anti-utopia, 119, 153; geographical utopia, 146. *See also* The West as (anti-)utopia of the East, 159; normalcy as post-totalitarian utopia, 141, 143, 153, 158, 162, 176; radical utopia, 135, 147, 148, 152, 153; utopia as reality, 67; utopia as text, 148; utopian project, 169; utopian vision as cosmic voluntarism, 167; anti-utopian, xix, 173; modernist project, 68, 78; party project, 66; Schlaraffenland and Gulag, 123

Vergangenheitsbewältigung und Vergangenheitsverdrängung, 157
violence, 136, 141, 142, 146, 150, 151, 153; suppressed violence, 137; violence and terror as synonymous, 150

war, 72, 176
will to power, 110
word vs. Word opposition, 173. *See* inflaming the Word, 173
work, 28, 29, 31, 32, 36, 39, 57, 58, 59, 60, 70, 84; life-work, 51; party work, 89; society as poetic work, 66; work-world, 76. *See also* chef d'oeuvre, 74
writing, 27, 28, 29, 40, 41, 42, 47, 52–53, 56, 59, 155; party and anti-party writing, 89; writing as experience of (utopian) limit, 164, 167, 169

zapadniki and potchveniki, 159

Index of Personal Names

Adorno, Theodor, 50
Aeschylus, 39
Andropov, Jurij, 109
Arendt, Hannah, 109, 117
Aristotle, 34

Barthes, Roland, 173
Battaille, George, 164
Baucis, 33, 54, 55, 61
Baudrillard, Jean, xviii–xix, xx, 110, 167
Benjamin, Walter, 31, 48, 50
Benvenist, Emil, 136
Berkley, George, 30
Bogdanov, Alexander, 71, 80, 81–82
Boyadjiev, Lutchezar, xvii
Brecht, Bertolt, 113–114
Brezhnev, Leonid, 117, 132
Burke, Samuel, 148
Butler, Samuel, 119

Cervantes, Miguel de, 25–30
Charles the Great, father of the Carolingian Renaissance, 26, 32
Chicherin, Georgi, 95, 96
Churchill, Winston, 153
Cicero, Marcus Tullius, 177
Cratylus, 136
Cyclops, 16, 73

Dante, Aligieri, 166
Danton, George Jacques, 149, 170
Delacroix, Eugene, 44
Demand, Alexander, 177
Derrida, Jacques, xx, 53, 149, 170

Descartes, Rene, 106, 107
Ditchev, Ivaylo, xii, xvii, xx
Dostoievsky, Fyodor, 127

Eckermann, Peter Johann, 33
Eco, Umberto, 34
Eisenstein, Sergei, 81
Euripides, 39

Fischer, Lewis, 97
Flaubert, Gustav, 29
Foucault, Michel, xx, 159, 160, 171
Fourier, Charles, 105
Freud, Sigmund, 50, 127, 134, 166, 175
Fyodorov, Nikolaj, xiv

Ginsburg, Moses, 83
Goethe, Johann Wolfgang, 33–62
Guillotin, Joseph Ignace, 151

Havel, Vaclav, xiii
Hegel, Georg Friedrich Wilhelm, 117, 122
Hitler, Adolf, 69

Janus, 4
Jean-Paul (Johann Paul Friedrich Richter), 31
Jillas, Milovan, 112

Kafka, Franz, 139
Kant, Immanuel, 120, 167
Karaliichev, Angel, xiii

Index

Kiossev, Alexander, x, xii, xvii, xx, 147–154
Klein, Melanie, 122
Krakauer, S., 118
Krassin, Leonid, 96
Kristev, Ivan, xi, xii, xx, 155, 168–171
Kristeva, Julia, 164
Kuleshov, Lev, 116

Lacan, Jacques, 138
Leforte, Claude, 150
Lenin, Vladimir Ilitch, 67, 68, 69, 89, 94, 95, 96, 111, 127, 130, 166
Luis XVI, king of France (Luis Capet), 98, 99, 100
Luxembourg (city), 15–23
Luxembourg, Rose, 15
Lyotard, Jean-Francois, xiv, xx, 140

Macpherson, Roland, 33, 34, 54–62
Madam Tussaud, 97, 98, 99
Marinetti, Philippo, 54–55, 72
Marx, Karl, 106, 127, 131
Menard, Pierre, 25–32, 168, 170
Meyerhold, Vsevolod, 81
Mirandola, Giovanni Picco della, 106
Molotov, Vyacheslav, 95
More, Thomas, 118
Morosov, Pavlik, 124

Napoleon, Bonaparte, 43
Nicholas II, (Romanoff) emperor of Russia, 98, 100, 101
Nietzsche, Friedrich, 110, 127

Orwell, George, 109
Ossian, 59–60

Philemon, 33, 54, 55, 61
Plato, 118, 136

Plautus, T. Maccius, 39
Polo, Marco, 38
Protagoras from Abdera, 137
pseudo-Dionysius the Aeropagite, xiv

Quixote, don, 25–32

Reich, Wilhelm, 151
Roland, Marie Jeanne (Manon) Philipon, 56, 60
Rousseau, Jean-Jaques, 151

Sade, de, xiv
Saint Just, Luis Antoine Leon, 99, 150
Sartre, Jean-Paul, 106
Saussure, Ferdinand, 51–53
Schiller, Friedrich, 33
Schönemann, Lilly, 44
Seneca, Lucius Aenaeus, 177
Shakespeare, William, 166, 177
Spielberg, Steven, 153
Stalin, Joseph, 69, 97, 111, 123, 126
Synthesis, group, xiii

Tell, Wilhelm, 44
Todorov, Vladislav, xi, xii, xvii, xviii, xx, 112, 142, 149, 154, 164, 166, 167, 168, 173

Vatimo, xiv

Wallenstein, 44
Weber, Max, xiv, 127, 131
Winckelmann, Johann, 41
Wittgenstein, Ludwig, 61, 164
Wutz, 31

Zeitler, 33
Zossima, 134